MERCHANT SHIPS' SEAWORTHINESS

MARITIME AND TRANSPORT LAW LIBRARY

Codification of Maritime Law
Challenges, Possibilities and Experience
Edited by Zuzanna Pepłowska-Dąbrowska and Justyna Nawrot

Transport Documents in Carriage Of Goods by Sea
International Law and Practice
By Caslav Pejovic

Maritime Law
Fifth Edition
Edited by Yvonne Baatz

Ship Operations: New Risks, Liabilities and Technologies in the Maritime Sector
Edited by Bariş Soyer and Andrew Tettenborn

Maritime Safety in Europe
Edited by Justyna Nawrot and Zuzanna Pepłowska-Dąbrowska

Fresh Produce Shipping
Damages and Compensation
Rex C. Tester

Freeports and Free Zones
Operations and Regulation in the Global Economy
Mark Rowbotham

Disruptive Technologies, Climate Change and Shipping
Edited by Bariş Soyer and Andrew Tettenborn

Responsibility and Accountability in Maritime Law
The Criminalisation of the Ship's Master
Simon Daniels

Cartner on the International Law of the Shipmaster
On the New Command at Sea
Second Edition
John A C Cartner

Illegal Charters and Aviation Law
Alena Soloveva

Commercial and Maritime Law in China and Europe
Shengnan Jia and Lijun Zhao

Offshore Floating Production: Law and Commercial Risk Management
Edited by Stuart Beadnall, Simon Moore and Max Lemanski

The Modern Law of Marine Insurance
Volume Five
Edited by D. Rhidian Thomas

Merchant Ships' Seaworthiness: Law and Practice
Xiankai Zhan and Pengfei Zhang

Inland Waterway Transport
The European Legal Framework
Massimiliano Grimaldi

For more information about this series, please visit:
www.routledge.com/

MERCHANT SHIPS' SEAWORTHINESS

LAW AND PRACTICE

XIANKAI ZHAN AND PENGFEI ZHANG

informa law
from Routledge

First published 2023
By Informa Law from Routledge
4 Park Square, Milton Park, Abingdon, Oxon OX14 4RN

and by Informa Law from Routledge
605 Third Avenue, New York, NY 10158

Informa Law from Routledge is an imprint of the Taylor & Francis Group, an informa business

British Library Cataloguing-in-Publication Data
A catalogue record for this book is available from the British Library

Library of Congress Cataloging-in-Publication Data
A catalog record for this book has been requested

ISBN: 978-1-032-24738-0 (hbk)
ISBN: 978-1-032-24740-3 (pbk)
ISBN: 978-1-003-27993-8 (ebk)

DOI: 10.4324/9781003279938

Typeset in Times New Roman
by Apex CoVantage, LLC

CONTENTS

TABLE OF CASES

PREFACE

Over 80 per cent of world trade by volume are carried by merchant ships, without which the global economy cannot function effectively. Therefore, the maritime industry has an essential role to play in world economic growth and sustainable development. To ensure that the maritime industry remains effective, safe, and environmentally friendly, it is crucial to make sure that all ships meet certain minimum standards in terms of safety, maintenance, crew competence and training, and so on; otherwise, enormous consequences could result from the failure to do so, such as loss of life, oil pollution, increases in insurance premiums, and instability of the commercial industry. It is here where the issue of ship seaworthiness comes to light.

The concept of seaworthiness has evolved over many years, and in common with similar concepts (for instance, the definition and application of "prudent seamanship"), its precise meaning has varied considerably. Seaworthiness deals with fitness and readiness, in all respects: human, physical, documentation, cargo-worthiness, ship management, maintenance, machinery and equipment of the vessel, and its ability to sail safely to its destination. It is one of the most important concepts in the maritime regulatory regime and takes many forms.

For instance, Article 94(1) of LOSC 1982 requires that flag states are under a categorical duty to exercise jurisdiction and control in relation to "administrative, technical and social matters" over ships that are permitted to fly its flag. Seaworthiness is clearly a crucial element in relation to this duty, and this is further set out in the remainder of the article, particularly in Article 94 (3) and (4).

Similarly, in the commercial context of the carriage of goods by sea, the Hague/Hague–Visby Rules require that the carrier has the obligation to exercise due diligence to make the ship seaworthy both before and at the beginning of the voyage. In marine insurance law, seaworthiness is an implied warranty of the shipowner, the breach of which results in the loss of insurance cover, even though there is no causal relationship between the breach and the loss. In the law relating to seafarers' employment contract, seafarers are guaranteed of the protection that originates from the legal implication that the ship on which he is employed to work is, in fact and law, seaworthy. For instance, section 458 of the UK Merchant Shipping Act (MSA) of 1894 has conferred upon seafarers a statutory right to an implied term of seaworthiness which cannot be displaced or exempted by contractual agreement.

However, seaworthiness is not an absolute concept but a relative one, dependent on the particular context and facts. This is primarily dependent on and determined by a variety of different contractual purposes and perspectives. A ship might be seaworthy as between the insurer and the shipowner, though unseaworthy as between shipowner and the shipper of a particular cargo. For instance, frozen cargo requires special freezing apparatus, though that does not affect the safety of the ship but may impair seaworthiness under a marine insurance policy. This was made clear in the Eurasian Dream, where it was held that "[seaworthiness] is relative to the nature of the ship, to the particular voyage, or even to the particular stage of the voyage on which the ship is engaged."

In the recent case the CMA CGM Libra, Teare J of the High Court of the UK held that the ship was unseaworthy at the time of its departure, and this was affirmed in the Court of Appeal. The Supreme Court, in agreement with the judge and the Court of Appeal, rejected the owners' novel and unsound case on due diligence. It seems that the carrier's obligation under the Hague Rules is not subject to a category-based distinction between a vessel's quality of seaworthiness or navigability and the crew's act of navigating. The crew's failure to navigate the ship safely is capable of constituting a lack of due diligence by the carrier which may result in unseaworthiness. This appears to be consistent with the Privy Council's view in the Maruinne that the ship was unseaworthy at the moment of the fire. It makes no difference that at the moment of on hire or before or at the beginning of the voyage, the undertaking of seaworthiness is an overriding obligation under the Rules.

The current law on seaworthiness, represented by the Hague/Hague–Visby Rules as the most commonly used regime, was sufficient for the era when it was introduced. However, laws in general need to be dynamic and able to evolve in tandem with the changing needs of the industry they govern, and the law on the Carriage of Goods by Sea is no different from any other law; it should be dynamic and able to adapt to meet the needs of the shipping industry.

Despite its important role of seaworthiness in maritime law and charterparties, there is a lack of existing literature and knowledge on seaworthiness. This work is an attempt to fill the gap. The authors investigated the relevant jurisprudence and drew a wide range of issues together from a theoretical study to the practical contexts operating in the maritime industry, offering a critical examination of merchant ships' seaworthiness.

Our thanks go to the International Group of P&I Clubs, Lloyd's Law Reports, West Law, Lexis Nexis, China Ocean Shipping (Group) Company, National Social Science Foundation of China on Ocean Governance (22AZD108), and seafarers who provided support and encouraged us to complete this work. Greatest thanks (and apologies) go to our respective families, as well as the editorial team at Informa Law, Taylor & Francis, and Routledge.

Xiankai Zhan and Pengfei Zhang
Hongkong and Shanghai

CHAPTER 1

Introduction

1.1 The historical development of seaworthiness

For hundreds of years, the shipping industry has continued to develop, but the obligation to provide a seaworthy vessel is still one of the cores of maritime cargo transportation. The carrier is obliged to provide a ship that is tight, staunch, strong, and properly manned; equips and supplies the ship; and is suitable for cargo carriage in all respects. These basic seaworthiness requirements have also been explicitly incorporated into different charterparties forms. Since seaworthiness is usually not clearly defined in the modern standard charter, whether it is a time charter, a voyage charter, or a bareboat charter, the specific meaning of the concept must be determined from the common law case.

As early as in the case of *Lyon v Mells*,[1] the defendant agreed to load a certain amount of yarn owned by the plaintiff from the hull wharf onto the barge at the wharf. The barge leaked and partially capsized, causing yarn damage. The defendant relied on the announcement, claiming to limit the liability of the barge in the Humber area. Lord Ellenborough CJ stated:

> In every contract for the carriage of goods between a person holding himself forth as the owner of a lighter or vessel ready to carry goods for hire, and the person putting goods on board or employing his vessel or lighter for that purpose, it is a term of the contract on the part of the carrier or lighterman, implied by law, that his vessel is tight and fit for the purpose or employment for which he offers and holds it forth to the public; it is the very foundation and immediate substratum of the contract that it is so: the law presumes a promise to that effect on the part of the carrier without any actual proof; and every reason of sound policy and public convenience requires it should be so.

Over the past hundreds of years, the implied obligations recognized in the *Lyon v Mells* case have become complex; in the *Eurasian Dream*,[2] it contains important statements about the main features of modern law. Cresswell J concluded that the vessel was unseaworthy before and at the beginning of the voyage for these grounds: the vessel was not suitably manned and equipped, and the documentation supplied to the vessel was inadequate. More details will be discussed in Chapter 5. Obligations stipulated in clear language are common and are usually described as standards required for careful handling. Or this prudent test is incorporated into the charterparty through the most important clauses, such as the relevant

---

1 See *Lyon v Mells* [1804] 5 East 428, per Lord Ellenborough CJ.

2 *Papera Traders Co Ltd. v Hyundai Merchant Marine Co Ltd., The Eurasian Dream* [2002] EWHC 118; [2002] 1 Lloyd's Rep.719.

DOI: 10.4324/9781003279938-1

clauses of the Hague or the Hague–Visby Rules or some international conventions or regulations that implement these rules.

Of course, the implied undertaking of seaworthiness is an innominate term, and the charterer's right to treat the contract as discharged in consequence of a breach of the undertaking depends on whether the breach goes to the root of the contract and deprives the charterers of whole benefits under the contract. If the initial unseaworthiness is sufficiently serious, the charterer may treat the contract at an end, even if the contract has been partially performed.[3]

1.2 The obligation of seaworthiness under the Hague/Hague–Visby Rules

The Hague/Hague–Visby Rules provided in article III, rule 1 that:[4]

> The carrier shall be bounded before and at the beginning of the voyage to exercise due diligence to:
> (a) Make the ship seaworthy;
> (b) properly man, equip and supply the ship;
> (c) Make the holds, refrigerating and cool chambers, and all other parts of the ship in which goods are carried, fit and safe for their reception, carriage and preservation.

However, as described in the next example, the test of seaworthiness stipulated in many charterparties is due diligence, and the absolute undertaking of seaworthiness implied by the common law is abrogated by this act. The first is the start time of the obligation, "before and at the beginning of the voyage"; it covers at least the period from the beginning of loading to the beginning of the voyage.[5] If the vessel is unseaworthy due to an earlier breach of due diligence, the carrier will be liable.[6] The second relates to the scope of the obligation, which, as already pointed out, is one of due diligence. The exercise of due diligence is equivalent to the exercise of reasonable care and skill. Lack of due diligence is negligence.[7]

If responsibilities are delegated to independent contractors or surveyors and all persons who are negligent, the carrier is still liable. Such as the *Fjord Wind*,[8] the case of the British Court of Appeal. The Court of Appeal ruled that the relevant clauses of the voyage charter contract stipulate that the shipowner has a reasonable duty to ensure that the ship is seaworthy before and at the beginning of the voyage, which is consistent with the requirements under the Hague Rules in the bill of lading. The vessel broke down when she left the loading port and could not resist ordinary navigation risks. At the same time, if the shipowner knows these deficiencies, they should take measures to rectify them. Therefore, it is not a potential defect of the vessel. The shipowner has not done enough to ensure the seaworthiness of the vessel. The vessel should carry out some inspections, but there is no evidence that inspections have been carried out.

3 See *Scrutton on Charterparties and Bills of Lading*, 24th ed, Sweet & Maxwell at para. 7–020.
4 *Hague–Visby Rules*, Article III, r1 (a), (b) and (c).
5 See *The Maruinne* [1959] 2 Lloyd's Rep.105 at p. 113.
6 See *The Kriti Rex* [1996] 2 Lloyd's Rep.171.
7 See *The Eurasian Dream* [2002] 1 Lloyd's Rep.719.
8 See *The Fjord Wind* [2000] 2 Lloyd's Rep.191 (C.A.).

It is settled law that the obligation arising under article III, rule 1 is overriding. However, the carrier's responsibility does not begin until the vessel comes into his orbit, and allows the carrier

> will be protected against latent defects, in the strict sense, in work done on his ship, that is to say, defects not due to any negligent workmanship of repairers or other employed by the repairers or others employed by the repairers, and, as I see it, against defects making for unseaworthiness in the ship, however, caused, before it became his ship if these could not be discovered by him, or competent experts employed by hi, by the exercise of due diligence.[9]

The third of the specific wording in (a), (b), and (c) is understood to include every different seaworthiness element recognized by the common law. This act requires the obligation to handle the manning, ship equipment, material supply and cargo hold, etc. with the duty of care. Although the obligation to provide seaworthy ships can be divided into the absolute and relative, the standards that vessels must meet are also relative. However, once the standard is determined, according to the common law, the lessor is obliged to meet the standard, which is absolute. The shipowner's ignorance of defects or failure to handle carefully to make the ship seaworthy is not a reason for exemption.[10] It is important to get clear the point to which criticism must be directed. Lack of due diligence is negligence, and what is at issue, in this case, is whether there was an error of judgment that amounted to professional negligence.[11]

1.3 The obligation under British Marine Insurance

As an ancient concept, the seaworthiness doctrine is very important in several different legal backgrounds of maritime law. It is used in maritime law to assume responsibility for certain consequences. It serves both as a defence mechanism and as a responsibility to impose a theory. For example, in addition to marine insurance, this principle plays a vital role in cargo carriage. The implied warranty of seaworthiness plays a vital role in marine insurance law because it is one of the most effective defence mechanisms for insurance companies. In many cases, even if there is no causal relationship between default and loss, the default will result in insurance compensation. The Marine Insurance Act 1906 states in section 39 that:[12]

> (1) In a voyage policy there is an implied warranty that at the commencement of the voyage the ship shall be seaworthy for the particular adventure insured.
> (3) Where the policy relates to a voyage which is performed in different stages, during which the ship requires different kinds of or further preparation or equipment, there is an implied warranty that at the commencement of each stage the ship is seaworthy in respect of such preparation or equipment for the, purposes of that stage.
> (4) A ship is deemed to be seaworthy when she is reasonably fit in all respects to encounter the ordinary perils of the seas of the adventure insured.

---

9 *Scrutton on Charterparties and Bills of Lading*, 24th ed, Sweet & Maxwell at para. 14–48.

10 *McFadden v Blue Star Line* [1905] 1 KB 697.

11 *Union of India v N.V. Reederij Amsterdam (The Amstelslot)* [1963] 2 Lloyd's Rep.223 (H.L.), per Lord Devlin at p. 235.

12 Marine Insurance Act 1906, Section 39 (1), (2) and (4).

S. 39(4) of the act does not specifically point out what seaworthiness should include but says instead that the vessel should be reasonably fit in all respects. Thus, no matter the type of loss suffered, the insured must still comply with the warranty obligations, such as maintaining the ship's class, which is a prerequisite for the association's underwriting. A ship's class is usually a condition, so if the ship does not obtain a class according to the date of the charterparty, the charterer has the right to treat the charterparty as discharged.[13] In the recent case of the British High Court, the maintenance of the ship's class under the bareboat charter contract has also been considered as a condition term.[14]

Time charters other than bareboat charters promise seaworthiness at the beginning of time, but Scottish law stipulates that there is no such warranty at the beginning of each voyage, and English law may also be the same. If the captain continues to perform such a voyage without the opportunity to repair the unseaworthy conditions of his ship, the shipowner will be liable for his negligence unless he is protected by an exception. For this rule, the charterparty for continuous voyages or round trips is not listed as a time charterparty. Therefore, the charterer under this type of charterparty is obliged to provide a seaworthy vessel at the beginning of each voyage or during the voyage. Therefore, it is difficult to determine what seaworthiness is within a certain period of time; it is also difficult to determine for an unknown voyage. These considerations do not apply so strongly to time charter contracts other than through bareboat charters, which usually (though not always) begin with the ship from a port of known voyage.[15]

In the insurance term insurance policy, it is difficult to warrant the initial seaworthiness because the shipowner is required to bear the seaworthiness of the ship when the vessel is out of its control.[16] If the insurance company investigates the matters covered by the maritime warranty during the negotiation, the situation is different. In this case, the disclosure of facts within the scope of the warranty will not become superfluous.[17] This is also the case if the implied warranty of seaworthiness is exempted from the implementation of the applicable seaworthiness clause.[18]

However the act used broad terms to define seaworthiness, it left to the courts the job of identifying what is a seaworthy vessel, according to the facts, particular wording, and circumstances of each case.

1.4 Clear seaworthiness provisions in the charter

1.4.1 Time charter

Under common law, the seaworthiness obligation in a time charterparty is attached to the shipowner when the ship is chartered; however, as in the case of a voyage charterparty, a standard time charterparty always contains a clear seaworthiness clause.[19] For example,

13 See *Routh v MacMillan* [1863] 9 L.T. 541, *The Apollonius* [1978] 1 Lloyd's Rep.53, per Mocatta J at p. 61, and *The Seaflower* (*No. 2*) [2001] 1 Lloyd's Rep.341, per Rix LJ at p. 63.

14 See *The Arctic* [2019] EWHC 376 (Comm).

15 See *Scrutton on Charterparties and Bills of Lading*, 24th ed at para. 17–31.

16 See *Gibson v Small* [1853] 4 HLC 353.

17 *Svenska Handelsbanken v Sun Alliance and London Insurance plc (No. 2)* [1996] 1 Lloyd's Rep.519 at pp. 553–554, per Rix J.

18 *Cantiere Meccanico Brindisino v Janson* [1912] 3 KB 452.

19 See *The Madeleine* [1967] 2 Lloyd's Rep.224; and *The Derby* [1984] 1 Lloyd's Rep.635.

NYPE46 stipulates in its preamble that the vessel, on her delivery or prior to its arrival on the first loading port after delivery, be ready to receive cargo with clean-swept and dried holds and be tight, staunch, strong, and in every way fitted for the service, having water ballast, winches, and donkey boiler with sufficient steam power, or if not, equipped with donkey boiler, then other power sufficient to run all the winches at the same time (and with a full complement of officers, and crew, seamen, engineers, and firemen for a vessel of her tonnage).[20]

NYPE 93[21] has made amendments to this aspect, which is no longer in the preamble; it is stipulated that the vessel, on her delivery, shall be ready to receive cargo with clean-swept holds and be tight, staunch, strong, and in every way fitted for ordinary cargo service,[22] have water ballast, and be with sufficient power to operate all cargo-handling gear simultaneously.

Similarly, lines 42–46 of the NYPE2015 provided:

> The vessel on delivery shall be seaworthy and in every way fit to be employed for the intended service, having water ballast and with sufficient power to operate all cargo-handling gears simultaneously, and, with a full complement of Master, officers and ratings who meet the Standards for Training, Certification and Watchkeeping for Seafarers (STCW) requirements for a vessel of her tonnage.

In addition, clause 1 of BALTIME 1939, which stipulates in line 25 the vessel being in every way fitted for ordinary cargo service, the same wording as in NYPE93: in every way fitted for ordinary cargo service.[23]

In a wet charter, such as Shelltime 4, clause 1 of Description and Condition of Vessel stipulated in detail:

1. At the date of delivery of the vessel under this Charter and throughout the charter period:
   (a) she shall be classed by the American Bureau of Shipping, and she shall be technically managed and operated by a technical manager/operator who has passed the Shell Time Charter Assurance Review (defined herein);
   (b) she shall be in every way fit to carry crude petroleum and/or its products, and she and the Owners shall be in full compliance with the requirements and regulations of the Oil Pollution Act of 1990, and as same may be amended from time to time ("OPA90");
   (c) she shall be tight, staunch, strong, in good order and condition, and in every way fit for the service, with her machinery, boilers, hull and other equipment (including but not limited to hull stress calculator, radar, computers and computer systems) in a good and efficient state;
   (d) her tanks, valves and pipelines shall be oil-tight;
   (e) she shall be in every way fitted for burning, in accordance with the grades specified in Clause 29 hereof:
      (i) at sea, fuel oil for main propulsion and fuel oil/marine gas oil (MGO) for auxiliaries;
      (ii) in port, fuel oil/marine gas oil (MGO) for auxiliaries;

20 NYPE46, Line 21–24.
21 NYPE 93, Line 33–35.
22 See *The Arianna* [1987] 2 Lloyd's Rep.376.
23 See *The Roberta* [1937] 58 Ll.L. Rep.231.

(f) she shall comply with the regulations in force so as to enable her to pass through the Suez and Panama Canals by day and night without delay;
(g) she shall have on board all certificates, documents and equipment required from time to time by any applicable law to enable her to perform the charter service without delay;
(h) she shall comply with the description in the OCIMF Harmonized Vessel Particulars Questionnaire appended hereto as Appendix A, provided however that if there is any conflict between the provisions of this questionnaire and any other provision, including this Clause 1, of this Charter such other provisions shall govern;
(i) she shall be owned by a US citizen for the purposes of owning or operating a vessel engaged in the US domestic Jones Act trades under 46 USC Chapter 121 and Section 2 of the Shipping Act of 1916, as each may be amended from time to time, and her US ownership structure, US documentation and registry status (with valid coastwise endorsement), classification society,
(j) Owners will operate:
 (i) a safety management system certified to comply with the International Safety Management Code ("ISM Code") for the Safe Operation of Ships and for Pollution Prevention;
 (ii) a documented safe working procedures system (including procedures for the identification and mitigation of risks);
 (iii) a documented environmental management system;
 (iv) documented accident/incident reporting system compliant with U.S. requirements;
(k) Owners shall submit to Charterers a monthly written report detailing all accidents/incidents and environmental reporting requirements, in accordance with the "Shell Safety and Environmental Monthly Reporting Template" appended hereto as Appendix B;
(l) Owners shall maintain Health Safety Environmental ("HSE") records sufficient to demonstrate compliance with the requirements of their HSE system and of this Charter. Charterers reserve the right to confirm compliance with HSE requirements by audit of Owners.
(m) Owners will arrange at their expense for a SIRE inspection to be carried out at intervals of six months plus or minus thirty days.

The clauses (a) to (g) of Shelltime 4 are, to some extent, a guarantee of the vessel's condition at the time of delivery; the general requirement of clause (c) that the vessel "shall be tight, staunch, strong, in good order and condition, and in every way fit for the service" constitutes undertaking of seaworthiness. The wording is similar to that of NYPE – except for only the word "fitted" instead of the word "fit," the wording is almost the same. It is suggested that this distinction is not important.[24]

Clause 1(g) of the original Shelltime 4 is considered to be a continuous undertaking, which applies to the entire charterparty, although clause 1 only consists of "on the date of delivery

24 See *The Derby* [1984] 1 Lloyd's Rep.635 at p. 641, Hobhouse J, whose decision was upheld by the Court of Appeal at [1985] 2 Lloyd's Rep.325.

specified in this charterparty." The interpretation of clause 1(g) seems doubtful. It is suggested that a better interpretation is that paragraph (g) describes the nature of the documents rather than the time when they were undertaken.[25] Paragraph (h) requires that the questionnaire survey of the International Maritime Forum of the Petroleum Company be satisfied. The survey document also includes the shipyard address and shipyard code of the vessel.[26]

These provisions of clause 1, if they contain an undertaking applicable on the date of delivery, impose absolute obligations and therefore have nothing to do with any compliance issues or to the exercise due diligence.[27] The question of "fit" is a preliminary question of fact. The lack of equipment has no impact on the safety of the vessel, its effective operation, or the safety of the cargo and has no practical commercial significance. Even if the equipment does not meet the requirements of the charterparty, it will not make the vessel unsuitable for the service.[28]

1.4.2 Voyage charters

Voyage charterparties, such as standard GENCON 94 form,[29] for vessel seaworthiness stipulate that:

> The Owners are to be responsible for loss of or damage to the goods or for delay in delivery of the goods only in case the loss, damage or delay has been caused by personal want of due diligence on the part of the Owners or their Manager to make the Vessel in all respects seaworthy and to secure that she is properly manned, equipped and supplied, or by the personal act or default of the Owners or their Manager.

This clause is rather an implied undertaking of seaworthiness under the common law to provide a seaworthy vessel, but with due diligence.

Absolute obligations are still highly relevant and may cause major problems in the context of generally worded exclusion clauses. Therefore, as far as deck cargo is concerned, the charterparty does not include that the ship is not responsible for any loss or damage to the cargo on deck. The English court ruled that the wording "for whatsoever reason and howsoever caused" could protect the shipowner, even in unseaworthy cases,[30] but it was not approved by the Singapore court.[31]

Clause 2 does not attempt to make any special definition of seaworthiness, so general law will be applied. For a seaworthy vessel, its equipment and systems[32] must be reasonably able to withstand the peril that may be encountered during sea passage, and the cargo must

---

25 See *The Elli and The Frixos* [2008] 2 Lloyd's Rep.119 (C.A.).

26 See *The Diana Prosperity* [1976] 2 Lloyd's Rep.621.

27 See *The Fina Samco* [1994] 1 Lloyd's Rep.153, per Colman J, on p. 158; and *The Trade Nomad* [1998] 1 Lloyd's Rep.57 [1999] 1 Lloyd's Rep.723 (C.A.).

28 *The Arianna* [1987] 2 Lloyd's Rep.376; See *Time Charters*, 7th ed, para. 37.4–37.8.

29 GENCON94, Clause 2/Owners' Responsibility Clause, Line 16–21.

30 See *Transocean Liners v Euxine Shipping (The Imvros)* [1999] 1 Lloyd's Rep.848, followed by Morison J in *Compania Sud Americana Vapores v ER Hamburg Schiff* [2006] 2 Lloyd's Rep.66 and considered in *The Socol 3* [2010] 2 Lloyd's Rep.221.

31 See *Sunlight Mercantile v Ever Lucky Shipping* [2004] 2 Lloyd's Rep.174.

32 See *Cia Sud Americana de Vapores v Sinochem Tianjin Import & Export Corp. (The Aconcagua)* [2010] 1 Lloyd's Rep.1, para. 367 and [2011] 1 Lloyd's Rep.386.

be reasonably safe from these perils.[33] The perils encountered include maritime risks but are not limited to these perils.[34]

Article 1 of part 2 of the SHELLVOY 6 Form of Oil Tanker Charter provided:[35]

> Condition of Vessel. Owners shall exercise due diligence to ensure that from the time when the obligation to proceed to the loading port(s) attaches and throughout the charter service –
>
> (a) The vessel and her hull, machinery, boilers, tanks, equipment and facilities are in good order and condition and in every way equipped and fit for the service required; and (b) The vessel has a full and efficient complement of master, officers and crew and the senior officers shall be fully conversant in spoken and written English language and to ensure that before and at the commencement of any laden voyage the vessel is in all respects fit to carry the cargo specified. . . . For the avoidance of doubt, references to equipment in this Charter shall include but not be limited to computers and computer systems, and such equipment shall (inter alia) be required to continue to function, and not suffer a loss of functionality and accuracy (whether logical or mathematical) as a result of the run date or dates being processed.

This clause required that the shipowner exercise due diligence at the beginning, and the obligation covers the entire charterparty period, which is a continuous undertaking; this kind of undertaking is rare under voyage charterparties. Subsequently, the various pieces of equipment of the vessel are listed in detail, and the problem of the vessel's hatch cover and sea valve can also cause the vessel to be unseaworthy.[36] The crew manning's and the senior crew's English proficiency is required; at the same time, the cargo suitability undertaking also covers the requirements for the vessel's computer equipment before and at the beginning of the voyage.

In the ASBATANKVOY form, part 2, article 1 stipulates:[37]

> The vessel, classed as specified in Part I hereof, and to be so maintained during the currency of this Charter, shall, with all convenient dispatch, proceed as ordered to Loading Port(s) named in accordance with Clause 4 hereof, or so near thereunto as she may safely get (always afloat), and being seaworthy, and having all pipes, pumps and heater coils in good working order, and being in every respect fitted for the voyage, so far as the foregoing conditions can be attained by the exercise of due diligence, perils of the sea and any other cause of whatsoever kind beyond the Owner's and/or Master's control excepted, shall load (always afloat).

The shipowners will be well protected by the last sentence of this clause, as the protection offered by article IV, rule 1 of Hague/Hague–Visby Rules, where owners have no responsibility for loss or damage whatsoever caused. The exclusion covers any cause, and there is no justification for excluding unseaworthiness as a cause.

However, when interpreting a contract, the court is concerned to find the intention of the party or parties, and it does this by identifying the meaning of the relevant words, (a) in the light of (i) the natural and ordinary meaning of those words, (ii) the overall purpose of the document, (iii) any other provisions of the document, (iv) the facts known or assumed

33 See *Fyffes v Reefer Express (The Kriti Rex)* [1996] 2 Lloyd's Rep.171, Moore-Bick J at p. 184.
34 See *Voyage Charters*, 4th ed at para. 11.17–11.18.
35 See *Shellvoy 6*, Part II, 1.
36 See *The Gundulic* [1981] 2 Lloyd's Rep.511.
37 See *Asbatankvoy,* Part II, 1.

by the parties at the time that the document was executed, and (v) common sense, but (b) ignoring subjective evidence of any party's intentions.[38]

As article III, rule 1 was an overriding obligation for any carrier under B/L contract, it is rather important to distinguish between the charter and the act. The owners will be liable for loss or damage caused by unseaworthiness, such as independent contractors he employs to make the vessel seaworthy.[39] Unlike the shipowner's obligation to maintain the vessel's class, the absolute obligation of seaworthiness under article III, rule 1 may only apply to the beginning of loading. Therefore, any previous seaworthiness obligations must be implied, and whether there is any implied seaworthiness obligation or not, it is suggested that this be read together with art III, rule 1, which requires the carrier to exercise due diligence to make the vessel seaworthy before and at the beginning of the voyage.[40]

In addition, it is also necessary to pay attention to the special provisions of clause 18 of the charter regarding the inspection clauses. The condition of the cargo hold needs to be satisfied by the charterer's inspectors. The owners will be liable for damages if those result from:

(a) Unseaworthiness existing at the time of loading or at the inception of the voyage which was discoverable by the exercise of due diligence.
(b) Error or fault of the servants of the owners in the loading, care, or discharge of the cargo.

On the other hand, if the condition of the cargo hold of the ship does not meet the requirements of the cargo to be loaded, it may also cause the ship to be unseaworthy, and the owners will be liable.[41]

38 *Marley v Rawlings* [2014] UKSC 2, per Lord Neuberger said at [19].
39 See *Voyage Charters*, 4th ed, 52.6.
40 See *Voyage Charters*, sup., 52.7.
41 See *Petrofina v Compagnia Italiana* [1937] 57 Ll.L. Rep.247 (C.A.).

CHAPTER 2

Seaworthiness of the vessel

2.1 The meaning of *seaworthiness* under common law

The classic definition of *seaworthiness*, as set out by Thomas Carver himself in the third edition of his original treatise, was approved in *McFadden v Blue Star Line*[1] and in *F.C. Bradley & Sons Ltd v Federal Steam Navigation Co Ltd.*[2] The test of seaworthiness is that the vessel

> must have that degree of fitness which an ordinary careful and prudent owner would require his vessel to have at the commencement of her voyage having regard to all the probable circumstances of it. To that extent the shipowner . . . undertakes absolutely that she is fit, and ignorance is no excuse. If the defect existed, the question to be put is, would a prudent owner have required that it should be made good before sending his ship to sea had he known of it? If he would, the ship was not seaworthy within the meaning of the undertaking.

Under common law, in the absence of any clear terms to the contrary, it is implied that the vessel is suitable for navigation and can perform the contract voyage. This is an "absolute" undertaking of seaworthiness, rather than making the vessel seaworthy with due diligence.

The shipowner's requirement to provide a seaworthy ship is that the ship be equipped with appropriate personnel and equipment to meet the common hazards that may be encountered when performing the required services. At the same time, it must be cargo-worthy and capable of loading designated goods.[3] As far as the first aspect of the concept of airworthiness is concerned, the promise implied in the common law includes not only the ship's conditions and equipment but also the capabilities of the crew and the adequacy of the ship's equipment and documents. Therefore, if the ship has a defective main engine[4] or a defective compass, or the storage method of deck cargo makes the ship lose its stability, the ship is unseaworthy.[5]

1 See *McFadden v Blue Star Line* [1905] 1 K.B. 697. per Channell J. A vessel must have that degree of fitness which an ordinarlly careful and prudent owner would require his vessel to have at the commencement of her voyage having regard to all the probable circumstances of it. To that extent, the shipowner, as we have seen, undertakes absolutely that she is fit, and ignorance is no excuse. If the defect existed, the question to be put is, Would a prudent owner have required that it should be made good before sending his ship to sea, had he known of it? If he would, the ship was not seaworthy within the meaning of the undertaking.

2 *Bill of Lading*, 2nd ed, 10.96; 3rd ed at para. 11.103.

3 John F Wilson, *Carriage of Good at Sea*, 7th ed at para. 2.1.2.

4 See *The Hong Kong Fir* [1961] 2 Llody's Rep.478; *The Amstelslot* [1963] 2 Lloyd's Rep.223.

5 See *The Friso* [1980] 1 Lloyd's Rep.469 (go ahead).

DOI: 10.4324/9781003279938-2

But if he hires an incompetent engineer or other personnel, the shipowner will also violate this rule.[6] Defects in the charts used for ship work[7] or lack of documents required for the voyage[8] will cause the ship to be unseaworthy. Therefore, the seaworthiness of a vessel embraces all matters that affect a vessel's ability to perform properly the contractual voyage. The expression covers not only the physical characteristics of a ship, such as her shell plating, but also other matters, such as her equipment and crew and the documentation for the intended voyage.[9]

2.2 Seaworthiness of the ship

Seaworthiness is primarily concerned with the nature of the vessel herself, and the fact that potentially hazardous activities are carried out on board, such as electric welding operations on decks causing fire,[10] crew not holding ITF Blue Cards,[11] or vessel failing to obtain RightShip approval,[12] does not make the ship unseaworthy. *Seaworthiness* is a relative term depending on its application to the type of vessel and the character of the voyage. The general rule is that the ship must be staunch and strong and well equipped for the intended voyage. And she must also be provided with a crew adequate in number and competent for the voyage regarding its length and other particulars, and have a competent and skilled master of sound judgment and discretion.[13]

In any event, depending on the nature and purpose of the contract, the owner implies and undertakes that the ship is in good condition to perform the voyage. The ship should be in a condition to encounter whatever perils of the sea a ship of that kind, laden in that way, may be fairly expected to encounter.[14]

One test of seaworthiness is: Would a prudent owner have required that the defect should be made good before sending his ship to sea had he known of it? If he would, the ship was not seaworthy.[15]

In contrast, there will be an inevitable presumption of fact that a vessel is unseaworthy if there is some characteristic of it that prima facie endangers the safety of the vessel or its cargo or which renders it legally or practically impossible for the vessel to go to sea or to carry its cargo safely.[16] On the other hand, defects that are capable of being quickly remedied on the passage do not render a ship unseaworthy.[17] The required seaworthiness

6 See *The Makedonia* [1962] 1 Lloyd's Rep.316; *The Farrandoc* [1967] 2 Lloyd's Rep.276.

7 See *The CMA CGM SA* [2019] EWHC 481 (Admlty).

8 See *The Madeleine* [1967] 2 Lloyd's Rep.224. See also *Golden Fleece Maritime Inc v St Shipping & Transport Corp* [2008] 2 Lloyd's Rep.119.

9 *Bill of Lading*, 2nd ed, 10.98; 3rd ed, 11.102.

10 See *The Apostolis* [1997] 2 Lloyd's Rep.241.

11 See *The Derby* [1985] 2 Lloyd's Rep.325.

12 See *The Silver Constellation* [2008] 2 Lloyd's Rep.440.

13 See *The Framlington Court* [1934] AMC 272 at p. 277.

14 *Bill of Lading*, 2nd ed, 10.100; 3rd ed, 11.104.

15 See *Scrutton on Charterparties and Bills of Lading*, 24th ed at 7–025. Also see *The Cape Bonny* [2017] EWHC 3036 (Comm) per Teare J at [118]: *"The usual test of unseaworthiness is whether a prudent owner would have required that the defect in question should be made good before sending his ship to sea. If he would then the ship is not seaworthy."*

16 See *Scrutton on Charterparties and Bills of Lading*, 24th ed at para. 7–025.

17 See *The Hector* [1955] 2 Lloyd's Rep.218; *The Aconcagua* [2010] 1 Lloyd's Rep.1 at [362]. Also see *Carver on Charterparties*, 2nd ed, 3–122.

is[18] relative to the nature of the ship,[19] for the particular voyage to be concluded, and for the particular phase of the voyage, for summer or winter voyages, rivers and lakes or sea voyages,[20] loading in port and sailing are different[21] and vary with the specific cargo agreed upon in the contract.[22] At the commencement of loading,[23] the vessel must be fit to receive cargo and as an ordinary peril vessel afloat in port at the time of receipt of cargo, but not necessarily fit to sail.[24] After completing each stage, the ship must have the level of fitness required for the next stage.[25] Navigation phases for this purpose are usually marked by different physical conditions, such as for rivers and seas.

Simply put this way, a seaworthy vessel must be in such a state at the start of the voyage that it can perform the contract voyage in safety, both as regards the vessel itself and the particular cargo to be carried on the voyage.[26]

2.3 Structure

In March 2017, the Marshall Islands–flagged very large ore carrier (VLOC) *Stellar Daisy*, owned by Korean company Polaris Shipping, was underway in the South Atlantic Ocean, carrying 260,003 t of iron ore cargo from the Vale Guaiba terminal, Brazil, to China, when it sank on 31 March.

Stellar Daisy was converted from a VLCC in China in 2008. There is a heavy history of the conversion of single-hull tankers to bulk carriers. On 18 March 1967, the supertanker the *Torrey Canyon* was loaded with 117,000 t of crude oil. On her final voyage, the *Torrey Canyon* left the Kuwait National Petroleum Company refinery at Mina Al-Ahmadi, Kuwait (later Al-Ahmadi), with a full cargo of crude oil, on 19 February 1967. The ship had an intended destination of Milford Haven in Wales. On 14 March, she reached the Canary Islands. Following a navigational error, the *Torrey Canyon* struck Pollard's Rock on the extreme western end of the Seven Stones between the Cornish mainland and the Isles of Scilly on 18 March 1967, spilling more than 100,000 t of crude oil into the English Channel. It was the first major oil spill in British and European waters, causing enormous damage to marine life and the livelihoods of local people. It also led to changes in the way people viewed the environment.

Since 1973, the Inter-Governmental Maritime Consultative Organisation ("IMCO" or, as it has been called since 1982, "IMO") has been concerned with minimising occurrences

18 See *Burges v Wickham* [1863] 3 B. & S. 669, Also see *Scrutton* sup. 7–021.

19 See *The Good Friend* [1984] 2 Lloyd's Rep.586.

20 See *Thin v Richards* [1892] 2 Q.B. 141; *Daniels v Harris* [1874] L.R. 10 C.P. 1; *Annen v Woodman* [1810] 3 Taunt. 299.

21 See *McFadden v Blue Star Line* [1905] 1 K.B. 697.

22 See *Scrutton on Charterparties and Bills of Lading*, 24th ed, 7–021.

23 For the position on the approach voyage see *Cie Algerienne v Katana Soc (The Nizeti)* [1958] 2 Lloyd's Rep.502; [1960] 1 Lloyd's Rep.132, holding that the implied warranty of seaworthiness does not attach until the commencement of loading, a decision questioned in Cooke, *Voyage Charters* [2014], para. 11.45–11.46.

24 See *Reed v Page* [1927] 1 K.B. 743; *Svenssons v Cliffe S.S. Co* [1932] 1 K.B. 490, where the stage of loading was held not to be completed when the last sling of pit props was on board but not stowed. Although it was unseaworthy at the time of the accident, there was no breach of warranty, the ship having been seaworthy at the commencement of the stage of loading. Cf. *The Stranna [1938]*, pp. 69, 77, 84. See also as to when loading is completed: *Argonaut Navigation Co v Ministry of Food* [1949] 1 K.B. 572.

25 See *Reed v Page* [1927] 1 K.B. 743. On the doctrine of stages in relation to a contract governed by the Hague–Visby Rules, see *Scrutton*, sup. para. 14–45.

26 *Shipping Law*, Simon Baughten, 7th ed at p. 82.

and consequences of pollution, and under its auspices, the Marine Pollution ("MARPOL") Convention has introduced internationally recognised regulations covering the prevention of pollution of the marine environment by ships. Before 1973, most ships were "single-skinned" or "single-hulled," and in the event of collision or grounding, pollution from the content of ruptured tanks could easily occur. The parties to the MARPOL Convention have gradually been requiring improvements in the design of tanker vessels. The first improvement was that, from 1973, segregated ballast tanks were required for new buildings of over 70,000 mt DWT, and the 1978 MARPOL Convention extended that to new buildings of over 20,000 mt. The next development was the requirement that segregated ballast tanks ("SBTs") should be fitted alongside the vessel in "wing tanks" while oil was carried in the central tanks of the vessel. These vessels were called double-sided vessels. The class description of these vessels was "SBT/PL" (segregated ballast tanks/protected location). The final logical step was to require the cargo tanks to be completely protected not only at the sides of the vessel but also concerning her bottom. These vessels are called "double-hulled" since they are effectively constructed as two hulls one inside the other. Amendments to the MARPOL Convention to secure this end were adopted in March 1992 and came into force in July 1993 by regulation 13F of annex 1 of the MARPOL Convention. They applied to new tankers delivered on or after 6 July 1996, and existing tankers were required to comply with regulation 13F not later than 30 years after the vessel had been delivered by the builder to its original owner.[27]

Some countries introduced these new regulations sooner than required by the convention itself. Thus, after the Exxon Valdez incident in Alaska, the United States promoted the use of double-hulled tankers in US waters by the Oil Pollution Act of 1990. After 100 mi of Atlantic coastline had been polluted by *Erika* in December 1999, the European Union decided that from 21 October 2003, there should be an absolute bar on the carriage of heavy grades of oil between EU ports and terminals on vessels that did not have a double hull as defined in regulations 13F, 13G, and 13H of the MARPOL Convention, other than on certain ice-strengthened vessels. This was achieved by EU Regulation 417/2002 of 18 February 2002, as amended by EU Regulation 1726/2003. IMO likewise decided to accelerate the phasing-out of single-hull tankers and, by annex 2 of MARPOL, adopted "Amendments to Annex 1 of MARPOL 73/78," which contained a regulation (regulation 13H) to that effect in December 2003, to come into force on 5 April 2005. This meant that only double-hulled vessels could carry fuel oil cargoes after that date. There were, however, exemptions from that regime contained in regulations 13H(5), (6), and (7).[28]

The 1969 International Convention on Civil Liability for Oil Pollution Damage has successively launched the 1976 Protocol (CLCPROT76) and the 1984 Protocol (CLCPROT84), 1984 edition (FUNDPROT84). In addition, the International Convention for the Prevention of Pollution from Ships, 1973 (MARPOL78), as amended by the 1978 Protocol, came into being during this period.

The 78th IMO MSC approved Circular No. 1117, Guidelines for Structural Inspection of Bulk Carriers, based on the opinion of the subcommittee on Flag State Implementation, providing PSC officers with guidelines for inspection of bulk carriers as soon as possible.

27 See *The Elli and the Frixos* [2008] 2 Lloyd's Rep.119 (C.A.) at p. 120.
28 Ibid, p. 121.

The purpose of this guide is to train PSC officers to conduct structural inspections of bulk carriers, explain how to verify documents and how to conduct inspections of the actual structure of bulk carriers, etc., reminding port state officials of the points that should be paid attention to during inspections so that they identify weak areas in the structure of bulk carriers, especially older bulk carriers. SOLAS Chapter XII, Additional Safety Measures for Bulk Carriers; Resolution A.862(20), Code of Practice for Safe Handling of Bulk Carriers; Resolution A.866(20), Seafarers and Terminal Personnel on Bulk Carriers Guidelines for Inspection of Cargo Ships; Resolution A.744(18) as amended, Guidelines for Enhanced Survey Procedures During Surveys of Bulk Carriers and Oil Tankers, etc. Those who are familiar with PSC port state inspection have experience. For those with problems with the hull structure, there are 30, and the ship will be detained. If those deficiencies, especially the extent of hull structure, will render the ship unsafe for the voyage, the ship will be detained under code 30 by PSCO.

On 3 June 1979, *Ixtoc I* was an exploratory oil well being drilled by the semi-submersible drilling rig *Sedco 135* in the Bay of Campeche of the Gulf of Mexico, about 100 km (62 mi) northwest of Ciudad del Carmen, Campeche, in waters 50 m (164 ft) deep. On 3 June 1979, the well suffered a blowout, resulting in one of the largest oil spills in history. In Asia, with the collision of the *Hebei Spirit* in South Korea in 2007, about 10,900 t of crude oil leaked into the sea, causing the most serious marine ecological disaster in South Korea's history.

The single-hull tanker became unseaworthy due to non-compliance with MARPOL 73/78. Around 2010, a large number of oil tankers were converted into bulk cargo. Similar to the company owned by *Stella Daisy*, there was also the *Stellar Unicorn*, which was built in 1993 and was about 338 m in length and 58 m in width. It was found that there were cracks in the hull. Emergency repairs are required in Cape Town. The *Stellar Cosmo*, built in 1992, was found defective and went to South Africa for repairs. *Stellar Queen*, built in Japan in 1994, is about 332 m in length and 58 m in width and has DWT of 300,000 mt. It was converted from an oil tanker to a bulk carrier in October 2010. Two cracks appeared on the deck of the ship.

Ships sank frequently due to hull structural problems. Earlier, *Leader L* sank in Canadian coastal waters due to a broken hull; the *Treasure* also sank in South African waters due to cracking of the hull plate, causing damage to the hull and flooding. The ship also caused fuel pollution. The most recent is the container *MOL Comfort*, which encountered heavy weather 200 mi off the coast of Yemen; the ship suffered a crack at midship and broke in two on 17 June 2013. The aft section sank on 27 June, and the bow section, after having been destroyed by fire, on 11 July. Ningbo Maritime Court issued a judgment on 25 May 2016 and dismissed a cargo insurer's (PICC Ningbo) recovery claim against Mitsui OSK Lines Ltd.

Most of the seaworthiness issues involved in the practice are managed by the ship herself. For example, the obvious corrosion of the ship's structure exists at the beginning of the voyage, and the shipowner should have handled it with care and should have found and repaired it during the ship survey, which would make the ship unseaworthy.[29] The ship will also be considered unseaworthy if the owner fails to exercise due diligence carefully,

29 See *The Torenia* [1983] 2 Lloyd's Rep.210 at pp. 230, 234.

causing damage to the ship's piping or bonding materials.[30] Of course, simply because the hatch cover and coaming are not completely watertight, sparks from gaps in the deck welding work can fall and cause a fire. But in any case, if the unproven fire is caused by welding, then the ship is not unseaworthy or unfit for carrying cargo.[31]

The leading case is the *Elli and the Frixos*.[32] By two time charters on the Shelltime 4 form dated respectively 30 May 2003 and 10 August 2004, the claimant owners chartered their oil tankers *Elli and Frixos* to the defendant charterers for the carriage of "all lawful merchandise crude and/or dirty petroleum products including fuel oil." The *Elli* charter, as amended and extended on 1 June 2004 and again on 10 August 2004, was for a period ending on 30 September 2006 plus up to 90 days in charterers' option. The *Frixos* charter was for two years plus 30 days in charterers' option. Elli was built in 1986, and Frixos in 1987. Both vessels were single-hulled. Each cargo tank was protected on the outside by wing ballast tanks which formed a "double-side."

There were two slop tanks in the aft of the cargo tanks. A small part in the aftermost section of each of the two slop tanks was protected on the outside by bunker tanks.

On 4 December 2003, new MARPOL regulations came into operation, setting out new requirements for the carriage of fuel oil from 5 April 2005. After that date, fuel oil could only be carried in double-hulled vessels, subject to certain exemptions, including an exemption under regulation 13H(5) relating to "double-sided" vessels.

At the time of the 2004 amendments and extensions to the *Elli* charter and of the conclusion of the *Frixos* charter on 10 August 2004, the vessels complied with the then-current MARPOL regulations. The parties knew of the impending changes to the MARPOL regulations, but they thought that because the vessels had "double-sides," they would obtain dispensation under the regulation 13H(5) exemption.

On 15 February 2005, the vessels' classification society informed the owners that the vessels were not eligible under the regulation 13H(5) exemption. The strict wording of the exemption required any cargo tank, including slop tanks, to be surrounded by spaces "not used for the carriage of oil." The presence of the bunker tanks meant that the vessels did not fully comply with the requirements of the exemption.

When they realised that the vessels were not entitled to the regulation 13H(5) exemption and that the vessels could not lawfully carry all the cargoes permitted under the charterparties, the charterers contended that the owners were in breach of the charters, and they withheld hire. The charterparties provided inter alia:

> 1. At the date of delivery of the vessel under this charter
>
> . . .
>
> (g) she shall have on board all certificates, documents and equipment required from time to time by any applicable law to enable her to perform the charter service without delay
>
> . . .
>
> 52. ELIGIBILITY & COMPLIANCE
>
> Owners warrant that the vessel is in all respects eligible under application [sic] conventions, laws and regulations for trading to and from the ports and places specified in Clause 4 of the Charter Party and that she shall have on board for inspection by the authorities all certificates, records, compliance letters and other documents required for such services. . . .

30 See *The Subro Valour* [1995] 2 Lloyd's Rep.509.

31 See *The Apostolis* [1997] 2 Lloyd's Rep.240 (C.A.), reversing [1996] 1 Lloyd's Rep.475.

32 *The Elli and the Frixos* [2008] 2 Lloyd's Rep.119 (C.A.).

> Owners further warrant that the vessel does, and will, fully comply with all applicable conventions, laws, regulations and ordinances of any international, national, state or local government entity having jurisdiction including . . . MARPOL 1973/1978 as amended and extended . . .

The owners denied they were in breach of charter and claimed a balance of hire and declarations of entitlement.

The charterers counterclaimed for loss of profits that they would have earned if the vessels had been able to carry fuel oil throughout the balance of the charters. They contended that the owners were obliged to provide vessels fit for the carriage of fuel oil and had not done so.[33]

In the first instance, Cooke J upheld the charterers' contentions. The owners appealed.

Longmore LJ gave the judgment and said:

> In order to carry fuel oil, the vessels needed, as from April 2005, an exemption under regulation 13H(5). That was a document required by law of the flag (Liberia). It was a document required at a particular time. The opening words of the clause, however, look to the time of delivery of the vessel under the charter, namely August 2004. There is thus an inconsistency between the opening words and the words "required from time to time" in the body of the clause. In my judgment, precedence should be given to the words in the body of (g) rather than the words in the introducing phrase on the basis that the "particular should prevail over the general" if that is an acceptable translation of well-known legal principle, "Generalia non specialibus derogant." This would be enough on its own to resolve the appeal in favour of the charterers.[34]

The first two paragraphs of clause 52 lead to the same conclusion. Both paragraphs are relevant. The warranty in the first paragraph is not stated to be a warranty applicable only on delivery of the vessel under the charter, and I would not construe it as such. The exemption required to enable the vessel to carry fuel oil was, after April 2005, a document required for the service of trading to the ports and places specified in clause 4 of the contract.[35]

Mr Kealey, for the owners, made the point that this proves too much in that, even at delivery, the vessels could not trade to European ports or (probably) the USA without being granted a 13H(5) exemption and the parties cannot have intended the owners to be in breach of the clause on the first day of the contractual service. He also pointed out that any particular country could, if it wished, refuse entry under the MARPOL Convention even if the vessel had the relevant exemption. Hong Kong and Australia did just that on a regular basis, so those countries were effectively out of bounds as well. One feels, however, that, if a claim for breach had been made by charterers on the basis that the vessels could not, if ordered to, proceed to, say, Rotterdam or Hong Kong, the case would have had an entirely different shape. As the judge records, it was always the parties' intention that vessels would trade from the Middle East to ports in India and Southeast Asia (perhaps apart from Hong Kong). It is by no means clear that any claim formulated on the national basis supposed by Mr Kealey's argument would have succeeded.

This warranty explicitly applies to the future and expressly refers to the MARPOL Convention as amended and extended. Without the 13H(5) exemption, the vessel did not,

33 Ibid.
34 Ibid, per Longmore LJ at p. 126.
35 Ibid.

in my judgment, comply with the MARPOL Convention, because she was designated fit to carry dirty petroleum products but could not do so unless she had the relevant exemption for double-sided vessels. The vessels were unable to obtain that exemption, and there was thus, on any view, a breach of clause 52 even if there was no breach of the other clauses of the charterparties.[36]

Mr Kealey submitted that this conclusion entailed the absurd result that in or before April 2005, owners would have to take the vessels out of service and rebuild them. On the facts of this case, that is something of an overstatement. Lloyd's solution to the problem was that the slop tanks should become void spaces. No doubt that would involve a measure of construction work to shut off the pipes that introduced the slops into the slop tanks or to seal off the tanks in some other way. To call that a rebuilding is hardly fair. No doubt problematic situations can be posed, for example, that a particular Southeast Asian country suddenly required all fuel oil–carrying vessels to be double-hulled, but the possibility of such a scenario cannot, in my view, be allowed to deflect one from the proper construction of these particular charterparties in the light of the events that have occurred. The doctrine of frustration is, in theory, available if events occur which render the contracts radically different from what the parties contemplated at the outset. One recognises that is a very long stop, but it is, at least, there for cases very different from this.[37]

In conclusion, the Court of Appeal upheld the judge's order and dismissed this appeal.

In this case, due to the new regulations of the MARPOL Convention on oil tankers, which require double hulls, the ships, in this case, are outside the exemption and cannot carry out further trade. The Court of Appeal upheld the judgment of the first instance, finding that the owners had breached the charterparty. The issue of whether the shipowner or charterer bears the risk where further requirements to conduct a particular trade is imposed by third parties after the charterparty is concluded is a matter of construction of the charterparty. The inclusion of an express provision as to seaworthiness may also have somewhat-unexpected consequences upon the application of exception clauses to cases of damage caused by unseaworthiness. If there is an implied obligation as to seaworthiness, exception clauses will, unless their wording is quite clear, be read as not applying to breaches of the implied obligation. If, however, there is an express undertaking of seaworthiness, exceptions will be read as applying to the consequences of a breach of it.[38]

From the charterer's perspective, however, in most cases, it is the date of delivery that is of vital importance. It is possible to postulate circumstances in which a ship might be altered to the benefit of the charterer between the date of the charterparty and the date of delivery, particularly in the case of a charterparty made many months or year or more prior to the agreed time of delivery, in which case it is suggested that the ship's compliance with her description ought to be answered with reference to the date of delivery. In some such cases, indeed, the shipowner may be obliged to carry out modifications to the ship between the date of charterparty and the date of delivery.[39]

---

36 Ibid, per Sir Anthony Clarke MR at p. 127.

37 Ibid, p. 127.

38 See *Scrutton on Charterparties and Bills of Lading*, 24th ed at para. 7–33.

39 See *Carver on Charterparties*, 2nd ed at para. 3–009.

2.4 Vessel broke in two and sank

As mentioned previously, especially for large bulk cargoes, once there is a problem with the ship's structure, it is likely to have catastrophic consequences. Such as the case of the *Hopestar.*[40]

The *Hopestar* was a cargo vessel of 5,267 gross and 3,192 net registered tonnage which belonged to the defendants. On 2 November 1948, she sailed from the Tyne in ballast to Philadelphia, where she was to load a cargo for a Mediterranean port. On 13 November, she ran into heavy weather, which was severe, but not exceptional. The wind was force 9, with gusts of force 10. At 1:00 a.m. (GMT) on the 14th, she reported heavy-weather damage in the way of the deep tank. It was sufficiently serious for her to request that Lloyd's Register surveyors and repairers should be available on arrival; but it can hardly have caused the master much anxiety, for he gave her expected time of arrival as 10:30 p.m. on the 17th, and that meant that he anticipated that she would complete the voyage at her normal speed of 10 knots. At about noon on the 14th, she sent out her usual weather message, which gave a position somewhere south of Newfoundland and showed that she was then making about 5 knots and the wind was still force 9. She was by then beginning to move out of the heavy weather; it moderated very quickly in the afternoon of the 14th. She might be expected to have sent her next message at about 4:00 p.m., but she did not. Her silence did not at first give rise to alarm, but when by the 19th there was no report of her arrival, inquiries were started and an aeroplane search began on the 22nd. She had disappeared completely without, so far as is known, giving any signal of distress and without leaving any trace and with the loss of all hands.[41]

The plaintiff is the widow of one of her crew and sues the defendants in what is in the nature of a test case, alleging that they knew or ought to have known that she was deficient in longitudinal strength and that the cause of the casualty was that, by reason of such deficiency, she broke in two. The alleged weakness was about amidships in the way of the stokehold at frames 90 and 91.

Devlin J (as he then was) began by considering how the vessel came to be designed and built, and I shall first state how the longitudinal strength of a ship is assessed. A ship which is built to the requirements of a classification society – for example, Lloyd's Register – is designed according to the rules laid by the society which provide for the necessary strength in all respects. The rules show what strength and thickness of the material are required in each part of the ship. The approval of the plan by Lloyd's Register before the building is begun shows that the rules have been complied with. But besides being a classification society, Lloyd's Register is also the assigning authority to allot a load line under the Merchant Shipping (Safety and Load Line Conventions) Act, 1932. One of the factors affecting the strength of the vessel at any given moment is her draught. The stronger the vessel, the larger the draught she can sustain, and so the smaller the freeboard. If a vessel is 100 A1 at Lloyd's or satisfies the requirements of any other recognized classification society, her strength is such as to entitle her automatically to the minimum freeboard. In the case of a cargo vessel, the owner naturally wants to get the largest draught he can and therefore qualify for the minimum freeboard. If a vessel does not comply with these

40 *The Hopestar* [1952] 2 Lloyd's Rep.105.
41 Ibid, p. 121.

requirements, then her strength must be calculated to see what freeboard she is entitled to have. This is done in accordance with a test laid down in the Act of 1932, and to be found in rule XXXVII of the second schedule to the act. The same test is set out in the Load Line Rules, 1941, [1941] S.R. & O., No. 1464 in Rule 44b, and it is by the latter number that it is generally identified. The test was prescribed as a result of the International Load Line Convention of 1930 and embodies the rules of leading classification societies.[42]

In considering the modulus as a useful standard, Devlin J observed that two qualifications have to be borne in mind. The first is that it is a general and simple designer's test. There are certain factors which may give strength to a vessel but which are not valued in the modulus. There is, for example, the shape of the vessel – whether she is full or fine. These and other matters would, if they were all to be taken into account, make too elaborate a calculation for general use, but if it is required to make a more exact assessment of an individual vessel, they may have to be taken into account. Whether there were any factors in the case of the *Hopestar* differentiating her actual strength from her strength calculated according to the modulus – which is described as her conventional strength – is a matter of controversy.[43]

Devlin J further considered how these errors in design came to be committed. The defendant company was formed in July 1935. Sometime before that, a Mr Mann, a director in a Newcastle firm of ship managers, who subsequently became a director of the defendant company and the registered manager of the *Hopestar*, had begun to interest himself in the building of the *Hopestar* and in the formation of a company to take her over. One of the objects of building her was to provide a vessel to try out a new and experimental form of machinery. The vessel was designed and built by Messrs Swan, Hunter, and Wigham Richardson, the well-known Tyne shipbuilders, at their Wallsend yard. There was nothing experimental about the hull design, which was taken from that of another ship which had given satisfaction.[44]

Devlin J observed that, in fact, it was an error of the Lloyd's Register surveyor, and if he was wrong in the general view which he had just expressed, he should hold that the employer was not under a duty to go behind, as it were, the Lloyd's Register certificate. This is on the ground that such an inquiry would involve a retrogression beyond the point to which a reasonable employer can be expected to go, rather than upon the ground that the duty of the Lloyd's Register surveyor is public or quasi-judicial.[45]

On the onus of proof, that the presumption that the sinking of a ship without apparent reason was due to unseaworthiness was a mere prima facie presumption; if there were two explanations equally consistent and one involved no liability on the defendants, the onus was on the plaintiff to prove the cause of the loss, and the burden was not transferred to the defendants unless the nature of the loss and its relationship to the defendants' negligence were first ascertained and proved.[46]

In a case where substantially all the facts have been brought to light, it is no doubt legitimate to argue that some cause must be found, and therefore the one that has the most

42 *The Hopestar* [1952] 2 Lloyd's Rep.105 at p. 122.
43 Ibid.
44 Ibid, p. 123.
45 Ibid, p. 130.
46 Ibid, per Devlin J at p. 130.

to be said for it should be selected. Where it can fairly be said that all possible causes have been canvassed, the strongest must be the winner. But in a case where all direct evidence is missing, there is no ground for saying that the most plausible conjecture must perforce be the true explanation. The answer that may well have to be given is that not enough is known about the circumstances of the loss to enable the inquirer to say how it happened. All that he can say is that no theory advanced has been able to collect enough support from the facts to make it more likely than not that it happened in that way and not in any other.[47]

Devlin J considered that the argument is put in two ways. First, it is said that this is an unexplained loss, and so unseaworthiness is to be presumed; alternatively – and this is another facet of the same argument – once the plaintiff has established structural weakness, the burden passes to the defendants to disprove that that weakness was the cause of the loss. In support of the first point, there was cited a passage from *Scrutton on Charterparties*, 15th edition, p. 98, in the following terms:

> The burden of proving unseaworthiness rests upon the party who asserts it and the party intending to rely upon unseaworthiness must plead it with sufficient particularity. But where a ship, shortly after leaving port and without any apparent reason sinks or leaks, the mere facts afford prima facie evidence of unseaworthiness, which must be rebutted.[48]

Devlin J does not think this involves anything more than the sort of presumption that is ordinarily raised by the res ipsa loquitur rule. The prima facie presumption is of value only if no further evidence is elucidated. As soon as further evidence is adduced, a plaintiff has to make out his case on the whole of the evidence. Since in the end the plaintiff has not satisfied that, on the balance of probability, the vessel was, at the material time, in a dangerous condition, she fails. Alternatively, the plaintiff fails if, at the end of the evidence, there are two possible explanations, each equally consistent with the evidence and one involving no liability. Here, Devlin J observed the defendants have advanced an alternative hypothesis which is at least as plausible as the plaintiff's hypothesis, and so her case fails. The res ipsa loquitur rule is designed to relieve the plaintiff in the first instance from proving negligence or breach of duty otherwise than by proof of the accident itself.[49]

Devlin J stated that this general statement must be read in relation to the facts of the case. It does not mean that, once a breach is proved, damage of any sort, however different in character from the ordinary consequences of such a breach, is presumed to be caused by it. The principle, Lord Wright says, applies only when the breach increases, or at least alters, the risk of loss or damage. You cannot tell whether the risk has been altered if you do not know what the loss or damage is. In this case, it was ice damage, and Lord Wright was dealing with that admitted fact. If the damage had been found at the end of the voyage and there was nothing to show whether it was attributable to ice or some other cause, Lord Wright might not intend to say that it was enough to prove that the defendants were in breach of their duty to provide icebreakers and that that breach was in operation.[50]

This type of question has recently been considered in the Court of Appeal in *Watts v Enfield Rolling Mills (Aluminium) Ltd.*,[51] where the burden of proof had to be determined

47 Ibid, p. 139.
48 Now *Scrutton on Charterparties and Bills of Lading*, 24th ed at para. 7–030.
49 *The Hopestar* [1952] 2 Lloyd's Rep.105, per Devlin J at p. 139.
50 Ibid, p. 141.
51 *Watts v Enfield Rolling Mills (Aluminium), Ltd.* [1952] 1 T.L.R. 733.

in the case of a breach of a statutory duty under the Factories Act, 1937. Lord Justice Denning, at p. 738, stated the principle as follows:

> The first burden which is always on the plaintiff is this: he must show that his injury was caused by the relevant danger, that is, by the danger against which Parliament intended to guard him, such as a circular saw, a flying fragment, a revolving belt or suchlike. . . . When that is proved or admitted then the second thing that the plaintiff must show is that there was a breach of a statutory duty which was intended to guard against that very danger. When both those are shown, the proper inference is that the breach was the cause of the injury unless the occupier proves that it was not.

As Devlin J noted, it would be surprising if, in a case which, as so many do, involves a breach of the Factory Act and also of a common law duty of an employer to an employee, the burden of proof should be different in the two causes of action. If the plaintiff had been able to establish from some extraneous source that the vessel actually broke in two, there would still have been a question to be argued whether the structural weakness was a cause of the breaking in two. The defendants might then have argued that the stresses to which the vessel was subject, notwithstanding her structural weakness, were never sufficient to cause the breaking in two, and that there must have been some further intervention, such as a mine, which would have caused the loss, whether she was structurally weak or not. But the burden of establishing all that would have been upon them. It is a burden which is not, in my judgment, transferred to them unless the nature of the loss or damage and its relationship to the breach have first been ascertained and proved. In the same way, it may be that, if the structural weakness was the cause of the loss, the defendants would have been held liable for it, notwithstanding that they were responsible for a part only of the weakness, unless they could show that, but for the additional weakness for which they were not responsible, the loss would not have happened. But this point does not now arose judgment for the defendants.

In a case where substantially all the facts have been brought to light, it is no doubt legitimate to argue that some causes must be found, and therefore the one that has the most to be said for it should be selected. Where it can fairly be said that all possible causes have been canvassed, the strongest must be the winner. But in a case where all direct evidence is missing, there is no ground for saying that the most plausible conjecture must perforce be the true explanation. The answer that may well have to be given is that not enough is known about the circumstances of the loss to enable the inquirer to say how it happened. All that he can say is that no theory advanced has been able to collect enough support from the facts to make it more likely than not that it happened in that way and not in any other.[52]

Similarly, if there are obvious corrosion defects in the steel structure of the ship, which existed at the beginning of the voyage, but the shipowner failed to exercise due diligence, it should have been discovered and repaired during the ship inspection, and if the result was that the ship was unseaworthy, the owners would have to take responsibility.[53] Owners are also responsible for failure to maintain adequate systems to inspect and repair damage and deformation of certain frames, etc., which are attached to the hull's shell plating, resulting in seawater entering the cargo hold through cracks in the plating.[54]

52 *The Hopestar*, sup., per Devlin J at p. 139.
53 *The Torenia* [1983] 2 Lloyd's Rep.210 at pp. 230, 234.
54 *The Toledo* [1995] 1 Lloyd's Rep.40 at pp. 50, 52–53.

The burden of proving unseaworthiness rests upon the party who asserts it, and the party intending to rely upon unseaworthiness must plead it with sufficient particularity. But where a ship, shortly after leaving port and without any apparent reason, sinks or leaks, the mere facts afford prima facie evidence of unseaworthiness, which must be rebutted.[55] However, the carrier's responsibility does not begin until the ship comes into his orbit. Accordingly, if he has a new ship built for him or buys or charters or takes over a ship from another, he will not be liable for damage by unseaworthiness due to existing defects which could not be discovered by him, or competent experts employed by him, by exercise of due diligence.[56]

2.5 Main engine breakdown

The main engine of a vessel is just like the heart of the human body. Common problems happen with the main engine, such as air leakage. Because the air control is constantly in an open position when the engine is in use, leakages in this area are often overlooked, like fuel leakage or fuel valve malfunction, sparks in the main engine exhaust, stuck fuel rack, and faulty alarms and sensors. Once there is a failure or breakdown that occurs during the sea voyage and it cannot be repaired in time, it will directly cause the ship to be out of control and cause an emergency; the vessel may aground and block the channel, and the vessel needs to be salvaged.

In the *Antigoni*,[57] the vessel was built by German shipbuilders in 1977. Her main engine was an 18-cylinder V-form 4-cycle diesel engine developing 2,610 bhp at 800 rpm built by Alpha Diesel A/S. Attached to the crankshaft of the engine were ten counterweights whose function was to balance the crankshaft and to prevent or counteract vibration. The ten counterweights were heavy steel blocks with projections or shoulders which slid into grooves machined in the crank web. The counterweights rotated with the crankshaft, and the centrifugal force thus generated had the effect that the shoulders of the counterweights were pressed against the grooves in the crankshaft. A single bolt was screwed through each counterweight. The end of the bolt pressed hard against the crank web and pushed the counterweight away from the crankshaft, thus keeping the shoulders of the counterweight in tight contact at all times with the grooves in the crankshaft.

To maintain the tightness of the counterweights and to prevent them from working lose, it was necessary, as a matter of routine maintenance and at regular intervals, to inspect the bolts and to ensure that they were keeping the counterweight pressed tight against the crankshaft. A small amount of wear could occur on the shoulders of the counterweight and the face of the securing bolts, and the effect of such wear was to reduce the pre-compression of the bolt. If this was not remedied, greater amounts of wear could occur, which in turn could lead to the pre-compression becoming lost altogether and to the counterweight becoming loose and being able to come in contact with the nearby connecting rods, thus causing major damage to the engine. Alpha Diesel, therefore, recommended that the bolts be checked and re-tightened about every 5,000 engine hours.

55 See *Scrutton on Charterparties and Bills of Lading*, 24th ed, 7–030.
56 Ibid, 14–046.
57 *The Antigoni* [1991] 1 Lloyd's Rep.209 (C.A.).

On 16 September 1986, while the vessel was steaming some 110 mi west of Freetown in the course of her cargo-carrying voyage, the vessel's engine sustained a major breakdown and the vessel became immobilized as a result. Subsequently, the owners needed to accept towage assistance on the terms of Lloyd's Open Form from another vessel, *Goldenay*. *Antigoni* was successfully towed to Las Palmas, where she arrived on 1 October 1986, and where the main engine was eventually replaced thus enabling the vessel to complete her voyage.

When the engine was inspected at Las Palmas, it was found that two of the ten counterweights could pivot axially on the crankshaft. It was found that the counterweight attached to the aft web of the no. 9 crank had struck a connecting rod. This in turn had caused the collapse of the connecting rod, which in turn had produced the result that the connecting rods and pistons of no. 9 unit on both the port and the starboard sides had broken their way through the engine entablature.

The cargo interests sought to recover from the owners the amount of the salvage which they had become liable to pay and had paid to the owners of *Goldenay*. The cargo interests contended that the ship's engineers had negligently failed to carry out the steps described in Alpha Diesel's service letter no. 153 dated 9 November 1981. The last occasion on which the ship's engineers had examined the securing bolts of the counterweights was on 2 July 1986, and it was common ground that this was only some 900 to 950 engine hours before the casualty. Cargo interests contended that the owners had failed to exercise due diligence to make the vessel seaworthy within article IV, rule 1 of the Hague–Visby Rules.

Considering all the evidence, Anthony Diamond QC, at first instance, observed that there was no doubt that the vessel's engineers had failed properly to carry out the very clear and detailed procedures described in Alpha Diesel's service letter no. 153 and that this failure was the direct cause of the engine breakdown; the cause of the casualty on 16 September 1986 was the owners' failure to exercise due diligence to make the vessel seaworthy, and both the salvage expenditure incurred by cargo interests and the general average expenditure incurred by the owners were caused by an actionable breach of the relevant contracts of carriage. There would be judgment for the cargo interests.

Anthony Diamond QC stated:[58]

> In the result I find that the cause of the casualty on Sept. 16, 1986 was the owners' failure to exercise due diligence to make the ship seaworthy. It follows that both the salvage expenditure incurred by cargo interests and the general average expenditure incurred by owners were caused by an actionable breach of the relevant contracts of carriage.

The owners appealed, contending that the unseaworthiness of the vessel was not caused by want of due diligence to make the ship seaworthy (article IV, rule 1), and that the casualty was caused by a latent defect not discoverable by due diligence (article IV, rule 2[p]).

The decision of the Court of Appeal, according to Staughton LJ, was:[59]

> On that view of art. IV, r. 1, it might be thought that the exception in r. 2(p) of latent defects not discoverable by due diligence is superfluous. That would not necessarily be an obstacle, since the rules were the product of an international Convention and have to be applied in

58 Ibid, per Anthony Diamond Q.C. [1990] 1 Lloyd's Rep.45 at p. 50.
59 Ibid, per Staughton LJ [1991] 1 Lloyd's Rep.209 (C.A.) at p. 213.

many countries throughout the world, which may not have the same predilection for avoiding surplusage. But Scrutton (p. 450) points to a case where r. 2(p) would be important:

> Another possible meaning for these words resulting in their giving the shipowner an immunity additional to that provided in Rule 1 of this Article is that they cover defects which would not have been discovered by the exercise of due diligence even though the shipowner could not show that he had in fact exercised such diligence.

That view had the support of Mr Justice Branson in *Corporacion Argentina de Productores de Carnes v Royal Mail Lines Ltd.*[60]

Staughton LJ turns to consider the shipowners' two defences and to see how they stand on that analysis of the law, taking first the defence of latent defect not discoverable by due diligence within rule 2(p). If one leaves aside the evidence relating to *Antigoni* in this case, there is nothing more than the speculation of experts and a meagre account of other casualties. The latent defect, to be relevant, must be a propensity of counterweight bolts in this type of engine to become loose in some period of less than 5,000 running hours since they were last tightened. I limit the definition in that way because the shipowners were warned that there was a possibility that bolts might become loose in a longer period, and due diligence required at least that after 5,000 hours, they should be checked.[61]

According to the decision of the Court of Appeal, the defendants had, on the evidence, failed to prove due diligence. The learned judge had considered what alternative explanation of the casualty there might be other than lack of due diligence and could find none; in those circumstances, he was fully entitled not to accept the evidence as to due diligence. The appeal would be dismissed.[62]

The main engine must be overhauled for a certain period of running hours; otherwise, it is likely to cause problems with the main engine bearing. In the *Fjord Wind*,[63] the vessel was voyage chartered on the Norgrain form to lift cargo on the River Plate. Clause 1 of the charter provided that the ship should be "tight, staunch and strong and in every way fit for the voyage" at the time of commencing its approach voyage. Clause 35 provided, in words echoing the terms of article 3(1) of the Hague Rules, that the "[o]wners shall be bound before and at the beginning of the voyage to exercise due diligence to make the ship seaworthy." The question arose whether clause 1 contained an absolute warranty that the ship was seaworthy when it commenced the approach voyage. It was held that, but for clause 35, clause 1 would have imposed an absolute duty. However, read together with clause 35, its meaning was different.

At the first instance, Moor-Bick J observed that clause 35 imported into this charter the fundamental scheme of obligations and exemptions in relation to the carriage of cargo contained in the Hague Rules; it was clear that the parties intended that the owners' liability for loss of and damage or delay to the cargo was intended to be governed by those terms. Insofar as clause 1 would impose on the owner a more onerous obligation about seaworthiness, the parties must have intended it to give way to clause 35 concerning the laden voyage.[64]

60 *Corporacion Argentina de Productores de Carnes v Royal Mail Lines Ltd.* [1939] 64 Ll.L. Rep.188 at p. 192.

61 *The Antigoni* [1991] 1 Lloyd's Rep.209 (C.A.) at p. 213.

62 Ibid, pp. 215–216.

63 *The Fjord Wind* [1999] 1 Lloyd's Rep.307 [2000] 2 Lloyd's Rep.191 (C.A.).

64 Ibid, per Moor-Bick J at p. 314.

Moor-Bick J continued that clause 1 governed the obligation of the shipowner about the seaworthiness of the vessel in respect of events occurring during the period prior to the commencement of loading, that being the point at which the cargo-carrying stage of the adventure began; clause 35 governed the obligation concerning events occurring thereafter, although the fulfilment of the owners' duty would depend on what had gone on before.[65] The obligations of the disponent owners about the seaworthiness of the vessel during the cargo-carrying voyage were limited to an obligation to exercise due diligence before and at the beginning of that voyage to make the vessel seaworthy, and in the event, the disponent owners' obligations about the carriage of the cargo were no more or less extensive than those of the registered owners under the bill of lading.[66]

The history of crankpin bearing failures was of particular significance about the question of whether the owners exercised due diligence to make the vessel seaworthy; as far as unseaworthiness at the commencement of the voyage was concerned, the most telling evidence was the very fact that there was a failure of the no. 6 crankpin bearing within a few hours of the vessel's departure from the loading port. There was nothing to suggest that the conditions which the vessel encountered in the river were, in any respect, unusual or that the casualty was the result of any outside intervention, and although it had been impossible to identify the precise cause of the bearing failure, the inference must be that there was a defect of some kind in the bearing itself or the lubricating system which rendered the vessel unfit to encounter the ordinary incidents of the voyage.

Where a vessel suffered a serious casualty without any outside intervention, the natural inference was that there was something wrong with her that a prudent owner would have rectified if he had known about it. It was clear that there was a defect in the vessel's propulsion equipment which was liable to result in a crankpin failure at some time during the voyage without warning and with potentially disastrous consequences. It had manifested itself as a propensity for crankpin bearings to fail at unpredictable intervals. if a prudent owner had become aware of the nature of the defect, he would have taken steps to correct it rather than risk the consequences. The vessel was unseaworthy both when she left Rosario and when she left Barcelona at the beginning of her approach voyage.

The Court of Appeal noted that the history of bearing failures was sufficiently serious to call for a thorough investigation into, among other things, the physical condition of the failed bearing shells, the lubrication conditions, and the operating conditions under which the failures occurred; it was for the owners to show that they and those for whom they were responsible exercised due diligence to make the ship seaworthy, or that any failure to do so, if there was one, did not cause or contribute to the casualty. Since the cause of the casualty remained unknown, the owners could only discharge that burden by showing that they and MAN, the engine builders, between them did not overlook any lines of inquiry which competent experts could reasonably be expected to have pursued; in the absence of what investigations were carried out, the court was not satisfied that that was so, and the owners were unable to discharge the burden of showing that they exercised due diligence to make the vessel seaworthy.[67]

65 Ibid.
66 Ibid, p. 315.
67 Ibid, p. 323.

Moor-Bick J stated that even if there had not been a want of due diligence about the failure to implement MAN's recommendations and the change of inlet temperature of the lubricating oil, the court was unable to find that the casualty would still have occurred; the plaintiffs were entitled to succeed in their claim on the ground that the loss was caused by the unseaworthiness of the vessel, for which the owners were liable under their separate contracts of carriage.[68]

In the Court of Appeal, Clarke LJ's view was that clause 1 provided that the vessel, being tight, staunch, and strong and in every way fitted for the voyage, should, with all convenient speed, proceed to one or more loading ports and there load; clause 35 expressly applied "before and at the beginning of the voyage," which must include the loading process, so that under clause 35, the owners had to exercise due diligence to make her seaworthy for the loading process and thereafter they must exercise due diligence to make her seaworthy for the cargo-carrying voyage itself. Clause 35 directly affected the true construction of clause 1 and was intended to affect the whole operation of the clause; the expression "before and at the beginning of the voyage" was apt to include the whole period before the beginning of the voyage.[69]

Clarke LJ noted it was extremely unlikely that the parties would have agreed on a different regime for cargo damage under the bill of lading and the charter; they would be expected to apply a Hague or Hague–Visby Rules' regime and not have agreed on an absolute warranty of seaworthiness, and in particular, they would not be likely to have agreed on a different regime for different voyages which were both subject to the same contract in respect of which the charterers were to pay the freight. The correct construction of clauses 1 and 35 of the charter, when read together in the context of the contract as a whole and in light of the commercial considerations, was that the disponent owners' obligations as to seaworthiness at each stage were the same, namely, to exercise due diligence to make the vessel seaworthy.[70]

Clarke LJ stated:[71]

> In these circumstances the Judge was in my opinion right to hold that the vessel was unseaworthy when she left Rosario because there was present a defect which meant that it could not operate on an ordinary voyage, since it failed on the voyage down-river, with the consequences described above, which were entirely foreseeable. Thus, if the owners had known that such a defect was present the bearing would fail in those circumstances, they would have rectified the defect.

Clarke LJ continued:[72]

> I agree with the Judge that seaworthiness is concerned with the state of the vessel rather than with whether the owners acted prudently or with due diligence. The only relevance of the standard of the reasonably prudent owner is to ask whether, *if he had known of the defect*, he would have taken steps to rectify it. In the instant case, there can I think be no doubt that he would if he had known that there was a defect which would cause the bearing to fail as it did, which it seems to me is the relevant state of knowledge for these purposes. It follows that

68 Ibid, p. 327.
69 Ibid, per Clarke LJ [2000] 2 Lloyd's Rep.191 (C.A.) at p. 196.
70 Ibid, pp. 196–197.
71 Ibid, p. 199.
72 Ibid.

> the vessel was unseaworthy when she left Rosario because she was not in a fit condition to withstand an ordinary voyage down the river Paraná.
>
> (emphasis added)

According to Clarke LJ, it is not in dispute that, once the claimants have proved unseaworthiness, the burden of establishing due diligence is on the owners. It is also common ground that they must establish that due diligence to make the vessel seaworthy was exercised, not only by themselves, their servants, and their agents, but also by their independent contractors. That has been accepted to be the correct position since the decision of the House of Lords in *Riverstone Meat Co. Pty. Ltd. v Lancashsire Shipping Co. Ltd.*[73] That is a very important principle in the facts of this case because the judge held that the owners had shown that they and their servants or employees had exercised due diligence but had failed to show that their independent contractors, MAN, had done so.

The principal problem which bedevilled this whole case was that, despite a considerable amount of investigation both before and after the casualty, the owners never succeeded in discovering the cause of the problem which led to the defect or defects in the no. 6 crankpin bearing, which in turn led to failure. As the judge pointed out, this made it difficult for the owners to prove that due diligence had been exercised. He referred in this connection to the following passage from the judgment of Lord Justice Staughton in the *Antigoni*:[74]

> Of course a Judge may be so impressed by the evidence of those whose task it was to exercise due diligence as to find that they did so, even though he is totally mystified as to how the vessel became unseaworthy; he may think it right to believe that evidence, while not being able to identify any possible latent defect which they can reasonably have overlooked. There may indeed be cases where a Judge has reached that result. But in practice the shipowner will wish, if he can, to lead evidence of such a latent defect and the Judge must necessarily have regard to that evidence before deciding whether due diligence has been exercised. If he concludes that there is no possibility of a latent defect which could be overlooked in the exercise of due diligence, he will find it very difficult to accept that due diligence was in fact exercised, if not wholly impossible. . . . There is not imposed on the shipowner in law any burden to establish a latent defect if he seeks to rely on art. IV, r. 1. But (I would not start the sentence with but) he will find it much easier to establish due diligence if he can point to the likelihood of a latent defect, and much more difficult if he can suggest none, or only one which is wholly implausible.

Clarke LJ noted that as the judge pointed out on p. 319, the problem facing the owners here was that they sought to show that they had exercised due diligence to make the ship seaworthy, but they were unable to identify that latent defect which was said to be responsible for the crankpin bearing failure. Clarke LJ observed that there was a problem causing bearing failures which had been identified before Durban. The casualty, in this case, demonstrated that the problem had not been cured; the existence of the problem called for detailed investigations in Durban, and the owners delegated the making of those investigations to MAN. The owners did not produce any evidence as to the extent of the investigations carried out by MAN and failed to discharge the burden of proof that was on them of exercising due diligence.[75]

The decision of the Court of Appeal, as Clarke LJ said, was:[76]

---

73 *Riverstone Meat Co. Pty. Ltd. v Lancashsire Shipping Co. Ltd.* [1961] 1 Lloyd's Rep.57; [1961] A.C. 807.
74 *The Antigoni* [1991] 1 Lloyd's Rep.209 at p. 213.
75 *The Fjord Wind*, sup. per Clarke LJ at p. 203.
76 Ibid, p. 204.

> For these reasons I am not persuaded that the Judge was wrong to hold that the owners had failed to discharge the burden of proving that they exercised due diligence, through themselves, their servants, their agents and their independent contractors, to make the vessel seaworthy before she sailed from Rosario by responding sufficiently to the earlier bearing failures. That conclusion makes it unnecessary to consider the other bases upon which the Judge found a failure to exercise due diligence. I shall not therefore further lengthen this judgment by doing so.
>
> It follows from the conclusion that the owners have failed to show that due diligence was exercised to make the vessel seaworthy before she sailed from Rosario that, given the further conclusion that the vessel was unseaworthy at that time, the defendants are liable for any loss caused by that unseaworthiness as damages for breach of the charter or of the contract of carriage contained in or evidenced by the bill of lading as the case may be. On that basis, I do not understand the defendants to challenge the conclusions reached by the Judge on questions of causation or quantum and none of the interesting questions arising out of the abandonment of the voyage and the law of frustration arise. In all the circumstances I would dismiss the appeal.

In this case, where the charter contained an express and unqualified warranty of seaworthiness at the date of the charter and a separate clause which obliged the owners to exercise due diligence to make the ship seaworthy, it was held that the owners' obligation at each stage was the same, namely, to exercise due diligence. Any implied warranty of seaworthiness on the approach voyage would, it seems, be similarly qualified. As Clarke LJ said on page 196, "The expression 'before and at the beginning of the voyage' is apt to include the whole period before the beginning of a voyage." The owners' obligation under clause 1 was therefore to exercise due diligence to make the ship seaworthy.

On 14 July 2011, in the course of a laden voyage from Argentina to China, a Suezmax oil tanker[77] suffered an engine breakdown. The timing of the breakdown was unfortunate; the vessel was seeking to avoid a tropical storm, or typhoon Ma-on. Towage assistance was required, and on 18 July 2011, the vessel was taken in tow by *Koyo Maru*. The vessel was not permitted to enter a Japanese port of refuge or to discharge her cargo in the Chinese port of discharge. She was therefore taken to Yosu in South Korea, where her cargo was transferred into another vessel by an STS operation on 2 and 3 August 2011. Due to the approach of another tropical storm, or typhoon Muifa, *Koyo Maru* took the vessel out to sea on 3 August and returned on 9 August 2011. *Koyo Maru* was then released, and the vessel was berthed for repairs.

A general average was declared. On 28 July 2011, the defendants provided a guarantee on behalf of the cargo interests by which they promised to pay any contribution to the general average, "which may hereafter be ascertained to be properly due." In due course, on 13 March 2013, an average adjustment was prepared which assessed the cargo's contribution to the general average for about US$2.5 million. The adjustment was later amended, assessing cargo's contribution to the general average at approximately US$2.1 million.

The owners accepted that the vessel was unseaworthy at the commencement of the voyage because of the presence of metal particles in the lube oil system lying downstream of the lube oil filters but not (at the commencement of the voyage) circulating within the lube oil itself. The burden, therefore, lies upon the owners, according to the Hague–Visby Rules, which were incorporated in the contract of carriage, to show that they exercised

77 *The Cape Bonny* [2017] EWHC 3030 (Comm); [2018] 1 Lloyd's Rep.356.

due diligence to make the vessel seaworthy before the commencement of the voyage. They say that they can discharge the burden of proof because the main engine failure was caused by sudden and catastrophic damage to the no. 1 main bearing caused in turn by the metal particles which had been present in the lube oil piping from the date of build (in 2005) – referred to as weld slag – breaking off from that piping during the voyage in a period of bad weather, working their way through the lube oil piping into the bearing assemblies over a period of weeks and then rapidly causing damage to the no. 1 main bearing.

By contrast, the defendants say that the particles had been generated by spark erosion or by damage to the vessel's chain drive gear or had been permitted to enter the engine by poor procedures when the crew were cleaning the filters. They further say that there was progressive wear to the no. 1 main bearing shells caused by damaged lube oil filters failing to remove the particles from the lube oil. Failing to maintain in good condition the shaft earthing device and the lube oil filters was also a failure of due diligence, as was the failure to use proper procedures when cleaning the lube oil filters. The defendants denied any liability to contribute to the general average, alleging that casualty was caused by actionable fault on the part of her owners, namely, a failure to exercise due diligence to make the vessel seaworthy.

Teare J commented on unseaworthiness:[78]

> The usual test of unseaworthiness is whether a prudent owner would have required that the defect in question should be made good before sending his ship to sea. If he would then the ship is not seaworthy; see Scrutton on Charteparties [*sic*] 23rd.ed.para.7–025. Had the Owners known that main bearing no.1 was suffering from an abnormal degree of wear I consider that they, acting as prudent owners, would have required that the bearing be repaired. The presence of abnormal wear exposes the bearing, and hence the main engine, to the risk of breakdown and a prudent owner would require that that risk be removed before the ship was sent to sea. These conclusions are supported by the evidence of Mr. Shortall, the Defendants' expert, who said that had the clearances been checked "it is highly likely that the bearing would have been repaired before the voyage in question." Although this comment was based upon MAN's assessment of the relationship between crankshaft deflections and bearing clearances the same conclusion must follow from MET's assessment of that relationship. In any event, in addition to the presence of wear, there was also the presence of foreign particles and the presence of damaged lub oil filters. There can be no doubt that the presence of all three rendered the vessel unseaworthy at the commencement of the voyage.

For due diligence, Teare J added:[79]

> The duty of due diligence imposed by Article III r.1 of the Hague–Visby Rules to make the vessel seaworthy is the equivalent of the common law duty of care. Thus, if an inspection conducted by the crew failed to reveal a defect there will be a failure to exercise due diligence if (1) the examination was, in the circumstances, of a character such as a skilled and prudent

78 *The Cape Bonny* [2018] 1 Lloyd's Rep.356.

79 Ibid, per Teare J at p. 373. Also see *Scrutton on Charterparties and Bills of Lading*, 24th ed, 14–047. "The standard imposed by the obligation to exercise due diligence appears to be equivalent to that of the common law duty of care. Thus, if an inspection of the vessel's machinery by or on behalf of the shipowner fails to reveal a defect, the question whether the failure amounts to want of due diligence must be answered by considering (1) whether the examination was, in the circumstances, of a character such as a skilled and prudent shipowner should reasonably have made, and (2) if so, whether the examination was carried out with reasonable skill, care and competence. There is no failure of due diligence merely because precautions are not taken which subsequent experience shows to be necessary."

> shipowner should reasonably have made and (2) if so, whether the examination was carried out with reasonable skill, care and competence.

According to Teare J, the burden of proving due diligence lies on the owners as carriers pursuant to article IV, rule 1 of the Hague–Visby Rules. But no onus as to due diligence arises except after proof of unseaworthiness and damage resulting therefrom.

Teare J views that a custom is a reasonable and universal rule of action in a locality followed not because it is believed to be the general law of the land or because the parties following it have made particular agreements to observe it but because it is, in effect, the common law within that place to which it extends, although contrary to the general law of the realm. Evidence of custom may be admissible both for interpreting express terms and as the basis for implying terms into the contract. To be enforced by the courts, a custom must be (1) reasonable, (2) certain, (3) consistent with the contract, (4) notorious in the sense of being universally acquiesced in, and (5) not contrary to law. Notoriety has been thus illustrated:

> In order that the shippers should be taken to have impliedly given leave to stow the goods on deck, the shipowners must prove a practice so general and universal in the trade, and in the particular port from which the goods were taken, that everyone shipping goods there must be taken to know that other people's goods, if not his goods, might probably be stowed on deck.

Teare J noted that this finding gives rise to two questions on due diligence. First, did the owners exercise due diligence to ensure that the filters were in seaworthy condition at the commencement of the voyage? Second, did the owners exercise due diligence when considering whether the deflection readings in May 2011 indicated abnormal wear of main bearing no. 1?

Teare J observed that it is unnecessary to consider whether the owners exercised due diligence to maintain the shaft earthing device in good condition because it has not been proved on the balance of probabilities that the particles were caused by spark erosion. Also, it is unnecessary to consider whether the owners exercised due diligence to maintain the chain drive gear in good condition, because it has not been proved on the balance of probabilities that the particles were caused by the shearing of the chain coupling bolts.[80]

Teare J concluded that a prudent engineer or superintendent would have decided, in light of the May 2011 deflection readings, that bearing clearance measurements should be taken. The failure to do so was a failure to exercise due diligence to make the vessel seaworthy. The chief engineer ought to have done so before the vessel left port and commenced her voyage. For the reasons I have already given, had the measurements been taken, the best evidence is that they would have revealed an increase in clearance of significantly more than 0.05 mm, which would have indicated abnormal wear, thus necessitating a repair before the voyage could safely be undertaken. The failure to exercise due diligence was, therefore, causative of the subsequent engine breakdown.[81]

For these reasons, the general average expenditure incurred by the owners was due to an actionable fault, and it follows that the cargo interests are not liable to make a general

80 Ibid, per Teare J at p. 373.

81 Ibid, p. 378.

average contribution. In the decision of Teare J, the claim against the defendants must therefore be dismissed.[82]

2.6 Vessel's boiler

The malfunction and breakdown of marine boilers are not new issues, although it is well known that only a very thin layer of oil on the surface of the boiler tubes can cause local overheating and possible damage to the boiler. Gard has recently seen a number of claims involving boiler damage caused by the presence of oil in the boiler feedwater system. In several cases, where a minor oil leakage has been discovered by the crew, the boiler has been blown down from the bottom instead of surface blowing, resulting in a boiler covered with oil. During cleaning after repairs, the oil has not been properly removed from the boiler or from the feedwater piping system, which again has led to cracks and an associated loss of integrity in high heat transfer areas. Many of the reported incidents have led to expensive and time-consuming repairs, including cleaning of the feedwater system and renewal of the boiler tubes. The purpose of this circular is therefore to remind shipowners and operators of the importance of proper boiler operation and maintenance and to highlight the relevant control measures for preventing and, where necessary, handling oil leakages into the feedwater system.

The most common sources of oil contamination are leaking heating coils in fuel tanks and fuel heaters or lube oil heaters. In one recent case, it was alleged that fuel oil had been detected in the hot well, which had come from a leak in the fuel oil purifier heater a few weeks earlier. The defective heater was replaced with a new spare, and the hot well was cleaned. The boilers were then put back in operation. A few weeks later, the crew noticed a low-level alarm in the hot well tank, and further investigation revealed water leaking inside the furnace. The opening of the boiler revealed several cracks in way of the fire tubes.[83]

In the *Waco*[84], the vessel arrived at Buenos Aires on 13 November, discharged her cargo by 4:00 p.m. on 24 November, began loading on 30 November, and completed it at 10:00 a.m. on 10 December. The charterers contended that they were entitled to cancel the charterparty and to refuse to load the ship on three grounds: (1) that in certain respects the holds were not ready; (2) that the ship could not provide steam for her winches and she was, on this ground, not ready to load within the meaning of the charterparty by 6:00 p.m. on 25 November; and (3) that the ship was not seaworthy at the time when she was, by express provision of the charterparty, required to be so.

On the first ground, the umpire decided in favour of the shipowners, that the holds were ready within the meaning of the aforementioned provision, and his decision in this respect was accepted by the parties. His findings are stated in paragraph 18 of the case. Findings 1 and 2 are the only findings dealing with the question whether the charterers were entitled to refuse to load. Findings 3 to 6 deal with the rights of the parties in the event of the charterparty being held to have been rightly cancelled, and the loading being treated as taking place under the special arrangement made between the parties as mentioned previously. Finding no. 7 is not questioned by either party.

82 Ibid.
83 Gard/Loss Prevention Circular No. 02–13.
84 *The Waco* [1922] 10 Ll.L. Rep.772.

In paragraph 20, the umpire states his award. The court is asked to say whether, on the facts as found by the arbitrator, the award is correct in law.

Greer J explained the matter:[85]

> If, once the loading commences, the ship is unable to do her share of the joint operation with proper despatch, that may disentitle her to claim demurrage, or may render her liable for damages: but that does not in my judgment make her unready to load so as to bring into operation the canceling clauses.

Greer J cited the judgment of Mr Justice Channel in *McFadden v The Blue Star Line*.[86] In the course of his judgment, the learned judge said at p. 704:

> It is clear that the warranty of the ship is fit to encounter the perils of the voyage does not attach before she sails, and while she is still loading her cargo. There is, of course, no warranty at the time the goods are put on board that the ship is then ready to start on her voyage; for while she is still loading there may be many things requiring to be done before she is ready to sail. The ordinary warranty of seaworthiness, then, does not take effect before the ship is ready to sail.

Greer J spoke of:[87]

> The law as thus stated is not open to question. It is obvious that in dealing with the effect of an implied term in a contract, an account must be taken of what is reasonable and necessary. In the case quoted the judge was dealing with the condition as to seaworthiness implied in a bill of lading. The umpire in the present case had to interpret and apply the express words of Clause 2 of the charterparty. In my judgment that clause means what it says, viz.: That when the ship proceeds to her loading berth she is to be tight and staunch and strong, and in every way fitted for the intended voyage, that is to say, she was to be so fit at latest at 3:45 p.m. on Nov. 25.

Greer J observed that there are other conditions as to seaworthiness, one that applies during the loading and another that comes into operation when she sails. There is one condition that applies when she starts on her chartered service. She is to be fit to commence her chartered enterprise, which consists of loading and sailing when loaded. If she is fit to be afloat and take in cargo but has some small defects which can, with reasonable certainty, be made right during the loading and without interfering with the due course of loading, she would, in my judgment, be in every way fitted for the intended voyage. But if she is in such a condition that she cannot be made ready by her cancelling date and there is no reasonable certainty that she will be ready by the time her loading is finished, as was the case here, she cannot be said to be "tight, staunch, and strong, and in every way fitted for the intended voyage."[88]

In the present case, the ship's boilers were in such a defective state that they could not have been made right for at least ten days. The loading, when it was done, took eight days, and though the ship had four or five days to begin her work on the boilers before the loading began, the work was not completed until about three days after the loading had finished.

---

85 Ibid, per Greer J at p. 772.
86 *McFadden v The Blue Star Line* [1905] 1 K.B. 697.
87 *The Waco*, sup. Greer J at p. 773.
88 Ibid.

Greer J concluded that the umpire was right in law in concluding that the charterers were entitled to refuse to load the ship. It was open to the umpire to conclude that there was no reasonable certainty that the repairs would have been completed in ten days.[89]

The case was held by Greer J that the express provision amounted to an undertaking of seaworthiness, that the ship was unseaworthy at the time the notice of readiness was given, and that the charterers were entitled to cancel.

Greer J said:

> She is to be fit to commence her chartered enterprise which consists of going to her loading berth, loading, sailing and unloading. If she is, in fact, fit to lie afloat and take in cargo, but has some small defects, which can, with reasonable certainty, be made right during the loading and without interfering with the due course of loading, she would, in my judgment, be in every way fitted for the intended voyage, notwithstanding those small defects.[90]

Whatever may be the position under the general law, certain forms of charter contain express provisions which make it clear that the warranty of seaworthiness attaches at the time the vessel embarks on the chartered service, including the approach voyage to the loading port.[91]

2.7 Breakage of propeller blades

Loss of one or more blades will induce propeller imbalance and result in severe vibration, necessitating the shutdown of the associated engine. This, in turn, can result in decreased performance and increased drag and may induce handling difficulties. Other potential effects of blade separation include loss of control.

In the *Yuri Maru*,[92] a dispute arose out of the charter of the Japanese steamship *Yuri Maru*, the plaintiffs' claim being for damages for alleged breach of undertakings contained in the charterparty with regard to the condition and seaworthiness of the vessel.

The Snia Company, of Turin, was an Italian company carrying on a shipping business. They were charterers of the *Yuri Maru*, belonging to the Teikoku Company, of Kobe, Japan, the first-named defendants being the owners' agents. The question of hire was raised by way of counterclaim, and the Japanese companies brought in by way of defendants to the counterclaim the Credito Italiano, whom they sued under a guarantee of the payment of hire. The vessel was built and completed sometime shortly before 11 August 1919. She was chartered to the plaintiffs for nine months from 19 December 1919, the charterparty containing the conditions that she should be in every way fitted for ordinary cargo service at the commencement of the service, and that she was to be maintained in a thoroughly efficient state in hull and machinery for and during the service.

The vessel was handed over under the charterparty to the plaintiffs at Cardiff on 19 December, and she started on her first voyage by carrying coal to Savona, and there she was ordered to go to Hampton Roads and take coal from there to the River Plate, and from there she had been chartered by the Italian government to take grain to Italy. These voyages

89 Ibid.
90 Also see *Time Charters*, 7th ed at para. 8.38.
91 See *Voyage Charters*, 4th ed at para. 11.48.
92 *The Yuri Maru* [1923] 17 Ll.L. Rep.78; [1924] 18 Ll.L. Rep.333 (C.A.).

would have taken the vessel to about the middle of the year in 1920. She got to Savona without any grave mishap. From Savona she went under ballast to Gibraltar, where she took in bunkers, and she then started for Las Palmas, which was reached in March 1920. On the way from Las Palmas, she shed a propeller blade, and she had to deviate and return to Las Palmas for repairs. Thereafter, there was a series of mishaps in connection with the propeller blades, and on 22 May, the plaintiffs cancelled the charter, claiming that they had lost both the contract to carry coals from Hampton Roads to the River Plate and the return charter for the Italian government.

At the first instance, Greer J found that the vessel was unseaworthy and that there was a failure to take reasonable steps within a reasonable time to put her into an efficient state. He accordingly gave judgment for the plaintiffs, the damages to be assessed, and also for the plaintiffs on the counterclaim.

Greer J spoke of:

> But here there is not only a condition about seaworthiness at the beginning of the enterprise but there is also the undertaking that the owners will maintain her in a thoroughly efficient state of hull and machinery during the service; and, though that does not mean that she will be in such a state during every minute of the service, it does mean that when she gets into a condition when she is not thoroughly efficient in hull and machinery they will take within a reasonable time reasonable steps to put her into that condition. I think, having regard to the great importance of the maintenance of vessels in a seaworthy condition, I am right in reading that, not merely as a term of the contract, but as a condition the breach of which would entitle the charterers to throw up the charter-party. I think the defendants, in this case, did commit a breach because they did not take reasonable steps within a reasonable time to put the vessel into a thoroughly efficient state in hull and machinery during the service.[93]

Mr Wright, for the appellants, said that the learned judge held that the ship was unseaworthy at the commencement of the charterparty because she had bad propeller blades that were not sufficiently strong. Against that finding, there was no appeal. The question was whether the notice cancelling the charterparty given by the charterers on 22 May was justified and, if it was, what was the true measure of damages.

In the decision of the Court of Appeal, Bankes LJ agreed with the conclusion of the learned judge, and it is entirely in accordance with what has fallen from other learned judges.

Bankes LJ refers to a passage of Scrutton LJ in *Embiricos v Reid & Co.*,[94] where he said:

> Commercial men must not be asked to wait till the end of a long delay to find out from what in fact happens whether they are bound by a contract or not; they must be entitled to act on reasonable commercial probabilities at the time when they are called upon to make up their minds.

Bankes LJ commented:[95]

> I think it is impossible to contend that, in a case like this of a time-charter, the charterer, simply because the vessel is off hire, is bound to wait an interminable time (if I may use that expression) without getting his vessel, and yet have no right to terminate the contract under circumstances which make it not only absolutely impossible for him to use the vessel, but quite conclusively

93 Ibid, per Greer J at p. 188.
94 *Embiricos v Reid & Co.* [1914] 3 K.B. 45 at p. 54.
95 *The Yuri Maru* [1924] 18 Ll.L. Rep.333 (C.A.), per Bankes LJ at p. 335.

> certain that he never will be able to make use of it for the purpose contemplated by both parties at the time they entered into the contract.

Bankes LJ continued:

> Having said that, if it had not been that the learned Judge, more in conversation than as part of his judgment, did say certain things in reference to the damages recoverable, I should have been content to leave the matter at large so far as the damages are concerned for the consideration of the Referee who has been appointed, and who has great experience in this class of litigation; but after the discussion which has taken place here I think it is desirable that this Court should say broadly speaking the lines upon which it thinks the Referee should proceed, without tying him down particularly to dates or items.

Then come to the third period, Bankes LJ added that it is open to the shipowners to say to the charterers:

> You were bound to do your best and to act reasonably in order to mitigate the damages, and if you could have got a vessel at the chartered rate, or anything in the neighbourhood of the chartered rate, by which vessel you could have earned the same profits as if you had had our vessel, you should have done so.

In conclusion, Bankes LJ stated:[96]

> I entirely agree with what the learned judge said (referring to the above statement of Mr. Justice Greer), that, in estimating the damages here, the measure was not to be calculated having regard to the special contracts which the charterers had in effect entered into, of which they had given the ship owner no notice; but I am not saying that those contracts may not be looked into, provided it is quite clear that they are not looked into, except for the possible purpose of arriving at what were the market conditions prevailing at the time they were entered into.

In the Court of Appeal, where the judgment of the lower court was affirmed, Scrutton LJ added:[97]

> The first question in the case is whether the charterers were entitled to cancel the charterer on May 22 on the ground that the ship had then been inefficient for so long a time as, for a commercial purpose, to frustrate the adventure – or whatever phrase one may use to express the doctrine of frustration. On this point I apply the reasoning and the principles which were applied by the House of Lords in the Bank Line case, [1919] A.C. 435; and it appears to me that the steamer had been unable to perform her contract for so long a time, and it was so uncertain when she would be able again to perform her contract, that the charterers were justified in saying "We decline to be bound any longer by the contract."

For stage 1 and 2 damages claim, Scrutton LJ put it:[98]

> It seems to me that the arbitrator should consider the matter in three stages. There is first of all the stage up to the end of the Savona voyage. The exact date seems to be in dispute, and I do not say which it is, during which, although the ship was unseaworthy, the unseaworthiness caused no damage. It appeals to me that no damage is recoverable for that stage.
>
> Then there comes a second stage, while the ship is waiting at Las Palmas for the unseaworthiness to be remedied; and I should say that that stage, in my view, begins from the time of leaving Savona, because the ship was not seaworthy when she left Savona. During that period the position seems to be this. The charterer can recover such hire as he has paid in advance and is attributable to that period.

96 Ibid, per Bankes LJ at p. 336.
97 Ibid, per Scrutton LJ at p. 336.
98 Ibid.

Where the unseaworthiness of the ship at the time of delivery causes or is likely to cause a delay that will frustrate the commercial object of the charter, the charterers may treat the contract as discharged. On the other hand, where initial unseaworthiness is not sufficiently serious to allow the charterers to treat the charter as discharged, a refusal or failure on the part of the owners to rectify the deficiency may show an intention no longer to be bound by the charter, giving the charterers the right to terminate.[99]

2.8 Broken tailshaft

Propeller shaft, tailshaft – the aftermost section of the propulsion shafting in the stern tube in single-screw ships and in the struts of multiple-screw ships to which the propeller is fitted. Propulsion shafting constitutes a system of revolving rods that transmit power and motion from the main drive to the propeller. The shafting is supported by an appropriate number of bearings.

In the Canada Supreme Court case the *Lake Chilco*,[100]

> the tailshaft had fractured and the propeller had dropped off. The vessel then was towed to Singapore, but it was found no suitable tailshaft; after made inquiries, the shaft was transported from other place by air at the cost of 22,018 dols. The appellant claimed 21,771.25 dols after excluded steamer freight 246.75 dols, as a general average item on the ground that the time saved by flying the shaft out resulted in avoiding port-of-refuge expenses estimated at 24,606 dols., and that the cost of air freight was, therefore, an "general average" within Rule F of the York/Antwerp Rules, 1924.[101]
>
> The learned trial Judge went on to find that the appellant had discharged the onus of proving that it exercised due diligence to make the ship seaworthy within the meaning of Arts. III and IV of the Schedule in respect of this defect, and he found also that the respondents had fallen far short of proving unseaworthiness with respect to the fenderlog incident, but that, in any event, due diligence had been exercised in that regard also. From this decision, the respondents appealed to the Court of Appeal for British Columbia, the members of which considered the fenderlog incident and the state of the appellant's knowledge as two separate issues as to which they were sharply divided in their opinions.[102]
>
> https://www.canlii.org/en/ca/scc/doc/1960/1960canlii40/1960canlii40.html

O'Halloran JA found that the learned trial judge did not err in holding that the shipowner had exercised due diligence in respect of the fender log incident and that there was not sufficient evidence to make it more likely than not that this incident was a causative factor in the loss of the propeller. He then went on to hold that the appellant had failed to exercise due diligence to make the ship seaworthy, having regard to its knowledge of the frequency of tailshaft failures in Victory-class ships.[103]

Davey JA, on the other hand, concluded that due diligence had been exercised by the shipowner except that it had failed to discharge the burden of proving that the fender log incident, when considered together with the weakness of the shaft, did not cause

99 See *Time Charters*, 7th ed at para. 8.45–8.47.
100 *The Lake Chilco* [1960] 2 Lloyd's Rep.313.
101 Ibid, p. 316.
102 Ibid, p. 317.
103 Ibid.

or contribute to the loss, and he held that due diligence had not been exercised in this regard.[104]

Sheppard JA agreed with the learned trial judge that, notwithstanding the appellant's knowledge of the tendency to weakness in these shafts, due diligence had been exercised before the commencement of the voyage, and he also found that the fender log incident must be disregarded for the reason that it had not contributed to the accident and, in any event, that the learned trial judge had found due diligence to have been exercised in respect thereof and that this finding should not be disturbed.[105]

The decision of Davey JA is based in large measure upon the conclusion which he reached as to the nature of this burden. In this regard, he expressed himself as follows:[106]

> In my opinion, [cargo-owner's] Counsel was right in his submission that once he proved, as he did, the ship was unseaworthy at the commencement of the voyage because of the weakened shaft, which caused the casualty, the statutory onus resting on the [shipowner] to prove due diligence required it to show the actual cause of the unseaworthiness, i.e., the cause of the weakened shaft, and that it had exercised due diligence in respect of that cause, or failing proof of the actual cause, to enumerate all probable causes and show that it had been diligent in respect of each.

This opinion is based on that portion of the judgment delivered by Fry LJ in *The Merchant Prince* (1892) P. 179, at p. 189, where that learned judge discussed the burden resting on a defendant who relies upon inevitable accident as an answer to a claim founded in negligence, which reads:

> They must either shew what was the cause of the accident, and shew that the result of that cause was inevitable; or they must shew all the possible causes, one or other of which produced the effect, and must further shew with regard to every one of these possible causes that the result could not have been avoided.

Ritchie J in Supreme Court, giving judgment, said:

> It seems to me that the distinction between the statutory burden of proof imposed by Art. IV, r. 1, and the burden which falls on a party to a collision who is required to rely upon "inevitable accident" by way of defence is that, in the latter case the issue to be determined is confined to "the cause" of the collision whereas, in the former, "unseaworthiness" must have already been determined to be a "cause" of the loss before any burden is cast upon the carrier at all.[107]

Ritchie J added, when, as in the present case, unseaworthiness has been shown to be the cause, the burden then arising under article IV is limited to that of "proving the exercise of due diligence to make the ship seaworthy before and at the beginning of the voyage." Notwithstanding the views expressed by Davey JA, this language does not, in my view, serve to shift to the carrier the onus of proving either the cause of the loss or the cause of the unseaworthiness and should not be treated as going so far "as to make him prove all the circumstances which could explain an obscure situation," such as the one here disclosed.[108]

---

104 Ibid.
105 Ibid.
106 Ibid, p. 318.
107 *The Lake Chilco*, sup., Ibid, p. 318.
108 Ibid.

Ritchie J continued:[109]

> The evidence presented at the trial of this action attributing the loss of the propeller to the effect of torsional vibrations in the propulsion machinery of the ship, is in my opinion, so strong as to exclude the probability of the fenderlog incident as a contributing cause of the loss, but it is to be remembered that, at the time of the striking, the appellant had no way of being sure that the shaft would not be weakened by contact with the log, and, accordingly, I think it would have been incautious to ignore the possible effect of this incident on the propeller and the shaft. In this regard, however, I am satisfied that the investigation and inspection carried out in May and the subsequent care and attention given to the matter by the ship's engineer constituted the exercise of due diligence within the meaning of Art. IV of the Schedule, and I am not satisfied that if any further steps had been taken any further evidence of damage would have been discovered.

Ritchie J observed that although the defect in the present case was in the design rather than in the shaft itself and it would not have been necessary to destroy the thing in order to discover the weakness, it is nonetheless apparent from the American Bureau of Shipping letter of 8 January 1948 that it was necessary to install "torsiograph" equipment on a ship and to conduct numerous experiments before the cause of the weakness could be determined, and in my view, the exercise of due diligence to make the ship seaworthy under the circumstances did not require the shipowner to install such equipment even if it had been available, or to make such tests.[110]

Ritchie J considered that the evidence discloses that due diligence was in fact exercised by the appellant in this case in the manner and for the purposes required by articles III and IV of the Schedule to the Water Carriage of Goods Act, 1936, and stated that the respondents are liable for contribution in general average in respect of the expenses consequent upon the loss of the ship's propeller in the manner and to the amount determined by the average adjustment statement which is an exhibit in this case.

The *Danica Brown*[111] was a new building vessel delivered into the possession of the plaintiffs in February 1986 with an integral clutch assembly in a coupling box to the propeller shaft and a single variable pitch propeller. On a voyage in ballast to Kolberg in February 1986, the vessel was stuck in ice for periods of time and light tremors were detected in the hull. On the cargo voyage to Exmouth in March 1986, the vessel was again stuck in the ice, and again during this voyage, tremors were detected in the hull. It was discovered that the propeller blade was bent towards the stern.

In the event, the vessel was dry-docked, and it was discovered that the propeller shaft was also bent, it being about 3 mm out at the aft end. It was decided to replace that shaft. The thrust bearings were also examined, but no damage was found.

In December 1986, the vessel was on a voyage from Northwest Europe to New Zealand, carrying the defendants' cargo of munitions. On 10 December 1986, off the coast of Canada, the coupling unexpectedly seized with overheating to the thrust roller bearing. The vessel drifted without propulsion and required to be salved and repaired before her onward voyage to New Zealand.

The plaintiffs claimed a general average contribution from the defendants.

109 Ibid, p. 322.
110 Ibid.
111 *The Danica Brown* [1995] 2 Lloyd's Rep.264.

Waller J commented on the exercise of due diligence:[112]

> I had my attention directed to two authorities, *Union of India v. mv Reederij Amsterdam*, [1963] 2 Lloyd's Rep.223 and *The Yamatogawa*, [1990] 2 Lloyd's Rep.39. I found the passage in Lord Devlin's speech in the Union of India case at p. 234 of assistance in indicating my approach to this case. He said in relation to that case:
>
> > "The plaintiffs" case, on appeal, was that there were three precautions that could have been taken by the surveyors which would have increased their chances of discovering any crack. These precautions were:
> >
> > (a) to remove the upper housing of the gears for the purpose of the examination;
> > (b) to wipe the teeth of the gears clean of oil before examining them; and
> > (c) to examine the teeth of one helix at a time instead of the teeth of four helices simultaneously.

In *Union of India v MV Reederij Amsterdam*, Lord Devlin said:[113]

> Your Lordships are not invited to say that these were the sort of precautions that were obviously necessary, whatever the experts might think. The respondents must rely on qualified witnesses who are prepared to criticize the survey as inadequate in one or more of the above respects. I do not think that this is a case in which the Judge has to keep it constantly in mind that the burden of proof of due diligence lies on the defendant. Proof of unseaworthiness fulfils, as Mr. Brandon says, the same function in this type of case as res ipsa loquitur does in the ordinary case of negligence. But where, as here, the defendant meets the prima facie case against him by calling two surveyors of unchallenged reputation who are found by the Judge to be impressive and who say what they did and why they did it and why they did not do more, then, unless they can be successfully criticized for their omissions, a Judge is entitled to say that due diligence was exercised. No doubt he must remember that if, in the end, he is unable to make up his mind whether or not the criticisms are weighty enough to disturb his confidence in the surveyors' judgment, he must find for the plaintiff and not for the defendant. But that is not the sort of situation that often arises.

And Lord Devlin continued:[114]

> It is important to get clear the point to which criticism must be directed. There is here no lack of care and no lack of skilled knowledge. The surveyors were quite familiar with the three methods of examination which it is said that they should have adopted; and they could easily have followed them if they had chosen to do so. What is said against them is that by deciding in effect that these methods were not appropriate to the sort of examination they were conducting, they made an error of judgment which a competent surveyor ought not to have made. Lack of due diligence is negligence; and what is in issue in this case is whether there was an error of judgment that amounted to professional negligence.

Waller J commented on the aforementioned authority and stated that the onus is on the plaintiffs to demonstrate due diligence. However, lack of due diligence is negligence, and what is at issue in this case is whether there was negligence.[115]

Waller J explained the matter. This latter philosophy, as it seems to me, is a reasonable and practical philosophy. Thus, the question to my mind becomes "Was it negligent to form the view which in my judgment was actually formed by Mr. Asmussen that there was no real possibility that the thrust bearings were damaged?" As I have said previously, in that view he was supported by those others who were present at that time, and he was

---

112 Ibid, per Waller J at p. 266.
113 *Union of India v mv Reederij Amsterdam* [1963] 2 Lloyd's Rep.223 (H.L.), per Lord Devlin at p. 235.
114 Ibid.
115 *The Danica Brown*, sup., per Waller J at p. 266.

supported by Mr Hudson and Dr Baker. Even Mr Edon, called for the defendants, was not in fact prepared to actually say that he thought that no reasonable engineer should have formed that view, even though he himself would have taken what he described as a more prudent view. This absence of evidence from the defendants is significant and, on one view, is really the end of the case.[116]

Waller J concluded:[117]

> In relation to the reliance placed on the absence of damage to the shaft bearing, it was pointed out and accepted that it is axial vibration that would affect the thrust bearing as opposed to radial vibration which affects the shaft bearing. But the absence of damage to the shaft bearing must have rightly given some comfort in considering the extent of the vibrations experienced, and the likely consequences.

The court held that there was no real possibility that the thrust bearings were damaged. Accordingly, the plaintiffs have discharged the onus that is on them to show that they acted with due diligence.

2.9 Steering gear

Steering gear, integrated with the rudder system, defines the complete "turning mechanism" mandatory for each ship irrespective of size, type, and operation. The steering gear system has been an indispensable part of the ship's machinery since the advent of the very early ships, which were operated by hand. The efficiency of the performance of the steering gear depends on some main aspects. Accidents because of steering gear failure are common in the maritime industry. Such incidents have led to some serious accidents in the past, causing heavy damage to the ship, their crew, and the environment. Periodic maintenance and checks are extremely important for the smooth functioning of the ship's steering gear. However, there are a few common issues which tend to occur in spite of taking all necessary precautions.

In the *Assunzione*,[118] the plaintiffs were the charterers and the owners of a cargo of grain carried on board the defendants' steamship *Assunzione* on a voyage from Dunkirk to Venice in October 1949. The vessel left Dunkirk on 21 October 1949. On the night of 24 October 1949, when she was in the Bay of Biscay, she encountered heavy weather, which, during the succeeding days, developed into a storm of great severity. On the morning of 25 October, her steam steering gear failed. The vessel was, therefore, left without steering, in a helpless condition, at the mercy of the weather in the Bay of Biscay. She fell off into the trough of the sea, and there is no doubt that she sustained quite a substantial amount of damage.

The vessel remained in the port of Ferrol for some considerable time, and while she was there, temporary repairs were carried out, both in relation to the steering gear and in relation to other damage which the vessel had sustained.

The plaintiffs claim to recover in respect of this damage to their cargo. The plaintiffs' case is that this vessel, the *Assunzione*, was unseaworthy, and it is further the plaintiffs' case that the damage was wholly attributable to the unseaworthiness of the vessel. Numerous

116 Ibid, p. 268.
117 Ibid.
118 *The Assunzione* [1956] 2 Lloyd's Rep.468.

allegations of unseaworthiness were made in the pleadings, some of which have been supported by evidence, others not.

Those heads of unseaworthiness are alleged quite apart from the question of defective steering. It is said that even allowing for the additional strains and stresses to which the vessel was exposed after her steering gear had failed when she was lying in the trough of the sea, the extent of the leakage is more than could properly be attributed to ordinary heavy-weather damage had the ship been in proper condition. In other words, it is said that some, at least, of the damage was caused by water penetrating through defects in the ship, and that if these aspects had not existed, water would not have penetrated to damage the cargo.

The defendants deny that the vessel was unseaworthy in any of the respects alleged. In particular, they deny that the breakdown of the steering was due to any unseaworthiness on the part of the vessel. On the contrary, it is contended that the breakdown was wholly due to the very heavy weather encountered. The defendants, accordingly, say that the whole trouble was due to the perils of the sea, and they rely on article IV, rule 2(c) of the rules scheduled to the act.

Willmer J commented:[119]

> The particular negligence alleged is that the steam steering gear was connected up again at a time when the hand steering gear was in operation, and that steam was then negligently turned on, or the wheel was negligently turned, with the result that the force exerted by the steam gear broke the hand gear and caused the latter to carry away. That, as I have said, the defendants contended was due to an act of negligence on the part of some member of the crew, and they rely in the alternative on Art. IV, r. 2 (a), of the Rules scheduled to the Act. The importance of that point is that the defendants, as I understand their argument, contend that, even if the breakdown of the steam steering gear was due to unseaworthiness, the subsequent breakdown of the hand steering gear was quite a separate and severable cause-a novus actus which would break any chain of causation there might otherwise be between the unseaworthiness, if any, in relation to the steam gear, and the subsequent damage. Furthermore, the defendants say that, if the vessel was unseaworthy in any of the respects alleged (which of course they do not admit), they nevertheless at all material times had exercised due diligence to make and keep the vessel seaworthy; and in such circumstances, they claim to be protected by the terms of Art. IV, r. 1, of the Rules scheduled to the Act. That, I think, is sufficient to state broadly the issues that I have had to try in this case.

Having reviewed all evidence before the court, Willmer J continued:[120]

> In the result, I find that this vessel was unseaworthy in the various respects I have described, and more particularly in relation to her steering gear. I further find that all the damage resulted from that unseaworthiness, because it was the defect of steering which caused the vessel to fall off into the trough of the sea and exposed her good plates as well as her bad plates to the full force of the sea. In those circumstances I do not think I need further consider the question of the extent to which the damage resulted from the unseaworthiness which I have found.

Willmer J concluded:[121]

> In such circumstances the defendants, by merely relying on such opportunities as the classification society surveyors had from time to time to observe and point out defects, have

119 Ibid, per Willmer J at p. 473.
120 Ibid, p. 474.
121 Ibid, p. 487.

> far from satisfied me that they exercised due diligence in relation to this particular ship. It seems to me that the history of the ship was such that it can fairly be said to have cried out for vigilant superintendence, whether by a superintendent permanently employed by the owners, or by a consultant acting for them and performing the duties of a superintendent. But there is no evidence before me at all to show that this vessel, during the material two or three years before the casualty ever received any superintendence at all, other than the non-technical supervision of Mr. Rizzuto himself. Bearing in mind that the burden of proof is on the defendants to prove affirmatively that they have exercised due diligence, I can only say that they have wholly failed to satisfy me.

Insofar as this question of due diligence raises a question of law, in the leading case of the *Cathay*,[122] Wright J (as he then was) made this observation:

> Again, the need of repairing a ship may cast on the carrier a special duty to see, as far as reasonably possible, by special advisers for whom he is personally responsible, that the repairs adequately make good the defects.

In *Winkleigh*,[123] it was a case, however, in which the question cropped up as to the right of an owner to rely on observations and recommendations made by classification surveyors. The learned judge Hilbery J, at the bottom of the first column on p. 267, says this:

> If I may say so, I, of course, respectfully agree that the shipowner does not discharge his duty of exercising due diligence to have his ship seaworthy merely by establishing to the Court that she passed her classification survey, or merely by showing to the Court that he has appointed someone who by qualification should be a skilled person to examine it; but both those things are elements to be considered, in my view, in considering whether the shipowner has exercised due diligence to make the ship seaworthy.

In his judgment in the case of the *Hopestar*,[124] after discussing to what extent an employer should go to somebody skilled to advise him about a technical matter of this sort, Devlin J (as he then was) makes this profound observation:

> The standard of care depends upon prudent practice in each case.

Willmer J discussed the previous authorities and commented:[125]

> That seems to me to bring in, and rightly to bring in, the particular facts of the particular case. That, I think, is the correct view. There may be cases in which the Court would be justified in concluding that a finding of a classification society surveyor was conclusive to show that an owner had done everything he reasonably could; but there are other cases, of which I am quite satisfied that this is one, in which quite the opposite conclusion must be reached.

In this case, as the evidence is insufficient to show that adequate classification surveys and repairs had been carried out prior to the commencement of the voyage, or that a qualified surveyor had been appointed by the defendants to superintend the maintenance and repair of their ship, they had failed to show that they had exercised due diligence to make the ship seaworthy at the commencement of the voyage. The defendants had failed to discharge the onus of showing that the subsequent breakdown of the hand steering gear was due to any factor which could be said to amount to *novus actus interveniens*.

---

122 *The Cathay* [1927] 28 Ll.L. Rep.20.
123 *The Winkleigh* [1939] 64 Ll.L. Rep.26.
124 *The Hopestar* [1952] 2 Lloyd's Rep.105.
125 *The Danica Brown*, sup., per Willmer J at p. 487.

2.10 Reduction gear breakdown

Most main propulsion reduction gearing in current combatant ships has double-helical gears. The use of double-helical gears produces a smoother action of the reduction gearing and avoids tooth shock. Since the double-helical gear has two sets of teeth at complementary angles to each other, end thrust, such as is developed in single-helical gears, is eliminated.

Reduction gears are classified by the number of steps used to bring about the speed reduction and the arrangement of the gearing. Some things are essential for the proper operation of reduction gears. Proper lubrication includes supplying the required amount of oil to the gears and bearings, plus keeping the oil clean and at the proper temperature. Locking and unlocking the shaft must be done in accordance with the manufacturer's instructions. Abnormal noises and vibrations must be investigated, and corrective action is taken. Gears must be inspected in accordance with current instructions issued by the Naval Ship Systems Command, the type commander, or other proper authority.

In the *Amstelslo*,[126] on 20 September 1957, the vessel, while in the course of her voyage from Portland to Bombay, and having reached a position about 900 mi from Honolulu, sustained an engine breakdown due to the failure of her reduction gear. As a consequence of that breakdown, she was unable to proceed further under her power and had to be towed to Honolulu, where she arrived on 1 October 1957. An examination of the reduction gear carried out in the vessel revealed that the damage to the reduction gear was so severe as to require extensive replacements. It was estimated that the replacement in Honolulu would take eight or nine months. As a result of negotiations between the interested parties, it was agreed that the vessel should be towed from Honolulu to Kobe, Japan, and that at Kobe the cargo should be delivered to Union of India into a vessel chartered by them for on-carriage to Bombay. In pursuance of this agreement, the vessel was so towed to Kobe, arriving on 14 December 1957. The cargo was there discharged into the Don Demetrio and carried to Bombay.

In the action, the plaintiffs were the Union of India, who, it was admitted, were entitled to enforce the rights under the bill of lading. The defendants were the operators of the *Amstelslot* and were admittedly the proper party sued under the bill of lading.

The plaintiffs admitted that if the original breakdown was not due to actionable fault on the part of the defendants, the voyage was properly abandoned, and that the expenses to which they had been put in providing for the on-carriage of the cargo from Kobe to Bombay were for their account and that they were liable for their proportion of the general average, for which on that hypothesis their cargo would be liable. They contended, however, that there was actionable fault on the part of the defendants in failing to exercise due diligence to make the ship seaworthy as required by section 3 (1) of the United States Carriage of Goods by Sea Act, 1936.

In the first instance, McNair J held:[127]

(1) that breakdown was due to fatigue crack; that cause of fatigue crack was unknown; and that crack was not detectable by visual inspection in 1956;

126 *The Amstelslot* [1962] 1 Lloyd's Rep.539; [1962] 2 Lloyd's Rep.336; [1963] 2 Lloyd's Rep.223 (H.L.).
127 Ibid, [1962] 1 Lloyd's Rep.539, per McNair J.

(2) that when vessel was taken over by defendants there was nothing in her history to suggest that any special inspection of her reduction gear should be carried out; (3) that inspection carried out in 1956 was carefully and competently performed; (4) that defendants had exercised due diligence to make Amstelslot seaworthy because they employed skilled and competent persons to carry out necessary inspections and those persons carried out those inspections carefully and competently; and that, therefore, defendants were entitled to protection of Act – Judgment for defendants on counterclaim (i.e., cargo's proportion of general average) with interest.

N the appeal by the plaintiffs, they contended that when the reduction gear was inspected in 1956, due diligence was not exercised, in that the following additional steps should have been taken: (a) upper housing should have been removed, permitting closer examination; (b) oil should have been wiped from the teeth of the gearwheels; and (c) one helix should have been examined at a time.

The decision of the Court of Appeal by Lord Denning MR and Donvan LJ, with Diplock LJ dissenting, held:[128]

> Onus was on defendants to show that crack was not discoverable by any inspection which they could reasonably be expected to make, or which any servant or agent of theirs could reasonably be expected to make; that there was greater likelihood of crack being discovered if those additional steps had been taken; that those were steps which defendants could reasonably have been expected to take; that, therefore, defendants had failed to discharge onus of proving that due diligence had been exercised, and that, therefore, plaintiffs' appeal should be allowed.

Appeal by defendant operators of the vessel.

Lord Reid, in the House of Lord, said:[129]

> So if the appellants are to escape from liability they must prove that due diligence had been exercised not only by themselves and their servants, but by the Lloyd's Register of Shipping surveyor who surveyed this gear, but failed to discover the crack.

Lord Reid further explained the matter. The crack was a fatigue crack, which begins in the metal and gradually gets larger. No one knows just how big it was at the date of the survey, but on the evidence, it had probably reached the surface, and possibly it was then visible on a careful inspection of a more thorough kind than that made by the surveyor. If it was sufficient to carry out an inspection of the kind made by the surveyor, it is not maintained that he did his work negligently or unskilfully. The case for the respondents is that he ought to have taken certain steps which he did not take, and that if he had done so, he might have discovered the crack. If it was his duty to take those steps, then the appellants could only succeed if they could prove that the crack still would not have been discovered if he had done so. But they cannot prove that. So the question comes to be whether a reasonable surveyor, exercising proper care and skill, would have taken those steps.[130]

According to Lord Reid, it is not enough to say that if those steps had been taken, there would have been a better chance of discovering the crack. In a great many accidents, it is clear after the event that if the defendant had taken certain extra precautions, the accident

128 Ibid, [1962] 2 Lloyd's Rep.336 (C.A.).
129 Ibid, [1963] 2 Lloyd's Rep.223 (H.L.), per Lord Reid at p. 229.
130 Ibid.

would or might have been avoided. The question always is whether a reasonable man in the shoes of the defendant, with the skill and knowledge that the defendant had or ought to have had, would have taken those extra precautions.

In the judgment of Lord Devlin, he said:[131]

> For myself, I should want more than a piece of textual criticism as a bait before I was tempted to swallow the idea that Mr. Justice McNair, who is the greatest English authority on the Hague Rules and more experienced than any other Judge in their application, misunderstood where the burden of proof lay in a "due diligence" case.

The plaintiffs' case, on appeal, was that there were three precautions that could have been taken by the surveyors which could have increased their chances of discovering any crack. These precautions were:

(a) to remove the upper housing of the gears for the purpose of the examination,
(b) to wipe the teeth of the gears clean of oil before examining them, and
(c) to examine the teeth of one helix at a time instead of the teeth of four helices simultaneously.

Lord Devlin continued:[132]

> Your Lordships are not invited to say that these were the sort of precautions that were obviously necessary, whatever the experts might think. The respondents must rely on qualified witnesses who are prepared to criticize the survey as inadequate in one or more of the above respects. I do not think that this is a case in which the Judge has to keep it constantly in mind that the burden of proof of due diligence lies on the defendant. Proof of unseaworthiness fulfils, as Mr. Brandon says, the same function in this type of case as res ipsa loquitur does in the ordinary case of negligence. But where, as here, the defendant meets the prima facie case against him by calling two surveyors of unchallenged reputation who are found by the Judge to be impressive and who say what they did and why they did it and why they did not do more, then, unless they can be successfully criticized for their omissions, a Judge is entitled to say that due diligence was exercised. No doubt he must remember that if, in the end, he is unable to make up his mind whether or not the criticisms are weighty enough to disturb his confidence in the surveyors' judgment, he must find for the plaintiff and not for the defendant. But that is not the sort of situation that often arises.

Lord Devlin stated:[133]

> It is important to get clear the point to which criticism must be directed. There is here no lack of care and no lack of skilled knowledge. The surveyors were quite familiar with the three methods of examination which it is said that they should have adopted; and they could easily have followed them if they had chosen to do so. What is said against them is that by deciding in effect that these methods were not appropriate to the sort of examination they were conducting, they made an error of judgment which a competent surveyor ought not to have made. Lack of due diligence is negligence; and what is in issue in this case is whether there was an error of judgment that amounted to professional negligence.

Lord Devlin further concluded:[134]

> My Lords, I fully accept these answers which were the only answers that on the facts of this case could have been made to such a question. After all, there would be a better chance of

131 Ibid, per Lord Devlin at p. 234.
132 Ibid, p. 235.
133 Ibid.
134 Ibid.

> avoiding road accidents if everyone drove at five miles an hour. This line of questioning is quite legitimate for the purpose of laying a foundation, but it does no more than that. The ultimate question is not whether there was a better chance of discovering the crack, but whether, on balance, one or more of the precautions ought to have been taken. What has to be balanced is in the one scale the extreme unlikelihood of there being any crack to be found and in the other scale the serious damage and loss that could occur if there were a crack.

According to Lord Devlin, this is a case in which the judge has to keep it constantly in mind that the burden of proof of due diligence lies on the defendant. Proof of unseaworthiness fulfils, as counsel says, the same function in this type of case as res ipsa loquitur does in the ordinary case of negligence. But where, as here, the defendant meets the prima facie case against him by calling two surveyors of unchallenged reputation who are found by the judge to be impressive and who say what they did and why they did it and why they did not do more, then, unless they can be successfully criticized for their omissions, a judge is entitled to say that due diligence was exercised. No doubt he must remember that if, in the end, he is unable to make up his mind whether or not the criticisms are weighty enough to disturb his confidence in the surveyors' judgment, he must find for the plaintiff and not for the defendant. But that is not the sort of situation that often arises.

It is important to get clear the point to which criticism must be directed. There is here no lack of care and no lack of skilled knowledge. The surveyors were quite familiar with the three methods of examination which it is said they should have adopted, and they could easily have followed them if they had chosen to do so. What is said against them is that by deciding in effect that these methods were not appropriate to the sort of examination they were conducting, they made an error of judgment that a competent surveyor ought not to have made. Lack of due diligence is negligence, and what is at issue, in this case, is whether there was an error of judgment that amounted to professional negligence.

2.11 Broken rivet points

With the development of the shipbuilding industry and the application of a large number of steel plates and welding techniques, rivets are rarely used in ships now instead of welding. Welding has therefore replaced riveting as the main process in shipbuilding, but hulls were still riveted earlier. It can be seen from an online query that riveting began in 1800 and is the most important process for human beings to cross from wooden ships to steel ships. Before the welding technology is mature, riveting has always been the most important process in ship processing.

The principle of riveting is to transmit force through rivets to tightly connect two or more elements. There are two types of riveting: cold riveting and hot riveting. In hot riveting, the protruding end of rivets is heated to an elevated temperature prior to hammering. In cold riveting, hammering is carried out at room temperature. No heating is performed. It requires a suitable heat source (like fuel or gas flame) for heating rivets.

In the *Dimitrios N. Rallias*,[135] the case arises out of damage to cargo shipped on a vessel, which was bought in July 1921 by her owner, who was also her master, she having been built about 1899 and having passed through various ownerships since that time. She was

135 *The Dimitrios N. Rallias* [1922] 12 Ll.L. Rep.434; [1922] 13 Ll.L. Rep.363 (C.A.).

surveyed in July 1921. She was inspected before Mr Rallias bought her by Mr Richards on his behalf.

According to the plaintiffs' case, 500 t of black cottonseed was shipped in bulk on board the defendants' vessel at Alexandria in good order and condition, but as to part of it, it was delivered in London so wet and damaged as to be valueless.

The plaintiffs denied that the damage to the cottonseed was caused by perils, dangers, or accidents of the sea or by latent defects in the hull of the vessel. Further, or in the alternative, the plaintiffs said that the steamship, when she sailed on the voyage, was unseaworthy by reason of the fact that the points of two frame rivets on the third frame abaft the collision bulkhead on the port side of no. 1 hold were broken off.

In the further alternative, they pleaded that if the damage, or any part thereof, was caused by latent defects in the hull of the vessel (which was denied), the defects resulted from want of due diligence of the owners or some or one of them, or of the ship's husband or manager, in that the points of the two rivets referred to were broken off in consequence of the metal between the shell plate and the frame becoming oxidised, owing to want of care in upkeep and lack of painting, thereby allowing a heavy rust scale to accumulate between the frame bar and the shell plating, forcing off the points of the rivets.

In the first instance, Hill J stated:[136]

> There was undoubtedly great negligence on board the ship in that respect, and that negligence was the cause of much of the damage. But the damage was by seawater flowing into the ship and not pumped out because of the negligence of the master or crew. That is within the exception of "perils, dangers and accidents of the sea . . . and other accidents of navigation . . . even when occasioned by negligence . . . of the master or mariners." (See the Cressington, [1891] P. 152.) It makes no difference that the aster was also the owner, for if the negligence in this respect was his (and it appears rather have been of the person whose duty it was to sound the bilges) it was his negligence as master and not his negligence as owner. (See the Westport Coal Co. v. McPhail, [1898] 2 Q.B. 130.)

The Master of the Rolls, Lord Sterndale, in giving judgment for the defendants with costs, said:[137]

> The first thing is that there must be a latent defect. We have been told there is no definition of a latent defect, and I am afraid that state of things will not be altered by this decision. I do not propose to give a definition of latent defect. But I think, at any rate, it is safe to say that if a defect such as appeared could be discovered by the exercise of ordinary care, it cannot be said to be latent. I do not mean to say that is a complete test. I think the Judge has treated the case rather as if the question of whether a defect was or was not latent is the same thing as whether the person charged with the care of the vessel was or was not negligent in not discovering it. I am by no means convinced it is the same. At any rate, I am not going to define latent defect any further than I have done.

Lord Sterndale continued:[138]

> Taking the whole of the evidence together I think it supports the advice given to us, that by the exercise of ordinary care by a competent person, the existence of the rust would have been found, and if it had been found everybody agrees that something should have been done. In face of these facts can this be said to be a latent defect? It seems to me it cannot. If it was not

136 Ibid, per Hill J [1922] 12 Ll.L. Rep.434 at p. 437.
137 Ibid, per Lord Sterndale [1922] 13 Ll.L. Rep.363 (C.A.) at p. 365.
138 Ibid, p. 366.

> this ship was unseaworthy and the owner cannot be excused on the ground that it was a latent defect not resulting from want of due diligence.

Lord Sterndale explained the matter:[139]

> It very difficult to reconcile some parts of the Judge's judgment with other parts-his finding that the cause of the trouble was the accumulation of rust, which put an undue strain on the rivets, and the necessary implication from that that there must have been at the beginning of the voyage substantially this amount of accumulation; his statement that he is advised that careful examination should have disclosed rust to the extent of 5–16 of an inch, and that it must have been the growth of a year or more-it seems almost impossible to reconcile these findings with the finding that this was a latent defect. Because if a thing can be found by careful examination it is not latent. I think he has a little mixed up the question of whether there was negligence on the part of certain surveyors and whether this defect was latent. Even assuming they were not negligent, if this could have been discovered by ordinary care then the defendant does not come within the protection of the bill of lading at all.

Atkin LJ spoke in a similar vein:[140]

> Under these circumstances it appears to me perfectly impossible to say that the defect was a latent defect. The Judge has so found; and it is necessary to inquire shortly what is the meaning of a latent defect. I suppose normally speaking it means some defect that lies hid as opposed to a defect that lies open. But it is suggested that it is not every defect that cannot be perceived by touch or sight or hearing exercised with the most minute examination or observation that is latent; and I can believe that when the word is used with reference to defects in a ship's hull and machinery it may not be capable of the very extreme meaning that they cannot be perceived by the most accurate and refined perception. It was suggested to us that the definition contained in a work of authority, Carver, gathered from American decisions, is a better statement of what is meant by latent defect. That definition is:
>
> A defect which could not be discovered by a person of competent skill and using ordinary care.

Atkin LJ continued and concluded:[141]

> In this case it is impossible to say this defect could not have been discovered by persons of ordinary skill. One has only to visualise what is meant by a degree of rust of 5–16 in. existing by the side of the opening between the flange of the frame and the side plate, an interstice into which a man could place his finger, to make it impossible to suggest that this defect was a latent defect. It seems to me to have been a latent defect to anyone looking out for rust.

For these reasons, the Court of Appeal stated that although correct in all his findings of fact, he was wrong in the conclusion he drew from them and that this was not a latent defect. In this case, Atkin LJ did not think it necessary to say whether that is the true and precise definition of *latent defect* which would meet every case. But Atkin LJ was prepared to say this, that a defect which does not comply at any rate with these words could not be a latent defect, and it is important in bearing in mind the effect of these words to remember that the phrase is "which could not be discovered," not "which would not be discovered" or "which might not be discovered." If these words were used, it would appear that there would be no difference between the test of what was a latent defect and the test of whether the person responsible had been negligent or not, and the court was quite clear that negligence is not a test of latency.

139 Ibid.
140 Ibid, per Atkin LJ at p. 366.
141 Ibid, p. 367.

2.11.1 Not necessary to check each

In the *Anglo Colombian*,[142] after various other voyages, she, in November 1935, undertook a voyage from Leningrad to Tacoma, on the West Coast of the United States, in the state of Washington. The ship reached Tacoma towards the end of December and sailed from Tacoma to Vancouver, where she was to load a cargo for London, on 3 January 1936. She reached Vancouver on 6 January, and loading then began. She took on board originally a certain amount of grain, and among that grain, there was the grain as to which the liability is in dispute in this action. With that cargo, she proceeded homewards via the Panama Canal and Port Royal to this country.

When she reached this country, it was found that the grain in no. 1 hold was badly damaged over a portion of its bulk, and an examination was made. It was then found that there were certain leaky rivets, and in one case – I think of a forward rivet – they found it was split by a very fine crack. That was in no. 1 hold by the stringer at the angle bar in the forward portion of the hold next to the collision bulkhead. There were further defects, one or two defective rivets in the 15th frame on the starboard side aft of the collision bulkhead, and one in the 11th frame on the port side again near the collision bulkhead. Those are the rivets through which the damage was done.

The question that the court has to determine is whether the defendants are liable in respect of those three defects.

Porter J, in giving judgment, said:[143]

> Now, I may dispose of the question of seaworthiness at once by saying that in my view, if I had to determine whether the ship was seaworthy or unseaworthy, I should say she was unseaworthy. It is an obligation which is put on the defendants to see that their ship is seaworthy, and a ship which is not capable of crossing the North Atlantic with the weather experienced at that time without rivets leaking is in fact unseaworthy. I do not think that any such weather has been proved as would enable me to say that the ship was a seaworthy ship. A ship must be capable of withstanding the ordinary perils which you may expect upon such a voyage as that, and this seems to me to have been a very ordinary voyage, and in my view if I had to determine, as I have said, whether the ship was seaworthy or not, I should determine that she was not seaworthy.
>
> But under the Canadian Act of 1910 that is not what I have to determine. I have to determine what very much has to be determined under the English Carriage of Goods by Sea Act, whether due diligence was used in order to make the ship seaworthy.

Porter J continued:[144]

> The question is whether some steps ought to have been taken at that time to discover whether the ship was suffering from any defects or not. I agree first of all that "latent defect" does not mean latent to the eye. It means latent to the senses, that is, it may be hammer-tested, or there may be any other test. The only question is whether by "latent" it means that you have to use every possible method to discover whether it exists, or whether you must use reasonable methods. I cannot myself believe that in every case it is obligatory upon a ship's officer on the commencement of a voyage to go and tap every rivet to find if it has a defect or not. If that were so, ships would be held up in port for a very long time while the rivets were being tapped and eyes used to determine whether a defect existed or not. I think it means such an

142 *The Anglo Colombian* [1937] 58 Ll.L. Rep.188.
143 Ibid, per Porter J at p. 191.
144 Ibid.

examination as a reasonably careful man skilled in that matter would make, and I think that such an examination as that was in fact made.

Porter J continued and said:[145]

> To my mind it is a question of degree. I can quite imagine that in certain cases it might be that you would not discover a latent defect unless you make a proper test. If it had been shown to me that it was a regular practice, or even a likely practice, that you should in the case of a ship of 20 years old or thereabouts either have a very special test of the rivets which were in a particular part of her, or if it were shown that the proper and prudent course was to remove the rivets from that part and to replace them, I think it might quite well be contended that there was not a latent defect, or I should think myself it might perhaps be better said that you do not in that case use due diligence to make the ship seaworthy. I do not think it matters for the purpose of my decision. I am bound to say that in dealing with these cases I always find a certain amount of difficulty in distinguishing between a particular latent defect and a particular due diligence to get rid of that latent defect, and I think it is safer in cases of this kind to regard the position with reference to using due diligence as being rather aimed at other types of seaworthiness than the particular type which caused the damage in this case; that is to say, suppose the ship were not given a proper compass she would be unseaworthy even though that had nothing to do with a loss by a latent defect. Under the Canadian Act the owners there could not protect themselves by saying that there had been due diligence exercised. That is the class of case that is meant. It is not meant to deal with a class of case where if you do not use due diligence to find a latent defect you shall not be protected by that latent defect. In that case, the question really is: Is the defect latent or is it not, because if it is latent you have used due diligence, and if it is not latent it is not a defect which protects you even if you have used due diligence?

In those circumstances, Porter J held that these particular defects come within the description, and that, therefore, the shipowners, having used due diligence to make the ship seaworthy, are protected against the latent defects in this case. That means there will be judgment for the defendants, with costs.

There is no doubt that the onus is on the defendants to prove both due diligence and that this was a latent defect. If they fail in either of those matters, they fail in the action.

2.11.2 Exercise due diligence

Similarly, in the *Winkleigh*,[146] the wheat was shipped at Vancouver, BC, for carriage to London under bills of lading dated 20 November 1937, of which plaintiffs were holders for value and endorsees to whom the property in the goods passed. The wheat, as the plaintiffs alleged, arrived in a damaged condition through the entry of seawater into the hold where it was stowed. They maintained that the vessel was unseaworthy. The defendants denied unseaworthiness and pleaded perils of the sea.

The plaintiffs alleged that the defendants failed to stow the wheat properly and that the *Winkleigh* was unseaworthy. In their particulars of unseaworthiness, the plaintiffs said that seawater leaked through a rivet hole in the bottom stringer angle lug in the forward frame space on the starboard side of the no. 1 lower hold; that the rivet hole was defective, in that it was wasted and corroded around the head and countersunk portion; that the shell plate was also corroded; that the ship was structurally weak in the neighbourhood of the rivet hole; that bolts were fitted instead of rivets in the adjustment of the middle stringer

145 Ibid.

146 *The Winkleigh* [1939] 64 Ll.L. Rep.264.

plate of the collision bulkhead and the bolts, seven in all, were loose; and that the seven rivets attached to the forward end of the bottom stringer plate of the tee bar of the collision bulkhead were all slack.

The shipowners, by their defence, denied breach of contract or duty. They also denied that the ship was unseaworthy, or that the damage was caused by any want of due diligence on their part. They said that the bills of lading expressly incorporated the Canadian Water-Carriage of Goods Act, 1936, and they relied on section 3 of the act, and article IV, rule 1 of the schedule.

It is to be observed that the article which the court used to decide puts beyond any question of doubt the onus upon the shipowner, where the damage does arise or results from unseaworthiness, of showing that he used due diligence to make the ship seaworthy. That onus was accepted by Mr Mocatta in this case. The question, therefore, to be considered is: Was this unseaworthiness in this particular case which I have mentioned caused by want of due diligence on the part of the carrier to make the ship seaworthy?

Hilbery J, in giving judgment, said:[147]

> I have come to the conclusion that it was not. I have come to the conclusion that these owners did exercise due diligence and care to make this ship seaworthy and to have it seaworthy at the commencement of this voyage. If I may say so, I, of course, respectfully agree that the shipowner does not discharge his duty of exercising due diligence to have his ship seaworthy merely by establishing to the Court that she passed her classification survey, or merely by showing to the Court that he has appointed someone who by qualification should be a skilled person to examine it; but both those things are elements to be considered, in my view, in considering whether the shipowner has exercised due diligence to make the ship seaworthy. No one can doubt, I think, that if this ship had, for example, been shown, let us say, in June of 1937, before this voyage began in November, to have passed her classification survey, it would have been very strong evidence indeed that at the time of this voyage there had been due diligence in the making of her seaworthy and seeing that she was seaworthy, even though in such circumstances it was not shown that there had been any further specially skilled examination made of the vessel. Those matters I have mentioned are, I am sure, elements to be considered in considering whether the shipowners have exercised due diligence. Again, of course, it is an element to be considered whether there has been a sufficiently frequent drydocking of the vessel for examination and report. That is another element to be considered, and it is an element to be considered to see into whose hands the owners have put the vessel for their periodical examinations and reparations – to see whether they are properly skilled people for the work.

Hilbery J was satisfied that on the way home, she did encounter some very rough weather, but not so rough as on any occasion to necessitate her heaving to. She made her run, and she made her run continuously day by day. On some days she made a much shorter run than on other days, and on some days she made an exceptionally long run.

Hilbery J continued and said:[148]

> I do not believe he would. It is conceded that it is not the ordinary thing to do, or an ordinary thing to do, to scale plating in order to ascertain if there happens to be somewhere in the side of a vessel one defective rivet, but it is said: "Ah! Here was an area of the ship which you knew was peculiarly susceptible to damage." It is one thing to say that, but it has to be remembered that this area of the ship where this forward collision bulkhead was, was said on the evidence

147 Ibid, per Hilbery J at p. 267.
148 Ibid, p. 269.

to be susceptible to panting damage. It is quite true that she had on two occasions cracked plates through panting strain. It is one thing to be on notice that the particular area is liable to the sort of damage that a panting strain gives and, therefore, of course, to say it is right that you should make such an examination as to show whether there is any other damage due to panting strains. It is quite another thing to say that because that part of the vessel is liable to such damage as occurs through panting strain you, therefore, are on notice that you may expect to find defective rivets there. If one thing is clear, I should have thought it is that this defective rivet, the defect that was present, had nothing whatever to do with panting strain. I am not satisfied that a reasonably careful owner would have scaled the plate round the area of this particular rivet. Indeed, I am satisfied that all the reasonably careful sort of examination was made.

Hilbery J explained the matter and said:

> [O]ne thing is clear, I should have thought it is that this defective rivet, the defect that was present, had nothing whatever to do with panting strain. I am not satisfied that a reasonably careful owner would have scaled the plate round the area of this particular rivet. Indeed, I am satisfied that all the reasonably careful sort of examination was made.

Hilbery J discussed and concluded:[149]

> Now, as I have come to the conclusion that this unseaworthiness is shown not to have been caused by want of due diligence on the part of the carrier to make the ship seaworthy, that really answers the claim. I need not deal with the question raised that the ingoing of the sea water into that hold was due to a latent defect within the words of Art. IV, r.2 (p)-that is to say, due to a latent defect not discoverable by due diligence-or whether it was due to perils of the sea; but I refer to what Lord Justice Atkin said about the definition to be used of "latent defect" in the case of the *Dimitrios N. Rallias*, 13 Ll.L.Rep.363, at p. 366. I think there would have been great difficulties in the way of saying, on the evidence here, that this was a latent defect within the strict meaning of that expression as it is used in the article in question, but I need not elaborate that topic because of my other finding; nor is it necessary for me, in my view of this question of fact which I have to determine, to go into the questions touched upon by Lord Wright, Mr. Justice Wright as he then was, in *Angliss & Co. v. Peninsular and Oriental Steam Navigation Company*, [1927] 2 K.B. 456. I have endeavoured to approach this matter, applying to the shipowners the principle stated-if I may use his words and quote his words-by Lord Wright in *Wilsons & Clyde Coal Company, Ltd. v. English*, [1938] A.C. 57, that the shipowner is absolutely held to the fulfilment of his obligations; that is to say, the shipowner has to exercise due diligence and to take reasonable care to provide a seaworthy ship, and I have endeavoured to apply the principle, as I have said, which Lord Wright there states, that it is the obligation which is personal to the shipowner and not the performance. In those circumstances, there must be judgment for the defendants, with costs.

In this case, the condition of the rivet upon inspection indicated that the vessel must have been unseaworthy at the commencement of the voyage, but that the unseaworthiness did not arise from want of due diligence on the part of the shipowners, and that therefore they were protected by the act-doubt expressed whether the defect was a latent defect not discoverable by due diligence.

Hilbery J agreed with what Mr Justice Porter said in the *Anglo Colombian*, mentioned previously, most heartily. "I cannot myself," he said (at p. 191), "believe that in every case it is obligatory upon a ship's officer on the commencement of a voyage to go and tap every rivet to find if it has a defect or not."

149 Ibid, p. 271.

2.11.3 Failure to exercise due diligence

In the *Bryntaw*,[150] evidence was given that the steamship *Bryntawe*, of 3,364 t gross, built at Stockton in 1917, proceeded from Port Talbot, South Wales, with a cargo of anthracite coal and, after a rough passage, reached Montreal about 13 October 1927. Her cargo was discharged, and after her holds had been prepared, she took in a cargo of grain in bulk. On her way back, she again encountered rough weather. She reached Millwall Dock on 15 November 1927, and it was then found that part of the cargo in no. 3 hold, abaft the engine room, had been damaged by water which had entered by way of two of the bolts used to hold down the starboard fairlead of the steering gear. Two bolts in particular were heavily rusted and appeared to have been in that condition for three or four months.

The defendants admitted (1) that the plaintiffs were receivers and holders of bills of lading; (2) that the cargo was shipped in good order and condition; (3) that some cargo was damaged by seawater in the course of the voyage; (4) that the seawater entered the hold from the deck through leaky bolt holes in the starboard lead block of the steering gear; (5) that the weather was as rough on the voyage to Montreal as on the voyage from Montreal; and (6) that the cargo was carried under the terms of the bill of lading.

The bill of lading was subject to the provisions of the Canadian Water Carriage of Goods Act, 1910, and included extracts from the United States Harter Act, which shortly imposed upon the owners of ships that they exercised due diligence to make their ships seaworthy at the port of departure.

The plaintiffs said that the defendants had given particulars of what they were pleased to call due diligence, but he contended that the examinations of the vessel were at too remote a date to enable them to claim an exemption under the Harter Act.

His Honour Chetwynd Leech J, in delivering judgment, said:[151]

> By the bills the owners undertook to deliver the wheat at the Port of London in the like good order and condition as it was shipped, but they were exempted from liability for loss occasioned by peril of the sea or unseaworthiness of the vessel, provided that the owners had exercised due diligence to make the vessel seaworthy. Such exemptions, however, were subject to the provisions of the Canadian Act to which he had referred, and Counsel for the defendants admitted that, having regard to the terms of the bills of lading and the said Acts and also to the case of the Royal Exchange Assurance and Another v. Kingsley Navigation Company 14 Ll.L.Rep.81, the onus lay on the defendants to prove affirmatively that they had used due diligence to see that the vessel was seaworthy before leaving Montreal.

The defendants went further, however, and sought to prove that the vessel must have been seaworthy in fact when it left Montreal and that the leakage originated on the voyage to London. In support of this latter contention, they tendered evidence to the effect that no traces of any leakage were seen in no. 3 hold when the cargo of coal, which had been carried to Montreal in that hold on the outward voyage, was discharged.

Chetwynd Leech J did not accept the evidence of the chief officer or of the master on that point. He was impressed by the evidence of Commander Pearman, marine surveyor, who gave it as his decided opinion that the rust on the nuts and washers showed that the leakage was three or four months old at least. The defendants had failed altogether to

150 *The Bryntawe* [1928] 32 L.l.L. Rep.155.
151 Ibid, per Chetwynd Leech J at p. 157.

satisfy him that the bolts were started on the homeward voyage, and he was of the opinion that Commander Pearman was right in his view that the mischief was present prior to the wheat being loaded at Montreal.

Chetwynd Leech J had, accordingly, to consider whether the defendants had exercised all due and proper diligence to ascertain that the vessel was seaworthy in that respect prior to leaving Montreal. It had to be borne in mind that that was not a case of a latent defect. The evidence went to show that an examination of the ends of the bolts and the washers and nuts made in the interior of the hold would have disclosed that two at least were loose. On that part of the case, the defendants relied upon surveys of the vessel made by the witnesses Robson and Burn in the years 1925 and 1926, respectively; upon a certificate of the port warden at Montreal; and upon the evidence of the chief officer.

Chetwynd Leech J did not consider that the surveys assisted him. The witness Robson stated that the steering and connections should be examined at least twice a year and after heavy weather. Accordingly, surveys made, the one two years ago and the other nearly 12 months prior to the vessel leaving Montreal, could not be relied on as evidence of due diligence. That was all the more so as heavy weather had been experienced on the outward voyage. The port warden at Montreal was not concerned with the steering gear. He did not appear to have gone down into the hold, from which alone a proper examination of the bolts and nub could be made.

Chetwynd Leech J was not disposed to place much reliance on any evidence given by the chief officer, who, in any event, seemed merely to have given a cursory glance at the bolts and certainly did not make any real examination of them. It was significant that the carpenter, whose duty it would have been to test and examine the bolts, was not called. There was evidence that the bolts and nub formed no part of the permanent structure of a vessel and that they needed to be periodically examined. He thought that was particularly the case when the bolts passed through the deck into a cargo hold, as any looseness must give rise to leakage and, consequently, to damage to cargo.[152]

Chetwynd Leech J concluded:[153]

> In the absence of any evidence that those bolts were tested or examined at Montreal or after December, 1926 (if then), he was of opinion that the defendants had failed to discharge the onus of showing that they exercised due and proper diligence and, accordingly, they could not rely upon the exceptions in the bills of lading.

2.12 Inadequacy of the stern doors

In the sinking of motor vessel *Princess Victoria*[154] during heavy weather in the Irish Sea – ship built in 1947 and operated by British Transport Commission as car ferry on the Larne-Stranraer service, with successive managers between commencement of service and date of loss in January 1953, P. being designated manager from 1948 to 1952, and R. being designated manager from 1952 – in the inquiry into the cause of loss, the finding of the Court of Inquiry was that the loss was due to her unseaworthiness, which resulted from

152 Ibid.
153 Ibid.
154 *The Princess Victoria* [1953] 2 Lloyd's Rep.619.

the inadequacy of her stern doors and freeing ports on the car deck, and that the loss was caused by the default of the owners and managers:

(a) In that they failed to provide stern doors sufficiently strong to withstand the onslaught of the heavy seas which may be reasonably expected to occur from time to time in the North Channel.
(b) In that they failed to provide adequate freeing arrangements for seas which might enter the car space from any source.
(c) In failing to take precautionary steps after the incident of November 1951.
(d) In failing to comply with the provisions of section 425 of the Merchant Shipping Act, 1894, insofar as they did not report the incident mentioned in (c) previously.

Lord Macdermott CJ, in giving judgment, discussed the question of seaworthiness and said:[155]

> A lack of seaworthiness does not necessarily connote default, but it so often does that it is desirable, in the grave and unusual circumstances of this case, to treat these issues separately and to deal first with seaworthiness as a matter of physical fact. The immediate question, therefore, is whether the vessel as she lay at her berth at Stranraer on the morning of Jan. 31 was fit in her construction to encounter the ordinary perils of the crossing for which she was then preparing. The expression "ordinary perils" has long been associated with investigations as to seaworthiness, but it is not to be limited, in this connection, to hazards that are commonplace or that lurk only in usual conditions. It also comprehends those worse than average blows and whims of the sea which may be expected of that element in conditions of wind and weather that are known or might reasonably be anticipated. On the conclusions already reached under Head I, the stress of the seas on the stern doors was a natural, if not a common or inevitable, consequence of a foreseeable state of the weather with which the vessel should have been able to cope. This and the conclusion that these doors and the freeing arrangements were in fact inadequate to meet what happened to mean, in the opinion of this Court, that Princess Victoria was unseaworthy in her construction on the occasion of her last journey. Whether her unseaworthy state was due to default is another matter and one to which consideration must now be given.

Lord Macdermott CJ observed that the authorities cited on this point to depend very much on their own particular facts and to afford little general guidance.

The owners naturally relied on the high repute of the builders, the fact that the vessel was built to the requirements of Lloyd's Register of Shipping for classification and assignment of load line, and the passenger certificate which was granted by the Ministry of Transport after each annual survey. These are relevant considerations and all the more weighty because the builders, Lloyd's Register, and the ministry discharged their respective duties and functions knowing that the *Princess Victoria* was to ply between Larne and Stranraer. But they are not conclusive on the issue of default either at the time when the ship was first put into service or subsequently.

Lord Macdermott CJ explained the matter and said:[156]

> It is now easy to see that the design of the vessel was not suitable for round-the-year service on this particular route across the North Channel. But this Court must be careful to discount the wisdom that comes so readily after the event. It is true that the design and construction of the car deck and stern opening were based on a very meagre experience; but the production of a new

155 Ibid, per Lord Macdermott CJ at p. 627.
156 Ibid, p. 630.

> type is not in itself negligent, though it demands expert skill and care. The point is a difficult one and different minds might well come to different conclusions upon it; but all things considered, this Court is not satisfied that the owners were guilty of default at the commencement of the Princess Victoria's service. They may have been too sanguine; they may have placed too much reliance on the high freeboard and buoyancy of the vessel; and they may have had the shortness of the crossing too much in mind. But in the absence of further experience it would; I think, be going too far to tax them with more than an error of judgment at that time.

Lord Macdermott CJ continued:[157]

> The duty under discussion did not, however, evaporate once the new service had been started. The very fact that the vessel was, in some degree, experimental made it all the more encumbent upon the owners to keep her design and construction under constant and expert review as experience was gained, and to see to it that this task was committed, not to the master or others whose energies were largely devoted to their own special functions, but to some official alert to what was required and having the competence and time to see beyond the routine of maintenance and administration. Did the owners discharge this continuing duty? Did they, in the light of their experience, exercise all due care to make the ship seaworthy? After an anxious survey of all the relevant material it is the opinion of this Court that they did not do so and. that their failure in this respect contributed to the disaster.

In the nature of things, it is impossible to say exactly when this default began and the initial error turned to negligence. But the court is satisfied that the default existed by the end of 1951, if not earlier. By then the owners should have appreciated that the ship was vulnerable in the manner and under the conditions already described and should have acted, at the very latest, so as to abate the danger before another winter was upon them.

Lord Macdermott CJ concluded:[158]

> The loss of the MV Princess Victoria was caused or contributed to by the default of the owners and the manager, Captain Perry, in that they were negligent before the disaster (a) in failing to appreciate that the vessel was unfit to encounter the full range of foreseeable weather conditions on the Larne and Stranraer route by reason of the inability of the stern doors to withstand heavy seas and the inadequacy of the freeing arrangements on the car deck; and (b) in not taking appropriate steps to provide adequate freeing arrangements on the said car deck or else to make the stern doors sufficiently strong and adequate to prevent heavy seas from flooding that deck.

For all reasons, the High Court upheld the findings of the Court of Inquiry, that the weather, though severe, was not so phenomenal or abnormal as not reasonably to have been foreseen; that the loss was due to the inadequacy of the stern doors and of the clearing ports and was contributed to by the shifting of cargo stowed on the car deck; that the *Princess Victoria* was, in consequence, unseaworthy in that, by reason of her defects, she was unable to cope with sea perils which should reasonably have been anticipated; that her owners, though not in default at the commencement of her service, by reason of the unsuitability of her design, were, in view of knowledge subsequently acquired of defects which manifested themselves during her service, guilty of "wrongful act or default" in failing to take steps to remedy such defects and were in breach of their common law duty to provide a seaworthy ship; and further, that the facts justified a finding of default against P. but (varying findings of the Court of Inquiry) that neither the owners nor the managers were in breach of their statutory duty either under the Load Line Rules, 1941, or under

157 Ibid.
158 Ibid, per Lord Macdermott CJ at p. 638.

section 425 of the Merchant Shipping Act, 1894, and that the facts did not justify a finding of default against R.

The duty under discussion did not, however, evaporate once the new service had been started. The very fact that the vessel was, in some degree, experimental made it all the more incumbent upon the owners to keep her design and construction under constant and expert review as experience was gained, and to see to it that this task was committed, not to the master or others whose energies were largely devoted to their own special functions, but to some official alert to what was required and having the competence and time to see beyond the routine of maintenance and administration. Did the owners discharge this continuing duty? Did they, in light of their experience, exercise all due care to make the ship seaworthy? After an anxious survey of all the relevant material, it is the opinion of this court that they did not do so and that their failure in this respect contributed to the disaster.

2.13 Gear

As far as dry bulk cargoes are concerned, handling facilities may be in the form of power-propelled conveyor belts, usually fed at the landward end by a hopper or grabs, which may be magnetic for handling ores, fixed to a high-capacity travelling crane or travelling gantries. These gantries not only move parallel to the quay but also run back for considerable distances, covering a large stacking area, and are able to plumb the ship's hold. These two types of equipment are suitable for handling coal and ores. General cargo is handled by cranes on the quay, floating cranes, or the ship's cargo gear (deck cranes, derricks, etc.). Attached to such lifting gear is a shackle which links the crane or derrick with the form of cargo-handling equipment being used. For most lifts, a hook is used.

In the *Ardgroom*[159], the charterparty (in Gencon form) was entered into between claimant charterers and respondent-owners of the steamship *Ardgroom* for a voyage from Melbourne and Sydney, to load a cargo of scrap, and to proceed to two safe ports in the Osaka–Yokohama range.

At Melbourne, *Ardgroom*'s cargo gear was found not to satisfy the requirements of the UK Factories Act and the Australian Department of Navigation, and loading was delayed while the gear was tested and repaired. Charterers claimed that shipowners were liable for the cost of testing and repairing gear, additional stand-by labour, and despatch money which would have been earned. Shipowners denied liability.

The dispute was referred to arbitration, and the umpire stated a special case. Question for court was whether shipowners were under any obligation to supply cargo gear in working order while the vessel was at Melbourne. Whether the court should refer to deleted words to find the intention of parties. The court started to consider whether on this charterparty, as it now stands, such an implication could be made. The first observation which the court would make on that was this: that if the owners were right in their contention, it would mean, in effect, that this charterparty can only operate in ports where there were provisions for discharging a scrap cargo otherwise than by the ship's gear, namely, by shore cranes. And even when the clause is altered to confine the discharging ports to the two ports Tokyo and Mizushima, it would seem to be wholly unreasonable to put upon the charterparty

159 *The Ardgroom* [1966] 1 Lloyd's Rep.511.

a construction which, in effect, meant that the discharge could not take place at the two named ports unless there were shore loading and discharging cranes present and available. One has to bear in mind – it was right to bear in mind – that in an ordinary way, apart from express provisions in the charterparty, the ship's duty of seaworthiness comprises a duty, whether it be absolute or qualified due diligence, to have her loading and discharging tackle available for the ordinary purposes of loading and discharging.

McNair J discussed the matter and concluded:[160]

> I should have thought that the clear inference from that was that it was contemplated that at some loading and discharging ports the loading and discharging had to take place out of reach of the shore cranes and that it was contemplated that if that was done, the lightering operation was to be carried out not only at the expense of the charterers but at their risk; whereas getting the cargo out of the ship or on to the ship was not stipulated to be done at their risk but only at their expense. It should further be borne in mind that even on this form of charter-party the master ultimately remains responsible for seeing that the ship is seaworthy or seeing that she is not unseaworthy by reason of bad stowage, and so he cannot wash his hands completely of the operation of loading, stowing and trimming. Accordingly, if I were left to decide this matter solely on the words of the charter-party as they stand, I would, without doubt, answer the question put to me by the special case that the owners were under an obligation to supply cargo gear in working order while the vessel was at Melbourne.

In this case, the court held that there was no express right in charterers to use the ship's gear and that, accordingly, if there were such right, it must be by implication and such implication would not be made unless it was necessary and was consistent with express words of contract;[161] that, apart from express provisions of the charterparty, a shipowner was under duty to have cargo gear available for ordinary purposes of loading and discharging;[162] that, although stowing, trimming, and discharging were to be performed and paid for by charterers, that was not sufficient to exclude shipowners' obligation to have cargo gear available for charterers' use and for which charterers would have to pay;[163] and that, therefore, on the wording of the charterparty as it stood, shipowners were under an obligation to supply cargo gear in working order while *Ardgroom* was at Melbourne.[164]

Regarding the problem of the ship's gear, if it is only necessary to replace some spare parts, it can be used normally, or if one of the gear is broken, it will not make the ship unseaworthy. However, if the crane must be used for loading and unloading operations and the crane is completely unavailable and damaged, it will make the ship unseaworthy, and the charterer has the right to claim damages. Anyhow, in each case, it depends on how the particular terms of the charter are drafted.

2.13.1 Gear's power failure

In the *Waco*,[165] the issue arising is out of a charterparty dated 10 November 1920. The principal question raised by the case is whether, on the facts found by the umpire, the charterers were entitled to cancel the charterparty and refuse to load the ship.

160 Ibid, per McNair J at p. 524.
161 Ibid.
162 Ibid, p. 523.
163 Ibid.
164 Ibid, p. 524.
165 *The Waco* [1922] 10 Ll.L. Rep.772.

The vessel arrived at Buenos Aires on 13 November, discharged her cargo by 4:00 p.m. on 24 November, and started to make ready her holds for the chartered cargo of grain. On 25 November, at some time before 3:45, the steamer proceeded to her loading place in no. 3 dock at Buenos Aires.

It is clear that when after discharge she started to move to no. 3 dock, she began her service under the charterparty and the expresses condition of the seaworthiness contract in clause 2 came into operation. The charterers refused to load the ship under the charterparty and cancelled the charterparty under the cancellation clause. After some days' delay, the parties came to an agreement that the vessel was to be loaded by the charterers at a reduced freight and that the difference between the reduced freight and the charterparty freight was to be paid into the joint names of the charterers' and the owners' legal advisers in Buenos Aires and should await the decision of the disputes.

The charterers contended that they were entitled to cancel the charterparty and to refuse to load the ship on three grounds: (1) that in certain respects the holds were not ready; (2) that as the ship could not provide steam for her winches, she was, on this ground, not ready to load within the meaning of the charterparty by 6:00 p.m., on 25 November; and (3) that the ship was not seaworthy at the time when she was, by express provision of the charterparty, required to be so.

On the first ground, the umpire decided in favour of the shipowners, that the holds were ready within the meaning of the previous provision, and his decision in this respect was accepted by the parties. Findings 1 and 2 are the only findings dealing with the question whether the charterers were entitled to refuse to load. Findings 3 to 6 deal with the rights of the parties in the event of the charterparty being held to have been rightly cancelled, and the loading being treated as taking place under the special arrangement made between the parties, as previously mentioned.

The court is asked to say whether, on the facts as found by the arbitrator, the award is correct in law.

Greer J, in giving judgment, said:[166]

> The law as thus stated is not open to question. It is obvious that in dealing with the effect of an implied term in a contract, account must be taken of what is reasonable and necessary. In the case quoted the judge was dealing with the condition as to seaworthiness implied in a bill of lading. The umpire in the present case had to interpret and to apply the express words of Clause 2 of the charter-party. In my judgment that clause means what it says, viz.: That when the ship proceeds to her loading berth she is to be tight and staunch and strong, and in every way fitted for the intended voyage, that is to say she was to be so fit at latest at 3 45 p.m. on Nov. 25.

Greer J discussed the question of seaworthiness and said:[167]

> There are other conditions as to seaworthiness, one that applies during the loading and another that comes into operation when she sails. There is one condition that applies when she starts on her chartered service. She is to be fit to commence her chartered enterprise, which consists of loading and sailing when loaded. If she be in fact fit to be afloat and take in cargo, but has some small defects which can with reasonable certainty be made right during the loading and without interfering with the due course of loading, she would in my judgment be in every way fitted for the intended voyage. But if she is in such a condition that she cannot be made ready

166 Ibid, per Greer J at p. 773.
167 Ibid.

> by her cancelling date, and there is no reasonable certainty that she will be ready by the time her loading is finished, as was the case here, she cannot be said to be "tight, staunch, and strong, and in every way fitted for the intended voyage."

Greer J further explained and concluded:[168]

> In the present case the ship's boilers were in such a defective state that they could not have been made right for at least 10 days. The loading when it was done took eight days, and though the ship had four or five days to begin her work on the boilers before the loading began, the work was not completed until about three days after the loading had finished. In my judgment the umpire was right in law in coming to the conclusion that the charterers were entitled to refuse to load the ship. It was open to the umpire to conclude that there was no reasonable certainty that the repairs would have been completed in 10 days. In my judgment the umpire is right in law in coming to the conclusion that the charterers were entitled to refuse to load the ship.

The court, therefore, awarded damages caused to them by reason of the ship's failure to receive the cargo with proper despatch by reason of her inability to use her winches. Thus, whatever may be the position under the general law, certain forms of charter contain express provisions which make it clear that the warranty of seaworthiness attaches at the time the vessel embarks on the chartered service, including the approach voyage to the loading port.[169]

2.13.2 Ramshorn hooks

In the *Happy Ranger*,[170] on 7 October 1997, the defendant contracted with the third claimant to carry a "process vessel" from Italy to Saudi Arabia on the defendant's heavy lift vessel *Happy Ranger*, then under construction in Holland. The process vessel was a large cylindrical object, weighing 833 t, and was required as part of a gas plant in Saudi Arabia. On 24 February 1998, the defendant had applied to Lloyd's and had been granted a special exemption certificate to allow the process vessel to be loaded.

The claimant claimed damages for breach of the contract of carriage. They submitted that the defendant was in breach of its non-delegable duty to exercise due diligence to make the ship seaworthy under article III, rule 1 of the Hague–Visby Rules in that the defendant was at fault in allowing the lift to go ahead and was also liable for the negligence of others, including the crane manufacturers and Lloyd's, both before and after the date of delivery of the vessel on 16 February 1998. They also submitted that in breach of article III, rule 2, the actual lifting operation was not carried out properly and carefully.

The defendant denied liability. In relation to article III, rule 1, it contended that the vessel did not come into its "orbit" until it was delivered on 16 February 1998 and that accordingly it could not be liable for the negligence of others prior to that date. It denied that it was itself negligent prior to 16 February 1998 and contended that on and at all material times after 16 February 1998, it exercised due diligence to make the vessel seaworthy. It also contended that the actual lifting operation was carried out properly and carefully within the meaning of article III, rule 2.

168 Ibid.
169 See *Voyage Charters*, 4th ed, 11.48.
170 *The Happy Ranger* [2006] 1 Lloyd's Rep.649.

The court found as a fact that no one from Lloyd's did attend on 16 February for the purposes of carrying out tests, not least because that was the date that the vessel set sail and the barge test took approximately a day to carry out.

Gloster J, in giving judgment, said:[171]

> The defendant's non-delegable duty under article III rule 1 attached when the vessel came into its "orbit," or under its ownership, possession or control. The term "orbit" was co-extensive with ownership or service or control, and was not to be construed in any looser sense. Under the terms of the shipbuilding contract the defendant did not assume responsibility for the vessel until 16 February 1998. Nor did the fact that the master and chief officer were on board the vessel prior to delivery for familiarisation purposes mean that the vessel passed into the defendant's orbit prior to 16 February. The evidence indicated that in contracts relating to shipbuilding and ship sale it was standard practice for a buyer to place officers on board the vessel for familiarisation prior to the completion of purchase. On the evidence, the vessel did not come under the defendant's control or service prior to 16 February 1998 and accordingly the defendant was not liable for the negligence of others prior to that date.

Gloster J explained the matter and continued:[172]

> I heard extensive evidence from witnesses on both sides, both factual and expert, and received lengthy detailed submissions, both written and oral, from counsel, both during and after the hearing. I have carefully considered all of these, but it is not feasible to attempt to summarise all the evidence and arguments. In my judgment, the defendant has failed to discharge the burden of showing that it did indeed exercise due diligence to make the vessel seaworthy, after it took delivery on 16 February 1998.
>
> The claimants can only succeed if the breaches by the defendant to make the vessel seaworthy were causative of the damage to the process vessel. In my judgment, such breaches were indeed causative of the damage. Each breach, taken separately and cumulatively, was one of the several legally effective causes of the accident.

Gloster J discussed the loading process and said:[173]

> In my judgment the loading of the process vessel was not carried out properly and carefully within the meaning of article III, rule 2. My reasons can be shortly summarised as follows. First I accept Mr Lord's submissions that the defendant was negligent in proceeding to plan and effect the loading when it knew or should have known that the hooks had not been tested to 110 per cent of swl or even close to it. I accept that the defendant/Mammoet did not apply their minds to hook loadings or slings angles at all. . . . However the calculation formula remained the same, and failed to take account of the change in the drawing. The "load per hook" stated on the drawing was not per hook, and Mammoet failed to factor in the actual load per hook at any point. However, this failure is in reality no different from the point which I have already decided against the defendant under Issue (iv) above. It was causative of the claimants' loss, because if the point had been appreciated, the lifting could not have gone ahead. However it adds nothing to my previous findings under article III, rule 1.

Gloster J also considered that it was negligent and a breach of the defendant's obligations under article III, rule 2 for Mr Peterse to authorise the carrying on of the loading operation after the read-out showed 426 t. Mr Peterse knew the read-out on the no. 1 crane (the forward crane) was more than the permitted maximum. His failure to consult Lloyd's was irresponsible. His excuse that it was 1730 and therefore too late in the day to contact Lloyd's was not persuasive in the absence of any attempt to do so on his part. The load was

171 Ibid, per Gloster J at p. 656. *The Muncaster Castle* [1961] 1 Lloyd's Rep.57 (H.L.) considered.
172 Ibid, per Gloster J at p. 657.
173 Ibid, p. 664.

only just off the trailer. It could have been replaced and the grommets removed/adjusted, as envisaged by the claimants in their plans.

Gloster J concluded:[174]

> I reject these submissions. What would have happened if Mr Peterse had not gone ahead with the load that evening, but instead waited for Lloyd's to grant a further extension (as it most probably would have done), or alternatively had directed the defendant/Mammoet's employees properly to rebalance the load, is entirely speculative. The likelihood is that the hook would have broken in any event, and significant damage caused. Accordingly, save in respect of the first point, as to the negligent planning of the loading, the claimants have failed to prove causation under this issue.

Finally, the court held that the defendant failed to discharge the burden of showing that it exercised due diligence to make the vessel seaworthy after it took delivery on 16 February 1998. That failure was causative of the damage.[175] The loading of the process vessel was not carried out properly and carefully within the meaning of article III, rule 2. The planning of the loading was negligent and causative of the damage. The defendant was also negligent in the execution of the operation, but such negligence did not cause the damage.[176]

It's settled law that the owners are not liable for any failure to exercise diligence by any person who has worked on it before it has come into the owners' "orbit," that is, into their ownership, possession, or control. However, they are liable for any defect in the ship which is reasonably discoverable when the ship comes into their "orbit."[177] The carrier's responsibility for the work itself does not begin until the ship comes into his orbit, and it begins then as a responsibility to make sure by careful and skilled inspection that what he is taking into his service is in a fit condition for the purpose and, if there is anything lacking that is fairly discoverable, to put it right. But if the bad work that has been done is "concealed" and so cannot be detected by any reasonable care, then the lack of diligence to which unseaworthiness is due is not to be attributed to the carrier.[178]

As to the non-delegable duty under article III, rule 1 of the Hague–Visby Rules, a shipowner will not, in principle, be liable for any defects in the construction of the vessel because this would involve "an almost unlimited retrogression" in relation to a shipowner's non-delegable duties, as Wright J stated in *W Angliss and Co (Australia) Pty Ltd v Peninsular and Oriental Steam Navigation Co.*[179] The same principle was applied more recently in the *Kapitan Sakharov*.[180] See also *Carver on Charterparties*.[181]

2.13.3 Mainmast collapsed

In the *San George*,[182] the vessel arrived at Buenos Aires with a cargo of Polish coal on 3 December 1948. In the early forenoon of 10 December, a fire was discovered in the engine

174 Ibid, p. 665.
175 Ibid, See 41, 65.
176 Ibid, See 70–71, 73.
177 Ibid, p. 653.
178 *The Muncaster Castle* [1961] 1 Lloyd's Rep.57 (H.L.), per Lord Radcliffe at p. 85.
179 *W Angliss and Co (Australia) Pty Ltd. v Peninsular and Oriental Steam Navigation Co.* [1927] 28 Ll.L. Rep.202.
180 *The Kapitan Sakharov* [2000] 2 Lloyd's Rep.255, per Auld LJ at p. 271.
181 *Carver on Charterparties*, 2nd ed at para. 4–153.
182 *The San George* [1950] 83 Ll.L. Rep.500; [1950] 84 Ll.L. Rep.354 (C.A.).

room storeroom, which spread rapidly and was not extinguished until the afternoon; at that time, the cargo was being discharged overside into lighters by the ship's gear. Shortly after the fire was extinguished, the mainmast collapsed, owing to the backstays being improperly slackened off to facilitate the discharge from the no. 5 hold, and the two wooden derricks at the no. 5 hold were broken by the fall of the mast.

The senior surveyor to Lloyd's Register of Shipping at Buenos Aires was immediately called in to survey the vessel; with his consent, the vessel returned to a United Kingdom port. Accordingly, temporary repairs were effected by cutting away the mast 2 in above the mast platform and lashing it to the port bulwarks of the after well deck; the two wooden derricks were similarly made fast on the starboard side of the after well deck.

The charterer contended that he was entitled to cancel the charterparty since the vessel was not ready to load at the cancelling time upon any one or more of the four grounds set out previously. The shipowners denied that any of the holds were damp at the cancelling time, namely, 6:00 p.m. on 27 December, and, as to the remaining three grounds, while admitting the facts, though not the conclusions therefrom relied upon by the charterer, contended that the vessel was ready to load at the cancelling time. The shipowners further contended that the charterer was stopped from relying upon the fact that the vessel had no mainmast as evidence that she was not ready to load by the cancelling time, because of the fact that the charterer's agents were, at all material times, aware of the position and condition of the vessel and, being so aware, ordered the vessel to proceed to the first port of loading, San Lorenzo, on 23 December.

At the first instance, Devlin J (as he then was) said:

> Charterer's right to the full reach and burthen of the steamer was subject to the proviso concerning space used for reserve bunkers; that No. 3 lower hold was space within that description; that in estimating the bunker space required it was necessary to take into account the bunkers required for the whole voyage, and that the charterer had failed to establish that No.3 lower hold could not reasonably be required for reserve bunkers.

Devlin J discussed and concluded:[183]

> In my judgment, a charterer who cancels on the ground that the ship's gear is defective must (in the absence of express or implied provisions about the gear) show that the defects were such that the ship would probably be unready when the time came to play her part in the agreed method of loading, if any, or in giving the necessary co-operation in any reasonable method that might be employed. I do not think that the case discloses sufficient evidence of unreadiness in this sense. Accordingly, I answer in the negative the question for the opinion of the Court and I uphold the alternative award for £19,607 6s. 1d.

The court held that the charterer was entitled to no more than the reasonable cooperation of the shipowners in selecting and working the most convenient method of loading, and that the evidence of the absence of a mainmast and after derricks (which defects could probably have been remedied in good time if the method of loading required their use) was inadequate to discharge the onus upon the charterer of showing that the defects in the ship's equipment were such that she would probably be unready or unable to employ or assist in any reasonable method of loading which might be decided upon.

183 Ibid, per Devlin J [1950] 83 Ll.L. Rep.500 at p. 508.

Tucker LJ, in the Court of Appeal, explained the matter and said:[184]

> No authority for this proposition was cited to us, and it seems to me to be contrary to the principle that he who seeks to enforce a forfeiture clause, which in effect this is, must strictly prove the existence of all the matters upon which he relies as justification of his conduct, and in my view Mr. Justice Devlin rightly placed the onus upon him. Furthermore, I think the right test is what is required for the whole voyage. It is true that it has been decided that the shipowner is not in breach of the warranty of seaworthiness if the master has elected to divide his voyage into stages for coaling purposes and only carries sufficient coal to carry the vessel on its first stage (see the Vortigern, [1899] P. 140). But this doctrine is in relief of the shipowner's liability under his warranty that the ship is seaworthy for the whole of the charter voyage, and cannot in my view be used as imposing upon him an obligation, at any rate in the absence of any election on his part so to do, to bunker in stages. For these reasons I agree with the conclusion of the learned Judge on this part of the case.

According to Tucker LJ, there is a real distinction to be drawn between the cargo space and the gear. The charterer is entitled to the control of the whole of the cargo space from the outset of the voyage. Tucker LJ continued and concluded:[185]

> In this state of the authorities, I am of the opinion that, in principle, a charterer who has cancelled on the ground of unreadiness to load by reason of the insufficiency of the loading gear, in a case where the obligation to load is on the shipowner and where there is more than one port of loading and different kinds of cargo which may be loaded at the option of the charterer, must at least prove that at the cancelling date the ship was in such a condition that the shipowner would necessarily be unable to comply with his obligation to load some cargo which the charterer was entitled under the charter-party to call upon him to take on board at the first or some subsequent port. It is, in my view, not enough for him to show that at the cancelling date the shipowner may be unable to load some particular cargo; he must prove that he could not do so. In the present case the charterer failed so to do. There is nothing in the facts found by the umpire to indicate that he could not have devised some temporary equipment to take bags on board from lighters in the unlikely event of his being required to load in this manner.

Cohen LJ added:[186]

> Where a charterer gives notice of cancellation, the onus is on him to prove the existence of a state of circumstances which justify him in giving such a notice. As regards ship's gear, I do not think he discharges that onus by proving that a part of the gear was not available at the first port of loading, if it is established, as in substance it was in the present case, that it could not be required for use at that port; nor do I think that the mere fact that it might be required at a subsequent loading port is enough to discharge the onus of proof which rests on the charterer or shift it to the shipowner. The charterer must, I think, at least prove that it might be required at the subsequent port and that it or a substitute for it would not be available if required.

In the present case, the Court of Appeal held that the charterer's right to the full reach and burden of the steamer was subject to the proviso concerning space used for reserve bunkers; that no. 3 lower hold was space within that description; that in estimating the bunker space required, it was necessary to take into account the bunkers required for the whole voyage; and that the charterer had failed to establish that no. 3 lower hold could not reasonably be required for reserve bunkers. Where the obligation to load was on the shipowners, and where there was more than one port of loading and different kinds of

184 Ibid, per Tucker LJ [1950] 84 Ll.L. Rep.354 (C.A.) at p. 361.
185 Ibid, p. 363.
186 Ibid, per Cohen LJ at p. 364.

cargo which might be loaded at the option of the charterer, a charterer who purported to cancel on the ground of unreadiness to load by reason of the insufficiency of the loading gear had at least to prove that at the cancelling date, the ship was in such a condition that the shipowners would necessarily be unable to comply with their obligation to load cargo which the charterer was entitled to tender, and that as the charterer's proof fell short of that requirement, he was not entitled to cancel. It's not enough for charterers to show that at the cancelling date the shipowner may be unable to load some particular cargo; he must prove that he could not do so. In the present case, the charterer failed to do so. There is nothing in the facts found by the umpire to indicate that he could not have devised some temporary equipment to take bags on board from lighters in the unlikely event of his being required to load in this manner.[187]

2.14 Radar

An electronic navigation aid using radio waves was sent out as a narrow beam to detect solid objects around the ship. Any solid object of a reasonable size reflects the beam and is detected on the radar screen as a bright spot. Radar systems for ship navigation operate at wavelengths of 3 and 10 cm. Two systems are usually required for larger ships, one main S-band and one auxiliary X-band. A system consists of a transmitter modulator, receiver, a rotatable directional antenna (scanner), required power supplies, a master indicator, and remote indicators (when desired). The radar video presentation displays relative motion data in plan position indicator (PPI) form on either a 12 or 16 in cathode ray tube. The display is a map presentation of an area of 360° around the ship. Radar now is an indispensable instrument for safe navigation and avoiding collision.

In the *Portland Trader*,[188] a Liberty-type steamship of 7,251 t gross and 4,455 t net register departed from Vancouver (Washington), bound for Calcutta, India, laden with 9,800 long t of bulk wheat. On 5 January 1961, while traversing the Sulu Sea, the vessel damaged her propeller on the Tubbataha Reef. She subsequently grounded on the reef, and her hull was so damaged that seawater entered the cargo holds and the cargo sustained damage.

The cargo owner claimed against the shipowner, contending that the loss and damage to the cargo were proximately caused by the unseaworthiness of the vessel in that she was not equipped with radar, or LORAN (long-range navigation). It further contended that the loss was caused by the respondent's negligence in that it failed to equip the vessel with radar or LORAN, knowing the probable route of the vessel was through the Sulu Sea; failed to give the master specific instructions for making a safe voyage through the Sulu Sea; and failed to take any precautions to safeguard the cargo after it had been advised of the damage to the vessel's propeller.

The respondent denied that the vessel was unseaworthy or that it was negligent and contended that the damage was caused without its privity or knowledge and that, under the United States Carriage of Goods by Sea Act, 1936, it was not responsible for the damage in that the act, default, or neglect of the master, mariner, pilot, or those in charge of the ship was the sole cause of the loss.

187 Ibid, p. 363.
188 *The Portland Trader* [1963] 2 Lloyd's Rep.278.

The first question presented is whether the absence of radar, or LORAN, rendered the vessel unseaworthy and, if so, whether such unseaworthiness was the proximate cause of the damage to the *Portland Trader*. The evidence is clear that both radar and LORAN are valuable aids to navigation. The vessel was equipped with all navigational aids which had been commonly used over the centuries.

John F. Kilkenny J dealt with this and said:[189]

> Although the duty to furnish a seaworthy ship is absolute and is a species of liability without fault, limited neither by concepts of negligence nor by those which might be contractual in nature, the obligation does not require the owner to furnish a ship or gear beyond that which is reasonably fit for the use intended. In other words, the standard is not an accident-free ship, nor an obligation to provide a ship or gear which might withstand all conceivable hazards. In the last analysis, the obligation, although absolute, means nothing more or less than the duty to furnish a ship and equipment reasonably suitable for the intended use or service.

John F. Kilkenny J continued:[190]

> Another statement of the doctrine is that the standard is not perfection, but reasonable fitness. It does not require a ship which will weather every conceivable storm or withstand every imaginable peril of the sea, but only a vessel reasonably suitable for the particular service. In examining the facts in this case we must keep in mind that the shipowner's warranty of seaworthiness does not extend to the negligent use of what would otherwise be a seaworthy ship or appliance.

John F. Kilkenny J noted the overwhelming weight of the evidence in the case is that there is no worldwide or American practice or custom with reference to the use of radar or LORAN as aids to navigation. Improvements in the means and modes of navigation frequently require new implements or new forms of old ones, and these, though not necessary at first, become so when there is an established usage on ships of a certain quality, or those to be sent on certain voyages or used for certain purposes. Here, we have no well-established usage. Some companies use radar or LORAN; others do not. The evidence shows that none of the hundreds of Liberty ships built during the war originally carried either LORAN or radar. Some have been so equipped in recent years. Most of those engaged in the tramp trade, such as the *Portland Trader*, were not so equipped.

John F. Kilkenny J discussed the matter and started with a premise that both parties, under the undisputed evidence, believed that the ship was sound in every respect and fit for the voyage. In John F. Kilkenny J's view,[191] this is not one of the rare cases where the ultimate conclusion must be based on expert testimony. To arrive at a proper conclusion, the court must recognize that for thousands and thousands of years, men went down to the sea in ships without navigational aids such as radar or LORAN. There was no general movement towards the use of this equipment until well after World War II and into the mid-1950s. With all the time-tested aids that a mariner has had available over the years, can it now be said that his ship is made unseaworthy because of the absence of either radar or LORAN? It seems that neither radar nor LORAN was ever meant to supersede or replace time-honoured navigational aids and naval equipment such as that with which the *Portland Trader* was equipped. This does not mean that the navigator may ignore or make improper

189 Ibid, per John F. Kilkenny J at pp. 280–281.
190 Ibid.
191 Ibid, p. 281.

use of radar equipment which he may have aboard, and such misuse of radar may be a foundation for a finding of negligence leading to liability.

John F. Kilkenny J discussed the question of COGSA and said:[192]

> In all of my approaches to a solution of the problems involved in this cause, I have kept in mind and invoked the general rule that under COGSA, 46 U.S. Code 1303, 1304, the burden of proof to establish seaworthiness or the exercise of due diligence is on the respondent, and, furthermore, the trier of the facts must be convinced beyond a substantial doubt that the vessel was in fact seaworthy and the owner free from negligence. I have no doubt that the *Portland Trader* was seaworthy in all respects and that the owner used due diligence and was free from negligence in equipping and manning the ship and has met the burden required under COGSA.

At that time of night, he might as well be attempting to locate the proverbial needle in a haystack. All this points to exceptionally poor judgment on the part of the master on this one occasion. This does not mean that the respondent knew or, by the exercise of reasonable diligence, should have known that the master might "panic" on an occasion such as this. The great weight of the evidence is otherwise. In conclusion, John F. Kilkenny J found that the respondent furnished an adequate and competent crew for the vessel but that the master and those under him lost their heads at the time they were making the search for the Tubbataha Reef and that the master did not act as a reasonably prudent person would act at the time of such search.

As the court explained, the sole proximate cause of the casualty in this case was the act, neglect, and default of the master in the navigation and management of the ship immediately before and at the time of contact with the reef.[193]

The court concluded that (A) (1) the ultimate conclusion on seaworthiness was for the trier of the facts rather than the experts and that the employment of radar and LORAN in navigation of tramp steamships was not so essential that their absence would give rise to a finding of unseaworthiness; (2) that the shipowner had appointed a competent master and was entitled to rely on his judgment, that alternative route was no less dangerous than the route through the Sulu Sea, and that, therefore, instructions to master for intended voyage were sufficient; (3) that the shipowner was entitled to rely on the master's judgment in navigation of the vessel, that there was no duty on the shipowner to give specific instructions on how to proceed, and that, therefore, the *Portland Trader* was seaworthy, the shipowner had exercised due diligence and was free from negligence in equipping and manning vessel, and the shipowner had met the burden required under US Carriage of Goods by Sea Act, 1936; (B) that the shipowner's claim as to waiver of cargo owner's right to claim unseaworthiness and want of due diligence was without merit in that the vessel was manned and navigated by the shipowner and any certificate of surveyors or inspectors as to seaworthiness should be disregarded, and that the shipowner and master acted reasonably after the vessel grounded; and (C) that proximate cause of casualty was act, neglect, and default of the master in the navigation and management of the vessel immediately before and at the time of contact with reef, and that, therefore, the cargo owner's claim failed.

---

192 Ibid, p. 283.

193 See *The Marjorie Seed* [1926] 24 Ll.L. Rep.36, deviation and aground case.

2.15 Compass

The ship's magnetic compass has been around in various forms for more than a millennium. Navigators all over the world discovered the properties of magnetic compasses. Since their development, ships carry compasses to help navigate when conditions required a reference aboard the ship to provide orientation. At night, or otherwise, out of sight of familiar landmarks, a compass provides vital information for the navigator.

Since the compass is one of the main navigation equipment of the ship, the stability of the compass operation is directly related to the navigation safety of the ship. Therefore, during the voyage, the navigator is required to take every opportunity to measure the compass difference so as to check whether the compass is working properly and to make necessary corrections to the heading and bearing. When the ship is sailing offshore, the compass difference can be determined by the specially designed overlapping mark or the natural overlapping mark with higher sensitivity. However, when the ship sails on the open sea, only celestial stars are used to determine the compass. But now it is estimated that not many people know how to use celestial stars to measure the compass difference.

In the *Thordoc*,[194] the respondent company was the owner of the vessel. In November 1929, the appellant company was the owner of a cargo of flour and other cereal products laden on board the vessel for carriage from Port Arthur (Ontario) to Montreal. The vessel with this cargo on board was stranded at Point Porphyry, on the north shore of Lake Superior, and was wrecked with great loss of and damage to cargo. In an action in respect of that loss and damage, the appellants obtained judgment for USD 146,326.29 against the respondents.

The question at issue in the courts in the following passages was whether the loss and damage took place without the actual fault or privity of the respondents, and the question in this appeal is whether those courts were right in deciding that they did take place without such fault or privity.

Before dealing with the specific points involved, the general scope and effect of section 503 of the Merchant Shipping Act, 1894, may be briefly stated. Its scope and effect are not to excuse or exempt a shipowner from liability for tort or breach of contract but to limit the amount for which he can be liable for the faults of others than himself. The meaning of fault and privity in section 502 of the act, which in that respect is identical with section 503, has been authoritatively declared by the Court of Appeal and the House of Lords in the case of *Lennard's Carrying Company, Ltd. v Asiatic Petroleum Company, Ltd.* [1914] 1 K.B. 419; [1915] A.C. 705.

> The words "actual fault or privity" in my judgment infer something personal to the owner, something blameworthy in him, as distinguished from constructive fault or privity such as the fault or privity of his servants or agents.
>
> (per Buckley LJ)

> Actual fault negatives that liability which arises solely under the rule of respondeat superior.
>
> (per Hamilton, LJ)

194 *The Thordoc* [1937] 58 Ll.L. Rep.33.

As to the condition of the compass, Lord Roche said:[195]

> In this respect again the question in this action under the statute is not the same as the question in the cargo action previously heard between the same parties. In that former action the question was whether the condition of the exercise of due diligence to make the vessel seaworthy had been fulfilled, as it was necessary that it should be fulfilled to bring into operation the protective provisions of Sect. 6 of the Water-Carriage of Goods Act. The condition is not fulfilled merely because the shipowner is personally diligent. The condition requires that diligence shall in fact have been exercised by the shipowner or by those whom he employs for the purpose – see *Dobell v. Steamship Rossmore Company*, [1895] 2 Q.B. 408. Therefore, with regard to the Thordoc in the cargo action, want of diligence in the compass adjuster who adjusted the compasses or in the captain who said he checked or verified the adjuster's work would be material, and a finding adverse to the shipowner could be arrived at upon the ground of want of diligence in these persons. In this action, personal fault or privity of the respondents being essential, both Courts have found that the respondent company, which employed a compass adjuster of repute and proved that before the accident it knew from his account requiring payment for his work that the work had been done, was entitled to be satisfied. The appellants did not attempt before their Lordships to attack this finding or to support the appeal on any question of the improper state of the compass.

Lord Roche discussed the question of the officers, saying:[196]

> These officers were apparently certificated officers and engaged as such, and the stranding was admitted to be caused by improper navigation, which prima facie seems to their Lordships to be much more consistent with negligence than with any other assumption and which at all events does not necessarily lead to any inference of incompetence in these officers.

Lord Roche discussed the remaining question of the wheelsman, saying:[197]

> It is unnecessary to decide whether he was incompetent. It is not correct to say that he was in charge of the vessel. He was steering it and keeping the course he was told to keep. There was a look-out man and the second officer was in charge of the vessel and its navigation. There was, indeed, negligence, great negligence, in the navigation, but it is at least open to question whether far the greater part of the responsibility did not rest elsewhere than with the wheelsman and whether it would be just or fair to describe him as incompetent. However that may be, and their Lordships do not decide any such matter, it is sufficient to say that their Lordships agree with Demers, J., that the engagement of the wheelsman and the putting of him at the wheel at the stage of the voyage now in question were alike the responsibility and the work of the captain. Even if the captain were wrong in either respect that was not the fault of the respondent company.

In this case, the Privy Council concluded that the deviation, if any, and even assuming that it was the fault of somebody for whose fault the respondents were responsible, had nothing to do with the cargo damage (which was due to improper navigation after the deviation was passed) and therefore was not relevant to the petition for limitation; that there was no actual fault or privity of the respondents regarding the condition of the compass; and that there was no evidence of any fault of the respondents in their selection of the master and crew.

Thus, where the carrier is entitled to the benefit of a statutory exception or limitation of liability, his statutory rights are not displaced by the deviation. Just like this case, the ship

195 Ibid, per Lord Roche at p. 40.
196 Ibid.
197 Ibid.

deviated with the privity of the owner but had returned to her course before stranding, as a result partly of a defective compass and part of a navigational error, neither cause occurring with the fault or privity of the owner. It was held that the shipowners were entitled to limit their liability. In principle, there seems no reason that the same result should not hold good even when the loss occurs when the ship is upon the devious course, unless the loss or damage may properly be attributed to the deviation.[198]

On the other hand, the shipowner is responsible for the acts or omissions of those whom it involves in the task of making or keeping the vessel seaworthy (whether they may be its servants, representatives, or independent contractors).[199]

2.16 Ship spare parts

The lack of spare parts still nails thousands of ships to the port every day and leads to many significant downtime costs for shipping. In west Australian ports, if the vessel has no spare parts on board, it may cause delay for berthing once there are main engine or other navigation equipment problems which crews could not rectify by themselves.

In the *Trione*,[200] a dispute arose between the owners and the charterers, and to save holding up the ship while it was decided, the owners paid for the shifting boards to be put in, without prejudice to the position. Counsel said that it appeared to be common ground that under Swedish law, shifting boards were required when bulk grain was the cargo. The claimants, by notice of motion, asked that the case be remitted to the umpire for him to correct a wrong finding on that matter.

The question for the opinion of the court was, On whom was the liability to pay for the provision of shifting boards to enable a bulk cargo of grain to be carried? The owners contended that in the circumstances, the expense appertained to the cargo, and claimed to be reimbursed the cost of the shifting boards. The charterers said that the expense appertained to the ship, and denied liability to pay for the provision of the shifting boards.

His Lordship held that the shipowners were liable to provide and pay for the shifting boards, and the shipowners appealed.

In the Court of Appeal, Wright LJ, in giving judgment, said:[201]

> I do not, however, feel able to accept that somewhat ingenious construction. I think the words "appertaining to the cargo," on any view, exclude shifting boards; but if, contrary to my opinion, we were thrown back on Clause 4 and had to construe Clause 4, then I think the owners' obligation to provide shifting boards, which is a very natural and primary obligation, is not nullified, as Mr. McNair has contended, by the words "as far as on board." In the first place, these words contemplate that there would be shifting boards on the ship, and obviously, if the ship was to be used as the charter-party says, the charterers would have the right to call for their use-and when carrying grain in bulk the ship must have had shifting boards in order to comply with the Swedish law. And, indeed, we are carried back in that connection to Clause 1 of the charter-party, which I have already read, and which says that the vessel is to be let "with clean and clear holds" – that means without any rubbish or cargo left in them – "and every way fitted to carry bulk and general cargoes." The word "fitted" there, I think, means "equipped," or "provided," or "furnished with" the necessary apparatus or equipment, which would include

198 See *Voyage Charters*, 4th ed at para. 12.31.
199 See *Carver on Charterparties*, 2nd ed at para. 11–084.
200 *The Trione* [1936] 55 L.I.L. Rep.149; [1937] 57 L.I.L. Rep.95 (C.A.).
201 Ibid, per Wright LJ [1937] 57 L.I.L. Rep.95 (C.A.) at p. 98.

> shifting boards – and if Clause 4 has the effect which Mr. McNair contends it has, that is to say, in relation to Clause 5, it would become necessary to reconcile the relevant words of Clause 4 with the relevant words of Clause 1 – and the only way in which they can be reconciled, so far as I can see, is to start with the primary obligation that the ship shall be equipped, that is, sufficiently equipped, for all practical purposes as a Swedish ship, subject to Swedish law, for the carriage (inter alia) of grain cargoes. If she is so provided, the words "as far as on board" have merely this limitation, that the owners are not bound to provide any further or unusual equipment of shifting boards beyond what, under the general words of Clause 1, and under the Swedish law, and according to the overriding duty of providing a seaworthy ship, the owners would have to provide.

Wright LJ continued and added that there can be no question here, in his judgment, of an implied obligation on the part of the charterers to provide these things, because they have entered into a contract under which the ship is to be equipped in the sense that he had stated with shifting boards, among other things, and in his opinion, it would be impossible to imply an indemnity proposing a further obligation on the charterers contrary to the terms of the charterparty merely because the charterers have required the owners to fulfil their contract.[202]

Romer LJ discussed and put it this way:[203]

> Clause 1 of the charter-party is, in my opinion, wholly unambiguous, and it contains a warranty on the part of the owners that the ship was in every way fitted to carry bulk and general cargoes – and it is plain that without these shifting boards the ship was not fitted to carry grain cargoes in bulk. When one comes to Clause 4 it is true that the language there does suggest an argument that the obligation was not thrown upon the owners to provide any further shifting boards than were on the ship at the time of the charter-party – and there were in fact none. In view of the plain terms of Clause 1, it is the duty of every Court of construction to put such a meaning on Clause 4 as to make that clause consistent with, and not contradictory to, Clause 1 – and that can be done, and can only be done, I think, by adopting the construction of Clause 4 which the Master of the Rolls has just indicated. In my opinion, this appeal fails and should be dismissed, with costs.

For these reasons, Their Lordship cannot find any ground for holding the charterers responsible for the cost of these shifting boards, held that this appeal fails and should be dismissed, with costs.

2.16.1 Unsuitable spare parts

In the *Kamsar Voyager*,[204] the vessel was a bulk carrier in the course of a voyage with a part cargo of soybeans shipped at Reserve and Westwego, Louisiana. Five bills of lading dated 27 July 1995 and eight bills of lading dated 30 July 1995 were issued for carriage to Inchon in Korea. The contract of carriage evidenced by the bills of lading included a clause paramount incorporating the US Carriage of Goods by Sea Act, 1936, with the consequence that the Hague Rules became terms of the contract.

On 28 August, cylinder no. 1 was opened up, and after the piston was withdrawn and cleaned, a visual examination revealed extensive cracking extending from the aluminium piston skirt up to the steel piston crown. The vessel had a spare piston on board which

202 Ibid, p. 99.

203 Ibid, per Romer LJ at p. 100.

204 *The Kamsar Voyager* [2002] 2 Lloyd's Rep.57.

had been ordered by Klaveness from MAN in March 1995 and delivered by MAN to the vessel at Piraeus in April 1995. The spare piston was fitted to cylinder no. 1, and the engine gradually worked up to its full-service speed in the early hours of 29 August, when unusual noises were heard from the engine, followed by a stoppage of the engine and severe physical damage to the no. 1 unit and consequential damage to the no. 2 unit caused by water leakage and hydraulic shock. The vessel was immobilized at sea and had to be towed to Yokohama for repairs.

The major damage to the engine had been caused after the spare piston had been fitted because the dimensions of the spare were not compatible with the ship's main engine. The owners proclaimed general average (GA) and claimed the balance of cargo interest's proportion said to be due under a GA adjustment made in London in March 1996.

The claim was made against the cargo insurers as defendants under the terms of the average guarantees given by the cargo insurers in respect of delivery of the cargo to the consignees against customary average bonds.

The defendants resisted the claim on the grounds that no contribution was properly due from the cargo interests, as the GA expenditure was caused by the actionable fault of the owners in failing to exercise due diligence to ensure that *Kamsar Voyager* was seaworthy before the beginning of the voyage, in breach of the terms of the contract of carriage contained in and evidenced by the bills of lading.

The issues for the decision were (1) whether the vessel was unseaworthy on sailing by reason of the presence on board of the spare pistons with dimensions that were not compatible with the MHI version of the MAN engine; (2) whether the vessel was unseaworthy by reason of the crack in the no. 1 piston, the defendants were relieved of the need to prove that this was a cause of the GA expenditure by reason of clause 5 in the bill of lading, and whether the failure of the no. 1 piston was a cause of the GA expenditure; and (3) whether the claimants had established that due diligence was exercised to make the ship seaworthy, notwithstanding the presence on board of the cracked no. 1 piston and/or the inappropriate spare piston.[205]

His Honour Judge Dean QC discussed the question of due diligence and concluded:[206]

> This is without doubt an important consideration to bear in mind when considering the practicalities of actual maintenance in the real commercial world. If I had been hesitating as to which expert's evidence to prefer it might even have been decisive. However, I am not in such a state of mind. I am not satisfied that the owners have satisfied the burden of proving that they exercised due diligence. They did not offer any explanation of the reason for, let alone abandonment of, service intervals of less than the minimum 8000 hours proposed by MHI in 1992 and 1993 apart from Mr. Sinclair's unsupported suggestion that it might have reflected class requirements.
>
> Nothing in the vessel's maintenance history could justify extending this period as Mr. Moraes himself recognized when giving evidence. If the routine maintenance prescribed had been followed the crack in the No. 1 piston would have been found and attended to before it made itself manifest in August during the voyage.

Judge Dean QC explained and added the experts agreed that the failure of the no. 1 piston did not cause consequential damage to the rest of the engine and that the no. 1 unit could have been isolated so that the vessel could have completed the voyage under her

205 Ibid, p. 57.
206 Ibid, per Judge Dean Q.C. at p. 64.

power; however, there would have been no need to install the spare if the original piston had not failed at sea. Although the installation of a defective spare was not reasonably foreseeable as such, if the vessel carried a spare, as a prudent shipowner would have done, its use was inevitable; accordingly, the failure of the original piston was not simply an occasion giving rise to the opportunity to install the spare whose causative force had been spent. It was an operative cause that was indeed the only reason for the use of the only relevant spare part on board the vessel. It was thus causative of the installation of the spare part and the subsequent immobilization of the vessel at sea.[207]

Judge Dean QC commented on unseaworthiness and stated:[208]

> I am satisfied that the vessel was unseaworthy in fact by the presence on board of the unsuitable spare piston which would damage the engine if fitted during the voyage. The more interesting question is whether this came to be on board by reason of any failure to exercise due diligence for which the owners are responsible in law.

In this case, the court noted that no criticism was or could have been made of the way the owners ordered the spare piston from MAN, and no criticism was made of the owners for failing to notice the difference in the height of the piston pin securing the top end of the connecting rod in the piston skirt, or of the installation of the spare during the voyage. On the evidence, if the owners bore the legal burden of proving that MAN exercised due diligence to supply the vessel with the correct spare piston, they were quite unable to do so.[209]

2.16.2 Insufficient spare part

In the *Pride of Donegal*,[210] on 18 December 1995, the vessel departed Detroit with a view to loading cargo at Norfolk, Virginia, and Brownsville, Texas, for delivery to Asia. The vessel encountered engine problems which resulted in her being towed to Norfolk for repairs and being unable to fulfil her obligations of carriage.

The insurers denied liability. The insurers contended that the vessel was unseaworthy because she did not have enough diesel oil to reach Norfolk when she departed Thorold; the vessel was unseaworthy on departure from Detroit because the fuel oil transfer pump was defective and therefore fuel oil could not be pumped from the double bottom tanks; the vessel was not seaworthy when she left Detroit because her oil-fired boiler was not operable; corrosion or erosion of the engine's aft turbocharger meant that the vessel was unseaworthy when she left Detroit; and the insurers further submitted that the vessel was not seaworthy both when she departed from Detroit and later in the voyage.

The insurers contended that the vessel was unseaworthy at the start of the voyage because her generators were not working properly; the vessel was unseaworthy at the start of the voyage because she failed to carry sufficient spare parts and the vessel did not carry a clamping device. The insurers also submitted that the vessel ceased to be maintained with a classification society after 27 December 1995; the vessel was not seaworthy at the start of

207 Ibid, pp. 64, 67.
208 Ibid, p. 67.
209 Ibid, pp. 68–69.
210 *The Pride of Donegal* [2002] 1 Lloyd's Rep.659.

the voyage because of excessive wear of the no. 6 cylinder and ring grooves in the nos. 5, 6, and 7 pistons; and the vessel was not seaworthy because her cargo constructions safety certificate was valid only until 30 December 1995.[211]

Andrew Smith J discussed the unseaworthiness and said:[212]

> To establish unseaworthiness, it is not necessary to identify the precise defect. I refer to the decision in *Eridania S.p.A. and Others v. Oetker and Others* (*The Fjord Wind*). In that case the vessel suffered crackpin bearing failures within a few hours of departing down the river Paraná from the loading port, Rosario. Mr. Justice Moore-Bick considered that the very fact that there was this failure, when there was nothing to suggest that the conditions encountered by the vessel were unusual or that the casualty was the result of outside intervention, was telling evidence that the vessel was unseaworthy at the commencement of the voyage, even though it was impossible to identify the cause of the failure. The Court of Appeal endorsed his approach. Lord Justice Clarke said ([2000] 2 Lloyd's Rep.191 at p. 199):
>
>> In these circumstances the Judge was in my opinion right to hold that the vessel was unseaworthy when she left Rosario because there was present a defect which meant that it could not operate on an ordinary voyage, since it failed on the voyage down-river, with the consequences described above, which were entirely foreseeable. Thus if the owners had known that such a defect was present, the bearing would fail in those circumstances, they would have rectified the defect.

Andrew Smith J continued:[213]

> I agree with the Judge that seaworthiness is concerned with the state of the vessel rather than with whether the owners acted prudently or with due diligence. The only relevance of the standard of the reasonable prudent owner is to ask whether, if he had known of the defect, he would have taken steps to rectify it. In the instant case, there can I think be no doubt that he would, if he had known that there was a defect which would cause the bearing to fail as it did, which it seems to me is the relevant state of knowledge for these purposes. It follows that the vessel was unseaworthy when she left Rosario because she was not in a fit condition to withstand an ordinary voyage down the river Paraná.

Andrew Smith J added:[214]

> A vessel is not seaworthy if she has insufficient fuel to enable her to proceed on her voyage. A vessel need not have sufficient fuel at the commencement of her voyage to complete the entire journey. Under the so-called doctrine of stages, the assured's obligation at each bunkering stage is to ensure that the vessel has enough fuel for that stage with a sufficient margin for contingencies. When this trial was opened, it seemed that I might have to determine whether or not initial seaworthiness on leaving the first port might be cured on passage by bunkering at an intermediate port. However, the issues between the parties about the vessel's bunkers have largely been resolved, and the only remaining question is one of fact, whether the vessel on leaving Thorold had sufficient diesel oil for the passage to Norfolk.

Andrew Smith J stated that it was established that the fuel heating boiler was out of action at the start of the voyage and had been for same time; it was clear from the evidence that this did not make the vessel unseaworthy, and this complaint did not assist the defendant in establishing a defence under the implied warranty of seaworthiness.[215]

---

211 Ibid, p. 659.
212 Ibid.
213 Ibid, per Andrew Smith J at p. 666.
214 Ibid.
215 Ibid, p. 674.

Andrew Smith J explained the matter and concluded:[216]

> I therefore conclude that the defendant has established that PAL were in breach of the implied warranty of seaworthiness at the commencement of the voyage in respect of the turbocharger casing and the generators, and therefore that the claim is to be dismissed. The defendant succeeds in his counterclaim.

By the way, the statutory definition of *seaworthiness*, as Andrew Smith J pointed out, is that "[a] ship is deemed to be seaworthy when she is reasonably fit in all respects to encounter the ordinary perils of the seas of the adventure assured." There is thus no fixed standard of seaworthiness, but it varies with the exigencies of the voyage. As it was put by Lord Cairns in *Steel v State Line S.S. Co.*, (1877) 3 App. Cas.72 at p. 77: "The ship should be in a condition to encounter whatever perils of the sea a ship of that kind, laden in that way, may be fairly expected to encounter" on the voyage.

2.17 Anchor

The anchor and the anchoring mechanisms and procedures are crucial elements in securing a ship. Damage and claim statistics show a rather high damage ratio due to loss of anchor, which is being reported on the rise in recent years. Grounding and collision as a result of anchor chain lost or dragging anchor have caused severe oil pollution. Investigation revealed most of these incidents could have easily been avoided by following the appropriate operational procedure, inspection, and periodic maintenance of anchoring equipment. An awareness of the limitations of the anchoring system would have also helped avoid some damage incidence. Loss of anchor and chain damage are a serious matter. If an anchor is lost, the vessel will suffer an economical loss. Loss of both anchors makes the vessel lose seaworthiness, as berthing/unberthing operation will not be permitted by port authorities.

In one London arbitration case in 2019,[217] the vessel arrived at the specified anchorage and tendered NOR at 0830 on 13 May 2018. The vessel waited there for a pilot until 2035 on 15 May 2018, when she weighed anchor and proceeded to the pilot station, where a pilot boarded the vessel. When he did so, the pilot discovered that the vessel only had one anchor available. That had not been reported in advance by the vessel to the port authorities.

On discovering the position, the pilot was unwilling to proceed upriver to the discharge port with just one anchor unless the owners hired an escort tug. However, the owners considered that too expensive and opted instead to replace the second anchor and then proceed. The vessel was therefore sent back to the anchorage at 2345 on 15 May 2018 to undertake the necessary work. Once that had been done, the vessel weighed anchor at 0600 on 18 May 2018, proceeding to the pilot station again, but this time with two anchors, and on to the discharge port, where she arrived at 2112 the same day before berthing at 1436 on 19 May 2018 to discharge.

There was dispute for NOR and laytime calculation. Both parties relied on expert evidence. The owners' expert acknowledged that if a port considered that having both anchors was necessary for a safe river passage, and if a vessel arrived with just one anchor, the most effective and common action was to provide a tug to escort the vessel to berth.

216 Ibid, p. 678.
217 LMLN/*London Arbitration 16/19*.

He did not, however, accept that it was normal that two anchors were required for river navigation.

The charterers' expert considered the pilot's request for a standby tug for the river passage to have been a perfectly usual and reasonable one. A request of that nature should have been anticipated if arrangements had not been made by the owners for the anchor to be replaced on arrival.

The tribunal preferred the evidence of the charterers' expert and accepted and found that two anchors were a normal requirement for river navigation and that, in a case of a missing anchor, it was usual and reasonable for a standby tug to be required. That was something that should have been anticipated by the owners, and the master's failure to report the missing anchor to the authorities was surprising.

Notwithstanding that, the difficulty with the charterers' case was that it required a finding that when the vessel tendered NOR on 13 May 2018, she was not in a condition, or able, to undertake the river passage to the discharge port. The absence of a second anchor was not the end of the story, or an absolute bar, as the possibility existed of proceeding to the discharge port with tug assistance. When the vessel tendered NOR, she was not, therefore, in a condition in itself that necessarily precluded her from completing the contractual voyage: what did so was the later decision of the owners not to employ a standby tug.

The owners acknowledged that it was that decision on their part that prevented the vessel from proceeding to the discharge port by agreeing to exclude time lost as a result of laytime. They were right to do so. That, however, was as far as the consequences of their decision extended. It did not retrospectively invalidate the NOR tendered at a time when the vessel was able to proceed to the discharge port, albeit with tug assistance rather than by having two anchors on board.

In the circumstances, and without condoning what might appear to have been the somewhat-cynical conduct of the owners, their decision not to proceed with an escort tug was appropriately addressed by the exclusion of time in the manner adopted in their calculations.

The rules regarding specifications of anchoring equipment are established by the class societies. It is important to be aware that these requirements are minimum requirements, and also to be aware of assumptions made in the calculations used. Class societies stress that anchoring equipment is only intended for temporary mooring of a vessel, within a harbour or a sheltered area, when awaiting berth, tide, etc. It is also underlined that the equipment is not designed to hold a ship off a fully exposed coast in bad weather or to stop a vessel from drifting.[218]

2.18 Hatch cover/coaming

Hatch covers are crucial for the safety of the vessel and cargo; hence, correct hatch cover operation, maintenance, and inspections are important and need to be carried out in a professional manner to reduce the risks of wetting damage to cargo and ensure the vessel's seaworthiness and safety of the crew and protect the environment. Further, adhering to rules, requirements, and best practices will help avoid disruptions of the cargo flow and

218 www.gard.no/web/updates/content/11831736/loss-of-anchors-and-chain.

ensure that shipping remains a viable and sustainable industry. If the hatch cover is not watertight, it may affect cargo seaworthiness.

In the *President Monroe*,[219] the plaintiffs are the owners or subrogated insurers on numerous articles of cargo that were shipped aboard the *President Monroe* in late July and early August of 1966. The cargo was loaded onto the ship at various ports in Japan, and its ultimate destination was Los Angeles. While the vessel was in San Francisco, loading cargo other than the plaintiffs' that were aboard the ship, the master of the *President Monroe* ordered the no. 6 forward deep tanks filled with seawater for ballasting purposes. All parties concede that it was during this ballasting operation that seawater entered the vessel's no. 6 lower hold and damaged the cargo in question.

The plaintiffs have sued APL for their losses and allege that APL was negligent and the vessel was unseaworthy. APL denies negligence, unseaworthiness, or any wrongdoing on its part. The plaintiffs contend that their cargo was damaged when seawater entered the lower no. 6 hold because of defective and malfunctioning coamings, lids, and closing mechanisms of the no. 6 deep tank hatches and because a hole existed in the aforesaid coamings. They also allege that the employees of APL were not given adequate or proper instructions as to the operation of the tank lids, hatch covers, and their hydraulic closing devices. The plaintiffs further allege a breach of an implied warranty of fitness of purpose on the part of NASSCO and MacGregor.

Defendant APL asserts that its personnel used all due care required of them in the operation of closing and securing the deep tank steel hatch covers. They deny any negligence and contend that the hatch covers supplied by MacGregor were inadequate and defective and, further, that MacGregor did not provide adequate instructions as to the operation of these hatch covers. APL further alleges that the overflow from the no. 6 deep tanks into the lower hold resulted from a hole situated in the coaming of the deep tank. APL believes that the hole was negligently placed there while the vessel was under construction by NASSCO. Defendant APL has cross-complained against NASSCO and MacGregor for indemnity and contribution against any sum that APL is required to pay the plaintiffs for damage to their shipments.

Defendant NASSCO denies any negligence or malfeasance and contends that the hole in the no. 6 tank is of unspecified origin and was not placed there by it. NASSCO further alleges that the contract between NASSCO and APL limits its liability and should bar any recovery by APL against NASSCO. Defendant NASSCO denies that any warranty of fitness for purpose exists as to the *President Monroe*.[220]

Carter DJ discussed the question of seaworthy and said:[221]

> The duty of a shipowner to supply a seaworthy ship is absolute and cannot be delegated. APL cannot contract away the burden of unseaworthiness and the owner of the vessel must bear the full responsibility of any act or omission that makes his ship unseaworthy. Liability for unseaworthiness is absolute and imposed regardless of fault. The fact that APL did not have actual or constructive knowledge of the hole nor the fact that it should not have known of its existence will not reduce its responsibility or liability. The shipowner has a non-delegable

219 *The President Monroe* [1972] 1 Lloyd's Rep.385.
220 Ibid, p. 387.
221 Ibid, per Carter DJ at p. 387.

> duty to furnish a seaworthy vessel, and no amount of due care will absolve him of that legal responsibility.

The task of ballasting is not a complex one, and it is a basic operation aboard a seagoing cargo vessel. The evidence presented at trial has shown that the crew of the vessel conducted the ballasting operation negligently and carelessly. It alleges that the flooding was a consequence of the hatch covers failing to close properly. Regardless of how the entire amount of water got into the cargo area, APL may have been negligent in its failure to properly close and secure the hatch covers in the no. 6 hold. It is entirely possible that the hatch covers were not adequately closed and secured and there was a leakage as a result of this. All the amount of water that entered the dry cargo area obviously could not have come from a small hole in the tank coaming. The court will not speculate as to how much water came from which source; it is probable that both the hole and the improperly closed hatch cover caused the flooding.

Carter DJ continued:[222]

> There was no one, other than NASSCO, that had either the opportunity or the capability to make a hole such as the one that existed in the no. 6 deep tank. The Court, therefore, finds that the hole was made and negligently left unsealed by NASSCO and it must bear the burden and responsibility for any damage caused by sea-water entering through the hole into the area where the plaintiffs' cargo was stowed.

APL should have either demanded that MacGregor draft new and clearer instructions or refused to accept the vessel until MacGregor complied with the demand. APL did not do this, and the actions of APL in revising and accepting its guidelines and directions of operation of the hatch covers without demanding that MacGregor either approve or disapprove, formally, of them are a cause that intervenes to relieve MacGregor from alleged liability for failure to properly warn of a defect in their product. Therefore, the court concludes that the rewriting of the instructions for the opening and closing of the hatch covers in the no. 6 hold deep tank relieved the defendant MacGregor from liability.[223]

Carter DJ explained the warranty and said:[224]

> It is a well-established rule that contracts for the building of ships are not maritime. However, there is a conflict of opinion between District Courts as to whether or not implied warranties of fitness and merchantability are recognized in admiralty. This Court can find no reason or logic that prohibits it from recognizing implied fitness warranties in admiralty. If either Sears or APL can make out an action based on an implied warranty then the fact that admiralty law is involved should not be a bar to recovery on that theory. This Court respectfully disagrees with the finding of the District Court of Delaware, when it held that warranties of fitness and merchantability are not recognized in admiralty. This Court will, in the alternative, look to the sound reasoning of the decisions. The Court quite clearly stated that "any action based on breach of implied warranty will lie in admiralty."

Carter DJ added that the distinctive feature of many cases involving product liability actions is the effort to widen the range of plaintiffs who may be entitled to relief from any given defendant and, at the same time, to increase the number of defendants who may be liable to a specific plaintiff. To accomplish these aims, established concepts of

222 Ibid, p. 389.
223 Ibid.
224 Ibid, p. 390.

liability must often be expanded, limiting concepts removed, and new theories developed. However, it is noted that as the common law developed, a limitation of liability existed as to who might sue whom. This limitation was called privity. It was, for a great many years, a well-established rule in both common law and maritime law that privity of contract had to exist for the maintenance of a tort action that involved negligence when the liability of the defendant appeared to depend upon the breach of a contractual obligation to the plaintiff.[225]

In this case, Carter DJ noted the court cannot possibly apportion damages among the two negligent defendants, as it is impossible to determine how much water came from what source or who is responsible for what damage. The precise extent that the joint tortfeasors contributed to the plaintiffs' damages is undetermined. The plaintiffs are entitled to compensation for their damages regardless of how the loss is apportioned among the wrongdoers. Therefore, the defendants that have not been relieved from liability in this case, NASSCO and APL, must bear the burden for the losses suffered by the plaintiffs. It is the ruling of this court that APL and NASSCO are jointly and severally liable to the plaintiffs in this action.[226]

Therefore, this case having been tried and the evidence having been heard, and the counsel having presented their oral arguments, and the matter having been submitted, it is the judgment of this court that the evidence has established that the vessel *President Monroe* was unseaworthy, and that the defendant APL further was guilty of negligence. It has further been shown that defendant NASSCO is guilty of negligence. The court further concludes that the defendant MacGregor is not guilty of any negligence as to the plaintiffs or co-defendants. Accordingly, MacGregor will be dismissed with prejudice from this action.[227]

Carter DJ concluded that the first defendants had not exercised due diligence to supply a seaworthy ship as required by the United States Carriage of Goods by Sea Act, 1936 (46 US Code, sect. 1303 [1] [a]), for the hole in the coaming could have easily been discovered (see p. 386, col. 2); they had been negligent in the operation of ballasting the deep tank, and this negligence was a contributing cause of the damage (see p. 388, col. 1), and therefore the first defendants were liable jointly with the second defendants.[228]

As we could note from this case, these inspections are required within the parameter of reasonableness. It is said that the question to be asked is not what kind of examination should have been made but what kind of examination could have been made.[229] The nature of the examination which a reasonably prudent man, skilled in the behaviour of reduction gears, would make involves striking a balance between the likelihood of there being a

225 Ibid, p. 391.
226 Ibid, p. 392.
227 Ibid.
228 Ibid.
229 See *The Anglo Colombian* [1937] 58 Ll.L. Rep.188, per Porter J said at p. 191: "The only question is whether by 'latent' it means that you have to use every possible method to discover whether it exists, or whether you must use reasonable methods. I cannot myself believe that in every case it is obligatory upon a ship's officer on the commencement of a voyage to go and tap every rivet to find if it has a defect or not. If that were so, ships would be held up in port for a very long time while the rivets were being tapped and eyes used to determine whether a defect existed or not. I think it means such an examination as a reasonably careful man skilled in that matter would make, and I think that such an examination as that was in fact made."

fatigue crack detectable by way of the methods suggested by the plaintiffs and the delay, expense, and possible risk involved by the use of such methods.[230]

2.18.1 Hatch cover not watertight

In the *Gundulic*,[231] the vessel was built in Seville in 1969. She had four holds with six hatches. The hatch covers were of the MacGregor type, each cover consisting of four panels which were secured to each other by wedges.

On 5 September, the vessel suffered heavy weather in the English Channel, and further heavy weather was encountered in the North Atlantic on 11 September. Further heavy seas were encountered on 23 October, and on 25 October, the vessel reached Japan.

The plaintiffs contended that the entry of seawater occurred early in the voyage, on 5 or 11 September, as a result of defects in the hatch covers, and the vessel was unseaworthy in two respects: (1) the condition of the rubber seals beneath the hatch panels and (2) the condition of the cross-joint wedges. They further argued that there was personal want of due diligence on the part of the defendants or their manager.

The defendants argued that the seawater had entered the holds between 12 and 18 October because some of the wedges had not been driven home after the hatches had been closed.

Lloyd J explained the matter and found as a fact that while there was undoubtedly some admixture, it was no more than is normal and unavoidable in discharging any bulk grain cargo. The great majority of the damage was caused while the cargo was still on board the ship.[232]

Lloyd J added, on the facts seawater in substantial quantities entered all four holds through the seams in the hatch covers due to defective cross-joint wedges on 5 or 11 September or both and there was a further entry of seawater on 23 October and possibly also on 16/17 October, the damage to the bulk stow in all four holds was therefore caused by the entry of seawater at the beginning of September and the surface damage seen on discharge was caused by the entry of seawater on 16/17 October or 23 October and the vessel was unseaworthy at the beginning of the voyage.

Lloyd J found as a fact that seawater in substantial quantities entered all four holds through the seams in the hatch covers due to defective cross-joint wedges on 5 September or 11 September or both. Those conclusions were expanded by Lloyd J. He stated:[233]

> On those findings there could, of course, be no dispute that the vessel was unseaworthy; for, though the weather at the beginning of September was bad, it was by no means exceptional. There was a faint suggestion that the wedges might have become defective during the voyage. But there was no evidence to support that suggestion.

Lloyd J explained, if he was right that the vessel was unseaworthy at the commencement of the voyage, the only remaining question is whether there was personal want of due diligence on the part of the defendants or their manager.

---

230 *The Amstelslot* [1962] 2 Lloyd's Rep.336 at pp. 367–368.
231 *The Gundulic* [1981] 2 Lloyd's Rep.418.
232 Ibid, per Lloyd J at p. 422.
233 Ibid, pp. 422, 424.

Lloyd J concluded:[234]

> I bear all these matters in mind. I also bear in mind that the time for renewing or repairing something which is subject to wear and tear must usually be a matter of judgment. In such cases it is always easy to be wise after the event. But the present case goes beyond that. The condition of the wedges on inspection at Rotterdam was such that any prudent surveyor should have foreseen a real risk that water would enter the holds through the seams in the hatch covers, and would have called for repairs. It was conceded that the burden was on the defendants to show that the damage occurred without any personal want of due diligence on the part of Mr. Radulovich. I hold that the defendants have failed to discharge that burden. It follows that there must be judgment for the plaintiffs.

Similarly in the *Baltic Mercur*,[235] the claimant successfully proved its prima facie case under COGSA by showing that the cargo of steel casings was loaded in good order and delivered in damaged condition. Even though the bills of lading contained remarks that the cargo had "rusty spots," the claimant proved to the arbitrator beyond reasonable doubt that the "heavy rust damage" was not present at loading but rather caused by the ingress of seawater through the vessel's hatch covers. The proof was established by means of survey reports, by chemical analysis reports, and by showing the presence of seawater in the container fittings on the vessel's tank top.[236]

On the other hand, the ship's structure also must be sufficiently strong to withstand the weather and sea conditions likely to be encountered on the voyage, and her hull plating, hatch covers, and ventilators must be sufficiently watertight to protect the cargo from the risk of damage. Fire extinguishing systems must be operable. Defects which can be reasonably expected to be easily remedied at sea in the normal course of the crew's duties will not necessarily render the ship unseaworthy. With the increasing risk of piratical attacks off the east coast of Africa, there is a need, for such voyages, to provide the vessel with proper facilities to repel boarders, such as installing concertina razor wire and water cannon, reinforcing windows, ensuring proper locking of doors, and even perhaps installing a "citadel" to which crew members can retire in safety to await the arrival of military aid.[237]

2.19 Fuel oil

Recently, the Maritime and Port Authority of Singapore (MPA) is investigating the suspected contamination of bunker fuel supplied to several ships in the port and has ordered the supply of the batch to stop. Throughout February–March 2022, VPS identified 34 vessels which received HSFO deliveries from two Singapore suppliers which were contaminated with up to 2,000 ppm of chlorinated hydrocarbons. These bunker fuel contaminations have affected 14 vessels so far, and the impact has led to the failure of the fuel system to the auxiliary engine, causing loss of power and propulsion creating a blackout. As a major bunkering hub, the MPA takes quality assurance seriously and is investigating the cause of the alleged bunker fuel contamination. Further investigations are currently ongoing. MPA will not hesitate to take action should there be any non-compliance.

234 Ibid, p. 425.
235 *The Baltic Mercur* SMA 3894 [2005].
236 See *Voyage Charters*, 4th ed at para. 11A.71.
237 See *Voyage Charters* at para. 11.28.

Contaminants in fuel oil can often be the source of damage to combustion power machinery. When the cause of damage to combustion machineries such as boilers, turbines, and engines is investigated, common causes are wear-and-tear, improper or inadequate maintenance, or improper use.

In the *Evanger*,[238] time charterparty was entered into on 12 October 1951 between plaintiff owners of steamship *Evanger* and defendant charterers for carriage of defendants' sugar charterparty, providing (inter alia) that vessel should be "in every way fitted for ordinary cargo service," and:

> The Owners only to be responsible for delay in delivery of the Vessel or for delay during the currency of the Charter and for loss or damage to goods on board, if such delay or loss has been caused by want of due diligence on the part of the Owners or their Manager in making the Vessel seaworthy and fitted for the voyage or for any other personal act or omission or default of the Owners or their Manager. The Owners not to be responsible in any other case nor for damage or delay whatsoever and howsoever caused even if caused by the neglect or default of their servants.

Oil fuel (in no. 5 tank) found to be unsuitable, steam not maintainable – a consequent general average expenditure. Claim by shipowners was for general average contribution from charterers. The contention by the charterers was that shipowners were in breach of the charterparty and that therefore the charterers were entitled to be indemnified by shipowners in respect of the charterers' liability for general average contribution. Evidence pointed that it was the chief engineer's duty to examine oil fuel before taking delivery.

Walsh J explained the matter and said:[239]

> I think it must be taken as established that, in order to take away the plaintiff's right to contribution from the defendant, the fault of the plaintiff must be one which is actionable at the suit of the defendant. If, therefore, having regard to their contract, the default on the part of the plaintiff is one in respect of which it incurred no legal liability to the defendant, the former can maintain its claim for contribution against the latter. But if it is a default in respect of which legal liability was incurred, then the claim for contribution fails and should be dismissed.

Walsh J discussed the question of seaworthy and stated:[240]

> In my opinion, it is clear that, unless the plaintiff be relieved from responsibility, by reason of Clause 13 of the charter-party, the defendant should succeed. For the cause of the trouble which led to the general average expense was the unsuitability of part of the oil which was handed over with the ship, when she was delivered to the defendant. I am of opinion that, by reason of having this oil in her tank, the ship was unseaworthy. If there was, in the contract, an implied term that, upon delivery, the ship should be seaworthy, there was a breach of this term. There was also a breach of the provision in the contract, that the ship should be "in every way fitted for ordinary cargo service." I do not agree with the submission that Mr. Street made, that there was a special and, so to speak, an independent contract in relation to the oil, because of Clause 5, and that, for that reason, any defect in the oil did not fall within the ambit of the general provision as to fitness of the ship for ordinary cargo service, nor within the ambit of an implied term as to seaworthiness, if such a term should be implied. It was suggested that this should not be implied because there is, in the contract, the express provision as to fitness for cargo service.

238 *The Evanger* [1960] 2 Lloyd's Rep.206.
239 Ibid, per Walsh J at p. 209.
240 Ibid.

Walsh J continued:[241]

> In my opinion, the prima facie liability of the owner (i.e., apart from Clause 13) is established, and for the purpose of determining the existence of that prima facie liability, it is immaterial to determine whether it should be regarded as founded upon an implied term as to seaworthiness, upon the express term as to be fitted for cargo service, or upon a breach of an obligation implied in Clause 5 itself, or upon all three. The critical question, therefore, is whether such liability, in whichever way it may be asserted, is excluded by the terms of Clause 13.

According to Walsh J, the first is that a shipowner may contract out of obligations which would otherwise rest upon him, including his implied obligation to provide a seaworthy ship. The second is that, for this purpose, it is essential that clear language be used, and if the exempting clause is ambiguous and two constructions of it are reasonably open, one of which will relieve the shipowner and the other will not, the owner will be held liable. The third is that if a clause is introduced by which, for the absolute obligation as to seaworthiness, there is substituted an obligation which is limited to the taking, by the owner, of due diligence to make the ship seaworthy, the owner will not escape liability merely because he has not personally failed to exercise due diligence. He will be liable if the persons employed by him to act in this respect have failed to exercise due diligence. (See *G. E. Dobell & Co. v Steamship Rossmore Company, Ltd.*, [1895] 2 Q.B. 408.) In other words, the limited obligation which is substituted in those terms will be construed as still rendering the owner liable for a failure, on the part of his servants, to take due diligence to make the ship seaworthy, in circumstances in which it was part of their duty to the owner to do so.[242]

Walsh J viewed this charterparty and added that it has not been contended, nor does he think it could be contended, that it is not open to the parties, by their contract to cut down the common-law obligation still more drastically, by substituting for it an agreement that the owner is to be liable if, and only if, he himself has been wanting in due diligence, and is not otherwise to be liable to any action for the ship not being seaworthy, whether this is caused by the neglect of his own servants or not. This is what the plaintiff contends has happened here. The cases show that this result is not attained by the use of a clause which restricts the obligation to an exercise of due diligence by the owner, without going on to indicate whether the reference is mere acts or omissions of the owner personally or extends to acts or omissions of his servants. But these cases do not apply if it is seen that the language of the exempting clause does not clearly refer to acts or omissions of the owner personally and limits the liability to the consequences of such acts.[243]

In this case, Walsh J viewed the clause "*The Owners not to be responsible in any other case nor for damage or delay whatsoever and howsoever caused even if caused by the neglect or default of their servants*" and concluded that the vessel was unseaworthy by reason of the unsuitable oil fuel in her tank, and there was a prima facie liability upon the shipowners.[244]

Similar to the *Elin*,[245] the provision on page 1 of the bill of lading provided, inter alia, that "*the carrier and/or Owners and/or vessel being not responsible for loss or damages*

241 Ibid.
242 Ibid.
243 Ibid, p. 210.
244 Ibid, p. 209.
245 *The Elin* [2019] Lloyd's Rep. Plus 71 [2019] EWHC 1001 (Comm).

howsoever arising." Accordingly, the judge Stephen Hofmeyr QC concluded that on a true construction of the bill of lading, the owner was not liable for any loss of or damage to any cargo carried on deck, including loss of or damage to any cargo carried on deck caused by the unseaworthiness of the vessel and/or the owner's negligence.

So also Lord Blackburn in *Steel v State Line SS Co*:[246]

> The shipowners might have stipulated, if they had pleased . . . [w]e will take the goods on board, but we shall not be responsible at all, though our ship is ever so unseaworthy; look out for yourselves; if we put them on board a rotten ship, that is your look-out; you shall not have any remedy against us if we do.

The language of the parties' agreement, read as a whole, is the only direct evidence of their intentions, which is admissible. It is a fallacy to say that language is meaningful only in relation to some particular background. Most languages and all properly drafted languages have an autonomous meaning.

2.19.1 Insufficient fuel

Under common law, a shipowner's obligation to provide a seaworthy ship is absolute, but not continuous. The warranty of seaworthiness must be construed by reference to the reasonable standard applicable to such a voyage, and the voyage would be divided into stages, with the standard adjusted accordingly. The vessel shall be seaworthy at the commencement of each stage. It requires the ship to be fit to receive its cargo at the commencement of loading for the ordinary perils of lying afloat in the harbour and need not be fit for sailing. Then on the completion of each stage, the vessel must have the degree of fitness which is required for the next stage.

In the *Vortigern*,[247] the owners of the vessel sued the defendants to recover the freight due under a charterparty under which shipowners had agreed to carry a cargo of copra to Liverpool from Cebu, Philippine Islands. The defence was that a portion of the defendants' cargo had been burned as fuel because insufficient coal had been loaded and that the shipowners were in breach of the implied warranty of seaworthiness under the contract of affreightment at the commencement of the voyage.

A. L. Smith LJ, in giving judgment, said:[248]

> The implied warranty which prima facie attaches to a charterparty such as the present is that the ship shall be seaworthy for the voyage at the time of sailing, by which is meant that the vessel shall then be in a fit state as to repairs, equipment, and crew, and in all other respects, sufficient to take her in ordinary circumstances to her port of destination, though there is no warranty that the ship shall continue seaworthy during the voyage.

A. L. Smith LJ explained that if the voyage in this case had been an ordinary voyage, as to which there was no necessity, as regards taking in coal, for dividing it into stages, it cannot be denied that the steamship was unseaworthy when she started from Cebu on her voyage to Liverpool, for the simple reason that she had not then on board equipment of coal sufficient to take her in ordinary circumstances to her port of destination.[249]

246 *Steel v State Line SS Co* [1877] 3 App. Cas. 72.
247 *The Vortigern* [1899], p. 140.
248 Ibid, per A. L. Smith LJ.
249 Ibid.

A. L. Smith LJ discussed the question of seaworthiness and concluded:[250]

> In my judgment when a question of seaworthiness arises between either a steamship owner and his underwriter upon a voyage policy, or between a steamship owner and a cargo owner upon a contract of affreightment, and the underwriter or cargo owner establishes that the ship at the commencement of the voyage was not equipped with a sufficiency of coal for the whole of the contracted voyage, it lies upon the shipowner, in order to displace this defence, which is a good one, to prove that he had divided the voyage into stages for coaling purposes by reason of the necessity of the case, and that, at the commencement of each stage, the ship had on board a sufficiency of coal for that stage – in other words, was seaworthy for that stage. If he fails in this he fails in defeating the issue of unseaworthiness which prima facie has been established against him. In each case, it is a matter for proof as to where the necessity of the case requires that each stage should be, and I think that in the present case the necessity for coaling places at Colombo and Suez has been established.

This question of dividing up voyages into stages, as regards the warranty of seaworthiness, is by no means destitute of authority. There are numerous cases decided upon policies of marine insurance when the voyage is divided into stages, and there is also a case in this court relating to the warranty of seaworthiness upon a contract of affreightment when the voyage was divided into stages.

As regards the first class of cases, it suffices to cite from a judgment of Lord Penzance when delivering the judgment of the Judicial Committee of the Privy Council, consisting of himself, Sir William Erle, and Giffard LJ, in the case of the *Quebec Marine Insurance Co v Commercial Bank of Canada*,[251] where the numerous prior authorities relating to voyages consisting of different stages are referred to. Lord Penzance said:

> The case of *Dixon v Sadler*[252] and the other cases which have been cited, leave it beyond doubt that there is seaworthiness for the port, seaworthiness in some cases for the river, and seaworthiness in some cases, as in a case that has been put forward of a whaling voyage, for some definite, well recognised, and distinctly separate stage of the voyage.

This principle has been sanctioned by various decisions, but it has been equally well decided that the vessel, in cases where these several distinct stages of navigation involve the necessity of different equipment or state of seaworthiness, must be properly equipped and, in all respects, seaworthy for each of these stages of the voyage respectively at the time when she enters upon each stage; otherwise, the warranty of seaworthiness is not complied with. It was argued that the obligation thus cast upon the assured to procure and provide a proper condition and equipment for the vessel to encounter the perils of each stage of the voyage necessarily involves the idea that between one stage of the voyage and another, he should be allowed an opportunity to find and provide that further equipment which the subsequent stage of the voyage requires, and no doubt that is so. But that equipment must, if the warranty of seaworthiness is to be complied with (that is, the warranty at the time of the commencement of the voyage), be furnished before the vessel enters upon that subsequent stage of the voyage which is supposed to require it.

Read into this judgment the word "shipowner" in the place of "the assured" and the judgment is in point in the present case. There is no difference between the implied

250 Ibid.
251 *Quebec Marine Insurance Co v Commercial Bank of Canada* [1870] LR 3 PC 234.
252 *Dixon v Sadler* [1841] 5 M & W 405.

warranty of seaworthiness which attaches at the commencement of the voyage in the case of an assured shipowner and the case of a shipowner under a contract of affreightment. In each case, the shipowner warrants that his ship is seaworthy at the commencement of the voyage.[253]

Similarly, in the *Newbrough*,[254] the vessel loaded wheat at Vancouver for Hull in November 1932 and proceeded via the Panama Canal for St. Thomas for bunkers. On 22 December, it was found that the vessel had no sufficient bunkers to reach St. Thomas, and she deviated toward Port Royal. On 24 December, while proceeding towards Port Royal, she was stranded on Morant Cays and, with her cargo of 8,389 t of wheat and bran, became a total loss.

The plaintiffs alleged that the stranding was due to negligent navigation and, further, that the vessel was unseaworthy because of insufficiency of bunkers. The defendant shipowners denied that the vessel was unseaworthy or unfit, or that their servants were negligent. Alternatively, they pleaded that they were protected from liability by the provisions of the bill of lading and of the Canadian Water-Carriage of Goods Act, 1910, which were incorporated therein.

Lord Justice MacKinnon held that the stranding was due to faults or errors in navigation; that the shipowners had failed to exercise due diligence to make the vessel seaworthy in regard to her bunkers, in that insufficient bunkers were carried either for the stage from Vancouver to St. Thomas or for the stage from Colon to St. Thomas; and that, therefore, they were precluded from relying on the provisions of the Canadian Act. The Court of Appeal affirmed the decision of Lord Justice MacKinnon.

The main question raised by the appeal was as to the meaning in relation to bunkers of the obligation cast upon a carrier by sea by the Canadian Water-Carriage of Goods Act, 1910, to exercise due diligence to make his ship seaworthy and properly supplied. A subsidiary question of fact also arose as to what quantity of bunkers the *Newbrough* had on board when she sailed from Vancouver.

Lord Wright, delivering the judgment, said:[255]

> Of these provisions, those in Sect. 6 were the only ones relied on by the appellants. This section, so far as material, is to the effect that if the owners of any ship transporting merchandise from any port in Canada should exercise due diligence to make the ship in all respects seaworthy and properly supplied, the owner should not be responsible for loss resulting from faults or errors in navigation of the ship. The appellants rightly for obvious reasons did not seek to found a defence on Sect. 7. Sect. 6 was considered by the *Privy Council in Paterson Steamships, Ltd. v. Canadian Co-operative Wheat Producers, Ltd.*,[256] where it was said, at p. 427:
>
> > "What is important to note in Sect. 6 is that the protection is conditional on the owner having exercised due diligence to make the ship seaworthy. At common law, seaworthiness of the ship in a contract for sea carriage has, if necessary, to be shown to have existed at the commencement of the voyage, but unseaworthiness involves no liability on the shipowner unless it has caused the damage complained of: *J. & E. Kish v. Charles Taylor, Sons & Co.*, [1912] A.C. 604; but the obligation to provide a seaworthy ship is absolute,

253 More details see *Cases & Materials on the Carriage of Goods by Sea* at p. 52.

254 *The Newbrough* [1937] 58 Ll.L. Rep.45; [1938] 60 Ll.L. Rep.191 (C.A.); [1939] 64 Ll.L. Rep.33 (H.L.).

255 Ibid, per Lord Wright [1939] 64 Ll.L. Rep.33 (H.L.) at p. 37.

256 *Privy Council in Paterson Steamships, Ltd. v Canadian Co-operative Wheat Producers, Ltd.*, 49 Ll.L. Rep.421.

and is not limited to due diligence to make it so. The matter which Sect. 6 deals with as the condition on which its privileges may be relied on is not seaworthiness, but due diligence to make the ship seaworthy: if, however, that condition is not fulfilled, the shipowner cannot, under Sect. 6, excuse himself from liability for loss due to negligence in the respects specified in the section."

Lord Wright commented on the doctrine of stages and said it has not been the subject of direct decision in this House but has been laid down or recognised by the Court of Appeal, where the rule was applied in the case of a voyage policy of marine insurance. It is a special application, to bunker supply, of a doctrine which has been applied in other connections, such as a stage of the voyage for loading in port, or for passages in inland waters, where different standards of fitness are required as compared with what is required in the open sea. The application of the doctrine of stages became particularly important when vessels came to depend for their propulsion on machinery, the fuel for which was necessarily consumed as the voyage went on.[257]

Lord Wright continued and stated:[258]

The rule which has been established is that a steamship or motor vessel starting from her port on a long ocean voyage need not carry enough coal (or oil or other fuel) for the whole voyage, but only sufficient to take her to a particular convenient or usual bunkering port on the way. That is treated as a section of the voyage and is called a stage of the voyage. Thus, the warranty or seaworthiness is subdivided in respect of bunkers. Instead of a single obligation to make the vessel seaworthy in this respect, which must be satisfied once for all at the commencement of the voyage, there is substituted a recurring obligation at each bunkering port at which the owners or those who act for the owners decide she shall bunker, thereby fixing the particular stage of the voyage.

Lord Wright viewed that the principle presupposes that the contract of affreightment permits this course and of deviating if necessary for this purpose. It has been said that this rule is a concession to the shipowners. Lord Wright preferred to say (with Collins LJ in the *Vortigern*, sup., at p. 159) that it is rather an adjustment of the requirements as to this type of seaworthiness to the commercial necessities of the case. If a steamship starting, for instance, from London for Australia had to start with enough coal or fuel to carry her to Australia, the amount she would have to carry on starting would reduce her cargo-carrying capacity to such an extent as to make the adventure uneconomic. Not only would the shipowners suffer, but so would the shippers and the community generally because of the high or prohibitive freights which would have to be charged.

Lord Wright continued:[259]

But in my opinion the stage must be determined when the vessel sails. Seaworthiness is no doubt relative to the nature of the adventure and the other circumstances of the case. But unless it is determined on sailing what the stage of the voyage is, it is impossible to say whether the ship is seaworthy or not. There is also the special difficulty under Sect. 6 that a vessel might be lost by negligent navigation soon after sailing from her first port with insufficient bunkers. . . . I think that this is true not only in general but also where it may be said that it is only a question of estimating the margin for contingencies. If the stage is determined, the quantity of

257 Ibid, per Lord Wright at p. 38.
258 Ibid.
259 Ibid, p. 40.

> bunkers sufficient to make the vessel seaworthy for that stage must be determined in view of all contingencies that a prudent shipowner ought to contemplate.

Lord Wright explained and said in the case not necessary here to consider these questions because the vessel did not, in fact, take coal at Colon, so that if it is right to talk of conditional seaworthiness, the condition was not fulfilled and the original unseaworthiness was unredeemed. Owners would be held bound to fulfil excessive requirements in the way of bunkers. Commercial law has always been ready so far as possible to sacrifice pedantic logical consistency in favour of convenience in the conduct of business. But I am not pressed by the suggested hardship or embarrassment. Owners, with the help of their masters and other agents acting for them, have full discretion to fix any reasonable stages for the voyage. It would involve grave difficulties in practice if the stage of the voyage were not definitely fixed on sailing so that the standard of what was sufficient in respect of bunkers was rendered vague and uncertain.[260]

Lord Porter added:[261]

> Prima facie a ship must be seaworthy on sailing from her starting point for the whole voyage upon which she is engaged, but it has long been established that the voyage may be divided into stages and that it is sufficient if she be satisfactorily equipped for each stage at its commencement. The principle is older than the age of steam. It has been held to apply to such stages as lying in harbour; proceeding down a river; and passing from one port to another. The doctrine was, however, of less importance in the days when vessels proceeded under sail. Once steam propulsion was adopted and bunkers had to be carried, it became important for the shipowner that he should not be compelled to carry so large a quantity of bunkers as to compel him unduly to diminish his cargo or should even force him to avoid certain voyages altogether.

In this case, Their Lordship concluded the vessel was not seaworthy when she started on that stage of her voyage, which lay between Vancouver and St. Thomas, and due diligence was not exercised to make her so.

2.19.2 Incompatible fuel oils

In the *Evje (No. 2)*,[262] on 14 January 1966, the owners let their vessel on a voyage charter in the Baltimore Berth Grain form C to the charterers for the carriage of a cargo of wheat from one safe port, US North Pacific to Bombay or Kandla. The charter included the Jason clause, which provided (inter alia):

> If the owner shall have exercised due diligence to make the steamer in all respects seaworthy and to have her properly . . . supplied, it is hereby agreed that in case of danger, damage or disaster resulting from . . . any latent defect in the steamer her machinery . . . or from unseaworthiness, whether existing at the time of shipment or at the beginning of the voyage . . . the [charterers] shall . . . contribute with the [owners] in general average.

The vessel loaded at Portland on 23 January 1966 and sailed for Bombay via Yokohama as a bunkering port but ran out of fuel oil and had to be towed to Yokohama. By an agreement dated 23 February 1966, the charterers undertook to pay any general average contribution that might be legally due.

260 Ibid.
261 Ibid, per Lord Porter at p. 42.
262 *The Evje (No. 2)* [1976] 2 Lloyd's Rep.714; [1978] 1 Lloyd's Rep.351 (C.A.).

The owners claimed a general average contribution, but the charterers contended that the Jason clause prevented recovery of such a contribution since there was a failure by the owners to use due diligence to make the ship seaworthy at the beginning, in that (a) the fuel oil was unsuited to the engine, (b) there had been a mixing of incompatible fuel oils before the beginning of the voyage, (c) the fuel valves were not in a proper state of repair, (d) the vessel was overloaded at the beginning of the voyage, and (e) a freshwater tank was corroded.[263]

In the judgment of Donaldson J in the Commercial Court, he stated:[264]

> The owners contend that fuel is only ordered by reference to viscosity, and the chief engineer says that he cannot analyse the oil and is only concerned to check the viscosity as shown on the documents. I accept that analysis is impracticable. However, in my judgment, where the maker of the vessel's engine specifies a maximum specific gravity, it is incumbent upon the owners, the master or the chief engineer to make this requirement clear when ordering supplies of bunkers, and it is the duty of the chief engineer to check the documents to see that the fuel delivered appears to meet this requirement. I do not know what was ordered, but the chief engineer should have been aware that the fuel delivered was outside the limits specified by the engine makers.
>
> It follows that in my judgment the vessel was unseaworthy at the beginning of the voyage either because she had insufficient bunkers, or because they were of the wrong quality, or for both reasons. This unseaworthiness was the cause of the casualty. Furthermore, each form of unseaworthiness could and would have been avoided if the owners had exercised due diligence to make the vessel seaworthy. Contribution in general average is, therefore, irrecoverable from the defendant and the claim fails.

In the Court of Appeal, Lord Denning MR said:[265]

> The first point is whether the ship was in fact seaworthy when she left Portland in Oregon en route for Yokohama. In order to be seaworthy she had to have enough fuel on board to take her safely across the Pacific at that time of year. It was the master's task to calculate how much fuel was needed according to the knots she could do on her way across and make sure that she had enough fuel for that purpose: and this was investigated.

Lord Denning MR commented on the crew:

> It is quite plain the master made another mistake there; because, according to the records for this engine, it is quite clear that the specific gravity of oil should be below 0.970; whereas in truth the density or specific gravity of the oil which was loaded on the ship – and the master had full notice of it because he signed the documents acknowledging it – was the higher figure of 0.993. So he took on oil which was of a higher specific gravity than that which was recommended.[266]

Dismissing the argument, Lord Denning MR concluded:[267]

> So that expert said he would take the risk; but it seems to me taking such a risk on a voyage of this kind was not permissible. He would be taking a chance. There was a want of due diligence in the master in setting off on a ship of this kind across the North Pacific with all this cargo aboard. On this matter also it is quite plain that, in taking this fuel oil aboard with too high a specific gravity, he was taking a chance and was wanting in due diligence. This is how the Judge put it on p. 720:

263 Ibid, [1976] 2 Lloyd's Rep.714 at p. 714.
264 Ibid, per Donaldson J at p. 720.
265 Ibid, per Lord Denning MR [1978] 1 Lloyd's Rep.351 (C.A.) at p. 353.
266 Ibid, p. 354.
267 Ibid, p. 355.

> It follows that in my judgment the vessel was unseaworthy at the beginning of the voyage either because he had insufficient bunkers, or because they were of the wrong quality, or for both reasons. This unseaworthiness was the cause of the casualty. Furthermore, each form of unseaworthiness could and would have been avoided if the owners had exercised due diligence to make the vessel seaworthy. Contribution in general average is therefore irrecoverable from the defendant and the claim fails.
>
> The Judge had been through all the circumstances and the facts, and it seems to me that his judgment cannot be faulted. His is a decision on the facts of this case after hearing all the evidence and considering it most carefully. I think this appeal should be dismissed.

Lawton LJ added:[268]

> In my judgment, on a winter voyage of this kind, it was not justifiable for either the master or the chief engineer to take the risk. There are, of course, circumstances in which untoward events happen and it is uneconomical and impractical for those faced with a decision to take remedial steps at once. That sort of situation had not arisen in this case. If oil can be pumped into the tanks of a ship, it can be pumped out; and, in my judgment, the failure to have it pumped out once the error had been discovered was negligence or, to use the appropriate terminology in this case, want of due diligence. I too would dismiss the appeal.

Goff LJ dismissed the appeal by saying:[269]

> It seems to me, with that evidence, the learned Judge was perfectly justified in the conclusion which he ultimately reached, which my Lord has already read:
>
> > "It follows that in my judgment the vessel was unseaworthy at the beginning of the voyage either because she had insufficient bunkers, or because they were of the wrong quality, or for both reasons. This unseaworthiness was the cause of the casualty. Furthermore, each form of unseaworthiness could and would have been avoided if the owners had exercised due diligence to make the vessel seaworthy. Contribution in general average is, therefore irrecoverable from the defendant, and the claim fails."
>
> In my judgment the learned Judge's conclusion is entirely correct and his reasoning impeccable.

Also, those bunkers must be suitable for use in the vessel's engines. If bunkers are of the wrong specification or are contaminated so that the engines will not function with reasonable reliability, the vessel is unseaworthy. When bunkers are intended to be taken at an intermediate port, she must set out for that port with enough bunkers to reach it in safety.[270]

On the other hand, as long as the owners have formed a definite intention, before sailing from the loading port, to bunker at a particular intermediate port, it is sufficient that the ship should have enough bunkers, with a suitable margin, to reach that port. The warranty will then re-attach, so far as concerns the adequacy of her bunkers, when she sails from the bunkering port. It seems, however, that each bunkering stage must be fixed not later than the time of sailing; the owners cannot simply authorise the master to take on bunkers wherever necessary and then, if the vessel runs short of fuel, claim that she was seaworthy on leaving the loading port because she had enough bunkers to get to an intermediate port where she could have bunkered if the master had so decided. Moreover, the presence en route of potential bunkering ports, at which the vessel may call if the need arises, does

268 Ibid, per Lawton LJ at p. 355.
269 Ibid, per Goff LJ at pp. 356–357.
270 See *Voyage Charters*, 4th ed at para. 11.37.

not mean that the owners are entitled to embark on the voyage with a smaller margin than would be prudent if no such optional bunkering ports existed.[271]

The rule which has been established is that a steamship or motor vessel starting from her port on a long ocean voyage need not carry enough coal (or oil or other fuel) for the whole voyage but only sufficient to take her to a particular or usual bunkering port on the way. That is treated as a section of the voyage and is called a stage of the voyage. Thus, the warranty of seaworthiness is subdivided in respect of bunkers.[272]

2.19.3 Bad-quality coal causes boiler damage

In the *British Monarch*,[273] the pursuers were a Swedish firm of manufacturers who, in the ordinary course of business, on 21 April 1939, purchased through their London agents a cargo of Manchurian soya beans from the Japanese firm of Messrs. Mitsui & Co. Ltd. The voyage from Rashin to Karlshamn, which normally should have taken this vessel about 60 days, was greatly protracted.

From the outset, the ship's boilers failed to produce the proper working steam pressure, with the result that the ship's speed was greatly reduced. Instead of the nine knots which she should have done, the logs showed that she averaged around about five. On 23 June, serious boiler trouble developed at sea and the master was forced to divert the ship to Colombo for repairs. The ship was repaired at that port between 30 June and 15 July, on which date she resumed her voyage. The boilers again gave trouble and she had to put into Aden for further repairs. Thereafter she proceeded, still at reduced speed, to Port Said, where she arrived on 31 August. Repairs were again found to be necessary, and while these were being carried out, the war began and the ship came under the directions of the Admiralty as regards her future movements. On 23 September, the repairs being completed, the ship left Port Said and, acting under Admiralty orders, made for Glasgow, where she arrived on 21 October 1939.

The main case made by the pursuers was that the *British Monarch* was unseaworthy at Rashin and that the subsequent delay in the voyage was due to that unseaworthiness. It was said that the ship's boilers, evaporator, and condenser were in a defective state.

In reply, the shipowners denied the defects and maintained that the ship's poor performance and subsequent troubles were due to defective coal shipped at the port of Karatsu for the voyage, which, they said, was the only coal then obtainable for bunkers.

Lord Sorn held that the vessel was unseaworthy when she sailed, that her owners were liable for all consequences arising from the delay, and that the pursuers were entitled to recover the cost of transhipment from the shipowners.

On appeal by the shipowners, Lord Normand LP (with whom Lord Carmont agreed) held that the undue prolongation of the voyage was due to unseaworthiness; that it was within the knowledge of the shipowners that there was a risk of war, with the inevitable consequence of an embargo being placed on such a voyage; that accordingly the coming

271 Ibid, para. 11.51.

272 *The Newbrough* [1939] 64 Ll.L. Rep.33 (H.L.), per Lord Wright at p. 38.

273 *The British Monarch* (1945/46) 79 Ll.L. Rep.385; (1946/47) 80 Ll.L. Rep.151; [1949] 82 Ll.L. Rep.137 (H.L.).

into force of the embargo must be viewed as a reasonable consequence of the excessive delay in the prosecution of the voyage; and that therefore the cargo owners were entitled to recover from the shipowners the cost of transhipment as a head of damage.[274]

Lord Porter, delivering the judgment, said:[275]

> Undoubtedly, deviation necessarily made to remedy unseaworthiness does not amount to unjustifiable deviation or destroy the right to rely upon the terms of the contract of carriage unless it is established that the owners knew of the vessel's state on sailing. As indicated above, no such knowledge has been brought home to the appellants and therefore they continue to be entitled to rely upon the war clause.

Lord Porter discussed the peril and stated:[276]

> It was urged, however, that it was the delay caused by her unseaworthiness which brought the vessel within the excepted peril. This argument was rejected on the ground that the delay was the occasion and not the cause of the operation of the embargo. It was, so the Court held, no more its cause than delay which caused goods to be brought within the path of a flood would be the cause of their destruction. To one other circumstance existing in that case attention must be called, viz., the statement in the judgment of Mr. Justice Stone, 31 Ll.L.Rep.200, at p. 202, where he says:
>
> > "There is no finding, nor is it suggested, that at the time when the contract of affreightment was entered into, or when the vessel broke ground, the embargo could reasonably have been foreseen, or that there were any special circumstances charging petitioners with the knowledge or expectation that the unseaworthiness or consequent delay would bring the vessel within its operation."

Lord Porter continued:[277]

> These circumstances have to be balanced one against the other, and I am not sure that, without the advantage of your Lordships' opinions, I should have come to the conclusion that a shipowner ought to have foreseen that within the course of the contemplated voyage, even if protracted, a war would be likely to occur, or, if it did, that the carriage of goods to the stipulated range of ports and in particular to Karlshamn would be prohibited.

Lord Porter concluded:[278]

> I conclude, therefore, that the diversion to Glasgow, brought about through the delay in carrying out the contract of carriage in the present case, is attributable to the default of the owners of the ship because in the conditions existing in April, 1939, they ought to have foreseen that war might shortly break out and that any prolongation of the voyage might cause the loss of or diversion of the ship.

Lord Wright dealt with this:[279]

> In general, all the authorities are in agreement in this respect and embody the same rule. The shipowner, of course, under the familiar general rule, is debarred by his breach of duty from relying on the specific exception. Though he would not be liable for the consequences caused by the specific excepted peril or the accident alone if he were not in default, and though the unseaworthiness existing at the commencement of the voyage might not be operative or known until the time when the accident occurs, yet then the breach of the warranty operates directly

---

274 Ibid, [1949] 82 Ll.L. Rep.137 (H.L.) at p. 138.
275 Ibid, per Lord Porter at p. 146.
276 Ibid, p. 147.
277 Ibid.
278 Ibid.
279 Ibid, per Lord Wright at p. 156.

as a cause and indeed as a dominant cause. Causation in law does not depend on remoteness or immediacy in time. But unseaworthiness as a cause operates immediately whenever it comes into effect; it has until then only been dormant. The maxim causa proxima non remota spectatur is either meaningless or misleading until remota and proxima are defined. Thus, unseaworthiness as a cause cannot from its very nature operate by itself; it needs the "peril" in order to evince that the vessel, or some part or quality of it, is less fit than it should have been and would have been if it had been seaworthy, and hence the casualty ensues. A fitter ship would have passed through the peril unscathed. In this way unseaworthiness is a decisive cause, or, as it is called, a dominant cause. If it is not expressly excepted, the shipowner cannot excuse himself by any specific exception for a loss for which he is himself responsible, because he is responsible for unseaworthiness.

Lord Wright noted that the bills of lading and charterparty exceptions, which are expressed to be conditional on the vessel being seaworthy, use "seaworthy" in the sense that the breach of warranty was a breach which caused the loss.

In the case, the result of the delay was to deprive the shippers and their endorsees of the goods at Karlshamn. Of course, if they could replace them by buying other goods there, it was their duty to diminish the damages by doing so. But they could not do so since no soya beans were procurable at Karlshamn, and in default, the only way of placing themselves in the same position as if the contract had been performed was to engage transport to carry the beans to that port. Accepting, then, the view that the appellants ought to have foreseen the likelihood of war occurring and of an embargo being imposed, the House of Lords found them liable to pay the damages claimed and would dismiss the appeal.[280]

2.19.4 Lubricating oil

In the *Kriti Rex*,[281] while operating under a contract of affreightment for the carriage of bananas from the Caribbean to the UK/Continent, which incorporated the Hague–Visby Rules, the vessel was ordered to load at three loading ports. She loaded the first cargo, but in breach of contract, she broke down before reaching the second and third loading ports. The bananas on board were irretrievably damaged, the second cargo which had, in accordance with the normal trade practice, been cut in readiness for loading was despatched to a different destination, and the third cargo had to be destroyed in the absence of an available substitute vessel to lift in time because bananas have only a short period during which they are able to be shipped before becoming commercially useless. The cargo owners claimed damages based upon the price of similar goods at the destinations, the so-called "Green Boat Price," giving credit for the net recovery in respect of the second cargo. The carriers argued that the loss was too remote and the only foreseeable, and hence recoverable, loss was the extra cost of obtaining a substitute vessel.[282]

Moore-Bick J discussed the question of casualty, saying:[283]

I was reminded by both Mr. Young and Mr. Glennie that the concept of seaworthiness is not absolute in the sense that a vessel will not be considered unseaworthy merely because with hindsight she can be seen to have been suffering from some deficiency which in due course led

280 Ibid, per Lord Porter at p. 147.
281 *The Kriti Rex* [1996] 2 Lloyd's Rep.171.
282 Also see *Voyage Charters*, 4th ed at para. 21.110.
283 *The Kriti Rex*, sup., per Moore-Bick J at p. 184.

to a casualty. In *F.C. Bradley & Sons Ltd. v. Federal Steam Navigation Co. Ltd.*,[284] the point was put by Viscount Sumner in this way at p. 396:

"In the law of carriage by sea neither seaworthiness nor due diligence is absolute. Both are relative, among other things, to the state of knowledge and the standards prevailing at the material time . . ."

and in *M.D.C. Ltd. v. N.V. Zeevart Maatschappij "Beursstraat,"*[285] Mr. Justice McNair applied what he regarded as the most common test, and is still regarded as a good test, namely:

"Would a prudent shipowner, if he had known of the defect, have sent the ship to sea in that condition?"

Moore-Bick J continued and put it this way:[286]

Another way of putting it is that the vessel must be fit in all respects to carry her cargo safely to its destination having regard to the ordinary perils to which such a cargo would be exposed on such a voyage. The general nature of the effect which particles in the lube oil may have on bearings and of the ability of bearing surfaces to deal with them is well known and has been for some time, and one of the reasons for undertaking regular expert analysis of lubricating oil is to ascertain whether there is an excessive build up of particulate matter. Of course it can be said that provided the filters are in good working order, as they were in this case, there is some assurance that the particles which are small enough to pass through them can be safely accommodated by the bearings. I do not think that a prudent owner would simply rely on the filters and assume that the quantity of fine particles was a matter of indifference. Whether he would have foreseen the particular sequence of events which occurred in this case, or would have appreciated the mechanism by which they occurred, does not matter. For these reasons I am satisfied that when she set out from Zeebrugge on her approach voyage to Manzanillo the vessel was unseaworthy because of the amount of fine particulate matter in the lubricating oil.

The next question is, whether the owners exercised due diligence to make the vessel seaworthy does not loom large in this case because they accepted that, having failed to have regular analyses of the lubricating oil carried out, it would be difficult for them to argue successfully that they had done all that they could reasonably have done to ensure that the oil was fit for service. Moore-Bick J observed that they were right to make that concession since a regular independent analysis of the lubricating oil is a standard precaution against contamination by water and other foreign matter.[287]

Moore-Bick J accepted that the sump tank was not easy to enter because of its size and construction, but he was not satisfied that it was completely inaccessible, much less that it was impossible to remove sludge from it by one means or another. Moore-Bick J concluded that the owners did fail to exercise due diligence in the respect he had mentioned and that their failure to do so caused or contributed to the casualty.[288]

The court viewed that the vessel became committed to the voyage to a particular port from the time REL accepted orders to load at that port; the vessel had loaded at the first port and was proceeding under orders to the second and third ports. She was therefore performing the service contemplated by the contract, and the Hague–Visby Rules applied to regulate REL's obligations during its approach voyage. The casualty having been caused by the unseaworthiness of the vessel resulting from a failure on the part of those for whom

284 *F.C. Bradley & Sons Ltd. v Federal Steam Navigation Co. Ltd.* [1927] 27 Ll.L. Rep.395.
285 *M.D.C. Ltd. v N.V. Zeevart Maatschappij "Beursstraat"* [1962] 1 Lloyd's Rep.180.
286 *The Kriti Rex*, sup., per Moore-Bick J at p. 185.
287 Ibid.
288 Ibid.

REL was responsible, REL was liable to Fyffes for such loss as they had suffered by reason of the vessel not loading at Santo Tomás or Big Creek.[289]

2.19.5 Failure of bunkering

In the *North Sea*,[290] on 10 August 1995, the vessel was at anchorage in Hong Kong and remained there, not proceeding to either the charterers' berth or to the outward-bound pilot station. Once the noon deadline was passed, the charterers purported to exercise their right of cancellation on the ground that the vessel was at neither of the two positions mentioned in the charter and was not ready to have insufficient bunkers. The dispute was referred to arbitration, and the arbitrator's award declared that the cancellation was lawful.

The owners appealed, contending that the fact that the vessel did not have the full quantity of bunkers stipulated by clause 56 on board at 1200 hours did not entitle the charterers to exercise their option to cancel the charter; the vessel was at the disposal of the charterers.

At first instance, Mance J (as he then was) held:[291]

> The making of delivery depended on the charterers identifying where delivery was to take place; unless and until charterers selected such a place owners could not deliver in accordance with the charter; charterers' failure to identify any place for delivery meant that delivery never became due at all and charterers' claim to invoke the cancellation clause was unjustified; the obligation regarding bunkers on delivery imposed by cll.3 and 56 was, if broken, readily capable of giving rise to a claim for damages; there was no reason to treat the charter as conferring in respect of it the more draconian remedy of cancellation.

The charterers appealed the issues for the decision, being (1) whether a time charterer was entitled to cancel the time charter which required the vessel to be placed at the disposal of the charterer and (2) whether a charter was breached by the owner of the obligation regarding bunkers on delivery, could give rise to a right of cancellation under clause 14.

The decision of the Court of Appeal held that clause 3 and 56 served or were capable of serving a number of purposes; they dealt with delivery and redelivery, the prices at which the bunkers were to be acquired by the charterers and reacquired by the owners and the maximum and minimum quantities. In the present charter, there was an agreement which did not follow the usual format in all respects, but that was not a reason for treating the variation as critical to the construction of the delivery obligation, and the learned judge's decision on the bunkers issue was correct.

In this case, as is axiomatic, this is not a concept of fault or acceptance of repudiation; it is the exercise of a contractual option which is exercisable even though the owner may not have been at fault. It may well be that the vessel had more than sufficient fuel to reach Japan or other suitable port and she could take on more bunkers there. If the bunker is insufficient to reach her next port, the position will be different; just lack of some certs will make the vessel unseaworthy.[292]

289 Ibid, p. 190.
290 *The North Sea* [1997] 2 Lloyd's Rep.324; [1999] 1 Lloyd's Rep.21 (C.A.).
291 Ibid, per Mance J [1997] 2 Lloyd's Rep.324 at pp. 327, 329.
292 *The Madeleine* [1976] 2 Lloyd's Rep.224, The Mihalis Angelos [1970] 2 Lloyd's Rep.43.

CHAPTER 3

Cargoworthiness

3.1 Cargoworthiness

This chapter concerns cargoworthiness, which is the second aspect of the legal concept of seaworthiness. A seaworthy vessel must be reasonably fit to receive and carry the cargo tendered, so the perils also include storage perils. They may even include the operation of sanitary or port regulations, where the enforcement of those regulations will inevitably cause damage to the cargo.[1]

It concerns itself with the vessel's capacity to receive and convey the cargo in good condition. The cargo compartments must be made fit for the carrier's servants or agents properly and carefully to perform their obligations under article III, rule 2. "Seaworthiness" includes cargoworthiness, such that the vessel should be reasonably fit to receive and carry the cargo and deliver it at the specified destination.[2] Thus, where a cargo requires heating, the vessel's coils must be operative.[3] Where the loading of cargo requires residues of previous cargo to be removed, those residues must be removed, whether it is in the sole interests of the cargo[4] or in the interests of the safety of the vessel and cargo together,[5] but contrast what is possible by the exercise of due diligence in cleaning.[6]

Unseaworthiness in the form of lack of cargoworthiness has been found in the following wide variety of circumstances: inadequate means of ventilation; the inadequacy of a ship's pumps to deal with cargoes such as wet sugar; defective refrigeration machinery; the failure adequately to clean holds so as to remove previous cargo residues; the failure adequately to clean a ship's lines of a previous cargo of condensate, leading to an explosion during subsequent loading of fuel oil; the need for fumigation, which will inevitably cause damage to the cargo carried on the current voyage because of the ship's previous cargoes or ports of call; the absence of heating coils to carry a cargo which required heating in order to be discharged; the lack of proper plank fastenings and use of improper dunnage for carriage of a cargo of bark; and the unsuitability of a ship's bullion room to carry species in a manner suitable to resist thieves.[7]

1 See *Voyage Charters*, 4th ed at para. 11.18.
2 *The Good Friend* [1984] 2 Lloyd's Rep.586 and see also *The Benlawers* [1989] 2 Lloyd's Rep.51.
3 *The Gudermes* [1991] 1 Lloyd's Rep.456; [1993] 1 Lloyd's Rep.311 (C.A.).
4 *The Liepaya* [1999] 1 Lloyd's Rep.649.
5 *The Fiona* [1994] 2 Lloyd's Rep.506.
6 *The Aditya Vaibhav* [1993] 1 Lloyd's Rep.63; See also *Voyage Charters*, 4th ed at para. 85.96.
7 *Carver on Charterparties*, 2nd ed at para. 3–112.

DOI: 10.4324/9781003279938-3

As Lord Blackburn said in *Steel v State Line*:[8]

> I take it my Lords, to be quite clear, both in England and in Scotland, that where there is a contract to carry goods in a ship, whether that contract is in the shape of a bill of lading, or any other form, there is a duty on the part of the person who furnishes or supplies that ship, or that ship's room, unless something be stipulated which should prevent it, that the ship shall be fit for its purpose. That is generally expressed by saying that it shall be seaworthy; and I think also in marine contracts, contracts for sea carriage, that is what is properly called a "warranty," not merely that they should do their best to make the ship fit, but that the ship should really be fit.

See also Romer LJ in *Rathbone Brothers & Co. v D. Maciver, Sons & Co.*:[9]

> It is said that in this bill of lading the word "unseaworthiness" ought not to receive its ordinary meaning, but should be limited to unfitness of the ship as a ship to meet the ordinary perils of navigation without special regard to the cargo. On full consideration, I think it would not be right in this bill of lading to cut down in this way the meaning of the term "unseaworthiness." In the first place, it is important to bear in mind that this word "unseaworthiness" is used in a mercantile document and by mercantile men, and it ought to receive its well-known meaning, unless there are other and overwhelming considerations which compel the Court to depart from that meaning. To my mind there is nothing in this bill of lading taken as a whole which prevents the Court from giving to the word "unseaworthiness" its ordinary meaning. . . . Such a limitation would practically take away from the term "unseaworthiness" the whole of its meaning.

A ship may be unfit to carry the contemplated cargo. For instance, she has no sufficient means of ventilation and yet be quite fit to make the contemplated voyage, as a ship.[10] The vessel is to be reasonably fit. It certainly need not have fittings or instruments which had not at that time been invented, because by subsequent inquiry a danger has been discovered which these fittings and instruments when invented might avert. While the shipowner may be bound to add improvements in fittings where the improvement has become well known or the discovery of danger established, the position is quite different where at the time of the voyage the discovery had not been made or the danger discovered. Further, it is well established that a ship is not unseaworthy because of a defect, at the beginning of the voyage, which can easily, in the ordinary course of management, be rectified on the voyage.[11]

3.2 Contamination

In the *Atrice*,[12] the defendants were the demise charterers (owners) of the gas carrier *Atrice*. The vessel was voyage-chartered by PMI on 16 June 1995 from her disponent owners to carry a full cargo of ethylene from Pajaritos to Northwestern Europe. The vessel arrived at Pajaritos on 24 June with tanks 1 and 2 P/S containing a mixture of ethylene and nitrogen vapour and with temperatures of the order of +30°C. Tanks 3 P/S, which should have contained ethylene, were only partly cooled down. The master directed that a coolant parcel of about 100 t be loaded into no. 3 tanks, as this would enable him to complete

8 *Steel et al. v The State Line Steamship Company* (1877–78) L.R. 3 App. Cas. 72.

9 *Rathbone Brothers & Co. v D. Maciver, Sons & Co.* [1903] 2 K.B. 378. Cited by Hobhouse J in *The Benlawers* [1989] 2 Lloyd's Rep.51 at p. 59.

10 *AE Reed & Co Ltd v Page, Son and East* [1927] 1 KB 743, per Scrutton LJ at p. 754.

11 *The Northumberland* [1926] 24 Ll.L. Rep.446 (C.A.), per Scrutton LJ at pp. 454–455.

12 *The Atrice* [2001] 2 Lloyd's Rep.1.

the gassing up and cooling down an operation more quickly. Although samples taken and analysed at the initial stage of loading and at first footing showed that the cargo was contaminated, loading continued and was completed on 28 June. The cargo was eventually sold as distressed cargo.

The defendant shipowners admitted that their vessel was unfit to carry the cargo in question, ethylene, the owners having failed in their duty to exercise due diligence to clean or purge the vessel's tanks and lines of a previous cargo of butadiene. However, the owners argued that the bulk of the loss sustained by the cargo interests was to be regarded as having been caused by their own decision to continue loading. That was a decision for which there was no rational basis and which could be characterized as reckless. The defendants argued that that decision was so aberrant it must be regarded as breaking the causal link between the owners' admitted breach and the ensuing contamination of the balance of the ethylene parcel thereafter loaded.

The claimants submitted that the measure of their loss was the difference between what they would have earned under the BP contract and what they achieved on the distress sale.

The defendants also say that the master was effectively under the orders of both the time charterers Cheminter and the voyage charterers PMI to load the cargo. He was contractually obliged to load and was not entitled to refuse to do so, whether or not there had been a prior breach of contract in presenting the vessel to load in the state in which he did. Moreover, because the vessel lacked spare tank capacity, once the contamination was discovered, the situation could be remedied only by discharging the cargo already loaded. The cargo obviously did not belong to the shipowners, and thus the master could do nothing to remedy the vessel's unseaworthiness without the instruction or cooperation of charterers and/or cargo interests.

Tomlinson J explained and said:[13]

> In the light of that conclusion it is strictly unnecessary for me to decide whether the decisions to resume loading after coolant and first foot level should properly be regarded as breaking the causal link between the initial unseaworthiness and the contamination beyond those parcels but I must nonetheless address that point in case I am wrong in my view as to the role played by the master or its causative effect.

In this regard, Tomlinson J added, it is also relevant to consider what might have happened had the charterers or the cargo interests in fact declined to continue loading beyond coolant or first foot level and required the shipowners to remedy the unseaworthiness, since any decision to continue loading should, in part, be informed by consideration of the consequences of not continuing loading.[14]

According to Tomlinson J, it was the master's duty to make clear that he could not, consistent with his owners' duty to cargo interests, load further cargo without first making his vessel fit to receive it; loading further cargo without rendering the vessel fit to receive it amounted without more to a breach of duty owed to cargo interests. The claimants succeeded in establishing that the defendants, in consequence of the master's inactivity, failed properly and carefully to load and/or care for the cargo.[15]

---

13 Ibid, per Tomlinson J at p. 13.

14 Ibid, p. 14.

15 Ibid, p. 12.

Tomlinson J continued and stated:[16]

> The defendants' breach in the latter respect should be regarded as an effective cause of the loss; the owners failed properly to load and care for the cargo precisely because the master abdicated his own responsibility; and in such circumstances the defendants' breach in this regard remained an effective cause of the loss notwithstanding it could be said that without the decisions to which the master was not party, the cargo would not have been loaded beyond coolant or first foot level; the master should not have allowed these decisions to be taken or have been put into effect without input from him.

In this case, Tomlinson J held the charterers' decision to continue loading, even though a "first foot" sample demonstrated the presence of contaminating residues of previous cargoes, was not such as to exclude the shipowners from liability since the master had a duty himself to stop loading. He did not consider the case where the master makes reasonable but vain efforts to stop the charterer's loading. In the absence of the ability to effect a reduction for contributory negligence, it seems that the tribunal will have to decide the case on whether there has been such conduct as breaks the chain of causation.[17]

3.3 Discoloration of cargo

In the *Gianna M*,[18] the ship arrived at Constantza to load on 30 October 1934. During the voyage to Constantza, the master took the opportunity of cleaning the tanks, which were washed by hand and the special pump, evaporating and then washing with hot water, making the main tanks 4, 5, 6, 7, and 8 and all the summer tanks, they said, fit to receive the cargo and the three forward tanks ready to receive the gas oil. At Constantza, the master requested the Concordia Company to inspect the tanks for the charterers. That was done on 30 October 1934, and the inspector wrote to the master, and the result of the inspection is shown in a copy of the letter which appears in the special case. The inspector of the tanks made certain suggestions and added that notice would be given that the ship's lay days would commence from the moment when the tanks were perfectly clean and ready to be loaded.

Accordingly, a considerable cargo of benzine and kerosene and gas oil was loaded, and the vessel left Constantza on 8 November and arrived at Ango-Ango about a month later, where a portion of the cargo was discharged. At that port, samples were taken of the cargo, and thereafter this dispute arose because it was said that some portion of the benzine in certain tanks had become discoloured, and the charterers seek to make the shipowners responsible in respect of it.[19]

In the first instance, Singleton J discussed the question of unseaworthiness and said:[20]

> If it can be said that the two Clauses 16 and 27 are in any way irreconcilable, then I think that in such a case the doctrine would apply that where there is an ambiguity the ambiguous document is no protection. It is a wholesome doctrine as applied to the question of sending unseaworthy vessels to sea. It can be derived from *Elderslie Steamship Company, Ltd. v. Borthwick*, [1905] A.C. 93. Still more from the judgment of Mr. Justice Bigham in the case of *Sleigh and Others*

16 Ibid, p. 13.
17 See *Voyage Charters*, 4the ed at para. 21.73.
18 *The Gianna M* [1936] 56 Ll.L. Rep.141; [1937] 57 Ll.L. Rep.247 (C.A.).
19 Ibid, [1937] 57 Ll.L. Rep.247 (C.A.) at p. 145.
20 Ibid, per Singleton J [1936] 56 Ll.L. Rep.141 at p. 147.

v. Tyser, [1900] 2 Q.B. 333. It was held that the ship was unseaworthy in both respects, that the implied warranty of seaworthiness was not excluded by the provision as to the approval of the fittings, and that the underwriters were not liable. Mr Justice Bigham, at p. 336, said:

> "The question then arises whether insufficient ventilation and an insufficient supply of men constitute a breach of the implied warranty – or, more correctly, the implied condition – of seaworthiness. I think they do. What is the implied warranty in a policy on cargo? It is, in my opinion, exactly the same as the warranty in a policy on ship – that the ship shall be seaworthy for the adventure on which she starts. Stating the warranty with particular reference to a policy on cargo, it may be defined as a warranty – or rather as a condition – that the ship shall be fit for the proposed service-fit, that is, in respect of all those things that appertain to the safe carriage of the cargo in question to its destination."

Singleton J continued and observed that, the oil having been shipped water white and discharged in part discoloured, the onus was on the shipowners to prove non-liability; that the express warranty of seaworthiness contained in clauses 1 and 16 were not affected by clause 27, which was intended to be an addition to and not in substitution for the other clauses; and that, the shipowners having failed to prove some excepted peril relieving them from liability, they were responsible to the charterers for the damage. Singleton J concluded:[21]

> In my view if the shipowner desires to exclude himself from the express warranty which exists in these clauses other than that clause, he must use terms much more express, pertinent and apposite than he has done in the present case.

In the Court of Appeal, Lord Wright MR concluded:[22]

> We are dealing here with a contract of affreightment and it is necessary to bear in mind the well-established view that has been stated so often, that if it is sought to effect a reduction or a general limitation of the overriding obligation to provide a seaworthy ship – whether that is express or implied for this purpose does not matter – by other express terms of the charter-party or contract of affreightment, that result can only be achieved if perfectly clear, effective and precise words are used expressly stating that limitation. I think the language of Clause 27 here is not sufficient. To make it sufficient I think it would need to be amplified in something like this manner. It would have to run: "Steamer to clean for the cargo in question to the satisfaction of the charterers' inspector and if that is done that shall be treated as fulfilment of the obligations under Clauses 1 and 16." Clause 27 does not say so. I think, on the contrary, it has a much more limited effect. It gives, as I think, an added right to the charterer. He is entitled before he loads the cargo to have an inspection and to have a certificate, or whatever the form of the evidence is, that his inspector is satisfied. But, without express words, the satisfaction of the inspector cannot be relied upon by the owners as a discharge and fulfilment of their obligations. From the point of view of the charterers this super-added right is something which it is worth their while to have. It gives them some sort of guarantee against their being involved in questions such as this, where unfortunately, notwithstanding the inspection, there has been a failure to provide tanks sufficiently clean and in proper condition.

The point may be stated very shortly in this way. The shipowner contracts to load a cargo and to deliver the same on certain terms, which means to deliver the same cargo in the same condition as shipped, unless the shipowner can justify the defective condition by bringing himself within an exculpating clause. The onus of doing so is upon him, and he can only do it by explaining how the accident happened and explaining it in such a way as

21 Ibid, p. 148.
22 Ibid, per Lord Wright MR [1937] 57 Ll.L. Rep.247 (C.A.) at p. 251.

enables him to escape liability under the terms of his contract. Nothing of the sort has been done here, and the same result, as at present advised, would have followed from this way of looking at the case.[23]

Thus, if intending to exclude the implied warranty of seaworthiness, the words used must be express, pertinent, and apposite.

3.4 Crude oil washing system

In order to achieve the purpose of fire prevention and explosion prevention, before the ship (mainly oil tanker) cleans the cargo tank, it is necessary to carry out crude oil tank washing and water tank washing successively. For the oil residue and sediment accumulated at the bottom of the cargo tank and around the bulkhead, for safety purposes, it is suggested to employ shore gang to conduct tank cleanings. If such cleaning will be done by crews, they should bear in mind that those tanks should be thoroughly ventilated.

In the *Trade Nomad*,[24] by a charterparty in the Shelltime 4 form, the owners let their vessel *Trade Nomad* to the charterers for the carriage of oil and liquid gas cargoes. While the vessel was discharging in Singapore on 30 June 1989, a boiler breakdown interrupted discharging at 2120 hours. That was repaired by 1800 hours on 1 July, but in the meanwhile, the ship had been ordered off the berth by the port authorities on 30 June. The ship would have reberthed at the terminal on 5 July, but the charterers ordered her to shift to a second berth. The vessel discharged at the second berth and returned to her first berth on 9 July.

The charterers contended that the vessel was off-hire from 30 June to 9 July. The owners conceded that the vessel was off-hire until 1800 hours on 1 July, when the boiler had been repaired, and argued that the ship was again ready and in an efficient state to resume service.

In August 1989, the vessel was inspected at Wilhelmshaven when the charterers discovered that the vessel was unfit to carry out crude oil washing and unfit to carry cargoes of crude oil. They claimed to be entitled to a deduction from hire under clause 3(iii) on the basis that the owners were in breach of their obligation to exercise due diligence to maintain or restore the condition of the vessel's crude oil washing system. On 26 February 1990, the vessel suffered an engine breakdown in New Orleans. She was subsequently involved in a collision, and she then went off-hire.

The disputes were referred to arbitration, and the arbitrator, in his award dated 31 January 1997, found that the defects in the crude oil washing system were in existence at the time of delivery and that clause 3(i) and 3(iii) had no application to those defects.

In the first instance, Colman J held that the arbitrator had not erred when he rejected the charterers' arguments and held that clause 3(i) and 3(iii) applied only to defects occurring after delivery of the vessel under the time charter; the phraseology of clause 3(i), "exercise due diligence so as to maintain or restore the vessel," strongly suggested that the vessel had become defective after the commencement of that service; and the concept of "restoring"

23 Ibid, p. 253.

24 *The Trade Nomad* [1998] 1 Lloyd's Rep.57; [1999] 1 Lloyd's Rep.723 (C.A.).

the vessel suggested that its condition was to be returned to what it once was, that is, on delivery, not to what it ought then to have been.[25]

Hirst LJ explained the question of obligation to maintain, saying:[26]

> Focusing first on the precise wording of cl. 3(i) taken in isolation, and leaving aside for the moment the crucial phrase "whenever . . . or any event" the obligation is to maintain and restore the cl. 1 and 2(a) conditions throughout the charter service.
>
> "Maintain" connotes keeping the vessel in the requisite condition; "restore" connotes putting the vessel back into that condition if it has not been so maintained. Both these verbs are to my mind more apt to refer to supervening defects, i.e. those occurring after delivery at any time throughout the service, rather than those already in existence before that period began.
>
> This view is strongly reinforced by the vital phrase "whenever (1) the passage of time, (2) wear and tear, or (3) any event require steps to be taken. . . . " I have for convenience inserted numbers for these three items which I shall describe as the three criteria. Mr. Collins sought to argue that the word "whenever" can be sensibly detached from the remainder of the phrase, but in my judgment such a construction, which would in effect strike out the three criteria upon which the remainder of cl. 3(i) hinges, is untenable.

Turning now to the wider context, Hirst LJ observed that most incongruous breach of an absolute obligation, such as clauses 1 and 2(a), should give rise to a mere due diligence requirement, a fortiori where the consequences of such a breach are already provided for in clause 3(ii).

Hirst LJ continued:[27]

> This approach it is my judgment in full conformity with Lord Justice Neill's ratio in *The Fina Samco* [1995] 2 Lloyd's Rep.34(C.A.), though I accept, as Mr. Baker candidly acknowledged, that the decision of the Court of Appeal in that case was not decisive in his favour.

In this case, the Court of Appeal construes this charterparty as it stands, not as it might have been interpreted if the obligations had been differently expressed, upholds Colman J's judgment, and dismisses this appeal.

The maintenance obligation obliges the owner to comply with class requirements as to surveys and inspections, and probably also to follow a prudent programme of his own of inspections and maintenance to avoid breakdown or damage, which could lead to a withdrawal of class. However, the obligation is probably not absolute, and if, after the date of the charter, the vessel does lose her class in spite of the precautions mentioned prior, there is no breach of the clause.[28]

The owners' obligation to maintain the ship has two aspects: (a) an obligation to keep up a prudent programme of inspections and surveys, replacements, and renewals (preventive maintenance) and (b) if the ship, its machinery, or its equipment becomes inefficient during the charter period, an obligation to take reasonable steps within a reasonable time to effect repairs (remedial maintenance). On the other hand, the question whether the owners have exercised reasonable diligence in maintaining the ship must depend to some extent on whether the charterers' use of the ship has allowed the owners a reasonable opportunity to carry out maintenance.[29]

25 Ibid, per Colman J [1998] 1 Lloyd's Rep.57 at p. 63.
26 Ibid, per Hirst LJ [1999] 1 Lloyd's Rep.723 (C.A.) at pp. 727–728.
27 Ibid, p. 728.
28 See *Voyage Charters*, 4th ed at para. 52.2.
29 See *Time Charters*, 7th ed at para. 11.7, 11.9.

3.5 Tank cleaning system

For bulk carriers, especially those loading and unloading iron ore and coal, including some Panamax vessels, no special cleaning system is required, and the cargo holds could be cleaned by crews. The residual sewage from cargo holds cleaning also could be discharged directly into the sea, unless the ship is in a restricted area and the pollution prevention requirements are not allowed to discharge the hold cleaning water. But if the position of the tanker is different, there is a whole complex system for cleaning the tank.

In the *Arianna*,[30] by a charterparty dated 3 October 1980, in an amended Esso time form, the owners let their newbuilding motor product carrier subsequently named *Arianna* to the charterers for ten years, two months, more or less, in charterers' option as from delivery ex the builders' yard at Busan.

The owners tendered the vessel for delivery in June 1982, but the charterers declined to take delivery upon the ground that the vessel did not comply with certain charterparty provisions.

The disputes between the parties were referred to arbitration. By their interim award, the arbitrators found that the charterers were not entitled to refuse to take delivery in that the vessel was in every way fitted for the service and carriage of all liquid cargoes that could safely be handled by product tankers. The charterers appealed.

Webster J, discussing the charterers' right to cancel the charter, observed:[31]

> In my view, the words "ready in accordance with the provisions hereof" in cl. 4 are to be construed as a reference to the provisions of cl. 3; and, in my view, those words are to be taken as a reference, therefore, to the words in cl. 3 beginning at the words "then ready" and ending at the words "attained by the exercise of due diligence."

Webster J observed that the reference to clause 57 in clause 3 was to be taken as a reference to the opening words and was intended to do no more than identify the employment required of the vessel. Webster J discussed the question whether the vessel was in every way fitted for the service and carriage of all liquid cargoes, stating that it was a question of fact and the arbitrators' award could only be interfered with if they misdirected themselves in law or the decision which they reached was such that no reasonable arbitrator could have reached.[32]

Webster J turned to the question of seaworthiness, saying:[33]

> In support of the view that it was prima facie a finding of fact, and assuming for the moment that the question of fittedness can be regarded as synonymous with seaworthiness, I rely upon the following dicta: that of Lord Esher in Vaughan (the question is really one of fact); the references in *The Waco* to defects which "with reasonable certainty," could be put right; Mr. Justice Branson's reference in *The Vendémiaire* to the evidence and to the fact that the vessel as proferred was "a different thing in substance" from that which had been promised.
>
> Mr. Justice Devlin's references in *The San George* at pp. 507 and 227 to elasticity and to the test of "readiness in a business and mercantile sense"; and at pp. 508 and 229 to whether the ship was "proved" to be unready, and to whether it would "probably be unready"; Lord Justice Tucker's use at pp. 363 and 237 of the word "prove"; Mr. Justice McNair's test of the prudent

30 *The Arianna* [1987] 2 Lloyd's Rep.376.

31 Ibid, per Webster J at p. 387.

32 Ibid, p. 388.

33 Ibid.

> shipowner in *The Westerdok*; Lord Justice Kerr's reference to that same test in *The Derby*; and his agreement with Counsel that issues as to a vessel's seaworthiness may involve questions of fact and degree on which the decisions of arbitrators could not properly be regarded as open to review.
>
> The question of whether a prudent owner would have required a defect to have been made good must, surely, be a pure question of fact.

Webster J observed that it was implicit in the award that the arbitrators must be taken to have directed themselves by implication that non-compliance with a provision of the charter, though, prima facie, relevant to the vessel's readiness and fittedness for service, would not necessarily, as a matter of law, render the vessel unfitted and would not do so if the non-compliance was, as a matter of fact, of no real significance from the commercial point of view.[34]

Webster J concluded:[35]

> In the absence of authority it was an inevitable presumption of fact that a vessel was unseaworthy if there was something about it which endangered the safety of the vessel or its cargo or which might cause significant damage to the cargo or which rendered it legally or practically impossible for the vessel to go to sea or unload its cargo; where the characteristic in question had none of these effects but was one which might only cause some delay to the movement of the vessel or to the loading or discharging of its cargo, what its likely effect would be and whether the effect was such as to render the vessel unseaworthy or unfitted were all questions of fact; and the weight of all the authorities favoured the proposition that there was no rule of law having the effect that a defect of no significance should nonetheless render a vessel unseaworthy or unfitted.

Webster J found that the arbitrators did not misdirect themselves if they decided that a defect which had no real commercial significance did not render the vessel unfitted for service and they did not misdirect themselves by assuming that it did not render the vessel unseaworthy; the charterers had not shown that the arbitrators had misdirected themselves in law or that their decision was such that no reasonable arbitrator could reach; the appeal would be dismissed.

In this case, the judge held that that was the type of deficiency which would not render the ship unseaworthy but might make it unfit. While seaworthiness and fittedness may often overlap, and while a ship can never be fitted if she is unseaworthy, nonetheless a vessel may be unfitted even though seaworthy.

3.6 Heating coils

Vessels carrying cargo oil in bulk may be fitted with steam heating coils in order to maintain the required temperature for pumping. By circulating steam through the coils, it is possible to increase the temperature gradually to the required level to facilitate pumping by reducing the liquid viscosity. Fuel oil tanks are also equipped with the necessary heating coils in order to ensure sufficient liquid fluidity for pumping at all times. Heating coils need to be installed around the tank bottom outlet valve of the ship's fuel tanks and the crude oil tanks.

---

34 Ibid, p. 389.

35 Ibid. *The Hong Kong Fir* [1961] 2 Lloyd's Rep.478, *The Waco* [1922] 10 Ll.L. Rep.772, *The Madeleine* [1967] 2 Lloyd's Rep.224 and *The Derby* [1985] 2 Lloyd's Rep.325, considered.

In the *Vendemiaire*,[36] the vessel was time-chartered for 12 months. The charterers intended to use the ship for carrying molasses, and the owners knew that that was the case. Carrying molasses is a special trade, requiring the ship to have pipes of large diameter and to have heating coils as close as possible to the bottom of the tanks. The vessel had not been designed for carrying molasses, but by the terms of the charter, the owners guaranteed that the ship had pipelines of no less than 30 cm diameter and heating coils "right at bottom of tanks." In fact, the ship's pipelines were at points less than 20 cm wide, and its coils were around 30 cm above the tank tops. These defects made the ship unfit for the carriage of molasses, and the charterers were held entitled to reject the ship. The ship, as presented, was "a different thing in substance" from the ship as described. The plaintiffs, charterers of the vessel from the defendants, also asked for a declaration that the charterparty dated 15 May 1934 was not and never was binding upon them. They asked further for rescission of the charterparty on the ground of misrepresentation.

Branson J discussed the representation and said:[37]

> In fact, it only becomes material in the present case on the question whether the arbitrator ever got jurisdiction to decide between the parties. Light is thrown upon it in the discussion of the distinction between representations inducing a contract and terms of a completed contract in Anson on Contract, 17th Ed., at p. 173 and following. It is there pointed out that at common law if an innocent misrepresentation did not afterwards become part of the contract its untruth was immaterial. In such a case equity might intervene to avoid or rescind the contract. But where the representation has been embodied in the contract, there the Courts of Common Law could deal with it according to whether it was a condition entitling the injured party to repudiate the contract or a warranty giving rise only to an action ex contractu for damages. The representation thus becomes merged in the higher contractual right and there was no need to resort to equity for rescission. The fusion of law and equity does not affect this result, as Anson correctly states at p. 183:
>
> > "It is perhaps well to add that the Judicature Act has not of course affected the common law rules regarding an innocent representation which has become a term of the contract, but the further discussion of this matter falls under the subject of breach of contract. The equitable remedy of rescission merely supplements these rules, as it can provide for the case, to which they did not apply, of an innocent misrepresentation which is not a term in the contract."

Branson J explained the question of condition, saying:[38]

> I approach it with the following principles in mind. First, that stated by Mr. Justice Blackburn in *Bettini v. Gye*, 1 Q.B.D. 183, at p. 187:
>
> > "Parties may think some matter, apparently of very little importance, essential; and if they sufficiently express an intention to make the literal fulfilment of such a thing a condition precedent, it will be one;"
>
> and, secondly, that stated by Tindal CJ, in *Glaholm v. Hays, Irvine & Anderson*, 2 M. & G. 257, at p. 266:
>
> > "Whether a particular clause in a charter-party shall be held to be a condition, upon the non-performance of which by one party, the other is at liberty to abandon the contract and consider it at an end . . . must depend upon the intention of the parties to be collected, in each particular case, from the terms of the agreement itself, and from the subject-matter to which it relates."

36 *The Vendemiaire* [1936] 55 Ll.L. Rep.271.

37 Ibid, per Branson J at p. 276.

38 Ibid.

Branson J observed that the word "guarantee" in 11 of the 52 clauses shows an intention to lay a special emphasis upon the obligations assumed under these clauses and to treat them as conditions of the contract as distinguished from mere warranties. To use the language of Tindal CJ in *Glaholm v Hays, Irvine & Anderson*, "the form of the stipulation is more nearly in the language of condition than in that of agreement."[39]

Branson J concluded:[40]

> The plaintiffs cannot get rescission of the contract on the ground of misrepresentation inducing it. It is unnecessary, therefore, to discuss the interesting question whether, had the misrepresentations not been incorporated in the contract, they would have been sufficient to entitle the plaintiffs to rescission. The plaintiffs were bound to perform the charter-party unless it contained conditions for the breach of which they became entitled to and did repudiate it.

In addition to imposing on the owners an obligation to tender the ship fit and ready for the charter service, the charter will often make further, more specific stipulations about the condition or description of the ship, either at the time the charter was concluded or at delivery. The general rule is that such stipulations are not conditions precedent to the owners' right to deliver the ship, unless the owners' failure to comply with those stipulations has rendered the ship unfit for the charter service when she is tendered for delivery.

However, just as the case, it will often be the case that compliance with a particular additional stipulation is essential to make a ship fit and ready for the charter service.

3.7 Hatch cover leakage

In the *Hermosa*,[41] the vessel was chartered on the New York Produce form for two years with options to extend the period for a further four months under certain circumstances. Following delivery in December 1974, there was serious damage to the cargo carried on her first voyage, as a result of unseaworthiness. Because of the repairs which were then carried out and which took from mid-January to the end of March 1975, the sub-charterers lost their next employment for the ship. The owners had refused to allow the sub-charterers to survey the ship after the first voyage, and the sub-charterers obtained a court order to survey the ship on 9 August 1975. This survey revealed deficiencies in the ship's hatch covers, which were the cause of the damage to the cargo on the first voyage, and they remained unrepaired and that the ship was in bad condition in other respects.

Nitrates applied for a declaration that the sub-charter had been justifiably terminated on the ground that MTC, in their capacity as disponent owners, had committed a breach or series of breaches of the contract and that the total of the time lost by Nitrates up to the moment of termination taken together with that which would inevitably have been lost if the charter had continued in existence was sufficient to go to the root of the charter and enabled them to treat the charter as repudiated.

39 Ibid.
40 See *Time Charters*, 7th ed at para. 8.69.
41 *The Hermosa* [1980] 1 Lloyd's Rep.638; [1982] 1 Lloyd's Rep.570 (C.A.).

It was held by Mustill J (as he then was) at first instance that:[42]

> It cannot be taken for granted that the interpretation adopted in *Adamastos Shipping Co. Ltd v. Anglo-Saxon Petroleum Co. Ltd.*, [1958] 1 Lloyd's Rep.73, in relation to voyage charters applies in all respects to time charters incorporating The Hague Rules. It is, however, unnecessary to tackle this problem in the present case, for on the findings which I have made, there was a breach of the initial warranty of seaworthiness or (if that warranty is to be regarded as qualified by The Hague Rules) of the obligation to exercise due diligence to make the ship seaworthy. The deficiencies which constituted, or evidence, this breach had not been put right by the time that the contract was cancelled.

Returning to the facts, Mustill J stated:[43]

> There must be such a change in the significance of the obligation that the thing undertaken would, if performed, be a different thing from that contracted for, or (to adopt the formulation of Lord Wilberforce, in *Federal Commerce & Navigation Co. Ltd. v. Molena Alpha Inc.*, (H.L.) [1979] 1 Lloyd's Rep.201; [1978] 3 W.L.R. 991), something which went to the root of the contract as depriving the charterers of substantially the whole benefit of the contract. I cannot find that anything of this kind existed in the present case. Some of the defects constituting the initial unseaworthiness had already been repaired at Dunkirk, although the repairs had not gone nearly as far as they should have done. The collision damage had been well and fully repaired.

In the Court of Appeal, Donaldson LJ concluded:[44]

> That was how matters stood when the contract was cancelled. What did it all amount to? Certainly to a picture of confusion, which could justify concern about the owners' true intentions, and a suspicion that M.T.C. (via the owners) might ultimately fail to repair the hatches at all, or (more likely) fail to repair them properly. But this is not enough. The test is whether M.T.C. and the owners acted in such a way as to lead a reasonable person to conclude that they did not intend to fulfil their part of the contract: see per Mr. Justice Devlin in *Universal Cargo Carriers v. Citati*, at pp. 193 and 436, and also per Lord Hewart, C.J., in *Maple Flock Co. v. Universal Furniture Products (Wembley) Ltd.*, [1934] 1 K.B. at p. 157, where a distinction is drawn between a possibility of breach and a reasonable probability. The time can of course come when a suspicion passes into a firm conclusion, reasonably inferred. I do not consider that such a moment had yet arrived on Aug. 29, 1975. Of course, M.T.C.'s conduct was not made more convincing by their failure to give a constructive answer to Nitrates' ultimatum of Aug.15. But the ultimatum had no formal legal status. It was not directed to making time of the essence. It did not, for example, purport to give the owners 10 days within which to commence repairs, and if it had done the time would, to my mind, have been too short. The letter was no more than a very strongly worded demand for reassurance. The fact that it did not provoke a helpful response was calculated to increase Nitrates' anxiety, but was not, in my judgment, enough to transform anxiety into conviction. Nitrates should have kept their patience and continued to wait and see whether the position was clarified, or whether, on the contrary, a further absence of response from the owners justified a firm conclusion that they were evading their responsibilities. If Nitrates had waited only a few days longer then (even allowing for the owners' reticence) they would have been bound to learn that the Hermosa was at Cartagena, and that the hatch covers were in a workshop on shore. I am quite satisfied that Nitrates did not in cold blood snatch at an opportunity to get rid of the ship on a falling market. Nevertheless, I consider that they acted too hastily and that since events have proved them wrong their cancellation on the ground of renunciation must be regarded as unjustified.

42 Ibid, per Mustill J [1980] 1 Lloyd's Rep.638 at p. 648.
43 Ibid, p. 649.
44 Ibid, per Donaldson LJ [1982] 1 Lloyd's Rep.570 (C.A.) at p. 580.

In this case, it was held by Mustill J, and the Court of Appeal, that:

(1) The sub-charterers were not justified in treating the charter as discharged by reason of the ship's unseaworthiness because the remaining defects were capable of being put right within a relatively short time and thereafter the sub-charter would still have had 16 to 20 months to run.
(2) There was no repudiation of the charter by the head charterers, because their conduct was not such as to lead a reasonable person to conclude that they did not intend to fulfil their part of the contract.

The sub-charterers were justifiably suspicious that the hatch covers might not be properly repaired, but that was not enough, and their action was premature.[45]

3.8 Cargo hold leakage

Reserve buoyancy is the potential buoyancy of the ship and depends upon the intact and watertight volume above the waterline. When the mass is added to the ship or buoyancy is lost due to bilging, the reserve buoyancy is converted to buoyancy by increasing the draught. If the buoyancy exceeds the reverse buoyancy, the vessel will sink. Reserve buoyancy is a very important factor in determining a ship's seaworthiness. Minimum freeboards are assigned to a ship to ensure that there is adequate reserve buoyancy at all times. Once seawater enters into cargo holds, it will cause cargo damage or for the vessel to divide into two and sink. The ship's structure must be sufficiently strong to withstand the weather and sea conditions likely to be encountered on the voyage, and her hull plating, hatch covers, and ventilators must be sufficiently watertight to protect the cargo from the risk of damage.

In the *Toledo*,[46] the plaintiffs were the owners of a cargo of 14,006.06 t of muriate of potash in bulk. The cargo was loaded on board *Toledo* on 11 and 12 February 1990 at St. John, New Brunswick, pursuant to a bill of lading dated 13 February 1990, for carriage to Fredericia in Denmark. The contract of carriage incorporated the Hague Rules.

The vessel sailed from St. John on 13 February 1990. On the night of 14/15 February, the weather became bad and remained bad thereafter. On 19 February, some water was found in the no. 4 ballast tank and in nos. 1, 2, and 3 holds. It was pumped out. On 20 February, the master noticed the vessel moving strangely and that the water astern of the ship was coloured red from time to time. Since the potash cargo was red, he concluded that there must be some form of leakage, and an investigation showed that there was water in the no. 4 hold. He assumed that there must be a crack in the shell plating which was allowing water to get into the hold. The initial cause of the casualty was the failure of the shell plating on the port side of hold no. 4.

The plaintiffs claimed damages from the defendants in respect of the total loss of their cargo, which they alleged was caused by the defendants' breach of contract. The plaintiffs contended that *Toledo* was unseaworthy before and at the beginning of the voyage and that the loss was caused by that unseaworthiness. The plaintiffs also alleged that the unseaworthiness was caused by want of due diligence on the part of the defendants. They argued that the defendants failed to lay down and carry out a proper system for the

45 See *Time Charters*, 7th ed at para. 8.47.
46 *The Toledo* [1995] 1 Lloyd's Rep.40.

inspection of their vessels, including *Toledo*, with the result that they failed to detect and repair the damaged brackets and frames.

The defendants contended that since the class did not comment or make recommendations, there could be no relevant damage requiring repairs. They further argued that their vessels were properly inspected both by their own personnel and, from time to time, by class, and that it was not reasonably foreseeable that damage to brackets and frames of the kind that existed would or might cause fatigue cracking of the kind or to the extent that occurred.[47]

Clarke J (as he then was) discussed the question of unseaworthy and observed that:[48]

> Even if those submissions were accepted in their entirety the correct conclusion would be that Toledo was unseaworthy at the commencement of the voyage since, as Mr Justice Hobhouse put it in *The Torenia* [1983] 2 Lloyd's Rep.210 at p. 225:
>
> > "... once one accepts that the weather conditions encountered would have been within the contemplation of a prudent shipowner, the proof of any pre-existing structural condition of the vessel which accounts for the loss of the vessel in those conditions must amount at the same time to proof that the vessel was unseaworthy."

Clarke J continued:[49]

> In these circumstances Toledo was not in such a condition at St. John as to be reasonably fit to encounter the ordinary perils which might be expected on the voyage. It follows that she was unseaworthy at the commencement of the voyage. It follows that the initial casualty was caused by unseaworthiness because it was caused by the fracture of the shell plating on the port side of No. 4 hold, which fracture was in turn caused by fatigue caused by the fact that the shell plating was not properly supported so that it could not withstand the stresses to which it was exposed during the voyage.

Turning to the question of due diligence, Clarke J observed that the burden of proving the exercise of due diligence is on the defendants. Based on findings of fact as to the state of the vessel at New Brunswick, Clarke J stated that the owners failed to exercise due diligence properly to maintain the vessel.

In all the circumstances for the reasons, Clarke J concluded:[50]

> The vessel was unseaworthy at the commencement of the voyage at St. John, that the casualty was caused by that unseaworthiness, that the defendants had failed to exercise due diligence to make her seaworthy and that if they had exercised due diligence the casualty would not have occurred. It follows that, whatever is the correct answer to the question of burden of proof referred to above, the plaintiffs have discharged the burden imposed upon them by art. III, r. 1 but the defendants have failed to discharge the burden imposed upon them by art. IV, r. 1 of the Hague Rules.

It followed that under arts III and IV of the Hague Rules, the onus rests on the charterer to prove unseaworthiness, but once this has been done, the burden of proving that the shipowner nevertheless exercised due diligence and is not liable for loss and damage resulting from the unseaworthiness shifts to the shipowner.[51] In short, once the claimant proves unseaworthiness, the burden of establishing due diligence is on the shipowner.[52]

---

47 Ibid.
48 Ibid, per Clarke J at p. 49.
49 Ibid, p. 50.
50 Ibid, p. 54.
51 See *Carver on Charterparties*, 2nd ed at para. 3–103.
52 *The Eurasian Dream* [2002] 1 Lloyd's Rep.719; *The CMA CGM Libra* [2019] 1 Lloyd's Rep.595.

3.9 Ballast tank leakage

Ballast and de-ballast operations on the ship must be carried out by an experienced and responsible officer, as it is directly related to its trim, stability, and structural integrity. A ballast system may differ from ship to ship, but the basics of all ballast systems remain the same: filling, removing, and transferring water from one tank to another to get the required stability for a ship. All valves in the ballast system are normally hydraulically operated from the remote operator station in the ship's control centre or the engine control room in manual mode or automatic sequence. The ballast pump suction and discharge valves, along with other valves, have their fail-safe in the open position so that if any valve malfunctions or gets stuck, it still remains open to carry out ballast operation.

In the *Torenia*,[53] on 14 April 1979, the master and the chief engineer noticed that the vessel was beginning to list to port and water was found in hold 3 port side and the port deep tank. It was clear that the leakage into hold 3 and the port deep tank was uncontrollable. There was a major failure of the vessel's portside shell plating in the way of the bulkhead between the deep tank and hold 3, and the list had increased. Water was also discovered to be getting from the deep tank into the accommodation amidships, and the master decided that the vessel was going to sink and should be abandoned, but in the event, the vessel sank on 19 April. She was a total loss, as was her cargo. The owners of the cargo of sugar at the time of its loss were the plaintiffs, the endorsees of the bills of lading. It was agreed that the bills of lading were, by their terms, subject to the Hague Rules. The plaintiffs claimed £1,071,232.81 against the defendants for the non-delivery of their cargo.

The defendants admitted non-delivery but contended that they had satisfied the burden of proof in (a) proving that the contract had become impossible of performance or, alternatively, (b) proving that perils of the sea operated so as to cause the loss of the goods, and it was for the plaintiffs to prove that the loss was caused or contributed to by the unseaworthiness of the vessel. The defendants sought to rely on article IV, rule 1 of the Hague Rules. Alternatively, the defendants claimed that they were entitled to limit their liability under the Merchant Shipping Act, 1894, and the Merchant Shipping (Liability of Shipowners and Others) Act, 1958.[54]

Hobhouse J discussed the question of unseaworthiness, saying:[55]

> The form in which the argument was developed was that if there was to be any question of unseaworthiness – specifically any breach of arts. III, r. 1, and IV, r. 1 – it was for the plaintiffs to allege and prove such breaches and their causative effect. Only the latter two authorities were concerned with Hague Rules contracts. No authority was cited to me as being binding on me with regard to a Hague Rules contract.

In the nineteenth century, before legislative intervention, two points were well established about contracts of carriage by sea. The first was that the typical liability of a carrier of goods by sea was that of a common carrier, and therefore his liability was absolute, subject only to the very limited common-law defences. Consequently, when exceptions were introduced into contracts of carriage of goods by sea, they were interpreted as applying only to the common carrier liability and not (in absence of express words) as applying to

53 *The Torenia* [1983] 2 Lloyd's Rep.210.
54 Ibid, p. 211.
55 Ibid, p. 217.

the implied duty to take reasonable care. Accordingly, the exceptions were construed as subject to an implicit proviso "unless the carrier has been negligent."

This was very clearly stated by Lord Esher in the *Glendarroch* at p. 230:

> Before you come to the exceptions the liability of the shipowner is absolute. He has contracted that he will deliver the goods at the end of the voyage. If there were no exceptions, it would be utterly immaterial whether the loss was caused by his servants or not. Even if there were no negligence whatever he would be liable. It cannot be, therefore, that this irresistible inference ought to be written into that part of the contract. It is not wanted there; therefore you must write it into that part which contains the exceptions.

Hobhouse J added, when you come to the exceptions, among others, there is that one, perils of the sea. There are no words which say "perils of the sea not caused by the negligence of the captain or crew." You have got to read those words in by a necessary inference. How can you read them? They can only be read, in my opinion, as an exception upon the exceptions. You must read in "except the loss is by perils of the sea, unless or except that loss is the result of the negligence of the servants of the owner."[56]

Hobhouse J discussed the question of negligence and observed that on ordinary principles, it was, on this construction of the contract, for the carrier to prove the peril of the sea and for the owner of the good to prove the negligence which would disentitle the carrier from relying on the primary exception. It is this reasoning which is referred to in the Joseph Constantine case in the passages cited previously from Viscount Simon and Lord Wright.[57]

Turning to the question of unseaworthiness, Hobhouse J said:[58]

> The common law implied a warranty of seaworthiness which, whilst not a condition of the voyage contract was treated as anterior to it; it was a kind of collateral contract to which the bill of lading contract did not apply unless the implied warranty had been superseded by an express warranty or the contract expressly referred to unseaworthiness. Thus the carrier could establish a contractual defence under the voyage contract, and it was left to the goods owner to say that the defence was not available because the loss or damage was caused by the breach of the warranty of seaworthiness. The goods owner had to allege this so he had to prove it.

Hobhouse J continued to discuss the burden of proof and stated:[59]

> With regard to the burden of proof in relation to negligence, the pre-Hague Rules law has unquestionably been qualified by art. IV, r. 2 (a) (*Gosse Millerd Ltd. V. Canadian Government Merchant Marine Ltd.*, (1928) 32 Ll.L.Rep.91; [1929] A.C. 223). With regard to unseaworthiness, in *Ministry of Food v. Reardon-Smith Line Ltd.* (sup.) Mr. Justice McNair, considering a case stated, applied the old law to the obligation under art. III, r. 1. He said that the burden of proving that the loss was caused by unseaworthiness was upon the goods owner and that it was not until that burden of proof had been discharged that any question of any burden of proof on the carrier under art. IV, r. 1, could arise. At an earlier part of his judgment he recognized that the Gosse Millerd decision had shown that there was a burden of proof on the carrier in connection with negligence and art. IV, r. 2 (a) (see p. 270 of [1951] 2 Lloyd's Rep.).

56 Ibid.
57 Ibid.
58 Ibid.
59 Ibid.

Hobhouse J concluded:[60]

> The vessel was unseaworthy by reason of corrosion at the commencement of the relevant voyage. That unseaworthiness was a cause, indeed the most significant cause, of the loss of the vessel and her cargo. This unseaworthiness was not latent nor was it undiscoverable by due diligence. Due diligence was not exercised. It follows that the defendants are liable.

In this case, the court found that the loss of the cargo was caused by the unseaworthiness of the vessel, that the defendants had not exercised due diligence, and that the defendants were not entitled to limit their liability under the Merchant Shipping Acts. It will therefore follow that the court give judgment for the plaintiffs for the agreed value of the cargo of £1,017,232.81.[61]

On the other hand, just as in this case a shipowner who relies on an excepted peril must show how much damage falls within the exception, so also a cargo owner who asserts unseaworthiness must show how much damage has resulted from the unseaworthiness. Once causative unseaworthiness is proved, the burden of proving the exercise of due diligence or latent defect lies on the carrier. Where loss or damage results from concurrent causes, one or more but not all of which fall within the list in article IV, rule 2, the shipowner is not relieved from liability; all the operative causes must fall within the list.[62]

3.10 Damage to frozen meat

A reefer ship is a special form of the cargo ship. As the name suggests, it is used to transport goods that must remain refrigerated during the entire transport or where the cold chain must not be interrupted. In other words, reefer ships are used for transporting perishable cargo overseas. This climate-controlled form of transit is vital for many products, including meat, fish, dairy, and vegetables. Anything that risks spoilage. Reefer ships are especially designed to provide temperature-controlled transportation. In turn, that allows safe and efficient shipping. Most of the time, reefer ships are hired as private carriers.

In the *Highland Monarch*,[63] the plaintiffs sue the defendants for damage sustained by a number of carcasses of frozen lamb which were loaded upon the defendants' vessel in Buenos Aires. The carcasses were loaded under a bill of lading which incorporated, among other things, the provisions of article IV of the Carriage of Goods by Sea Act, 1924. When the ship arrived in England, it was found that trouble had been caused by a leak in the no. 1 orlop trunk, and in the lower hold underneath that spot, there were found these damaged carcasses of lamb. Prima facie, the carcasses having been shipped, as is admitted, in good order and condition, and having arrived damaged by brine, the defendants are liable; and in order to discharge their liability, they must bring themselves within the immunity given by article IV in paragraph 1 or in paragraph 2 thereof. The defendants rely upon those two paragraphs, paragraph 1 and paragraph 2(p) and 2(q), but Mr Willink, in putting his case before me, did not press paragraph 2(q) in any way, saying that he could not see how, in the circumstances of this case, that subparagraph could carry him any further. Article IV, paragraph 1 provides:

---

60 Ibid, p. 230.
61 Ibid, p. 234.
62 See *Voyage Charters*, 4th ed at para. 85.262.
63 *The Highland Monarch* [1939] 64 Ll.L. Rep.188.

> Neither the carrier nor the ship shall be liable for loss or damage arising or resulting from unseaworthiness unless caused by want of due diligence on the part of the carrier to make the ship seaworthy, and to secure that the ship is properly manned, equipped and supplied, and to make the holds, refrigerating and cool chambers and all other parts of the ship in which goods are carried fit and safe for their reception, carriage and preservation in accordance with the provisions of par. 1 of Art. III.

The first question, therefore, which arises in this case as a matter of fact is whether the ship has discharged the onus which is placed upon the carrier by paragraph 1 of article IV of proving the exercise of due diligence in the matter of making this hold fit to carry the cargo which was loaded into it. Branson J, in giving judgment, observed that she has succeeded in discharging that onus.[64]

The evidence upon the matter is, first of all, directed to showing what was the particular spot in the ship's refrigerating machinery which failed in this particular instance and from which there escaped the brine which admittedly damaged the plaintiffs' goods.

Branson J continued:[65]

> I think that unless one is going to dismiss that evidence as false, the matter is conclusively established. Whatever Mr. Scott may think of the difficulty of making a brine-tight joint with this particular flange in the position in which it now is, they did make a brine-tight joint. So I have come to the conclusion that the brine escaped through the fabric of this flexible connection.

Turning to the next question is whether that which constituted unseaworthiness in this ship for the carriage of frozen cargo was caused by any want of due diligence on the part of the owners of this ship. Branson J stated:[66]

> It appears to me that that fact might be used in another way; it shows an amount of care when you find a responsible engineer, not content with testing the connections to 50 per cent. Above their working pressure, will yet reject any which, according to his experienced eye, look as if they were approaching a point at which they might create a danger.
>
> For these reasons I have come to the conclusion that there was no lack of due diligence in the tests that were made when the ship set sail from London.

Branson J continued:[67]

> Supposing that one had a tail-shaft which had a flaw in it which nobody could possibly discover by any examination short of destroying the thing, and that tail-shaft broke, it would be no answer to the shipowner's defence that there was a latent defect not discoverable by due diligence, to say that it might be he had not exercised any diligence to look at that tail-shaft at all. If the defect is such that it cannot be discoverable by due diligence it becomes immaterial to consider whether due diligence was exercised or not, because *ex hypothesi* if it had been exercised it would have been useless.

For reasons that have just been given, the court held that the shipowners had discharged the onus of showing that they had exercised due diligence to make the refrigerating hold fit and safe for the carriage of frozen meat and that, therefore, the claim failed.

As noted in this case, the Hague and Hague–Visby Rules exception is linked with the obligation to use due diligence to provide a seaworthy vessel. It is difficult to conceive of

64 Ibid, per Branson J at p. 189.
65 Ibid, p. 190.
66 Ibid, p. 191.
67 Ibid, p. 192.

many situations where a shipowner could raise the exception under the rules, and for that reason, the exception might be thought redundant. It has, however, been suggested that the exception provides additional immunities for the shipowner.[68]

3.11 Sludge tank

A slop tank means a tank specifically designed for collection, which also is the focal point of the load-on-top system used on crude oil tankers to prevent pollution of the sea. The design of these tanks and their operating procedures strongly affect the degree of oil–water separation achieved. Slop tanks in an oil tanker are used to collect drainings, tank washings, and other oily mixtures.

In *VTC v PVS*,[69] on 23 September 2005, the vessel was chartered on an amended Shelltime 4 form for a period of about ten years. On 9 December 2010, the vessel was sub-chartered to load a cargo of gasoline at Rotterdam for carriage to a range of ports in Mexico, the USA, and the Caribbean with a laycan of 18 to 20 December 2010. The vessel sailed from Boston on 10 December 2010 for Falmouth to bunker on the way to Rotterdam. On 14 December 2010, before it reached Falmouth, oil was found on the surface of the ballast water in one of the ballast tanks. Investigations revealed that that was due to a 12 mm crack in the port-side slop tank.

On 17 December 2010, the sub-charterers cancelled the sub-charter. The vessel sailed to Rotterdam nevertheless on 20 December 2010, arriving at 2200. She was repaired there over the next two days. Following her repairs, the charterers ordered the vessel to the UK west coast to load an alternative cargo.

The charterers deducted US$455,432 from hire on the basis that the owners were in breach of clause 64 when they informed the charterers that, by reason of the need to carry out repairs to the crack in the slop tank, the vessel would not meet her cancelling date under the sub-charter.

The owners brought arbitration proceedings to recover the sum deducted. The arbitrators held that the owners were not in breach of clause 64 and awarded the owners US$455,432 together with interest and costs. They concluded that the phrase "cargo tanks" in clause 64 could not be read as including ballast tanks or slop tanks.[70]

The charterers appealed, submitting that the phrase "all cargo tanks" encompassed the vessel's slop tanks.

The owners objected to any reference being made to any factual background matters that are not the subject of findings in the award. See, for example, *The Savina Caylyn*[71] at paragraph 30, in which Simon J stated as follows:

> Although all contracts must be construed against the commercial background which would have been available to the parties at the time the contract was made, the only admissible findings in relation to the commercial background are those in the award.

---

68 See *Carver on Charterparties*, 2nd ed at para. 5–119.

69 *VTC v PVS* [2012] 2 Lloyd's Rep.527.

70 Ibid.

71 *The Savina Caylyn* [2011] 1 Lloyd's Rep.550.

Hamblen J accepted that this was the correct general approach, but he considered that it was open to the charterers to contend that the charterparty itself contemplated the possibility of carriage of cargo in the slop tanks.[72]

Hamblen J continued:[73]

> The main difficulty facing the charterers, however, is that even if "cargo tanks" may include slop tanks the charterers do not have any findings to support the conclusion that this is how the clause should be applied in this case. If a case arose where cargo was ordered to be loaded into the slop tanks and those tanks were the subject of an inspection by the charterers' representative and/or independent surveyor, arguments could arise as to whether in that context "cargo tanks" should be construed as encompassing slop tanks.

Hamblen J explained and concluded:[74]

> The charterers are therefore driven back to the argument that "cargo tanks" in clause 64 must be construed as always including slop tanks, an argument that has been firmly rejected by the arbitrators. It is clear from the arbitrators' reasons that they considered that there is an important distinction between the cargo tanks and the other parts of the ship, such as the slop tanks, and that clause 64 is generally to be considered as referring to the cargo tanks only. That is consistent with clause 110 which itself draws a distinction between "cargo tanks" and the "slop tanks." The natural reading of clause 64 is therefore that it is referring to cargo tanks in contradistinction to other ship's tanks.

In the present case, it is not in dispute that (i) when the vessel arrived there, Rotterdam was not a loading port (the sub-charter having been cancelled on 17 December and the vessel only arriving at Rotterdam on 20 December for repairs), and (ii) the vessel's cargo tanks, pumps, and lines were never inspected at Rotterdam by, or found not to be suitable to the satisfaction of, the charterers' representative or an independent surveyor.[75]

As noted in this case, it would be impermissible to adopt a construction of the clause which robs the decision of the charterer's inspector of all significance and simply allows the court or arbitrator to substitute its own decision as to whether the tanks have been cleaned satisfactorily. It is probable, therefore, that a term should be implied that in reaching his decision, the inspector should act in good faith and on reasonable grounds. The effect of such a term is that the inspector's decision will prevail, even if the tribunal would have reached a different decision, as long as it falls within the range of reasonable opinion. Under the not dissimilar provisions of the sugar charter, it has been held in a London arbitration that a term is to be implied that the inspector shall judge the condition of the holds on proper and reasonable grounds and make his decision on the basis of an objective assessment of the holds.[76]

3.12 Cargo residues

Cargo residues will be a big problem if the vessel will load grain – the vessel mostly will fail to pass hold inspection.[77] In order to avoid losses caused by failure to pass hold

72 *VTC v PVS*, sup., per Hamblen J at p. 530.

73 Ibid.

74 Ibid.

75 Ibid, p. 531.

76 See *Voyage Charters*, 4th ed at para. 68.2.

77 See *London Arbitration 13/86, London Arbitration 13/86, London Arbitration 10/98, London Arbitration 6/07, London Arbitration 7/10, The Bunga Saga Lima* [2005] EWHC 244 (Comm).

inspection, for example, at a COFCO terminal in Argentina, a fine of USD 3,000 per hour is charged. Therefore, the holds must be properly cleaned of rust, residues of previous cargoes, insects, and the like which might contaminate the contemplated cargo and may also render the vessel unseaworthy.

In the *Good Friend*,[78] On 12 June 1980, part cargo of 6,016 t of soya bean meal in bags was shipped at Hamilton, Ontario, on board the defendants' vessel *Good Friend* for carriage to Havana. The shippers were Canada Packers Inc., who had agreed to sell the goods to the plaintiffs (Alimport), and in due course, the bill of lading was endorsed and delivered to Alimport.

The vessel had four holds and six hatches, and the soya bean meal was loaded in no. 2 tween deck and lower hold and no. 4 tween deck and lower hold. A further part cargo of timber was loaded in the remaining cargo spaces, and the vessel arrived in Havana on 28 June 1980. After the timber was discharged, complaints were made that the soya bean meal suffered from insect infestation. In particular, it was said to contain two kinds of insects which were the subject of quarantine in Cuba, that is, *Trogoderma variabile* and *Latheticus oryzae*.

The Cuban phytosanitary authority prohibited discharge, and as a result, the soya bean meal could not lawfully be discharged in Cuba. On 6 October 1980, the vessel sailed from Havana for Las Palmas and Tenerife, where the cargo was discharged, having been resold to salvage buyers.

Alimport alleged the vessel was unseaworthy before and at the beginning of the voyage, and they claimed a substantial loss because the meal could not be landed in Cuba. They had to buy a further quantity to fulfil their requirements.

The owners denied that the vessel was unseaworthy. They claimed that they had exercised due diligence to make the vessel seaworthy and relied on a number of excepted perils, principally quarantine, latent defect, and inherent vice. The owners counterclaimed for hire lost and fuel consumed while the vessel was at Havana.[79]

Staughton J, in giving judgment, said:[80]

> It was not disputed that the Hague Rules as enacted in Canada by the Water Carriage of Goods Act, 1936, were incorporated in the bill of lading and the contract of carriage. There was, however, some dispute as to the burden of proof; and I was referred to the case of *Aktieselskabet de Danske Sukkerfabrikker v. Bajamar Compania Naviera S.A.*, [1983] 2 Lloyd's Rep.210. In the present case it seems to me that the burden is initially on Alimport, to prove that the cargo was not delivered at Havana in accordance with the terms of the bill of lading; that was established without difficulty, and indeed it was not in dispute. Next, it was for the owners to show that they were protected by one of the exceptions in art. IV, r. 2, of the Hague Rules. The most obvious candidate is (h), quarantine restrictions. (It was not disputed that 'loss and damage' in art. IV, r. 2, included the kind of loss claimed by Alimport here, which did not comprise any physical damage to the soya bean meal.) It is proved that the discharge of the cargo at Havana was prevented by quarantine restrictions. Then Alimport have the burden of proving that the loss was caused by unseaworthiness. If they achieve that, the owners are liable (subject to the question of due diligence), since the exception in art. IV, r. 2, are subject to the obligation as to seaworthiness in art. III, r. 1: *Maxine Footwear Company Ltd. V. Canadian Government Merchant Marine Ltd.*, [1959] 2 Lloyd's Rep.105; [1959] A.C. 589. Finally, if

78 *The Good Friend* [1984] 2 Lloyd's Rep.586.
79 Ibid.
80 Ibid, p. 588.

Alimport prove that the loss was caused by unseaworthiness, the owners are excused if they can prove that they exercised due diligence to make the ship seaworthy before and at the beginning of the voyage.

Staughton J continued and observed that there was one aspect of the case which does not fit easily into that analysis. This was the exception of loss or damage arising from inherent defect, quality, or vice of the goods in article IV, rule 2(m), which was one of the exceptions relied on by the owners. If there was an inherent vice, and if it has the effect that the vessel was unseaworthy, the *Maxine Footwear* case would seem logical to lead to the conclusion that the owners were not protected unless they can establish due diligence. The explanation might be that inherent vice and unseaworthiness are mutually exclusive as potential causes of damage: either it was caused by the state of the cargo or by the state of the ship, but it cannot have been caused by both. In that respect, inherent vice would differ from many of the other exceptions in article IV, rule 2, such as perils of the sea, fire, quarantine restrictions, etc., which can be, and often are, concurrent causes with unseaworthiness.[81] At all events, it is first necessary, in considering the facts of this case, to determine whether the source of any infestation found at Havana was the ship or the soya bean meal.

Staughton J found it proved that there were substantial residues in the trunking just mentioned and on the balance of probabilities that these were infested before loading with *Trogoderma variabile*. There was also a considerable weight of evidence as to cargo residues elsewhere in the vessel, but some doubt as to whether they were substantial and not such as ought to be found in a well-run ship prepared to load soya bean meal. Staughton J inclined to the view that they were, in places, significant, but need not reach a firm conclusion on that point, because the residues in the no. 2 tween deck trunking were the major cause of the troubles which the vessel encountered. If they had not existed, discharge of the soya bean meal at Havana might well have been completed without incident.[82]

Staughton J discussed the question of seaworthy, saying:[83]

> If the Hague Rules fell to be construed in a vacuum, without any antecedent history, I would have had some sympathy with that argument. The natural meaning of the word "seaworthy" is fit to withstand the perils and incidents of a sea voyage. In *The Aquacharm* [1982] 1 Lloyd's Rep.7(C.A.) at p. 12, Lord Justice Shaw said that he would enter a caveat against any artificial extension of the concept of seaworthiness. Furthermore, the express provision in part (c) of the rule as to what shall be done about the state of the vessel's holds tends to suggest that the obligation in part (a) to make the ship seaworthy does not of itself already include fitness of the ship to carry and discharge the cargo safely.

Staughton J considered earlier cases and concluded:[84]

> The condition of the ship constituted a major and permanent obstacle to the completion of the contract voyage. I hold *Good Friend* to have been unseaworthy within art. III, r. 1. I also find that unseaworthiness caused Alimport's loss.

Turning to due diligence, Staughton J stated that:[85]

81 See *Monarch Steamship Co. Ltd. v Karlshamns Oljefabriker A/B* [1948] 82 Ll.L. Rep.137; [1949] A.C. 196, per Lord Wright at pp. 155, 226.

82 *The Good Friend*, sup. at p. 591.

83 Ibid.

84 Ibid, p. 593.

85 Ibid, p. 596.

> It follows that there was lack of due diligence on the part of the owners, through their master and crew, in failing to look inside the trunking, to detect the residues there, and to take measures to deal with them.

It is worth repeating cases which were cited in the case. In *Ciampa v British India Steam Navigation Co. Ltd.*,[86] a ship loaded a cargo of lemons at Naples for carriage to London. Because she had previously called at Mombassa, a plague-contaminated port, she was subjected to fumigation when she called at Marseilles in the course of the voyage. That damaged the lemons. It was held that the ship was unseaworthy when the voyage began at Naples. The case was not, of course, concerned with the Hague Rules but with the warranty of seaworthiness implied in common law. Mr Justice Rowlatt said (at p. 780):

> The ship was therefore in my opinion unfit to receive and carry the cargo. That is what is meant by unseaworthiness, quite apart from the fitness of the ship to traverse the ocean.

In the *Madeleine*,[87] the charterparty required the vessel to be delivered by a cancelling date, *she being in every way fitted for ordinary cargo service*. On the cancelling date, the vessel had no valid deratisation exemption certificate and so had to be fumigated. It was held that the charterers were entitled to cancel. Mr Justice Roskill (at p. 241) said:

> There was here an express warranty of seaworthiness and unless the ship was timeously delivered in a seaworthy condition, including the necessary certificate from the port health authority, the charterers had the right to cancel.

In *Tattersall v National Steamship Co. Ltd*,[88] cattle were loaded on board a ship which had previously carried animals infected with foot-and-mouth disease and which had not been properly disinfected. The shipowners were held liable for damage to the cattle. Mr Justice Day said (at p. 300):

> I take it to have been clearly established . . . that where there is a contract to carry goods in a ship there is, in the absence of any stipulation to the contrary, an implied engagement on the part of the person so undertaking to carry that the ship is reasonably fit for the purposes of such carriage.

In *Rickards v Forestal Land Timber & Railways Co. Ltd*,[89] loss of the adventure was considered a total loss of the good, per Viscount Maugham at p. 183:

> I consider that the more limited undertaking of due diligence in art. III, r. 1, uses "seaworthy" in the same sense. It would be surprising if a shipowner were obliged to use due diligence to provide a ship with holds that were fit and safe for the reception, carriage and preservation of the goods, but not one which was fit to discharge and deliver them at the specified port of destination. I do not reach that conclusion.

Also, as Staughton J suggested, bear in mind what Lord Reid said in *Union of India v N. V. Reederij Amsterdam*,[90] at p. 230:

> In a great many accidents, it is clear after the event that if the defendant had taken certain extra precautions the accident would or might have been avoided. The question always is whether a

86 *Ciampa v British India Steam Navigation Co. Ltd.* [1915] 2 K.B. 774.
87 *The Madeleine* [1967] 2 Lloyd's Rep.224.
88 *Tattersall v National Steamship Co. Ltd.* [1884] 12 Q.B.D. 297.
89 *Rickards v Forestal Land Timber & Railways Co. Ltd.* [1941] 70 Ll.L. Rep.173.
90 *Union of India v N.V. Reederij Amsterdam* [1963] 2 Lloyd's Rep.223 (H.L.).

> reasonable man in the shoes of the defendant, with the skill and knowledge which the defendant had or ought to have had, would have taken those extra precautions.

As noted in this case, the obligation to make a ship seaworthy itself includes an obligation to see that the ship is fit for cargo service. Where the particular service is specified in the contract, it is an obligation to see that the ship is fit to carry the specified cargo on the specified voyage.[91]

The undertaking of seaworthiness at common law includes, under the heading of what is sometimes called cargoworthiness, an undertaking that the ship shall be reasonably fit to receive and carry the cargo and deliver it at the specified destination. If the ship's condition is such that she is not reasonably fit for those tasks, the undertaking has been broken, even if the cargo suffers no physical damage and it is only the adventure that is lost.

3.13 Infested

In the *Tres Flores*,[92] the charterers ordered the vessel to Varna for the carriage of maize. She arrived on the roads there at 0500 hours on Sunday, 22 November. No berth was available for her. At 1000 hours, the master gave notice of readiness to load. On Friday, 27 November, at 1515 hours, the vessel was inspected by the port authorities. Pests were found in the cargo spaces, and fumigation was ordered. This took place between 1500 hours and 1930 hours on Monday, 30 November, whilst the vessel was still on the roads. At 1100 hours on Tuesday, 1 December, the charterers accepted the notice of readiness.

The shipowners claimed (i) demurrage, contending that the laytime started at 1400 hours on Monday, 23 November, whereas the charterers maintained that it started at 1400 hours on Tuesday, 1 December, and (ii) damages for detention on account of delay by the charterers in inspecting the vessel. The dispute was referred to arbitrators, who made an award in the form of a special case in favour of the shipowners, the questions for the court being whether:

1. (a) Laytime commenced at 1400 hours on Monday, 23 November.
   (b) Laytime commenced at 1400 hours on Tuesday, 1 December.
2. If the answer to 1 in the previous passage is (b), whether the owners are entitled to damages for detention on account of delay by the charterers in inspecting the vessel.

The arbitrators made an alternative award if the court were to decide that their decision had been wrong. The decision was appealed by the charterers.[93]

On the evidence, Mocatta J stated that the vessel was not ready to load on Sunday, 22 November, and could not give notice of readiness to load on that day, for her holds were infested; and clause 21 did not appear to make any difference to the common-law obligations of the shipowner prior to his being able to give a valid notice of readiness. Mocatta J observed that the facts did not show that the amount of infestation fell within

91 See *Scrutton on Charterparties and Bills of Lading*, 24th ed at para. 7–026: "*The undertaking of seaworthiness involves not only that the ship is herself fit to encounter the perils of the voyage, but also that she is fit to carry the cargo safely on that voyage.*"

92 *The Tres Flores* [1972] 2 Lloyd's Rep.384; [1973] 2 Lloyd's Rep.247 (C.A.).

93 Ibid, [1972] 2 Lloyd's Rep.384 at p. 385.

the de minimis principle. Mocatta J concluded that the laytime started at 1400 hours on Tuesday, 1 December.[94]

The Court of Appeal held that in order for a notice of readiness to be good, the vessel must be ready at the time that the notice is given and not at a time in the future; in this case, it could not be said that at the time when notice of readiness was given, the ship was, in a business and mercantile sense, ready to load. The vessel must be completely ready in all her holds to receive the cargo at any moment when she is required to receive it; under clause 6 and at common law, the presence of pests in the hold invalidated the notice of readiness.[95]

As noted in this case, the charterers were under no contractual duty to inspect the holds before loading and were entitled to rely on the owners fulfilling their obligations to provide a vessel which was fit to receive the contractual cargo.

3.14 Plague

In *Tattersall v National Steamship Co*,[96] the plaintiff shipped cattle on board the defendants' ship *France* for carriage from London to New York under a bill of lading which, among other things, provided that the defendants should not be liable "for accidents, disease, or mortality, and that under no circumstances shall they be held liable for more than £5 for each of the animals." The ship had, on a previous voyage, carried cattle suffering from foot-and-mouth disease. Some of the cattle shipped under the bill of lading were infected during the voyage. It was found that this was caused by the negligence of the defendants' servants in not cleaning and disinfecting the ship before loading the plaintiff's cattle on board.

Day J said:

> I take it to have been clearly established that where there is a contract to carry goods in a ship there is, in the absence of any stipulation to the contrary, an implied engagement on the part of the person so undertaking to carry that the ship is reasonably fit for the purposes of such carriage. In this case it is clear that the ship was not reasonably fit for the carriage of these cattle.
>
> There is, therefore, a breach of their implied engagement by the defendants, and the plaintiff having sustained damage in consequence must be entitled to recover the amount of such damage, unless the defendants are protected by any express stipulation.

Day J continued:

> I have considered the terms of the bill of lading, and, as I construe it, its stipulations which have been relied upon all relate to the carriage of the goods on the voyage, and do not in any way affect the liability for not providing a ship fit for their reception. If the goods had been damaged by any peril in the course of the voyage, which might be incurred in a ship originally fit for the purpose of the carriage of the goods, the case would have been wholly different, but here the goods were not damaged by any such peril, or by any peril which, in my opinion, was contemplated by the parties in framing the bill of lading. They were damaged simply because the defendants' servants neglected their preliminary duty of seeing that the ship was in a proper condition to receive them, and received them into a ship that was not fit to receive them. There

94 Ibid, per Mocatta J at p. 393.
95 Ibid, per Lord Denning MR [1973] 2 Lloyd's Rep.247 (C.A.) at p. 249.
96 *Tattersall v National Steamship Co* [1884] 12 QBD 297.

> is nothing in the bill of lading that I can see to restrict or qualify the liability of the defendants in respect of the breach of this obligation.

A ship which can navigate safely may still be unseaworthy in law if it is not fit to carry the agreed cargo. Some commentators prefer to treat cargoworthiness as a distinct obligation, while others regard it as an example of the wider duty to ensure seaworthiness, as it is treated here. This difference is, in practice, one of presentation rather than substance.[97]

In an earlier case, the *Matiana*,[98] a vessel was loaded lemons in Naples for carriage to London. Owing to the fact that she had previously been to a plague port, it was inevitable, because of existing French law, that she would have to undergo deratisation by sulphur fumigation if she did call at any French way port, as she had liberty to do. As intended by the owners, she called at Marseilles, where she underwent the required sulphur fumigation, which inevitably damaged the lemons.

Rowlatt J observed that it was beyond all doubt that the vessel was going to be subjected to fumigation on arrival at Marseilles, and in those circumstances, he did not think that the mere application of French law that existed at the date of loading amounted to a "restraint of princes." Whilst he disavowed any intention of holding that the application of the ordinary law of a country could not, in some cases, amount to a "restraint of princes," he said that where the facts exist at the date of loading showing that the vessel was "inevitably doomed" to be subject to the restraint, that did not bring the case within the exception. He continued to hold that the vessel was unseaworthy because she had come from a port contaminated by plague, necessitating fumigation of the vessel at her next port; she was unfit to receive and carry the cargo. On p. 780, he concluded:[99]

> The defendants therefore received the lemons on board their ship for carriage, the ship being at the time free from sulphurous fumes, but circumstances existing which rendered it inevitable that the ship and cargo would in the course of the voyage be subjected to them. The ship was therefore in my opinion unfit to receive and carry the cargo. That is what is meant by unseaworthiness, quite apart from the fitness of the ship to traverse the ocean.

As noted in this case, if a port or place is the subject of a fever epidemic which would result, were the vessel to call there, in her being blacklisted, detained, or impounded at a subsequent port, then that port would be unsafe, for it would render the vessel unseaworthy and would thus pose a physical threat.[100]

Cargoworthiness is an aspect of seaworthiness, and so a seaworthy vessel must be reasonably fit to receive and carry the cargo tendered, so the perils also include storage perils. They may even include the operation of sanitary or port regulations, where the enforcement of those regulations will inevitably cause damage to the cargo.[101]

---

97 For more details see *Cases & Materials on the Carriage of Goods by Sea*, by Martin Dockray, 3rd ed at p. 48.

98 *Ciampa v British India Steam Navigation Co. Ltd* [1915] 2 K.B. 774. This case was also cited in *Induna v British Phosphate Commissioners* [1949] 82 L.l.L. Rep.430 at pp. 436–437; *The Angelia* [1972] 2 Lloyd's Rep.154, itself commented on by Parker LJ in *Channel Island Ferries v Sealink* [1988] 1 Lloyd's Rep.323 at p. 328. *The Derby* [1985] 2 Lloyd's Rep.325 (C.A.), per Kerr LJ at p. 332.

99 See *Bills of Lading*, 3rd ed at para. 11.118.

100 See *Voyage Charters*, 4th ed at para. 5.66.

101 Ibid, para. 11.18.

3.15 COVID-19

A vessel's condition of unseaworthiness might arise from any number of circumstances. Her gear might be defective, her appurtenances in disrepair, her crew unfit. The number of men assigned to perform a shipboard task might be insufficient. The method of loading her cargo, or the manner of its stowage, might be improper. For any of these reasons or others, a vessel might not be reasonably fit for her intended service.

At common law, in the absence of any express term to the contrary, there is an implied term in the contract of carriage that the ship will be seaworthy to undertake the contractual voyage. It is an "absolute" warranty of seaworthiness, not one to use due diligence to make the vessel seaworthy. The shipowner is, by the nature of the contract, impliedly and necessarily held to warrant that the ship is good and is in a condition to perform the voyage then about to be undertaken, or, in ordinary language, is seaworthy, that is, fit to meet and undergo the perils of the sea and other incidental risks to which she must, of necessity, be exposed in the course of the voyage.[102]

The warranty is that the ship will be seaworthy at the commencement of the voyage for the particular voyage. A seaworthy ship is one that is reasonably fit in all respects to encounter the ordinary perils of the adventure. The warranty of seaworthiness relates not only to the hull but also to the machinery and equipment, the crew, and how a ship is loaded. Owners should be aware that a vessel may become unfit to receive and carry the cargo if she is chartered after calling at an area affected by the COVID-19 infectious disease.[103]

If the vessel is required to carry out compulsory fumigation as a result of calling at an infected area, this may cause cargo damage if it is perishable. Similarly, if a vessel is delayed due to quarantine regulations, which in turn cause damage to cargo, the vessel may be considered unseaworthy. Just as remnants of previous cargo may render a vessel unseaworthy if they are likely to affect or contaminate the cargo to be loaded, the infectious disease may therefore inadvertently put owners in breach of their obligations to provide a vessel that is seaworthy.[104]

Next question is whether a vessel may no longer be seaworthy if some or any member of the crew is suffering from COVID-19. On the other hand, the contracts for a number of the ship's crew have already expired or are due to expire soon, and owners may not be able to arrange the necessary crew changes in accordance with the terms of the crew contract due to the outbreak of COVID-19 and the restrictions in place in various Chinese ports. Provided that safe manning levels for the ship are maintained in accordance with flag state requirements and on mutually agreed extended contracts, this will not affect seaworthiness. But if no crew change plan, the vessel will be detained by AMSA in west Australian ports.

Now, turning to whether COVID-19 can make a vessel unseaworthy. The concept of seaworthiness applies to both time and voyage charterparties. The classic definition of *seaworthiness*, as set out by Thomas Carver himself in the third edition of his original

102 See *Bills of Lading*, 3rd ed at para. 11.100.

103 See *Tattersall v National Steamship Co* [1884] 12 QBD 297. Also see *Carver on Charterparties*, 2nd ed at para. 4–480, *Examples of qualifying diseases include Ebola and Covid-19.*

104 See *Ciampa v British India Steam Navigation Co. Ltd* [1915] 2 K.B. 774.

treatise, was approved in *McFadden v Blue Star Line*[105] and in *F. C. Bradley & Sons Ltd v Federal Steam Navigation Co Ltd.*[106] It is that a vessel:

> must have that degree of fitness which an ordinary careful and prudent owner would require his vessel to have at the commencement of her voyage having regard to all the probable circumstances of it. To that extent the shipowner . . . undertakes absolutely that she is fit, and ignorance is no excuse. If the defect existed, the question to be put is, would a prudent owner have required that it should be made good before sending his ship to sea had he known of it? If he would, the ship was not seaworthy within the meaning of the undertaking.

One test of seaworthiness is: Would a prudent owner have required that the defect should be made good before sending his ship to sea, had he known of it? If he would, the ship was not seaworthy. The warranty of seaworthiness that existed at common law is one of "the ship being fit to encounter the perils of the voyage" and subsequently expounded the well-known "prudent owner" test, as set out in the then-current edition of *Carver on Charterparties*.[107]

The concept extends to cargoworthiness and the fitness of the crew. It has also been modified by, inter alia, the Hague Rules/Hague–Visby Rules, which reduced the absolute seaworthiness obligation under common law to an obligation to exercise due diligence to make the vessel seaworthy.

Whether a vessel is seaworthy also has to be judged in the context of the increased sophistication of vessels, new technology, and the greater regulation of the industry generally. With COVID-19, seaworthiness issues are most likely to arise in cases where the vessel has called at a port that is affected by COVID-19 and/or where members of the crew have, or are suspected of having, COVID-19. Many issues arise when the vessels are isolated at anchorage for 14 days or 21 days since she left the last international ports, including Australian ports, Singapore, etc., especially Indian ports.

In the case of the crew, it is clear that a vessel may be unseaworthy if the crew members are infected with COVID-19.[108] This may also be a valid ground on which to place the vessel off-hire or to dispute the validity of a notice of readiness. In the context of disease and/or contamination, a vessel has been held to be unseaworthy because its previous port was contaminated by plague and it was detained and required fumigation due to its trading history.[109]

Next to deal with is the effect on charterparties of the COVID-19 pandemic. COVID-19 has stopped contract performance in its tracks in many instances. Does that mean the contract is suspended or even terminated because of force majeure or an act of God? A force majeure clause allocates the risk of loss if performance is hindered, delayed, or prevented because of an event that the parties could not have anticipated or controlled. It provides a contractual defence, the scope and effect of which will depend on the express terms of a particular contract. The starting point for parties is to review their contracts to ascertain whether there is a force majeure clause and if the definition of "force majeure"

105 *McFadden v Blue Star Line* [1905] 1 K.B. 697 at 703.

106 *F.C. Bradley & Sons v Federal Steam Navigation* [1926] 24 Ll.L. Rep.446 at 454, per Scrutton LJ. The decision of the majority of the Court of Appeal was upheld by the House of Lords at [1927] 27 Ll.L. Rep.395.

107 See *Carver on Charterparties*, 2nd ed at 3–075; *Scrutton on Charterparties and Bills of Lading*, 24 ed at 7–025; *Bills of Lading*, 3rd ed at 11.103.

108 *The Eurasian Dream* [2002] 1 Lloyd's Rep.719.

109 *Ciampa v British India Steam Navigation Co Ltd* [1915] 2 K.B. 774.

is broad enough to cover COVID-19 and its effects. Force majeure is a contractual remedy under English law. So if a contract is silent on force majeure, English law will not imply it in the contract. Similarly, undefined references to force majeure in an English law contract, without any contractual definition or interpretation, will not have an implied definition in law.

It's settled that a man should not be allowed to take advantage of his own wrong,[110] or neither party shall be entitled to take advantage of his own breach as against the other party.[111] These words have to be approached with the aid of the cardinal rules of construction that they must be read contra proferentem and that in order to escape from the consequences of one's wrongdoing, or that of one's servant, clear words are necessary.[112]

It has been said that, as a matter of construction, unless the contract clearly provides to the contrary, it will be presumed that it was not the intention of the parties that either should be entitled to rely on his own breach of duty to avoid the contract or bring it to an end or to obtain a benefit under it. This presumption applies only to acts or omissions which constitute a breach by that party of an express or implied contractual obligation, or (possibly) of a non-contractual duty, owed by him to the other party. Breach of duty, whether contractual or non-contractual, owed to a stranger to the contract will not suffice. However, such a "principle of construction" appears to be somewhat different in nature from the principle that a document will be construed against the grantor. It may therefore be that it is better regarded as depending on an implied term of the contract in question or as one illustration of a more general principle that "[a] man cannot be permitted to take advantage of his own wrong."[113]

So if a party who sustains loss by reason of a breach of contract is to be placed, so far as money can do it, it's in the same position as if the contract had been performed.[114]

It's suggested to keep in mind that, at common law, liability for breach of contract is often strict: that is, a party may be in breach even though his failure or inability to perform is not due to any want of care or diligence on his part. The mere fact that supervening events occurring without his fault has interfered with or prevented performance is therefore not sufficient to bring the doctrine of discharge into operation. This point is most readily illustrated by the case of a seller of unascertained generic goods who is cut off by supervening events from the only source of supply to which he could reasonably have been expected to resort or who cannot ship the goods from the contractually designated country of origin because it turns out that no shipping space is available there during the time specified in the contract for shipment.[115] The burden of proof is on the seller to prove the facts bringing the case within the clause. He must therefore prove the occurrence of one of the events referred to in the clause and that he has been prevented, hindered, or delayed (as the case may be) from performing the contract by reason of that event. He must further prove (i) that his non-performance was due to circumstances beyond his control and (ii)

110 *The Hong Kong Fir* [1961] 2 Lloyd's Rep.487.

111 *The Bonde* [1991] 1 Lloyd's Rep.136.

112 *Photo Production Ltd v Securicor Transport Ltd* [1980] 1 Lloyd's Rep.545 (H.L.).

113 See *Chitty on Contracts*, 34th ed at pp. 15–113.

114 *Hadley v Baxendale* [1854] 9 Ex. 341; *The Hong Kong Fir, sup.*; also see *Arnold v Britton and others* [2015] UKSC 36, per Lord Neuberger at [20]; *Bunge SA v Nidera NV* [2015] 2 Lloyd's Rep.469, per Lord Sumption at para. 14, 23.

115 See *Frustion and Force Majeure,* 4th ed at para. 1–003.

that there were no reasonable steps that he could have taken to avoid or mitigate the event or its consequences.[116]

The crucial factor here was that of delay: the contract expressly provided for suspension where performance was "hindered," and it was held that performance need not be resumed when, some years later, shipping conditions returned to normal. A similar point can be made in relation to the failure of a charterer to provide cargo. His liability for such failure is strict, but if he provides the cargo, the contract may be discharged as a result of delays in loading caused by events beyond his control, such as strikes at the port of loading. Again, it can be said that the charterer undertakes that there will be cargo, but not that manpower will be available to load it.[117]

There is a standard somewhere between a requirement to take every conceivable precaution, however extreme, within the limits of the law and a duty to do no more than act reasonably in accordance with prudent current practice; the words "could not avoid" were to be treated as comprising the rider even with the utmost care, and in deciding whether this criterion was satisfied in the individual case, the court would need to look at all the circumstances and not simply at any constraints which might be imposed by the criminal law on steps which would have prevented the loss.[118]

The word "reasonable" might be read as suggesting that the mere absence of fault is sufficient to demonstrate irresistibility for the purposes of force majeure. There is a very real difference between the absence of fault or negligence and a standard of conduct referable to reasonable and practical possibility. The mere fact that a defendant has not been negligent or at fault does not, in itself, prove that he took all measures that were reasonably possible in the sense of being reasonably and practically available to him. In other words, a concept of irresistibilité, which incorporates a standard of reasonable and practical possibility, still requires a defendant to do much more than prove that he was not negligent. On the contrary, he must go further and show that once the event was foreseeable, he did everything which was reasonably possible and practicable, not only that which it might have been reasonable for him to do.[119]

The general principle exemplified in these cases is not altogether easy to define in that if a party has a period of time within which, at his option, to perform, the principle does not seem to require that in order to escape liability for non-performance, he must show prevention by reason of the operation of the exception throughout the whole period. If he has arranged to perform at the end of his optional period or could have then performed and the inhibiting event occurs, he can, it would seem, escape from liability for non-performance by showing that nothing he could do, or perhaps reasonably do, after the occurrence of the inhibiting event would have enabled him to perform within the contract period. This shows that even when the general principle applies, regard is permissible to the intentions or arrangements made by the party seeking relief.[120]

116 See *Benjamin's Sale of Goods*,11th ed at para. 8–075.

117 See *Frustion and Force Majeure*, 4th ed at para. 1–003.

118 *Islander Trucking Ltd. v J. J. Silber Ltd. and Other & Patenta G.m.b.H. and Others* [1985] 2 Lloyd's Rep.243.

119 *General Construction Limited v Chue Wing & Co Ltd and another* [2013] UKPC 30.

120 *Classic Maritime Inc v Limbungan Makmur Sdn Bhd* [2019] EWCA Civ 1102.

The phrase "resulting from" required a "but for" test to be satisfied.[121] In the COVID-19 case, one must prove that but for COVID-19, he could perform a further obligation under the contract. The general principle is also clear. If a contract provides for alternative methods of performance and one such method comes to be prevented by an excepted peril, then the party affected must generally perform or seek to perform by one of the alternative methods.[122]

It's clear that English law has no intention to lay down any general principle; each must be directed to the facts and circumstances of the respective cases.[123] The only general rule that can be laid down is that one must consider the wording of the clause in every case.[124] The remaining question is whether charterers could not claim unseaworthiness if an owner fails to disclose crew was infected by COVID-19. It's the owner's overriding obligation to make the vessel seaworthy.[125] When unseaworthiness has been proved, the burden moves to the carrier to prove reasonable diligence.[126]

In conclusion, the seaworthiness required is relative to the nature of the ship, to the particular voyage contracted for, and to the particular stages of that voyage, being different for summer or winter voyages, for river and lake, or for sea navigation, whilst loading in harbour and when sailing, and varies with the particular cargo contracted to be carried.[127]

121 *The Furness Bridge* [1977] 2 Lloyd's Rep.367.

122 *The Loch Dee* [1949] 82 L.l.L. Rep.430; *The North Anglia* [1956] 2 Lloyd's Rep.367; *The Pacific Voyager* [2018] EWCA Civ 2413.

123 *European Grain & Shipping v J. H. Rayner* [1970] 2 Lloyd's Rep.239.

124 *The Berge Sund* [1993] 2 Lloyd's Rep.453.

125 *The Maruinne* [1959] 2 Lloyd's Rep.105.

126 *The Polessk and The Akademik Iosif Orbili* [1996] 2 Lloyd's Rep.40 at p. 45. Also see *Carver on Bills of Lading*, 1st ed at para. 9–143.

127 See *Scrutton on Charterparties and Bills of Lading*, 24th ed at para. 7–021.

CHAPTER 4

Cargo stowage

4.1 No tween deck bad stowage

It has been said that unseaworthiness must relate to some attribute of the ship itself. On this basis, it has been suggested that the fact that a hold contains cargo which threatens damage to other cargo stowed in proximity is not an attribute of the ship and does not render the ship unseaworthy. However, bad stowage which endangers the safety of the ship, rather than risks damage to nearby cargo, may amount to unseaworthiness, and residues from previous cargo may render a ship unseaworthy. But bad stowage which affects nothing but the cargo damaged by it is bad stowage and nothing more and still leaves the ship seaworthy for the adventure, even though the adventure is the carrying of the cargo. The undertaking of seaworthiness involves not only that the ship is herself fit to encounter the perils of the voyage but also that she is fit to carry the cargo safely on that voyage.[1]

Where cargo is so badly stowed as to imperil the safety of the vessel, a difficult question arises as to how any resulting loss or damage, to either the vessel or its cargo, should be categorized. Is it due to the bad stowage or to the unseaworthiness caused by the bad stowage? The answer to this question will prove critical to the question of who should bear responsibility for the loss under a time charter under which the charterers have accepted responsibility for stowage.[2]

In the *Ovington Court*[3], clause 8 was held also to effect a transfer to the charterer of legal responsibility for, and risk of, any loss or damage resulting from the specified acts of cargo handling. This was explained in the context of the contractual interests of the shipowner and charterer by Lord Wright as follows:[4]

> It is, apart from special provisions or circumstances, part of the ship's duty to stow the goods properly, not only in the interests of the seaworthiness of the vessel, but in order to avoid damage to the goods, and also to avoid loss of space or dead freight owing to bad stowage. In modern times the work of stowage is generally deputed to stevedores, but that does not generally relieve the shipowners of their duty, even though the stevedores are under the charterparty to be appointed by the charterers, unless there are special provisions which either expressly or inferentially have that effect. But under clause 8 of this charterparty the charterers are to load, stow and trim the cargo at their expense. I think these words necessarily import that the charterers take into their hands the business of loading and stowing the cargo. It must

1 *Scrutton on Charterparties and Bills of Lading*, 24th ed at para. 7–026.
2 Simon Baughan, Bad Stowage or Unseaworthiness? [2007] L.M.C.L.Q. 1.
3 *The Ovington Court* [1940] 67 Ll.L. Rep.161 (H.L.).
4 Ibid, per Lord Wright at p. 168.

DOI: 10.4324/9781003279938-4

> follow that they not only relieve the ship of the duty of loading and stowing, but as between themselves and the shipowners relieve them of liability for bad stowage. . . . The charterers are granted by the shipowners the right of performing a duty which properly attaches to the shipowners. Presumably, this is for the convenience of the charterers. If the latter does not perform properly the duty of stowing the cargo, the shipowners will be subject to a liability to the bill of lading holders. Justice requires that the charterers should indemnify the shipowners against that liability on the same principle that a similar right of indemnity arises when one person does an act and thereby incurs liability at the request of another, who is then held liable to indemnify.

The weight of the authorities supports the proposition that where the responsibility for the stowage has been contractually passed from the shipowner to the charterer (or the cargo owner), the shipowner will not be liable for damage arising from improper stowage even if it renders the vessel unseaworthy, unless it is established that the bad stowage leading to the damage arose from a significant intervention by the shipowners or their master. In this respect, it seems that the "intervention" must be significant in the sense that it operated to tie the stevedores' hands and was caused only by the captain's orders or was the result of matters of which the captain was, but the charterers were not, aware.[5]

Now turning to the *Grelwen*.[6] The vessel of the Isherwood type contains deep holds but no tween decks. The *Grelwen* proceeded to the Sherbro River, where she loaded from the respondents casks or butts of palm oil, which were stowed in two or three tiers at the bottom of holds 2, 3, and 4. She also loaded there from the respondents and other shippers about 51,800 bags of palm kernels, which were stowed partly over the casks of palm oil in holds 2 and 4 (thus completely filling those holds) and partly in other parts of the ship. The vessel then proceeded to Konakri, where she loaded from the respondents a further 147 butts of palm oil, which were stowed at the bottom of no. 3 hold, and also loaded from the respondents and others about 11,400 more bags of palm kernels, which were stowed partly over the palm oil in no. 3 hold (thus filling that hold) and partly elsewhere. When the vessel arrived at Hull, which was her destination, it was found that the casks and butts of palm oil in holds 2, 3, and 4 had been crushed by the palm kernels stored above them, which were very heavy.

The respondents accordingly commenced action against the appellants, claiming damages for breach of the contract entered into by the bills of lading under which the palm oil was shipped, or for negligence or breach of duty. The defendants at the trial attempted to prove that the casks and butts were frail or leaky, but this attempt failed, and it is not now denied that the damage was caused by the altogether unreasonable and excessive weight placed upon the casks. This being so, the contest resolved itself into the question whether the damage was due to bad stowage or to the fact that the vessel was structurally unfit or unseaworthy for the carriage of the palm oil by reason of the depth of her holds and the absence of tween decks. It was not denied that if the damage was due to bad stowage, the charterers are protected against liability by the conditions contained in the bills of lading, but if it was due to unseaworthiness, then it was contended that the charterers were not protected by any of the conditions of the bills of lading and were liable to make good the damage.[7]

---

5 *The Eems Solar* [2013] 2 Lloyd's Rep.487.
6 *The Grelwen* [1924] 18 Ll.L. Rep.319 (H.L.).
7 Ibid, p. 320.

The case was tried by Rowlatt J without a jury. He found that the vessel was not fit for the carriage of West African cargoes on the ground that she had no tween decks or substitute therefor, and he gave judgment for the plaintiffs. His decision was affirmed by the Court of Appeal, Scrutton LJ dissenting on the ground that in his opinion the damage was the result of bad stowage and that the bill of lading exempted the defendants from liability on this ground.

According to Viscount Cave:[8]

> The general principles which should govern the decision are not in doubt. It is well settled that a shipowner or charterer who contracts to carry goods by sea thereby warrants, not only that the ship in which he proposes to carry them shall be seaworthy in the ordinary sense of the word-that is to say, that she shall be tight, staunch and strong, and reasonably fit to encounter whatever perils which may be expected on the voyage-but also that both the ship and her furniture and equipment shall be reasonably fit for receiving the contract cargo and carrying it across the sea. The latter obligation, which is sometimes referred to as a warranty of seaworthiness for the cargo, was formulated by Lord Ellenborough in the year 1804 (see *Lyon v. Mells*, 5 East 428), and was affirmed by this House in *Steel v. State Line Steamship Co.*, 3 App. Cas. 72, and *Gilroy v. Price*, [1893] A.C. 56. The rule, as it applies to equipment, is well illustrated by such cases as Owners of Cargo on the *Maori King v. Hughes*, [1895] 2 Q.B. 550, where a ship with defective refrigerating machinery was held unseaworthy for a cargo of frozen meat; and *Queensland National Bank v. Peninsular and Oriental Steam Nav. Co.*, [1898] 1 Q.B. 567, where a ship with a bullion room not reasonably fit to resist thieves was held unseaworthy for a consignment of bullion. Reference may also be made to *Hogarth v. Walker*, [1899] 2 Q.B. 401; [1900] 2 Q.B. 283, where it was said by Bigham, J., and A. L. Smith LJ, that a ship without dunnage mats (which are usually laid on the floor of a grain ship to protect the grain from being damaged by wet) was unseaworthy for the carriage of a cargo of wheat.

Viscount Cave discussed unseaworthiness and bad stowage, saying:[9]

> It is hardly necessary to add that unseaworthiness and bad stowage are two different things. There are cases (such as *Kopitoff v. Wilson*, 1 Q.B.D. 377, where, a ship having been injured in consequence of bad stowage, the warranty of seaworthiness of the ship has been held to be broken; but in such cases it is the unseaworthiness and not the bad stowage which constitutes the breach of warranty. There is no rule that, if two parcels of cargo are so stowed that one can injure the other during the course of the voyage the ship is unseaworthy (per Swinfen Eady LJ, in the *Thorsa*, [1916] P. 257).

Applying these principles to the present case, Viscount Cave came to the conclusion that:[10]

> [T]he damage complained of was not due to unseaworthiness but to improper stowage. If the fitness or unfitness of the ship is to be ascertained at the time of loading, there can be no doubt about the matter. At the moment when the palm oil was loaded, the Grelwen was unquestionably fit to receive and carry it. She was a well-built and well-found ship, and lacked no equipment necessary for the carriage of palm oil; and, if damage arose, it was due to the fact that after the casks of oil had been stowed in the holds the master placed upon them a weight which no casks could be expected to bear. Whether he could have stowed the cargo in a different way without endangering the safety of the ship is a matter upon which the evidence is conflicting: but, if that was impossible, he could have refused to accept some part of the kernels; and the oil would then have travelled safely. No doubt that course might have rendered the voyage less profitable

8 Ibid.
9 Ibid, p. 321.
10 Ibid.

> to the charterers: but that appears to me for present purposes to be immaterial. The important thing is that at the time of loading the palm oil the ship was fit to receive and carry it without injury; and if she did not do so this was due not to any unfitness in the ship or her equipment, but to another cause.

Viscount Cave further concluded:[11]

> There is some authority for the proposition that the implied warranty of "seaworthiness for the cargo" extends to fitness for the cargo not only at the time of loading but also at the time of sailing. But it is unnecessary to pursue the point, for the proposition if established will not avail the present respondents. The evidence of the log is conclusive to show that the injury to the casks was caused at or immediately after the time when the cargo was loaded and before the ship sailed, and accordingly that it was not due to any unseaworthiness at the time of sailing. And in any case nothing occurred between the time when the oil was loaded and the time when the ship sailed to make the ship structurally less fit to carry the oil; and it is with reference to the contract cargo, namely, the oil, that the question of fitness must be considered.

Lord Sumner discussed the question of unseaworthiness and said:[12]

> The contract of carriage excepts liability for damage by improper stowage: but, if there was a breach of the implied warranty of seaworthiness, which there is nothing in the contract to limit or to oust, none of the exceptions or limitations contained in the bill of lading avails to prevent the cargo-owner from recovering. Two things must, therefore, be shown, (1) that the ship was unseaworthy in the sense of the word established by the decisions, and (2) that the damage complained of was caused thereby and would not have arisen but for that unseaworthiness.

Lord Sumner observed that a ship perfectly fit to carry one cargo may be unfit to carry another and so be unseaworthy in that connection, but a ship does not become unseaworthy merely because her construction or appliances are not foolproof or because she does not carry about the world contrivances for preventing by anticipation the consequences of any want of care or skill of which those in charge of the cargo may be guilty. If a captain, having a perfectly good hold at his disposal, puts cargo into it in the wrong way, or puts more cargo into it than is consistent with the safety of individual packages, the result is not that he makes his ship unseaworthy but that he proves himself to be an incompetent officer. One result of improper stowage is that damage will result thereby, and the cargo will be discharged at its destination more or less injured during the voyage; but such a loss is not caused by unseaworthiness merely because it happens during the voyage. It is the direct result of bad stowage, even though in a different ship that particular error in stowing could not have been committed.

Lord Sumner continued and concluded:[13]

> Accordingly I have thought it right to resist the impulse to take the injured plaintiffs' part and have ventured to examine the facts closely, lest I should arrive at a conclusion that would be seriously inconsistent with the way in which this class of ship is and necessarily must be employed in commerce. Ships built under the Isherwood patents are a numerous and, so far as I know, an accepted type of ship; and, in their freedom from 'tween decks and tween deck beams, they have an advantage for carrying larger cargoes, which is part of their design. I shrink, as Scrutton, LJ, shrank, from saying on this evidence that in the ordinary West African trade such a ship is an unseaworthy ship by reason of her construction and design. If the question had

11 Ibid, per Lord Sumner at p. 327.
12 Ibid, p. 331.
13 Ibid, p. 332.

> not been encumbered with the technicalities and refinements of modern bills of lading, it would not have occurred to anyone acquainted with practical shipping to affirm that this ship was unseaworthy, or to dispute that her cargo was improperly stowed. I could have understood that it might be argued, perhaps paradoxically, that the ship was not reasonably fit to load and carry this oil because she was in charge of a captain and mate who were without experience of such a cargo and knew their business no better than to overload the puncheons till they inevitably collapsed: but the argument which actually has been advanced, is, I think, one which begins and ends with the circumstance that improper stowage is here the subject of an exception, unless the ship was what is called unseaworthy, whereby the loss occurred.

In the judgment of Viscount Finlay, it reads:[14]

> I take it, my Lords, to be quite clear, both in England and Scotland, that, where there is a contract to carry goods in a ship, whether that contract is in the shape of a bill of lading, or any other form, there is a duty on the part of the person who furnishes or supplies that ship, or that ship's room, unless something be stipulated which should prevent it, that the ship shall be fit for its purpose. That is generally expressed by saying that it shall be seaworthy; and I think also in marine contracts, contracts for sea carriage, that is, what is properly called a warranty, not merely that they should do their best to make the ship fit, but that the ship should really he fit. I think, therefore, that it may be fairly said that it is clear that there is such a warranty or such an obligation in the case of a contract to carry on board ship.

As explained by Viscount Finaly, the mere fact that the ship was unseaworthy does not make the shipowner liable unless the loss was caused by the unseaworthiness. Bad stowage does not, in itself, constitute unseaworthiness, but it may be such as to render the vessel unseaworthy. The vessel is considered unseaworthy for this purpose if she has some defect which renders her unsuitable for the reception and carriage of the particular goods in question. For instance, the absence of a bullion room properly equipped for the carriage of bullion makes the vessel unseaworthy for the carriage of bullion, and so the room provided for the carriage of passengers' luggage is unfit for the purpose. Where the vessel is infected from the carriage on a previous voyage of sheep suffering from foot-and-mouth disease, she is unseaworthy for the purpose of the carriage of other sheep. Many other illustrations of the application of the principle are to be found in the books.[15]

Viscount Finlay concluded:[16]

> Seaworthiness, in its proper sense, relates to the condition of the vessel as regards its capacity to perform the voyage with safety to itself and the goods and persons on board. Is the vessel fit to cope with the perils of the seas? The seaworthiness which is in question in the present case is of a totally different nature, and relates to the fitness of the vessel for the reception of particular goods; and the absence of such fitness is described as unseaworthiness. It is unfortunate that for this purpose no more suitable term has been devised, as the use of the term unseaworthiness in this connection is apt to lead to confusion. The term "unseaworthy" is not apt to describe the unfitness of the vessel for the carriage of particular goods. For instance, a vessel which has no strong room for the carriage of bullion is described as unseaworthy for the purposes of bullion, and a vessel which has carried sheep suffering from foot and mouth disease without being disinfected at the close of that voyage is described as unseaworthy for the carriage of another cargo of sheep. The expression is at once awkward and misleading. The unseaworthiness alleged in the present case is the absence of a tween deck.

14 Ibid, per Viscount Finaly at p. 322.

15 Ibid, p. 322.

16 See *Voyage Charters*, 4th ed at para. 11.32.

Thus, where bad stowage affects only the cargo and leaves the vessel otherwise seaworthy, it does not necessarily render the vessel unseaworthy. But presumably, the result would have been different if the shift in cargo and the flow of oil had adversely affected the vessel's stability, causing her to capsize. The result would likewise have been different if the vessel had been a tweendecker and a corroded tween deck had collapsed, though not if the collapse was due to simple overloading.

4.2 Overloaded

In *AE Reed & Co Ltd v Page, Son and East*,[17] the plaintiffs were the consignees of 500 t of wood pulp which arrived at Erith on the *Borgholm*. They employed the defendants to lighter it to Nine Elms. One of the defendants' barges, *Jellicoe*, had a carrying capacity of 170 t; 190 t were put on board. While she was lying alongside the steamer, waiting for a tug to tow her to Nine Elms, she sank and her cargo was lost. The plaintiffs succeeded in an action for damages. The defendants appealed.

Scrutton LJ discussed the warranty of seaworthiness, saying:[18]

> There is some confusion in the authorities as to the warranty of seaworthiness, due, I think, to two causes: firstly, the word "seaworthiness" is used in two senses: (1) fitness of the ship to enter on the contemplated adventure of navigation, and (2) fitness of the ship to receive the contemplated cargo, as a carrying receptacle. A ship may be unfit to carry the contemplated cargo, because, for instance, she has not sufficient means of ventilation, and yet be quite fit to make the contemplated voyage, as a ship. Secondly, the fact that there are these two meanings of seaworthiness, and that there may be different stages of seaworthiness according to different stages of the adventure, has led to some confusion in statements. As the Court of Queen's Bench said in *Cohn v. Davidson*, 2 Q.B.D. 455, at p. 461:
>
> > "Seaworthiness is well understood to mean that measure of fitness which the particular voyage or particular stage of the voyage requires."

Scrutton LJ observed[19] that a ship, when she sails on her voyage, must be seaworthy for that voyage, that is, fit to encounter the ordinary perils that a ship would encounter on such a voyage. But she need not be fit for the voyage before it commences and when she is loading in port. It is enough if, before she sails, she has completed her equipment and repair. But she must be fit as a ship for the ordinary peril of lying afloat in harbour, waiting to sail. She must, in my view, be fit as a ship, as distinguished from a carrying warehouse, at each stage of her contract adventure, which may, as in *Cohn v Davidson*, commence before loading. And she may, as a ship, after loading, be unfit to navigate because of her stowage, which renders her unsafe as a ship. The case of *Kopitoff v Wilson*, 1 QBD 377, is a good example of this: there, armour plates were so stowed that there was danger of their going through the ship's side, and they did. As Lord Sumner says (in *Elder Dempste*'s case, 18 Ll.L. Rep.319, at p. 332):

> Bad stowage which endangers the safety of the ship may amount to unseaworthiness, of course: but bad stowage which affects nothing but the cargo damaged by it is bad stowage and nothing more, and still leaves the ship seaworthy for the adventure, even though the adventure be the carrying of that cargo.

17 *AE Reed & Co Ltd v Page, Son and East* [1927] 27 Ll.L. Rep.114 (C.A.).

18 Ibid, per Scrutton LJ at p. 119.

19 Ibid.

Looked at from the point of view of a ship sailing the sea, the highest measure of liability will be when she starts on her sea voyage, and this is often spoken of as the stage when the warranty attaches; but what is meant is that it is the time when that highest measure of liability attaches. There are previous stages of seaworthiness as a ship applicable to proceeding to the loading port, loading, and waiting to sail when loading is completed. On the other hand, the highest measure of liability as a cargo-carrying adventure, that is, of "cargoworthiness," is when cargo is commenced to be loaded. It has been decided that if at this stage the ship is fit to receive her contract cargo, it is immaterial that when she sails on her voyage, though fit as a ship to sail, she is unfit by reason of stowage to carry her cargo safely.[20]

It was argued that the doctrine of stages was only a question of difference of equipment, and that overloading was not equipment. But damages unrepaired at the commencement of a new stage, collision during loading, and starting on the voyage with that damage unrepaired may obviously be unseaworthiness at the commencement of the voyage stage. Scrutton LJ found no reason for defining stages only by difference of equipment.[21]

It is clear that the vesel was quite unfit to lie in the river for any time, exposed to the wash of passing vessels and the natural "send" of the water. It is still clearer that she was quite unfit to be towed, and that she was in such a condition that she would soon go to the bottom. The barge was unseaworthy as a barge from the time loading finished, unfit to lie in the river, and still more unfit to be towed. In the present case, when the loading was finished and the man in charge, apparently in the ordinary course of his business, left her unattended in the river, waiting for a tug, and unfit, in fact, either to lie in the river or be towed, there was a new stage of the adventure, a new warranty of fitness for that stage, and a breach of that warranty which prevented the exceptions from applying.[22]

The Court of Appeal held that at the commencement of a stage, this vessel was, and was rightly found to be, unseaworthy. As was said by Lord Sumner in the House of Lords in the case of *Atlantic Shipping & Trading Co. v Louis Dreyfus & Co.*,[23] per Lord Sumner at p. 708:

> Underlying the whole contract of affreightment there is an implied condition upon the operation of the usual exceptions from liability, namely, that the shipowners shall have provided a seaworthy ship. If they have, the exceptions apply and relieve them; if they have not, and damage results in consequence of the unseaworthiness, the exceptions are construed as not being applicable for the shipowners' protection in such a case.

4.3 Faulty stowage and reinsurance

In the *Hyannis*,[24] the plaintiffs, of New York, claimed, as original insurers, to be reimbursed by defendants, as reinsurers, in respect of a loss under a policy of insurance issued by plaintiffs upon 300 cases of gunpowder shipped on board the American steamship *Hyannis*, on a voyage from a United States Atlantic port to La Plata. Plaintiffs claimed as for a total loss from jettisoning while the ship was at Barbados, they having paid the original assured

20 Ibid.
21 Ibid.
22 Ibid, p. 120.
23 *Atlantic Shipping & Trading Co. v Louis Dreyfus & Co.* [1922] 10 Ll.L. Rep.707.
24 *The Hyannis* [1927] 28 Ll.L. Rep.243.

on that basis on 13 October 1921. The amount claimed from the first-named defendants was £1034 17s. 11d., and from the Atlantic Company, £517 8s. 11d. The defendants denied liability and set up various defences, including unseaworthiness and the restraint of princes.

Bateson J, in giving judgment, said:[25]

> It is a claim by original underwriters, the plaintiffs, against reinsurers, the defendants, for reimbursement of a claim paid by them, the original underwriters, to their assured. Before the plaintiffs can succeed there must be a liability on the original policy for payment. Here there is no liability because the ship was unseaworthy.

Discussing the reinsurance policy, Bateson J observed that it is quite clear that that is a reinsurance policy covering the original insurers against their liabilities. It is also clear that on the original policy, if the owner of goods lost the goods, the original underwriter could avoid payment if, in fact, the ship was unseaworthy.[26]

Bateson J continued and said:[27]

> Now those being the facts, I have no doubt that the ship was so loaded and stowed with such a cargo as to affect her as a ship and that she was unfit to perform the voyage when the cargo in question was put on board her. So far as the stowage was bad, it endangered the safety of the ship. So far as the cargo shipped was unfit for carriage, that is, the acid, it also endangered the ship; and, as I understand the law, if the stowage is such as to endanger the safety of the ship as a ship, the vessel is unseaworthy. *Elder, Dempster & Co., Ltd. v. Paterson, Zochonis & Co., Ltd.*, [1924] A.C. 522, 18 Ll.L.Rep.319; *Ingram & Royle, Ltd. v. Services Maritimes du Tréport*, [1913] 1 K.B. 538, are really not very much more than decisions following the old case of *Kopitoff v. Wilson and Others*, 1 Q.B.D. 377, and the facts of this case bring the case within those decisions. I think a wooden hip loaded with sulphuric acid which can escape and destroy metal pumps, her injections and other parts of her machinery, and destroy the oakum in the seams so that she cannot perform her voyage in ordinary weather, is unseaworthy.

Bateson J adopted the approach in *Ingram & Royal, Ltd. v Services Maritimes du Tréport* [1913] 1 K.B. 538, where at p. 543 the remarks of Scrutton J might almost be read as the observations on the facts in this case. There is no ground for cutting down the meaning of the words in a policy; "seaworthiness" is the same whether it is in a policy or in a contract of carriage. He referred to a passage in Lord Sumner's judgment in the case of *Becker, Gray & Co. v London Assurance Corporation* [1918] A.C. 101, at p. 114:

> Again, it is important that the same words should mean the same thing when used in a mercantile contract, whether that contract be of one description or another. Perils of the seas do not mean one thing in a bill of lading and something else in a policy; restraints of princes do not bear a different interpretation in the one or in the other.

Bateson J found that one might quite fairly go on to say that *seaworthiness* does not mean anything different in one case or in the other. As I understand it, a contract of reinsurance is a contract to indemnify against liability and a payment. There must be both liability and payment, and the precise liability must be covered in each case. Clause 8, seaworthiness admitted, does not prevent the reinsurer from saying that the original underwriter suffered no loss for which he could be made responsible; he had a complete

25 Ibid, per Bateson J at p. 247.
26 Ibid.
27 Ibid, p. 250.

defence against the assured, the defence of unseaworthiness, and there was no necessity to plead unseaworthiness in this case.[28]

Reading the two clauses together, Bateson J observed that those clauses mean this: "If you are liable I will indemnify you; if you have to pay on unseaworthiness under this policy I will have to pay too."

As noted in this case, the original underwriter was not liable at all, and if he was not liable, there is nothing for which he can claim over. The contract for reinsurance is on goods limited to the liability of the original underwriter. The reinsurer's liability is limited to the original insurer's liability under the original policy. It is only a different way of saying the same thing. Another way of putting it is to say that the contract of reinsurance properly understood is a contract to indemnify against losses which the original underwriter has suffered, but not against gifts. This was a voluntary payment so far as the original underwriter is concerned, and he did not insure himself for gifts that he might choose to make to his assured. The contract is expressed to be a reinsurance on the same term as the original policy to indemnify against liability for goods lost, not an insurance of the goods.[29]

4.4 Failure tarpaulin

In the *Hector*,[30] shipment was made at Brisbane and Melbourne of 4,400 cartons of tinned meat in no. 2 hold of the defendants' vessel for delivery to plaintiffs at Glasgow (via Fremantle). Tarpaulins stripped from hatch covers of no. 2 hold by heavy sea shipped during the voyage to Fremantle, seawater entering the hold.

Plaintiffs alleged that the defendants failed in breach of their duty to provide a seaworthy ship and failed to exercise due diligence before or at the beginning of the voyage to make her seaworthy, in that the no. 2 weather deck hatch was not securely battened down and/or the tarpaulins covering the same were inadequate and/or improperly secured, thereby permitting the entry of seawater into no. 2 hold, in which plaintiffs' goods were stowed.

They alleged that if the tarpaulins covering the hatch had been adequate and properly secured, they could not have been stripped or rolled off by a heavy sea, as alleged by the defendants. They also alleged that the tarpaulins were improperly secured in that they were not held in place by locking bars, as they ought to have been, and also in that (a) the wedges or some of them used in the cleats in the hatch coamings were not, at the material time, securely or tightly driven home, and in that (b) no lashings or nets were used over the tarpaulins and secured to the eyebolts provided around the hatch coamings so as further to secure the tarpaulins and prevent any displacement thereof. Plaintiffs further alleged that defendants failed in their duty properly and carefully to carry, keep, and care for their goods, in that although defendants knew or ought to have known that the goods or some of them had been immersed in seawater on the voyage between Melbourne and Fremantle, they took no or no adequate steps to inspect or restow the goods or in any way to protect them from the effects of such immersion.[31]

28 Ibid, p. 251.
29 Ibid.
30 *The Hector* [1955] 2 Lloyd's Rep.218.
31 Ibid, p. 220.

Defendants denied liability, contending that any damage sustained by the goods in transit was caused by perils of the sea within the meaning of article IV (2) I of the Schedule to the Sea-Carriage of Goods Act, 1924, namely, a sea taken over the port bow of the *Hector* at about 6:15 a.m. on 15 August 1953, and by following waves which swept over the no. 2 hatch, or by another cause within the meaning of article IV (2) (q). Defendants further denied that the vessel was unseaworthy or that they had failed to use due diligence before or at the beginning of the voyage to render her seaworthy, and they further said that if the tarpaulins were not properly secured at any time, that did not constitute unseaworthiness but was negligence by the master and mariners in the management of the ship, and that they were protected by article IV (2) (a). Defendants also said that they did not fail in their duty properly and carefully to carry, keep, and care for the plaintiffs' goods. There was no reasonable possibility of re-stowage before arrival at Fremantle, and at Fremantle, all reasonable steps were taken to obtain and follow the advice of an expert surveyor.[32]

McNair J commented on seamanship:[33]

> If I had been satisfied that good seamanship required that locking bars should in all circumstances be fitted when a ship leaves port for the open sea, I should without doubt have held that in the case of a ship manned by officers who had no intention of shipping them because they misunderstood their function, it would be wrong to say that the fact that in other hands they could be fitted at short notice meant that the failure to fit them before sailing did not amount to failure to exercise due diligence to make the ship seaworthy; but it is, I think, clear that good seamanship only requires them to be fitted on leaving port if there is a real indication of anticipated heavy weather and that the decision when to fit them must ordinarily be left to the discretion of the master or other officers in charge.

McNair J discussed the weather forecast and said:[34]

> Though the Australian Bight has a bad reputation, the voyage to Fremantle traverses a part of the Australian Bight which was just within the permanent summer zone under the Load Line Rules. I therefore hold that there was no lack of due diligence in this respect. I venture, however, to make the comment that owners who refrain from giving their masters adequate instructions as to the use of locking bars, the provision of which is required both by Lloyd's Register and the Load Line Rules, knowing that their officers regard them primarily, if not wholly, as anti-pilferage devices, may find themselves in difficulties if disaster occurs through failure to use this method of protection. But I express no final opinion upon this matter, because I have not heard the owners' explanation of their policy.

McNair J discussed the diligence and found that:[35]

> Having regard to the evidence also given by the chief officer that the wedges even if firmly driven in may work loose in heavy weather, I am not prepared to hold that the subsequent loosening of the wedges, which I shall examine later, compels me to disregard the direct evidence of fact given by the carpenter, who impressed me as a witness of truth. I accordingly hold that there was no failure to exercise due diligence to make the ship seaworthy on or before leaving Melbourne.

32 Ibid.
33 Ibid, per McNair J at p. 230.
34 Ibid, p. 231.
35 Ibid.

McNair J continued and added:[36]

> I cannot see how by any possibility this quantity of water could have entered the hold through the interstices in, or gaps between, the slab covers in the short time which elapsed before the water cleared from the weather deck through the freeing ports. I am accordingly driven to the conclusion, and so find, that the stripping of the tarpaulins and the resultant entry of sea water must have been a gradual process extending over some hours, probably starting with the worsening of the weather at or before midnight and continuing through the hours of darkness.

The master, representing the shipowner, has the duty of taking reasonable care of the goods entrusted to him, by doing what is necessary to preserve them on board the ship during the ordinary incidents of the voyage, for example, by ventilation, pumping, or other proper means. He has also the duty of taking reasonable measures, though necessitating expense, to prevent or check the loss or deterioration of the goods even by reason of accidents for the necessary consequences of which the shipowner is, by reason of the bill of lading, under no original liability, and the shipowner will be liable for any neglect of such duty by the master.

McNair J concluded:[37]

> I can see no difference in principle between the shipowner's obligation under Art. III, r. 1, and that under Art. III, r. 2. As a matter of law, therefore, I would hold that the defendants would be liable if the surveyor gave negligently wrong advice. A fortiori the shipowners would be liable if the advice was the result of incorrect or inadequate information given to the surveyor by the ship's officers, or if the action taken (which for this point of law must be assumed to be negligent) was the joint act of the ship's officers and the surveyor.

In conclusion, the court held that there was no breach by defendants of their duty under article III, rule 1, to provide a seaworthy ship on or before leaving Melbourne (although the main purpose of locking bars was to provide security for the hatches at sea in heavy weather, the weather experienced at the time of sailing did not then require that they should be fitted or that other precautions should be taken); that the weather experienced on the voyage to Fremantle was such as to require added precautions to be taken to secure the hatches (such as by the use of locking bars, etc.); and that the defendants, in failing to take such steps, were in breach of their duty of care of cargo under article III, rule 2; but that that failure to do so was negligence in the management of the ship and was excused by article IV, rule 2 (a).[38]

The court further held that a shipowner's duty of care of cargo under article III, rule 2 (as was his duty to provide a seaworthy ship under article III, rule 1) was non-delegable and that the defendants were liable if they acted on what turned out to be wrong advice given by their surveyor (a fortiori would they be liable where, as here, that advice was in part based on incorrect information supplied by the ship's officers and the negligent action taken was the joint action of the surveyor and the ship's officers), and that, accordingly, the defendants were liable for the increased damage caused by the on-carriage from Fremantle.[39]

It is clear beyond doubt that Lloyd's Register and those responsible for the Load Line Rules regard locking bars or their equivalent as part of the necessary defences of a ship against the entry of *sea*water in heavy weather.

---

36 Ibid, p. 233.
37 Ibid, p. 236.
38 Ibid, p. 219.
39 Ibid.

4.5 List lost stability

In the *Friso*,[40] on 10 November 1972, the defendants' *Friso* sailed from Leixões in Portugal with the plaintiffs' cargo of 349 packages of Portuguese pinewood and 3,000 cartons of wine, for carriage to Watchet in the UK.

The cargo was shipped pursuant to a contract of carriage evidenced by bills of lading which were incorporated in the Hague Rules. Cargo which weighed 170 t and comprised of softwood boards or slats of varying sizes secured by steel bands in rectangular bundles was stowed on deck in a shape described as prismatoid, since the varying size of the bundles made it impossible to produce a solid block stow as recommended by IMCO. On 12 November, during the course of her voyage, *Friso* encountered heavy weather, with the result that she was pitching and rolling heavily. At about 1630, when the master attempted to turn the ship's bows to port and heave to in the wind, the ship suddenly fell over and developed a list which was not more than 40–45°. The master thought the ship would not survive and, fearing for the safety of his crew, gave the order to abandon the ship. The whole crew took to an inflatable raft, from which they were rescued and landed at Lisbon. On 13 November, *Friso* was sighted by the ship *Cornelia B I*. Three men were put on board *Friso* to make fast a towing hawser. The cargo lashings were cut, and the majority of the deck cargo was jettisoned to reduce the list. *Friso* was then towed to Brest, where she was joined by her master. On 19 November, *Friso* sailed from Brest to complete her voyage to Watchet. On discharge, it was found that no water had entered the holds, that the stow in the forward end of the no. 1 hold had been disturbed, and that some of the deck cargo was in a saturated condition, samples of which were found to have a moisture content of 50 per cent.

The plaintiffs claimed in respect of the loss of and damage to their cargo, contending that the loss or damage did not result from loss by perils of the sea and the defendants were not entitled to the protection of article 4 of the Hague Rules, in that the defendants were in breach of article 3, rule 1, since they had failed to exercise due diligence to make the ship seaworthy before and at the beginning of the voyage.[41]

The defendants, however, argued that the explanation of the list which developed in *Friso* was (1) that there was an asymmetrical increase in weight of the deck cargo due to water absorption being greater on the port side than on the starboard side and (2) a small shift to the port of the deck cargo.[42]

Sheen J, in giving judgment, said:

> At the time when *Friso* took a list to port the weather was bad, but it was not unusually bad. It was just the sort of weather which any mariner would expect to encounter in the Bay of Biscay during the month of November. In truth the real cause of the damage and loss suffered by the cargo-owners was not the weather but the fact that *Friso* took an unusually heavy list to port.

Sheen J observed that if the vessel was seaworthy when she left Leixões, she ought to have been able to cross the Bay of Biscay in the prevailing weather conditions without taking a severe list to port. Sheen J accepted that a deck cargo of timber would increase in weight due to wetting in bad weather, but just how much of an increase to allow for cannot be clearly defined.

---

40 *The Friso* [1980] 1 Lloyd's Rep.469.

41 Ibid.

42 Ibid, p. 470.

Sheen J continued:[43]

> The defendants have not satisfied me that the additional weight of water absorbed by the cargo can have been distributed asymmetrically to an extent which could have made other than a marginal difference. The defendants have not sought to establish any other cause of the list, or to show that anything else occurred during the voyage which would explain it. It follows that at the beginning of the voyage *Friso* was not fit in condition or equipment to encounter the ordinary perils of the voyage. There is no absolute standard by which her stability characteristics can be judged. The recommendations of I.M.C.O. are a useful guide. But the defendants face this dilemma. On the one hand, if *Friso* had adequate stability when she sailed, then the heavy list could only have been produced by a very large shift of cargo, and such a shift of cargo could only have occurred if the cargo was so inadequately lashed as to endanger the ship. On the other hand, if the list was produced by a small shift of cargo, then *Friso* must have had inadequate stability. There is no escape from this dilemma. Whichever is the correct solution, *Friso* was not seaworthy on sailing.

As explained, Sheen J concluded:[44]

> *Friso* was not seaworthy at the beginning of the voyage. If that unseaworthiness was solely due to the manner in which the cargo was lashed, with the result that it was able to shift substantially, it must follow that the failure to lash the cargo was a failure to exercise due diligence to make the ship seaworthy. If, on the other hand, as I have found to be more probable, *Friso* was unseaworthy because she lacked adequate stability, that also was by reason of a failure to exercise due diligence to make her seaworthy.

As noted in this case, the defendants had failed to show that the additional weight of water absorbed by the cargo could have been distributed asymmetrically to an extent which could have made other than a marginal difference, and the defendants had not sought to establish any other cause of the list or to show that anything else occurred during the voyage which would explain it and, therefore, at the beginning of the voyage vessel was not fit in condition or equipment to encounter the ordinary perils of the sea. The only explanation for why the vessel had taken a substantial list to port was that her double-bottom tanks were slack, and on the balance of probabilities, this was the most likely explanation for her inadequate stability.[45]

4.6 Improper stowage

In the *Panaghia Tinnou*,[46] on 4 July 1974, the respondents, the disponent owners of the vessel *Panaghia Tinnou*, entered into a voyage charterparty with the applicant charterers for the carriage of a cargo of oil cakes in bags from India to Poland. A cargo of bagged oil cakes required to be stowed with particular care because of the propensity of such cargo to self-heating.

The cargo was loaded and stowed at Bedi Bunder by stevedores appointed by or on behalf of the charterers. The cargo was stowed in a manner which was wholly improper for its safe carriage in that (a) no or no adequate ventilation channels were built into the stow, (b) the cargo was not adequately insulated from contact with steel surfaces, (c) the cargo was not adequately protected from condensation, and (d) the cargo was not adequately

43 Ibid, p. 474.
44 Ibid, p. 476.
45 Ibid, p. 474.
46 *The Panaghia Tinnou* [1986] 2 Lloyd's Rep.586.

insulated from a heat-producing surface, that is, the engine room bulkhead in hold 4. The cargo suffered damage by condensation, heating, and spontaneous combustion during the course of the voyage, and the owners failed to prosecute the voyage with reasonable despatch so that the voyage was prolonged by 33.5 days. The cargo was discharged in Gdynia in October/November 1974.

The charterers sought to recover their loss in respect of the damaged cargo, and the dispute was referred to arbitration. The arbitrator concluded that the charterers were only entitled to nominal damages, but stated his award in the form of a special case, the question of law for the decision of the court being (a) whether the charterers or the owners were obliged to ensure that the cargo was properly stowed and (b) whether the unjustified prolongation of the voyage for 33.5 days entitled the charterers to recover damages (i) for all the cargo found damaged, (ii) for none of such cargo, or (iii) only for such of the cargo so damaged as a result of the said prolongation.[47]

Steyn J, in giving judgment, commented on improper stowage:[48]

> The first question raises a simple point which is covered by high authority. It is trite law that, at common law, the responsibility for stowing the goods rests on the owners. Both under the Hague Rules and the Hague Visby Rules, as respectively enacted in this country in 1924 and 1971, the owners and the charterers were free to determine what part, if any, either shall play in the stowage of the cargo: *Pyrene Co. Ltd. v. Scindia Navigation Co. Ltd.*,[1954] 1 Lloyd's Rep.321; *Renton (G.H.) & Co. Ltd. v. Palmyra Trading Corporation of Panama*, [1956] 2 Lloyd's Rep.379. That is a liberty of which the parties availed themselves in the present case. Clause 18(c) unambiguously provides that "the Charterers shall load and stow the cargo". It was pointed out on behalf of the charterers that this provision appears under the heading "Costs". That cannot, however, by itself negative or qualify the obligation undertaken in terms of cl. 18(c).

Turn to the question whether clause 18(c) has been qualified in any relevant sense by other provisions of the charterparty. The provision in clause 4 that owners are to supply dunnage to charterers' satisfaction is irrelevant since there is no finding that adequate dunnage had not been supplied. Steyn J took an example which is to be found in *Ismail v Polish Ocean Lines*. In that case, the following typewritten clause was added:

> Dunnaging and stowage instructions given by the charterers to be carefully followed, but to be executed under the supervision of the master *and he is to remain responsible for proper stowage and dunnaging*.

Steyn J observed that as confusing as this clause undoubtedly is, it nevertheless represents an attempted qualification of clause 18(c). No such wording is to be found in the present charterparty. Steyn J concluded that the charterers' obligation to stow was not qualified in any sense relevant to the issues in this case.[49]

Canadian Transport Co. Ltd. v Court Line Ltd[50] is directly in point. In that case the relevant words of the New York Produce Exchange charterparty were:

> The charterers are to load, stow and trim the cargo at their expense under the supervision of the Captain.

47 Ibid, p. 587.
48 Ibid, per Steyn J at p. 589.
49 *Ismail v Polish Ocean Lines* [1976] 1 Lloyd's Rep.489.
50 *Canadian Transport Co. Ltd. v Court Line Ltd.* [1940] 67 Ll.L. Rep.161 (H.L.).

In that case, Lord Atkin stated:[51]

> The supervision of the stowage by the captain is in any case a matter of course; he has in any event to protect his ship from being made unseaworthy and in other respects no doubt he has the right to interfere if he considers that the proposed stowage is likely to impose a liability upon his owners. If it could be proved by the charterers that the bad stowage was caused only by the captain's orders, and that their own proposed stowage would have caused no damage no doubt that might enable them to escape liability. But the reservation of the right of the captain to supervise, a right which in my opinion would have existed even if not expressly reserved, has no effect whatever in relieving the charterers of their primary duty to stow safely.

Lord Wright said:[52]

> But under clause 8 of this charter-party the charterers are to load, stow and trim the cargo at their expense. I think these words necessarily import that the charterers take into their hands the business of loading and stowing the cargo. It must follow that they not only relieve the ship of the duty of loading and stowing, but as between themselves and the shipowners relieve them of liability for bad stowage, except as qualified by the words "under the supervision of the captain", which I shall discuss later. The charterers are granted by the shipowners the right of performing a duty which properly attaches to the shipowners. Presumably this is for convenience of the charterers. If the latter do not perform properly the duty of stowing the cargo, the shipowners will be subject to a liability to the bill of lading holders. Justice requires that the charterers should indemnify the shipowners against that liability on the same principle that a similar right of indemnity arises when one person does an act and thereby incurs liability at the indemnity arises when one person does an act and thereby incurs liability at the request of another, who is then held liable to indemnify. . . . The master is responsible for the seaworthiness of the ship and also for ensuring that the cargo will not be so loaded as to be subject to damage, by absence of dunnage and separation, by being placed near to other goods or to parts of the ship which are liable to cause damage, or in other ways. . . . It follows that to the extent that the master exercises supervision and limits the charterers' control of the stowage, the charterers' liability will be limited in a corresponding degree.

Lord Porter, giving the speech, said:[53]

> Speaking for myself, however, I am in agreement with what I understand to be not only his view in that case but also the view of all the tribunals which in the present case have had to consider the meaning of the charter-party. In my opinion by their contract the charterers have undertaken to load, stow and trim the cargo, and that expression necessarily means that they will stow with due care. Prima facie such an obligation imposes upon them the liability for damage due to improper stowage. It is true that the stowage is contracted to be effected under the supervision of the captain, but this phrase does not, as I think, make the captain, primarily liable for the work of the charterers' stevedores. It may indeed be that in certain cases, as, e.g., where the stability of the ship is concerned the master would be responsible for unseaworthiness of the ship and the stevedore would not. But in such cases I think that any liability which could be established would be due to the fact that the master would be expected to know what method of stowage would affect his ship's stability and what would not, whereas the stevedores would not possess any such knowledge. It might also be that if it were proved that the master had exercised his rights of supervision and intervened in the stowage, again the responsibility would be his and not the charterers. The primary duty of stowage, however, is imposed upon the charterers and if they desire to escape from this obligation they must, I think, obtain a finding which imposes the liability upon the captain and not upon them.

51 Ibid, per Lord Atkin at p. 166.
52 Ibid, per Lord Wright at p. 168.
53 *Government of Ceylon v Chandris* [1965] 2 Lloyd's Rep.204.

Steyn J commented on the aforementioned authorities and held that there are accordingly no findings of fact which could give rise to a duty, owed by the master to the charterers, to intervene.

Turning to the question of burden of proof, in *Government of Ceylon v Chandris*, Mocatta J summarized the counsels' propositions as follows:[54]

> First, the general rule is that the burden of proof rests upon the party claiming relief, be he plaintiff in an action or claimant in an arbitration, and this applies both to the liability of the other party and the damages recoverable. Secondly, in a claim for damages for breach of contract of carriage by sea, once it is proved that the goods in question were shipped in good condition (as is the case here) and that a known quantity of those goods is proved to have been delivered damaged, the carrier is liable to pay damages measured by the difference between the sound and damaged value of the goods at the date and place of delivery unless the carrier can establish, and the burden is on him to do so, that the goods were damaged through the operation of an exception in the contract of carriage. Thirdly, and this is a qualification upon the second proposition, if the carrier can only show that some part of the damage to the goods was due to a cause within the exception, he must also show how much of the damage is comprised in that part, otherwise he is liable for the whole. Fourthly, if part of the damage is shown to be due to a breach of contract by the claimants, then the general rule stated in the first proposition applies, and the claimant must show how much of the damage was caused otherwise than by his breach of contract, failing which he can recover nominal damages only.

In *A/S. Rendal v Arcos Ltd*,[55] Lord Wright spoke for all Their Lordships. He said:[56]

> In my opinion under these circumstances all the ice damage without distinction (except for trifling damage sustained on her inward journey), is properly attributable to the breach of contract, since so far as appears it was all caused while the breach was operating, as it necessarily operated from the time when the delay commenced. I apply here the Judge's finding in the similar case of The Oddvar, that "the vessel would have had quite a good passage for a winter passage if she had been got out and helped in the earlier part of January."

Later in his judgment, he explains the reasoning behind his conclusion. Lord Wright said:[57]

> The principle thus applies whenever the breach of contract has the consequence of exposing the subject matter to conditions of risks different from those which would have operated if the contract had not been broken. The thing exposed to the risks in this case was a ship, which it is true was in the possession and control of the shipowner. The charter-party exposed the ship necessarily to certain sea perils including perils of ice, but the respondents' breach of the obligation to furnish reasonably the means necessary for the ship to pass through the ice, needlessly increased the hazards, so that in such a case when damage ensues after such a breach, the onus of proof is shifted. The defendant must show (if he can) that there must have been the same damage if the contract had not been broken.

Considering the aforementioned authorities, Steyn J concluded:[58]

> It was not established that any but nominal damages was attributable to the owners' breach in failing to prosecute the voyage with reasonable despatch and it was not right to equate an argument based on inevitability of loss with loss caused by the charterers' own breach in failing

54 Ibid, per Mocatta J at p. 216.
55 *A/S. Rendal v Arcos Ltd.* [1937] 58 Ll.L. Rep.287 (H.L.).
56 Ibid, per Lord Wright at p. 297.
57 Ibid, p. 298.
58 *The Panaghia Tinnou*, sup. at p. 593.

to ensure that the cargo was properly stowed; the arbitrator had correctly directed himself as to the legal burden of proof.

The absolute duty at common law to provide a seaworthy ship is displaced by article III, rule 1 of the rules, which requires the carrier to exercise due diligence to provide a seaworthy ship "before and at the beginning of the voyage." This is an "overriding obligation."[59]

For the question of burden of proof, as Cresswell J summarized in the *Eurasian Dream*:[60]

(1) The burden of proof is on the claimants to prove that the vessel was unseaworthy, pursuant to article III, rule 1, before and at the beginning of the voyage.
(2) The claimants must then also prove that the loss or damage was caused by that unseaworthiness.[61]
(3) If the claimants discharge the burden in respect of (1) and (2), the burden passes to the defendants to prove that they and those for whom they are responsible exercised due diligence to make the ship seaworthy in the relevant respects.[62]
    (a) If they fail to do so, the defendants are not entitled to rely upon the exceptions in article IV, rule 2, including the "fire" exception.
    (b) If the defendants are able to do so, they can rely upon the "fire" exception as a defence to breach of article III, rule 2, subject to the claimants proving that the loss or damage was "caused by the actual fault or privity of the carrier."[63]
(4) In relation to due diligence, proof of unseaworthiness fulfils the same function as *res ipsa loquitur* does in ordinary cases of negligence.[64]

4.7 Bad stow and list

In the *Lilburn*,[65] the vessel was chartered for a voyage from Soroka to Garston in September 1935, with timber cargo. She proceeded towards Garston until 18 September, when she put into Stornoway to take more bunker coal. When she had taken some 16 t, she heeled over, and to prevent her sinking, she was beached. In consequence, a good deal of her cargo was lost and some of it was damaged, and the shipowners brought their claim. The insurance company denied liability and counterclaimed, alleging short delivery by damage and loss when the vessel's list increased at Stornoway while she was taking in bunkers. The insurance company contended that if the vessel was unseaworthy, the guarantee did not hold, and they alleged that the vessel was unseaworthy by reason of her excessive deck cargo, a 5° list which was bound to increase in leaving Soroka, and insufficient tarpaulins.

The question raised by the appeal was whether appellants could recover general average contribution and whether they were liable for damages in circumstances where the loss

59 *Maxine Footwear Co. Ltd. v Canadian Government Merchant Marine* [1959] 2 Lloyd's Rep.105.
60 *The Eurasian Dream* [2002] 1 Lloyd's Rep.719, per Cresswell J at p. 735.
61 *The Europa* [1908] at pp. 84, 97–98.
62 *The Toledo* [1995] 1 Lloyd's Rep.40 at p. 50.
63 *The Apostolis* [1996] 1 Lloyd's Rep.475 at p. 483; *Scrutton on Charterparties and Bills of Ladng*, 24th ed at para. 1–092.
64 *The Amstelslot* [1963] 2 Lloyd's Rep.223 at p. 235, per Lord Devlin; *The Fjord Wind* [2000] 2 Lloyd's Rep.191 at p. 205.
65 *The Lilburn* [1939] 64 Ll.L. Rep.87 (C.A.); [1940] 67 Ll.L. Rep.253 (H.L.).

and expense and damage arising on the voyage was, as alleged by respondents, due to the unseaworthy condition of the ship.[66]

It was held by Mackinnon LJ and the Court of Appeal that:[67]

> I think the cause of the disaster at Stornoway was quite clearly due to the unstable condition of the ship, the unstable condition in which she had sailed from Soroka, which, so far from ever being remedied, had naturally got worse by the inevitable incidents of the voyage and the using up of her bunkers; and all that can be said about the master is that it was perhaps his act or, possibly, his default in not doing something to prevent the disaster, but, none the less, if he had been ideally wise and as skilled as Dr. Telfer, he might have prevented the disaster by something he did, or by doing something he did differently. I think the cause of the disaster was the instability of the ship-that condition in respect of which she had been unseaworthy from the beginning.

Mackinnon LJ discussed another test of unseaworthiness, saying:[68]

> This ship was unseaworthy in another respect when she sailed from Soroka bound for Garston. In order to be seaworthy she ought to have been supplied with sufficient bunker coals to take her to Garston – and there was no evidence that it had been arranged that the voyage should be carried on in stages for the purpose of bunkering her. As a matter of fact, she left Soroka with only 154 tons of bunkers on board, although to get to Garston she would need at least 182 tons and, therefore, would want a reasonable margin beyond the 154 tons she had on board. If the captain had not put into Stornoway and had carried on in order to get to some port in Scotland, and had found he had used up his bunkers and had had to burn his cargo, and the shipowner claimed that the burning of cargo was a general average sacrifice and the cargo-owners claimed for the loss of their cargo by reason of its being burned, could it then be said that the destruction of the cargo by burning it was not due to the fact that the ship had been in an unseaworthy condition, having insufficient bunkers on board, but was due to the act or neglect of the captain in not putting into Stornoway, as he could have done, to get further supplies? I think it would be impossible to say that the burning of the cargo would be the consequence of the fact that she left Soroka unseaworthy, having insufficient bunkers.

Mackinnon LJ concluded:[69]

> I would add that the shipowners are bound under this charter-party to use due diligence to provide a seaworthy ship, and if they fail to do so they ought not to be encouraged to say: "The master was making the best of a bad job, and must do his best with an unseaworthy ship, and if he does not make the best of a bad job and does not use this unseaworthy ship with such a degree of skill and with such care that we come out of it as well as if she was a seaworthy ship, then we are to be excused." I do not think that is the right construction of this exceptions clause, and I agree with my Lord in saying that this appeal must be allowed.

It was held by Lord Wright and the House of Lord, saying:[70]

> From the nature of the contract, the relevant cause of the loss is held to be the unseaworthiness or the negligence as the case may be, not the peril of the sea, where both the breach of the fundamental obligation and the objective peril are co-operating causes. The contractual exception of perils of the seas does not affect the fundamental obligation, unless the contract qualifies the latter in express terms.

---

66 Ibid, [1940] 67 Ll.L. Rep.253 (H.L.) at p. 254.
67 Ibid, per Mackinnon LJ [1939] 64 Ll.L. Rep.87 (C.A.) at p. 92.
68 Ibid.
69 Ibid, per Mackinnon LJ at p. 94.
70 Ibid, per Lord Wright [1940] 67 Ll.L. Rep.253 (H.L.) at p. 258.

To consider these rules in relation to unseaworthiness, Lord Wright found that:[71]

> I think the contract may be expressed to be that the shipowner will be liable for any loss in which those other causes covered by exceptions co-operate, if unseaworthiness is a cause, or, if it is preferred, a real, or effective, or actual cause. The law is, I think, correctly stated by the late Judge Carver in Carriage of Goods by Sea, Sect. 17. I quote from the Fourth edition, published in 1905, which was the last edition revised by the learned author. The words of the section are:
>
> > "And further, the shipowner remains responsible for loss or damage to the goods, however caused, if the ship was not in a seaworthy condition when she commenced her voyage, and if the loss would not have arisen but for that unseaworthiness. . . . If her unfitness becomes a real cause of loss or damage to the cargo, the shipowner is responsible, although other causes from whose effects he is excused, either at common law or by express contract, have contributed to produce the loss."

Lord Wright observed that the author relied for that proposition not only on *Kopitoff v Wilson*, cited by MacKinnon LJ, but also on the *Glenfruin*, 10 P.D. 103, and *Steel v State Line*, 3 App. Cas.72. In truth, unseaworthiness, which may assume according to the circumstances an almost-infinite variety, can never be the sole cause of the loss.

Lord Wright continued:[72]

> There is precise authority for this in the judgment of the Court of Appeal delivered by that great authority on mercantile law, Scrutton, L.J., with the concurrence of Bankes and Atkin, L.JJ., in the *Christel Vinnen*, (1924) 19 Ll.L.Rep.272. Cargo in that case was damaged by leakage through a leaky rivet; the damage might have been checked but for the negligence of the master in not detecting the water in the hold and pumping it out. It was held that the shipowners were responsible for the whole of the damage, not merely for such proportion as must have been incurred before the inflow of water could have been checked. No distinction was drawn between damage due to perils of the seas alone and that due to perils of the seas and to negligence combined.

Lord Wright concluded:[73]

> This is clearly so in the facts of this case. The acts of the master in bunkering as he did, and in pumping out the forepeak, whether negligent or not, were indeed more proximate in time to the disaster, and may be said to have contributed to the disaster, but the disaster would not have arisen but for the unseaworthiness, and hence the shipowners are liable.

Lord Porter added:[74]

> In such circumstances it is unnecessary to decide what would be the result if the loss were attributable partly to the coaling and partly to the unseaworthiness, or to determine whether the fact that the unseaworthiness was a substantial cause, even though some other matter relied upon were a substantial cause also, would be enough to make the owners liable for failure to use due care to make the vessel seaworthy.

The House of Lords held that she was unseaworthy on sailing because of her stow and that that unseaworthiness, not the miscalculation, was the cause of the loss. Bad stowage that endangers the safety of the ship and cannot readily be cured on the voyage is unseaworthiness. Even the best-found, best-equipped ship can be rendered unseaworthy if she is so loaded or stowed that she is, or will become, unstable during the voyage, for

71 Ibid.
72 Ibid, per Lord Wright at p. 259.
73 Ibid, p. 260.
74 Ibid, per Lord Porter at p. 262.

example, through the consumption of bunkers or the handling of cargo. If cargo, whilst properly stowed, is not properly lashed and, in consequence, shifts so as to undermine the vessel's stability, the vessel will be unseaworthy at the outset. So also, if cargo is properly stowed and lashed but is an obstruction to part of the vessel's appliances which affects the proper working of it as a part of the vessel, she is unseaworthy.[75]

4.8 Ventilation/apples

Wet damage, as the name suggests, is damage to cargo due to water and wet conditions. Wet damage could be related to moisture, condensation, rain, seawater ingress into cargo holds. Bulker vessels are required to have a system in place that will give a warning of water ingress as per the SOLAS convention. The purpose of a water ingress detection system is to provide an early warning of a condition that may seriously threaten the safety on board. Especially grain cargo damage claim relating to the ventilation system. This situation can arise when allowing the ambient air into a cargo space which can be injurious to the cargo. If the humidity of the air outside of the cargo space is higher than the humidity of the air inside, ventilation will worsen the conditions inside the holds.

However, a vessel is not necessarily unseaworthy just because some cargo damage is inevitable on the voyage. The test is often expressed as follows: Would a prudent owner have required that the defect should be made good before sending his ship to sea, had he known of it? Seaworthiness must be judged by the standards and practices of the trade in question, at least so long as those standards and practices are otherwise reasonable.[76]

In the *Northumberland*,[77] the plaintiffs, as consignees of a large number of apples, claimed damages from the defendants, the owners of the steamship *Northumberland*, in which the apples had been carried in the spring of 1921 from Hobart, Tasmania, to London and Liverpool. The complaint was that whereas the apples had been shipped in good order and condition, they arrived, to use the language of the points of claim, "decaying and/or rotten." The apples formed part only of a much larger quantity carried by the *Northumberland*. The total number of cases carried was 150,000; the number involved in the present action is 15,272 cases. The apples were carried under bills of lading which contained all the usual exceptions and which, if they could be relied upon by the defendants, would relieve them from any responsibility for the damage which is complained of.

In the judgment of Bankes LJ in the Court of Appeal, he said:[78]

> In my opinion the charge of unseaworthiness also fails. The defendants no doubt undertook that the Northumberland should be reasonably fit for the carriage of apples, but if she was fitted with sufficient means for providing the necessary amount of ventilation in the holds and spaces in which the apples were carried, she did not become unseaworthy because those means were not used. The holds had ventilating shafts and also had thermometer tubes, and if either or both had been kept open, or opened occasionally, sufficient ventilation would have been provided. This appears to have been accepted by the scientists, and the fact that these means of ventilation were kept carefully closed, may or may not have been due to an error of judgment:

75 See *Voyage Charters*, 4th ed at para. 11.31.
76 Ibid, para. 11.19.
77 *The Northumberland* [1926] 24 Ll.L. Rep.446 (C.A.); [1927] 27 Ll.L. Rep.395 (H.L.).
78 Ibid, per Bankes LJ [1926] 24 Ll.L. Rep.446 (C.A.) at p. 448.

> but it does not, in my opinion, constitute unseaworthiness of the ship. So much, therefore, of the case of the plaintiffs as depended upon negligence and upon unseaworthiness failed and, I think, rightly failed.

Scrutton LJ discussed the question of seaworthiness, saying:[79]

> There remains the general law as to unseaworthiness and inherent quality of the goods. Sect. 8 (1) of the Act imposes on the shipowner an absolute warranty of seaworthiness at the commencement of the voyage, which in the case of carriage of goods in a refrigerated hold includes fitness of the refrigerated holds to carry the cargo. The law is I think correctly stated by the late Mr. Carver in the passage approved by Channell, J., in *McFadden v. Blue Star Line*, [1905] 1 K.B. 697:
>
> > "The ship must have that degree of fitness which an ordinary careful owner would require his vessel to have at the commencement of her voyage having regard to all the probable circumstances of it. Would a prudent owner have required that it should be made good before sending his ship to sea, had he known of it?"

Scrutton LJ concluded:[80]

> I respectfully agree with these views. The vessel is to be reasonably fit. It certainly need not have fittings or instruments which had not at the time been invented, because by subsequent inquiry a danger has been discovered which these fittings and instruments when invented might avert. While the shipowner may be bound to add improvements in fittings where the improvement has become well known or the discovery of danger established, the position is quite different where at the time of the voyage the discovery had not been made or the danger discovered. It is not enough in my view to say, "we have now after the event discovered that there was a danger to which the cargo was exposed, the nature of which was unknown at the time; and, the danger being known, we have thought of a remedy, which was not common knowledge at the time, and which a prudent owner would not be imprudent in neglecting, having regard to the existing state of knowledge." Further, it is well established that a ship is not unseaworthy because of a defect, at the beginning of the voyage, which can easily in the ordinary course of management be rectified on the voyage.

The decision of the Court of Appeal, that bad stowage which does not endanger the safety of the ship is not unseaworthiness, is shown by the case of *Bond v Federal Steam Navigation Co.*, 22 T.L.R. 685, as explained and approved by the House of Lords in *Elder, Dempster*'s case, sup. The case of a latent defect is something that, if known, would be known to be dangerous and would be remedied by a prudent owner. But there are other cases where the facts, if known, would not be considered by a prudent owner, in the existing state of knowledge, dangerous, and also where, if the danger were known, the existing appliances on the ship could be used to remedy it, even if more suitable appliances were, after the danger was known, inserted. In such a case, the ship would be seaworthy, though subsequent knowledge would have required different use of the existing appliances and even of more suitable appliances.[81]

Viscount Sumner, who delivered the judgment, said:

> In the law of carriage by sea neither seaworthiness nor due diligence is absolute. Both are relative, among other things, to the state of knowledge and the standards prevailing at the material time. The words "properly equipped" in the Commonwealth Act also, in my opinion, import no absolute propriety, whatever that may be, but must be read as being relative only.

79 Ibid, per Scrutton LJ at p. 454.
80 Ibid.
81 Ibid, p. 455.

> For seaworthiness, the material time is the date of sailing; for due care, the period of the voyage. There was, to say the least of it, no real reason at the time to condemn or to decry the unscreened grid arrangement adopted on the Northumberland, or the exclusion of ventilation, and it is only against these that any attack is made. They were in general and successful use. The other arrangements and systems were not markedly superior, if at all, and the damage now in question was virtually unknown under both. Nor could the ship be said to have been sent to sea in an unseaworthy condition, on the ground that the stoppage of ventilation could not be undone in case of need – if, for example, damage was found to be extending in the cargo – for, if ventilation was required, the ship had very ready means of admitting air when necessary, by opening hatches and so forth; and to the extent to which, according to the knowledge of the time, this might be requisite, the officers were free and able to do so. They were not sent to sea fettered by inviolable orders never to alter the ventilation system at all, but they were instructed in what was believed to be the better system, and in general they kept the holds sealed. Accordingly, they could not be negligent in acting, like their masters, according to one of the accepted views of the time. In fact, during the voyage they were unaware that any damage was in progress.

Viscount Sumner observed that when, in addition to this, proof is given of a mode of carriage well known and in general use which would have prevented the inherent quality of the apples in the widest sense of the term from resulting in damage at all, that damage cannot be shown to have resulted without liability to the ship even though seaworthiness and care be proved.[82]

Viscount Sumner concluded:[83]

> My Lords, I am not able to assent to this contention. It appears to raise the old controversies about *causa causans* and *causa sine qua non* and to force into undue prominence the words "resulting from." I think it may be answered in either of two ways. Branson, J., argued thus. The evidence has eliminated the operation of an excessive concentration of carbon dioxide, to which the disease of "brown heart" was ascribed. If the apples did not die a natural death some other failing must have caused it, and as they are not said to have been otherwise ill-treated on board ship that failing must have been at least latent before shipment. The negation of the one establishes the other. It appears to me that this was a legitimate train of reasoning and your Lordships are not called upon to dissent from it. The similarity of the appearances in the case of "brown heart" and of "breakdown," and the common knowledge of mankind that apples are but perishable things, afford material for saying that the damage was caused ashore and might well have arisen there without its having been possible to prove when it arose or where or how.

As noted in this case, it's not disputed that neither does a defect that can be quickly remedied at sea necessarily make the ship unseaworthy,[84] or defects that are capable of being quickly remedied on the passage do not render a ship unseaworthy,[85] or where a particular matter can be put right quickly and easily at sea, the ship need not be unseaworthy in sailing without its having been rectified.[86]

Bailhache J dealt with this in *Moore and Another v Lunn and Others*:[87]

> The lashings were put in place so that they could be applied after leaving Baltimore, because the chains or ropes were placed underneath the logs, so it would not be necessary to shift the logs. But the cargo was not lashed. It is quite clear that, if a vessel is to be seaworthy for an

---

82 Ibid, p. 399.

83 Ibid, p. 400.

84 *Scrutton on Charterparties and Bills of Lading*, 24th ed at para. 7–025.

85 *Carver on Charterparties*, 2nd ed at para. 3–122.

86 *Carver on Bills of Lading*, 4th ed at para. 9–015.

87 *Moore and Another v Lunn and Others* [1922] 11 Ll.L. Rep.86 at p. 91.

> ocean voyage, and particularly for a North Atlantic voyage in the winter, it is essential that a deck cargo of logs should be securely lashed. If they are not, they are not only a danger to the life and limbs of the sailors, but to the structure of the ship. They may get loose and carry away ventilators and things of that sort. A vessel which has not got these logs securely lashed is not seaworthy for an ocean voyage.

So also Lord Blackburn in *Steel Al. v the State Line Steamship Company*,[88] at pp. 90–91:

> I think, on the other hand, if this port had been, as a port in the cabin or some other place would often be, open, and when they were sailing out under the lee of the shore remaining open, but quite capable of being shut at a moment's notice as soon as the sea became in the least degree rough, and in case a regular storm came on capable of being closed with a dead light – in such a case as that no one could, with any prospect of success, ask any reasonable people, whether they were a jury or Judges, to say that that made the vessel unfit to encounter the perils of the voyage, because that thing could be set right in a few minutes, and there is always some warning before a storm comes on, so that they would have plenty of time to put it all right, and it would have been put right. If they did not put it right after such a warning, that would be negligence on the part of the crew, and not unseaworthiness of the ship. But between these two extremes, which seem to me to be self-evident cases as to what they would be, there may be a great deal of difficulty in ascertaining how it was here.

4.9 Ventilation/potatoes

It's settled law that the shipowner is not liable for loss of or damage to the goods caused by their "inherent vice." By inherent vice meant is the unfitness of the goods to withstand the ordinary incidents of the voyage, given the degree of care which the shipowner is required by the contract to exercise in relation to the goods. Thus, a tendency of the goods to heat, discolour, rot, or evaporate, or to destroy their packing, or the inherent restiveness or phrensy of an animal, or defective packing, may all constitute inherent vice. It may be that the exception does not apply to the extent that the damage has been aggravated by the shipowners' unjustifiable deviation. Where the inherent vice has rendered the ship unseaworthy, the court will consider whether the loss was caused by the state of the ship or the state of the cargo.[89]

The shipowner may rely on the exception even if he knew of the inherent vice although his knowledge may affect the degree of care required of him. A shipowner who asserts that loss or damage was caused by inherent vice bears not only the burden of demonstrating that the cargo suffered from an inherent vice but also that this caused the loss in question. The shipowner, therefore, bears the legal burden of disproving negligence on his part, because if he cannot do so, he cannot show that the cause of the loss was the inherent vice.[90]

In the *Westerdok*,[91] the plaintiffs, MDC Ltd., who are the shippers in Malta of the potatoes with which this case is concerned, bring this action against the owners of a small motor vessel called the *Westerdok* to recover damages for breach of the contract contained in a bill of lading issued by the defendants to the plaintiffs bearing the date 30 May 1959. By this bill of lading, the defendants acknowledged having received on board their vessel

88 *Steel Al. v the State Line Steamship Company* (1877–78) L.R. 3 App. Cas.72.
89 *Scrutton on Charterparties and Bills of Lading*, 24th ed at para. 11–055.
90 Ibid, para. 11–056.
91 *The Westerdok* [1962] 1 Lloyd's Rep.180.

22,000 half-bags of Malta spring potatoes for delivery at Liverpool in the same good order and condition. That bill of lading incorporated the Carriage of Goods by Sea Act of Malta, 1954, with the rules scheduled to that act which are identical to the rules contained in the English Carriage of Goods by Sea Act, 1924. In this action, the plaintiffs claim the sum of £815 11s., which they allege is the loss they have suffered by reason of the fact that the defendants, in breach of their contract and duty, delivered the potatoes so heavily wasted that the plaintiffs suffered the damage alleged. The plaintiffs relied upon the breach by the defendants of rule 2 of article III of the schedule, which requires the shipowners properly and carefully to load and stow, carry, keep, care for, and discharge the goods, and in the alternative in the pleading, as originally delivered, they alleged that the damage was caused by negligence and the nature of the negligence relied on was the failure of the defendants, their servants, or their agents as carriers to take reasonable care for the safety of the goods. As the case developed, that allegation was developed as an allegation of faulty stowage.[92]

As explained by McNair J in this case, there was not any substantial damage to the potatoes themselves, but there were signs of condensation damage on the bags by way of staining the bags and producing a condition in which they disintegrated through rotting, but the condensation which had fallen upon the bags had not gone on long enough to produce any serious damage to the potatoes themselves. The condensation, of course, occurs when the atmospheric conditions inside the hold have reached a dew point, so that the moisture contained in the atmosphere, probably supplemented by some moisture given off by the potatoes themselves, descends in the form of water either onto the cargo below or may run down the ship's sides. If in the tween decks, it would then be taken by the scuppers from the tween decks down into the bilges. It is clear that the condensation on the deck beams cannot have penetrated through the whole of the cargo, because much of the cargo was sound throughout and undamaged.[93]

McNair J continued:[94]

> In my judgment the much more likely cause of the apparent damage in the lower tiers of the cargo was the fact that this particular class of cargo can get damaged by stevedores necessarily standing upon the cargo in the course of their operations, so that you get a considerable body of handling damage without negligence on anybody's part. Indeed, it has been generally agreed that you may have handling damage up to two per cent. of a perfectly good sound cargo properly stowed, properly carried, properly ventilated and properly discharged. It seems to me that the damage in the lower hold must primarily have been of that character.

The law, as McNair J observed in this case, is this: that it is quite clear from the evidence that there is inevitably a certain degree of damage in the sense of staining damage, and possible disintegration of bags from moisture in this trade, however well the cargo may be stowed and however well it may be ventilated, and that customarily that amount of damage is accepted by receivers without complaint, it being recognized that a cargo of this nature carried on small ships of this kind cannot be expected to arrive in identically the same condition as when shipped.[95]

---

92 Ibid, p. 182.
93 Ibid, per McNair J at p. 184.
94 Ibid.
95 Ibid, p. 185.

In this case, the shipowner who knew that these cargoes inevitably suffered minor damage by way of condensation staining or wasting of a few bags would not have hesitated to send this vessel to sea, although he knew she might run into weather necessitating the closing of hatches for longer periods than usual; that, although weather was worse than normal, it was not abnormal; and that, therefore, the cargo owners had failed to prove that the vessel was unseaworthy or that shipowners had failed to exercise due diligence to make the vessel seaworthy.

As McNair J observed, the test in a case of this kind, of course, is not absolute: you do not test it by absolute perfection or by an absolute guarantee of successful carriage. It has to be looked at realistically, and the most common test is: Would a prudent shipowner, if he had known of the defect, have sent the ship to sea in that condition?

4.10 Condensation/burden of proof

Article IV, rule 1 of the Hague and Hague–Visby Rules lays down a specific burden of proof in relation to claims falling under article III, rule 1 of the rules. The same is not, however, true of article III, rule 2, which is also concerned with the standard of performance expected from the carrier but does not deal with the burden of proof. Until recently, the normal common-law burden of proof favoured by the English courts was as outlined by the Court of Appeal in the *Glendarroch*. However, an alternative bailment explanation, that the carrier must disprove its own fault or neglect or that of its servants, has now come to the fore.[96]

Further, the principle that the custodian of goods had a legal responsibility to justify their loss or redelivery in a damaged condition was common to both common-law and civil jurisdictions. It was also incoherent for the law to impose a burden on the carrier for the purposes of article IV, but on the cargo owner for the purposes of article III, rule 2. On that basis, the legal burden was on the carrier to show either that the damage occurred without fault in the various respects covered by article III, rule 2, or that it was caused by an excepted peril. If the carrier was able to show that the loss or damage to the cargo occurred without a breach of the carrier's duty of care under article III, rule 2, it would not need to rely on an exception.[97]

The *Volcafe v Compania*[98] case is important to the question of the burden of proof. In this leading case, six claimants were the owners and bill of lading holders for nine separate consignments of bagged Colombian green coffee beans shipped at Buenaventura in Colombia between 14 January and 6 April 2012 on various vessels owned by the defendant shipowners for carriage to Bremen. They were stowed in a total of 20 unventilated 20 ft containers. These were transhipped at Balboa in Panama and discharged at Rotterdam, Hamburg, or Bremerhaven for on-carriage to Bremen. Each consignment was covered by a bill of lading covering the entire carriage to Bremen. When the containers were opened at Bremen, however, the bags in 18 of them were found to have suffered water damage from condensation.

96 *Carver on Charterparties*, 2nd ed at para. 5–066.

97 Ibid.

98 *Volcafe Ltd and Others v Compania Sud Amerciana De Vapores SA* [2019] 1 Lloyd's Rep.21; [2018] UKSC 61.

The cargo owners pleaded their case in what has, for many years, been standard form. Their primary case was that in breach of their duties as bailees, the carriers failed to deliver the cargoes in the same good order and condition as that recorded on the bill of lading on shipment. Alternatively, they pleaded that in breach of article III, rule 2 of the Hague Rules, they had failed properly and carefully to load, handle, stow, carry, keep, care for, and discharge the cargoes.

The case was tried by David Donaldson QC, sitting as a deputy High Court judge. He held that there was no legal burden on the carrier to prove that the damage to the cargo was caused without negligence or by an excepted peril. There was only a factual presumption that damage ascertained on discharge was due to negligence.

The Court of Appeal allowed the carrier's appeal, holding that where the carrier set up a case within a relevant exception, the legal burden was on the cargo owners to establish that the exception did not apply because of the carrier's negligence and that the cargo owners had failed to discharge that burden. The cargo owners appealed to the Supreme Court. The principal issue of law was, On whom was the burden of proving whether the cargoes were damaged by (i) negligent preparation of the containers or (ii) inherent vice?[99]

Lord Sumption JSC, delivering the judgment in the Supreme Court, said:[100]

> The burden of proof arises on this appeal at two stages of the analysis. The first is concerned with article III.2. Does the cargo owner bear the legal burden of proving breach of that article, or is it for the carrier, once loss or damage to the cargo has been ascertained, to prove compliance? The second relates to article IV.2, and particularly to an exception (m). The carrier accepts that he must bear the burden of proving facts which bring the case within an exception, but submits that once he has done so it is for the cargo-owner to prove that it was the negligence of the carrier which caused the excepted peril (in this case, inherent vice) to operate on the cargo.

Article III.2 imposes on the carrier a general duty to take reasonable care of the cargo during carriage. Lord Supmtion considered that, in principle, where the cargo was shipped in apparent good order and condition but is discharged damaged, the carrier bears the burden of proving that that was not due to its breach of the obligation in article III.2 to take reasonable care.[101]

In relation to article IV, rule 2(m), Lord Sumption pointed out that the leading modern case is the *Maltasian* [1966] 2 Lloyd's Rep.53 (H.L.). It is authority for the proposition that the standard of care by reference to which the exception for inherent vice is to be assessed may depend on the nature of the service contracted for. The issue was whether a cargo of fish was capable of withstanding carriage in unrefrigerated spaces, that being the service stipulated in that case. The ratio can conveniently be taken from the speech of Lord Reid, at p 23:

> Article IV, rule 2(m), provides that the carrier shall not be responsible for damage arising from "inherent defect, quality, or vice of the goods." . . . "This cargo was not damaged by reason of the shipowner committing a breach of contract, or omitting to do something which he ought to have done, but it was deteriorated in condition by its own want of power to bear the ordinary transit in a ship." By "the ordinary transit" I would understand the kind of

99 Ibid, [2019] 1 Lloyd's Rep.21 at p. 22.
100 Ibid, per Lord Sumption JSC at p. 27 [13].
101 Ibid, p. 28 [20].

> transit that the contract requires the carrier to afford. I agree with the Lord President when he says: "rule 2(m) is in my opinion intended to give effect to the well-settled rule in our law that if an article is unfitted owing to some inherent defect or vice for the voyage which is provided for in the contract, then the carrier may escape liability when damage results from the activation of that inherent vice during the voyage." It follows that whether there is an inherent defect or vice must depend on the kind of transit required by the contract. If this contract had required refrigeration there would have been no inherent vice. But as it did not, there was inherent vice because the goods could not stand the treatment which the contract authorised or required.

The effect of these statements, and others to the same effect, are accurately summarised in *Scrutton on Charterparties and Bills of Lading* 24th ed, paragraphs 11–55:

> By "inherent vice" is meant the unfitness of the goods to withstand the ordinary incidents of the voyage, given the degree of care which the shipowner is required by the contract to exercise in relation to the goods.

Lord Sumption stated:[102]

> It follows that if the carrier could and should have taken precautions which would have prevented some inherent characteristic of the cargo from resulting in damage, that characteristic is not an inherent vice. Accordingly, in order to be able to rely on the exception for inherent vice, the carrier must show either that he took reasonable care of the cargo but the damage occurred nonetheless; or else that whatever reasonable steps might have been taken to protect the cargo from damage would have failed in the face of its inherent propensities.

Lord Sumption concluded:[103]

> I would hold that the carrier had the legal burden of proving that he took due care to protect the goods from damage, including due care to protect the cargo from damage arising from inherent characteristics such as its hygroscopic character. I would reinstate the deputy judge's conclusions about the practice of the trade in the lining of unventilated containers for the carriage of bagged coffee and the absence of evidence that the containers were dressed with more than one layer of lining paper. In the absence of evidence about the weight of the paper employed, it must follow that the carrier has failed to prove that the containers were properly dressed.

In this case, Lord Sumption held that nothing in the Hague Rules changed the status of a contract of carriage by sea as a species of bailment for reward on terms. Therefore, where the cargo was shipped in apparently good condition but was discharged damaged, the burden of proof was on the carrier to show that it did not breach its obligation in article III.2 to take reasonable care.[104]

So also, as Hobhouse J pointed out in the *Torenia*:[105]

> The relationship between the present parties is contractual. It follows that the question of legal burden of proof has ultimately to be decided by construing the contract between them. In ascertaining the effect of the contract one must take into account the nature of the contract. The contract here is a contract in a bill of lading; it is a contract of carriage – that is to say, a species of a contract of bailment.

102 Ibid, per Lord Sumption JSC at pp. 33, 37.

103 Ibid, pp. 34, 43.

104 Ibid, pp. 28, 19.

105 *The Torenia* [1983] 2 Lloyd's Rep.210, per Hobhouse J at p. 216.

4.11 Improper lashing

Cargo is loaded onto a ship when she is floating steadily in the water, upright, or with a practical trim astern. When the ship sails out to sea, it encounters external forces which result in six forms of motions acting on the ship. These motions are a threat, especially for those ships which require cargo lashing and securing it on the open deck. Improper cargo lashing and failure to adhere to the procedures required for cargo stowage on ships is dangerous to property, life, and the environment at sea.

The SOLAS 1974 convention, as it is known commonly in the related circles, specifies standards for the construction, equipment, and operation of merchant ships. The provisions included in the SOLAS include the survey of ships and their certification and the control of ships while at the ports of other governments. Each member nation is responsible for following these standards and ensuring the safety and security of its marine vessels. Chapters VI and VII of this convention are all about the carriage of cargo. It specifies the requirements for stowage and securing almost all types of cargo and those that require special handling.

> In the *Imvros*,[106] by a charterparty dated 10 July 1995 on the NYPE form, the owners let the vessel to the charterers for one-time charter trip (min. duration 70 days). Under the charter and as instructed by the charterers, the vessel proceeded to the river Para in Brazil and, at four separate berths, loaded a cargo of sawn timber in bundles for carriage to Durban, Kohsichang, and Manila. The timber was loaded both above and below deck. The loading and stowage of the cargo were carried out under the directions of the charterers' supercargo, and the lashing of the cargo was carried out by the crew. The bills of lading were not claused as required.[107]
>
> The lashings were spaced at about 3 m intervals. Such spacings for deck cargoes of the height to which the timber was loaded were in contravention of the IMO Code of Practice for Ships Carrying Timber Deck Cargoes, which required the lashings to be at 1.5 m intervals. In the course of the voyage to Durban, on the evening of 23 August 1995, part of the deck cargo was lost, and the vessel damaged.
>
> https://vlex.co.uk/vid/transocean-liners-reederei-g-793137021

The dispute between the parties was referred to arbitration. The arbitrators found that the cause of the loss of the cargo was insufficiency of lashings, that the vessel was unseaworthy due to the insufficiency of her lashings, and that the charterers had assumed responsibility for securing the cargo. They awarded that the owners' claims succeeded.[108]

The charterers appealed, the issues being (1) the responsibility for safe loading and unseaworthiness between owners and charterers under an NYPE charterparty (the construction issue) and (2) the circumstances in which an owner was entitled to be indemnified in respect of cargo claims (the indemnity issue).

The owners submitted that the terms of the charter made it clear that the responsibility for the proper loading and lashing lay with the charterers and that was so whether or not the consequences of bad loading or lashing were to make the vessel unseaworthy in any sense of the word.[109]

The charterers argued that there was an absolute obligation on the owners who were under an overriding duty to intervene to prevent the vessel from sailing in an unseaworthy

106 *The Imvros* [1999] 1 Lloyd's Rep.848.
107 Ibid, p. 848.
108 Ibid.
109 Ibid.

condition, and so the owners were in breach of the charter and the authors of their own loss. As to indemnity, the issue was whether had the bill of lading been claused as required by clause 62, it would have been effective to exclude the owners' liability to cargo interests for the loss of the timber.

Langley J accepted the owners' submission and said:[110]

> [B]ad stowage which endangers the safety of the ship and crew constitutes unseaworthiness and that in law the responsibility for the seaworthiness of the vessel remains "the overriding responsibility" of the owners in the absence of a clear exclusion clause or a clause which clearly transfers the responsibility to the charterers by reference to the decision of the House of Lords in *Canadian Transport Co. Ltd. v. Court Line Ltd.*, (1940) 67 Ll.L.Rep.161; and in particular the speeches of Lord Atkin at pp. 166–167; Lord Wright at pp. 168–169; and Lord Porter at pp. 172–173; The charter-party there in issue contained a clause substantially in the same terms as cl. 8. The damage to the cargo was caused by improper stowage and there was no reference to unseaworthiness.

Langley J continued:[111]

> The passages relied upon refer to the right of the owners by the captain both to supervise stowage and to intervene if the manner of stowage is likely to impose liability on the owners. The argument that the words "under the supervision of the captain" had the effect of making the captain responsible for stowage or placed the onus on the owners to show that the damage was not due to an omission by the master to exercise proper supervision was rejected, at least unless it was proved that the bad stowage was caused only by the captain's orders or was the result of matters of which the captain was but the charterers were not aware. Insofar as the speeches do refer to unseaworthiness they do so not in terms of that giving rise to any material distinction such as to lead to different result, but only to explain how the master's right to intervene exists in any event and indeed regardless of contract.

The indemnity issue was explained by Langley J saying:[112]

> There is no dispute that the charterers were in breach of cl. 62(a) and (c) in failing to clause the bills of lading in respect of deck cargo with the words carried on deck at Shippers' risk without responsibility for loss or damage however caused.
>
> It follows (and again it is not disputed) that the owners are expressly entitled under cl. 62(b) to an indemnity against any losses, damages or other consequences arising as a result of this breach of the charter-party by the charterers.

In *Ingram & Royle Ltd. v Services Maritimes du Tréport Ltd.* [1913] 1 K.B. 538, it was established that to exclude liability for unseaworthiness, clear and unambiguous terms were needed because of the fundamental nature of the obligation. *The Galileo* [1914] P. 9 is an authority that the words "at shippers risk" alone are not sufficient to exclude liability for unseaworthiness or negligence. The addition of the words required by the present charterparty has been held to be effective to exclude liability for negligence causing the loss of cargo: *The Danah* [1993] 1 Lloyd's Rep.351 and *Travers v Cooper* [1915] 1 K.B. 73. But the charterers submitted, in neither of those cases was it sought to argue that the facts amounted to unseaworthiness or that if they did, the exclusion would not then have been effective.

110 Ibid, per Langley J at p. 851.
111 Ibid, p. 852.
112 Ibid.

For cargo carried on deck, the owners have no responsibility for loss or damage, however caused. The exclusion covers any cause, and there is no justification for excluding unseaworthiness as a cause. The bills of lading incorporated the Hague Rules, and thus, in respect of cargo carried on deck, the parties were free to exclude the carriers' liability under the rules. Mr Crookenden submitted that since the widespread adoption of the Hague Rules, there was no need for the courts to be astute to restrict the usual meaning and extent of words of exclusion where the rules permitted exclusions to be agreed, and particularly so where under the rules the obligation to provide a seaworthy ship is not an absolute one but a due diligence one.

Langley J concluded:[113]

> I, like the arbitrators, prefer and accept Mr. Crookenden's submissions. In my judgment they are supported by the logic of the reasoning of the Courts in *The Danah* and *Travers v. Cooper*, as stated in *Carver's Carriage by Sea* 13th ed., vol. 1, par.201. In my judgment the words are clear and cannot be qualified by in effect adding "but not if the loss is caused by unseaworthiness of the vessel."

In this case, the charter contained no paramount clause, and even if it had, the clause would probably have been construed as having no application to the deck cargo. If the provisions in question had related to under-deck cargo, the issue would have arisen whether a provision which effectively removes from the owner and transfers to the charterer the duty to exercise due diligence about certain aspects of seaworthiness is rendered null and void by article III, rule 8 of the Hague Rules. It is submitted that this is a result that the court would seek to avoid, in the ground that article III, rule 8 does not forbid a division of responsibility which reflects a division of function and performance.[114]

Thus, in the case where inadequate lashing of the deck cargo made the ship unseaworthy, it was held that the owner was not responsible. Langley J, in this case, expressed the view that the effect of the *Ovington Court*[115] was that the owner was not responsible for any lack of proper supervision by the master "at least unless it was proved that the bad stowage was caused only by the captain's orders or was the result of matters of which the captain was but the charterers were not aware." The supervision of the stowage by the captain is, in any case, a matter of course; he has, in any event, to protect his ship from being made unseaworthy, and in other respects, no doubt he has the right to interfere if he considers that the proposed stowage is likely to impose liability upon his owners.

4.12 Howsoever arising or cause

Some deck cargo clauses, such as that in the *Imvros* and the *Danah*, *sup*., use language of such width that it makes it clear that the owner is under no liability even if the loss results from the negligence of those for whom he would otherwise be responsible, and even if the improper stowage of the deck cargo renders the ship unseaworthy, but even such clauses have not always proved effective in all circumstances.[116]

113 Ibid, p. 853.
114 See *Voyage Charters*, 4th ed at para. 14.43–14.44.
115 *The Ovington Court (H.L.)* [1940] 67 Ll.L. Rep.161.
116 See *Voyage Charters*, 4th ed at para. 6.35.

In the *Sunlight*,[117] the appellant cargo owners owned a cargo of timber being carried on the deck of the respondents' vessel from West Africa to Tuticorin, India. During the course of the voyage, there was an explosion in the vessel's main engine crankcase. The vessel was towed to Cape Town, with the intention of carrying out repairs, but in the event, no repairs were carried out there and the vessel was towed from Cape Town to Tuticorin. The shipowners asserted that they had incurred general average expenses totalling US$910,288.78, of which US$746,967.18 was attributable to the cargo under the York–Antwerp Rules, 1974. The shipowners claimed the latter sum from the appellants as a general average contribution or, alternatively, as damages.

The cargo owners submitted that as the shipowners had failed to ensure that the vessel was seaworthy before and at the beginning of the voyage, the question of a contribution for general average expenses did not arise. The shipowners contended that even if the vessel had not been seaworthy at the commencement of the voyage, the bills of lading for the deck cargo contained exceptions that were wide enough to allow them to claim a contribution for general average expenses. The bills of lading provided that the shipowners should not be responsible for loss or damage "howsoever arising" or "howsoever caused."

As for the meaning of the term "fault" in Rule D of the York-Antwerp Rules, the trial judge referred to the *Granhill*, where Mr Justice Pearson explained that "fault" in Rule D refers to an actionable fault. For the purpose of determining whether or not there was an actionable fault in this case, much depended on whether or not the vessel was seaworthy at the commencement of the voyage and on the effect of exceptions in the bills of lading. The trial judge found that the vessel was unseaworthy when she left Port Gentil for her contractual voyage because of defects in her main engine. She also found that the explosion in the main engine was not caused by a latent defect. The breach of the absolute undertaking of seaworthiness by the respondents amounted to an actionable fault that would deprive the respondents of a general average contribution from the appellants unless there was an exception in the contract of carriage that altered the position. After noting that the deck cargo was outside the scope of the Hague–Visby Rules, the trial judge added that the issue before her was one of construction of the exceptions in the bills of lading for the deck cargo.[118]

The trial judge laid great emphasis on the words "howsoever arising" in the first batch of bills of lading, and the words "howsoever caused" in the second batch of bills of lading. Relying on the decision of Mr Justice Langley in the *Imvros* [1999] 1 Lloyd's Rep.848, she held that these words were wide enough to absolve the respondents from liability for unseaworthiness. As such, there was no actionable fault on the part of the respondents and the appellants were obliged to contribute their share of the general average expenses. The appellants, who were dissatisfied with this ruling, appealed against the trial judge's decision.[119]

As explained by Tan Lee Meng J in the Court of Appeal:[120]

> As the contract for the carriage of the appellants' deck cargo is outside the ambit of the Hague–Visby Rules, it ought to be borne in mind that at common law, a shipowner has an absolute

117 *The Sunlight* [2004] 2 Lloyd's Rep.174.
118 *The Granhill* [1957] 2 Lloyd's Rep.207.
119 *The Sunlight*, sup. at p. 176.
120 Ibid.

obligation to send his ship out to sea in a seaworthy state at the commencement of the agreed voyage. In *Atlantic Shipping and Trading Co. Ltd. v. Louis Dreyfus & Co.*, [1922] 2 A.C. 250, 260, Lord Sumner explained the effect of this obligation on exceptions in the contract of carriage by sea in the following succinct terms:

> "Underlying the whole contract of affreightment there is an implied condition upon the operation of the usual exceptions from liability namely that the shipowners shall have provided a seaworthy ship. If they have, the exceptions apply and relieve them; if they have not and damage results in consequence of the unseaworthiness, the exceptions are construed as not being applicable for the shipowner's protection in such a case."

Tan Lee Meng J continued:[121]

> It is well established that an exception that is intended to relieve a shipowner from the consequences of the unseaworthiness of the vessel at the commencement of the voyage must be "express, pertinent and apposite" (per Mr Justice Bigham in *Sleigh v. Tyser*, [1900] 2 Q.B. 333, 337). Innumerable cases have shown how difficult it is to frame an exception that would be applicable in cases of unseaworthiness. In *Steel v. State Line SS Co.*, [1877] 3 A.C. 72, 89, Lord Blackburn gave an indication of what a shipowner might do to escape liability for unseaworthiness when he said as follows:
>
> "The shipowners might have stipulated, if they had pleased. . . . We will take the goods on board, but we shall not be responsible at all, though our ship is ever so unseaworthy; look out for yourselves; if we put them on board a rotten ship, that is your look-out; you shall not have any remedy against us if we do."

In the *Makedonia* [1962] 1 Lloyd's Rep.316, one of the rare cases where an exception was applicable even though the loss was caused by unseaworthiness, the exception in question was almost as exhaustive as that suggested by Lord Blackburn. It is provided as follows:

> The carrier shall not under any circumstances of any kind whatsoever be liable for any loss of or damage or delay thereto, whether or not such loss, damage or delay may be due to the act, neglect or default of the carrier or the master, pilot, officers, crew, stevedores . . . or other person whomsoever for whom the carrier may be responsible, whether in the service of the carrier or not, and whether or not the above-named vessel . . . was unseaworthy at the time of loading or sailing or at any other time.

Reviewing various cases, Tan Lee Meng J observed:[122]

> Apart from the fact that we are presently dealing with the common law obligations of a shipowner and not the Hague Rules, it cannot be overlooked that the case before us concerns the effect of exceptions and not provisions that limit liability. In *The Happy Ranger*, [2002] 2 Lloyd's Rep.357, 364, Lord Justice Tuckey, with whom Lord Justices Rix and Aldous agreed, rightly pointed out that a provision that seeks to limit liability is different in character from an exception. That is why under the Hague and Hague–Visby Rules, the exceptions in art. IV, r. 2 cannot be relied upon where unseaworthiness has caused loss because, as Lord Somervell put it in *Maxine Footwear Co. Ltd. v. Canadian Government Merchant Marine Ltd.*, [1959] A.C. 589, art. III, r. 1 of the Rules, which requires a carrier to exercise due diligence to have the ship made seaworthy before and at the beginning of a voyage, creates an overriding obligation.

121 Ibid.
122 Ibid, p. 178.

Tan Lee Meng J concluded:[123]

> As we held that the exceptions in the bills of lading for the deck cargo in the present case are inapplicable because the vessel was unseaworthy when she commenced on her contractual voyage, it followed that there was an actionable fault on the part of the respondents. In view of this, the question of a contribution from the appellants for general average expenses did not arise. We thus allowed the appeal with costs. As for the costs in the Court below, we decided that the matter should, in the circumstances of the case, be dealt with by the trial Judge.

The Court of Appeal held that the exceptions "howsoever arising" and "howsoever caused" in the bills of lading could not be relied upon by the respondents as they had failed to fulfil their overriding obligation to provide a seaworthy ship at the commencement of the voyage. However, the English court declined to follow the approach adopted in this case, instead confirming that, as a matter of English law, a clause providing that a carrier will not be liable for loss or damage to deck cargo, "howsoever arising," will be effective to exclude liability for the carrier's negligence or its failure to exercise due diligence to make the vessel seaworthy.[124] Clear wording will, of course, ensure that unseaworthiness is covered, and wording directed to causation and covering all losses "howsoever arising," or similar, is effective to cover loss arising from unseaworthiness as it is a loss arising from negligence.[125]

4.13 Deck cargo/howsoever

In the *Elin*,[126] during the voyage, between around 2 and 6 July 2016, the vessel encountered heavy seas and some of the cargo was lost and/or damaged. A part of the cargo which was lost and/or damaged was indisputably carried in the vessel's holds. The damage to this cargo is not relevant for present purposes. There is a dispute as to whether the balance of the cargo which was lost and/or damaged was carried in the vessel's holds or on deck. The owner alleges that the balance of the cargo which was lost and/or damaged was carried on deck. The cargo interests do not admit that this was so. That dispute may need to be determined hereafter. However, for present purposes, the parties have agreed that the court must assume that the balance of the cargo which was lost and/or damaged was, in fact, carried on deck.

The owners submitted that the relevant provisions of the bill of lading were to be interpreted as excluding all liability for the carriage of deck cargo. The phrase "howsoever arising" referred to all causes of loss or damage.

The cargo interests contended that the implied obligation of seaworthiness was a fundamental and overriding obligation, and exclusion clauses did not affect it unless clearly worded. The words relied on by the owners did not specifically refer to liability for unseaworthiness or negligence and should not be interpreted as covering the owners' liability arising from its negligence. They should be given a restricted meaning by excluding

123 Ibid.
124 *The Elin* [2020] 1 Lloyd's Rep.111.
125 See *Carver on Charterparties*, 2nd ed at para. 4–275.
126 *The Elin* [2020] 1 Lloyd's Rep.111.

the owners' arguable strict liability for any loss or damage to the cargo, or by varying the owner's obligation from an absolute obligation to one of due diligence.[127]

Stephen Hofmeyr QC, sitting as a judge of the High Court, commented on the terms of articles I(c) and II of the Hague/Hague–Visby Rules, summarized here:[128]

> At first blush, this conclusion may be thought to be somewhat surprising because it results in the carriage of deck cargo and under-deck cargo being governed by different regimes. Second, and as a consequence of the first, the Owner's obligations in respect of the deck cargo are those found in the terms of the Bill of Lading (including the Charterparty which is assumed to apply for the purposes of the preliminary issue) and terms (if any) implied at common law. Third, at common law, in the absence of any express term to the contrary and subject to the proper construction of the relevant contract.

Stephen Hofmeyr QC commented on deck cargo and said:[129]

> As a general rule, the deck of a ship is not a proper place for the stowage of cargo and a shipowner is therefore not entitled to stow goods on deck. Deck cargo is also in a special category in relation to claims for general average. Further, goods carried on deck and stated to be so carried in the bill of lading are not "goods" within the meaning of the Carriage of Goods by Sea Act 1971, the Hague Rules or the Hague Visby Rules. Perhaps surprisingly, where the bill of lading states that the goods are carried on deck but, in fact, the goods are carried below deck, the Rules apply. Similarly, the Rules apply where the bill of lading is silent as to the location of the goods but, in fact, the goods are carried on deck.

Stephen Hofmeyr QC discussed the question of instruction, saying:[130]

> The correct legal approach to issues of the construction of commercial contracts is not seriously in issue. The Supreme Court (and House of Lords before it) has provided guidance which is now well settled. See *Rainy Sky SA v Kookmin Bank* [2011] 1 WLR 2900 at paragraphs 14–23 (per Lord Clarke of Stone-cum-Ebony); *Arnold v Britton and others* [2015] AC 1619 at paragraphs 14–21 (per Lord Neuberger of Abbotsbury PSC) and *Wood v Capita Insurance Services Ltd* [2017] AC 1173 at paragraphs 8–15 (per Lord Hodge). Clauses limiting or excluding liability are to be interpreted in precisely the same way.

Stephen Hofmeyr QC continued:[131]

> Viewed as a question of the construction of the terms of the Bill of Lading, free from authority and with the above guidance in mind, in my view the Owner is correct in its contention that the words of exclusion are effective to exclude liability for both negligence and unseaworthiness. The words of exclusion are clear. The Owner has no responsibility for cargo carried on deck whatever the cause. It is difficult to conceive of wider words of exemption. The exclusion covers any and every cause and there is no justification for excluding either negligence or unseaworthiness as a cause.

Turning to relevant authorities, first, in *Joseph Travers & Sons, Limited v Cooper*,[132] Lord Justice Phillimore reconciled two existing lines of authority in this way:

> If you say "any loss" you are directing attention to the kinds of losses and not to their cause or origin, and you have not sufficiently made it plain that you mean "any and every loss"

127 Ibid.
128 Ibid, per Stephen Hofmeyr QC at p. 115.
129 Ibid.
130 Ibid, p. 117.
131 Ibid.
132 *Joseph Travers & Sons, Limited v Cooper* [1915] 1 K.B. 73.

> irrespective of the cause, and therefore you have not brought home to the person who is entrusting the goods to you that you are not going to be responsible for your servants on your behalf exercising due care for them or possibly even for your own personal want of care. But if you direct attention to the causes of any loss, if you say "any loss", "howsoever caused" or "under any circumstances", you give sufficient warning, and it is not necessary to say in express terms "whether caused by my servants' negligence" or in the bill of lading phrase, "neglect or default or otherwise."

Second, in the *Danah*,[133] Saville J referred to *Travers v Cooper* and held that so long as it can be shown that had the charterers complied with the clause in their dealings with the shippers, the cargo interests concerned would have been in no better position, the clause is apt to exclude loss of or damage to deck cargo caused by want of care on the part of the owners in and about the carriage of such cargo.

Third, in the *Imvros*,[134] *sup.*, Langley J rejected the charterers' contentions. He concluded that the words were clear. For cargo carried on deck, the owners have no responsibility for loss or damage howsoever caused – whether caused by negligence or by unseaworthiness. In his view, the exclusions cover any cause and there is no justification for excluding unseaworthiness as a cause. The words cannot be qualified in effect by adding "but not if the loss is caused by the unseaworthiness of the vessel." In his view, the logic of the reasoning of the courts in *Travers v Cooper* and the *Danah* also supported his conclusion.

Stephen Hofmeyr QC therefore concluded:[135]

> It will therefore be apparent that, for the reasons stated above, I see nothing in the authorities to justify departing from what in my view is a point of construction on which both as a matter of plain language and good commercial sense the Owner is right. As I have shown, the same or similar words of exclusion have been held to be effective to exclude both liability for negligence causing the loss of cargo (*Travers v Cooper* [1915] 1 K. B. 73 and *The Danah* [1993] 1 Lloyd's Rep.351) and liability for unseaworthiness causing the loss of cargo (*The Imvros*) and the logic of the reasoning in those cases is compelling. Words of exemption which are wider in effect than "howsoever caused" are difficult to imagine and, over the last 100 years, they have become "the classic phrase" whereby to exclude liability for negligence and unseaworthiness.

According to Stephen Hofmeyr QC, it followed that on a true construction of the bill of lading, the owner is not liable for any loss of or damage to any cargo carried on deck, including loss of or damage to any cargo carried on deck caused by the unseaworthiness of the vessel and/or the owner's negligence.

It's clear that under English law, commercial parties are entitled to allocate between them the risks of something going wrong in their contractual relationship in any way they choose. Nor is it simply to be mechanistically applied wherever an ambiguity is identified in an exclusion clause. The court must still use all its tools of linguistic, contextual, purposive, and common-sense analysis to discern what the clause means.[136] The courts have become more accepting of such clauses, recognising (at least in commercial contracts made between parties of equal bargaining power) that exclusion and limitation clauses are an integral part of pricing and risk allocation.[137]

---

133 *The Danah* [1993] 1 Lloyd's Rep.351.

134 *The Imvros* [1999] 1 Lloyd's Rep.848.

135 *The Elin*, per Stephen Hofmeyr QC at p. 123.

136 As Briggs LJ put it in *Nobahar-Cookson v Hut Group Ltd* [2016] EWCA Civ 128 at p. 19. See also *Jackson LJ in Persimmon Homes Ltd v Ove Arup & Partners Ltd.* [2017] EWCA Civ 373 at p. 57.

137 *Interactive E-Solutions JLT v O3B Africa Ltd.* [2018] EWCA Civ 62, per Lewison LJ at p. 14.

CHAPTER 5

Fire

5.1 Introduction

There are reported cases in the past year. The MSC *Flaminia* is a German container ship which caught fire on 14 July 2012, forcing the crew to abandon ship in the middle of the Atlantic Ocean. After the fire had been brought under control, the stricken container ship was towed to Europe and arrived at Wilhelmshaven, Germany, on 9 September 2012. Then there was the explosion on board the *Hanjin Pennsylvania* while it was sailing between Singapore and Suez. The vessel was 88 mi south of Sri Lanka. The fire was under control on 25 November 2002. The vessel was towed to Singapore, where she arrived on 4 January 2003. The *Sanchi* oil tanker collision occurred on 6 January 2018 when the Panamanian-flagged, Iranian-owned tanker *Sanchi*, with a full natural gas condensate cargo, sailing from Iran to South Korea, collided with the Hong Kong–flagged cargo ship CF *Crystal* 160 nmi off Shanghai, China. *Sanchi* caught fire shortly after the collision; after burning and drifting for over a week, it sank on 14 January. None of *Sanchi*'s 32 crew members survived.

On 6 March 2018, *Maersk Honam*, one of Maersk's ultra-large containerships, caught fire in the Arabian Sea while en route from Singapore to Egypt.

In the early hours of 3 January 2019, a fire broke out in a container stowed on the deck of the *Yantian Express* above hold 2 while she was underway in the North Atlantic. With winds of force 8–9, cold temperatures, and rain, the conditions on deck were challenging for the firefighting team. The roll-o, -roll-off car carrier *Felicity Ace*, transporting luxury vehicles from Germany to Rhode Island, caught fire. The fire spread, requiring the crew to abandon ship, while crossing the Atlantic Ocean and lost stability and sank on 1 March, after attempts to be towed to safety.

There are numerous disputes arising from the carriage of Indonesian coal, and many issues relating to B/L and/or charterparties, such as cargo damage, laytime calculation, and off-hire. Since China unofficially banned Australian coal, Indonesia's coal exports rose sharply with shipments to China. As we are aware, most of those cargoes were loading at anchorage via barges, and many shippers are shipping coal without good practice, including misdeclaring the cargo as not being prone to self-heating, or providing no details of the self-heating or methane-emitting characteristics of the cargo. As a potentially hazardous bulk cargo, it is essential that coal is always loaded, carried, and discharged in accordance with the requirements of the International Maritime Solid Bulk Cargoes (IMSBC) Code. The IMSBC Code contains a detailed schedule for the carriage of coal and provides information on the associated hazards, such as asphyxiation and exposure of crew members to toxic gases, as well as the precautions which need to be taken when carrying coal.

DOI: 10.4324/9781003279938-5

Fire is potentially one of the greatest threats to ships at sea and is feared by crews. Vessels catching fire will cause cargo damage and time loss, and these risks and responsibilities as between receivers, owners, and charterers, can be avoided or mitigated or not by incorporating well-drafted clauses into B/L and charterparties.

Under charterparties issue, common-law authority for the possibility of a carrier obtaining a right of redress where it suffers damages as a result of complying with the express request, or order, of a charterer or another party is found in cases like *Dugdalge and Others v Lovering*, where it was held that:[1]

> It is a general principle of law when an act is done by one person at the request of another which act is not in itself manifestly tortuous to the knowledge of the person doing it, and such acts turn out to be injurious to the right of a third party, the person doing it is entitled to an indemnity from him who requested him that it should be done.

It has long been recognised that, if owners are to place their vessel and crew at the disposal of the charterer, it is entirely reasonable to seek protection against the adverse consequences of compliance with the charterers' orders by stipulating for an indemnity. As stated by Delvin J in the *Ann Stathatos*:[2]

> Dangerous cargoes, trades, ports and places can all be prohibited by express provision, but many cases may arise which are outside the rigid framework of a prohibition cause, but where an owner, if he were free to choose, might prefer not to go to a particular place or take a particular cargo, not necessarily because he foresees any definite danger but because he feels that it might lead to trouble. If he is to surrender his freedom of choice and put his master under the orders of the charterer, there is nothing unreasonable in his stipulating for a complete indemnity in return.

For many years, it was assumed by maritime practitioners and arbitrators that that was the case, but the only authority which clearly so stated was the 1979 decision of Mustill J in the *Athanasia Comninos*, in which it was stated that this was "long-established," without citing any authority to that effect – a striking example of the willingness of the Commercial Court to recognise and act upon accepted industry understanding[3].

It is well established that, as a general rule, a shipowner has an implied right of indemnity against a time charterer in respect of the consequences of complying with the charterer's orders as to the employment of the ship, even if the orders were ones the charterer was contractually entitled to give. However, it is equally well established that such indemnity does not extend to the usual perils of the voyage in respect of which the owner must be taken to have accepted the risks.[4]

The implication of such an indemnity as a matter of law was confirmed by the Supreme Court in its decision in the *Kos*.[5] Lord Sumption took the same approach to the scope of a shipowner's indemnity, expressly recognising that the indemnity did not apply to marine fouling occurring in the course of contractual trading.

A number of cases have stressed the need for there to be an unbroken chain of causation between the charterers' order and the loss, damage, or liability – see, for example, the *Ann*

1 *Dugdalge and Others v Lovering* [1875] LR 10 CP 196.
2 *The Ann Stathatos* [1950] 83 Ll.L. Rep.228.
3 Sir Nicholas Hamblen, Under Charterers' Orders-to Indemnify, or not to Indemnify [2019] L.M.C.L.Q. 200.
4 *The Island Archon* [1994] 2 Lloyd's Rep.227 (C.A.); *The Coral Seas* [2016] 2 Lloyd's Rep.293.
5 *The Kos* [2012] UKSC 17; [2012] 2 Lloyd's Rep.292.

Stathatos, *sup*., and the *Athanasia Comninos*.[6] Also many other cases relating to unsafe ports issue.

Causation in fact or "but for" causation is insufficient. As stated by Donaldson J in the *White Rose*:[7]

> It is necessary in every case to establish an unbroken chain of causation, although I would not accept as a generalization that "if some act of negligence intervenes or some marine casualty intervenes then I think the chain of causation is broken and the indemnity does not operate" (per Mr Justice Roche in Portsmouth Steamship *Company, Ltd. v. Liverpool & Glasgow Salvage Association*, sup., at p. 462). A loss may well arise in the course of compliance with the time charterers' orders, but this fact does not, without more, establish that it was caused by and is in law a consequence of such compliance and, in the absence of proof of such causation, there is no right to indemnity.

As the *Kos* establishes, it is not necessary to show that the charterers' order is the sole effective cause of the loss, damage, or liability. It is sufficient to show that it is an effective cause. As Lord Sumption stated:[8]

> The real question is whether the charterers' order was an effective cause of the owner having to bear a risk or cost of a kind which he had not contractually agreed to bear. I use the expression "effective cause" in contrast to a mere "but for" cause which does no more than provide the occasion for some other factor unrelated to the charterers' order to operate. If the charterers' order was an effective cause in this sense, it does not matter whether it was the only one.

It's common ground that coal is self-heating cargo. Charterers' order to wait for berthing to cause cargoes to catch fire is within the general right of indemnity, subject to proof of causation. As Lord Sumption observed in the *Kos* in relation to causation:[9]

> Like all questions of causation, this one is sensitive to the legal context in which it arises. It depends on the intended scope of the indemnity as a matter of construction, which is necessarily informed by its purpose. We are not therefore concerned with questions of remoteness and foreseeability of the kind which would arise in the law of damages, where the object is to limit the range of consequences for which a wrongdoer may be said to have assumed responsibility in the eyes of the law.

The implied obligation not to carry dangerous cargo without informing the carrier extends beyond the case of common carriage to the case of carriage in pursuance of statutory duty. It was stated that this obligation is not confined to cases where the goods are tendered to a common carrier, but is capable of applying, in appropriate circumstances, to all contracts for the carriage of goods by sea. Therefore, even if the charterer is not the actual shipper of the cargo, the charterers will also be in breach of an undertaking implied at common law if they load dangerous cargoes without notice of their dangerous nature, unless the owners or their master knew, or ought, reasonably, to have known, of the danger they pose. The implied duty is a means of risk allocation between shipper and carrier. Neither party may in fact be aware of any general or special characteristics rendering the cargo dangerous. The fact that the shipper had no opportunity to inspect the cargo is irrelevant. The duty is strict

6 *The Athanasia Comminos* [1990] 1 Lloyd's Rep.277.
7 *The White Rose* [1969] 2 Lloyd's Rep.52, per Donaldson J at p. 59.
8 *The Kos* [2012] UKSC 17; [2012] 2 Lloyd's Rep.292 at p. 12.
9 Ibid.

and absolute. The same logic applies to the relationship between charterer and owner, with the former bearing the loss.[10]

Where bills of lading incorporated the Hague/Hague–Visby Rules, it is well known that the "fire defence" under article IV, rule 2(b) should come to the aid of a carrier who exercised due diligence to make the vessel seaworthy at the commencement of the voyage. Alternatively, there is article IV, rule 2(p), which provides a carrier with a defence in the event of latent defects not discoverable by due diligence, and article IV, rule 2(q), which provides a defence in the event of any other cause arising without its actual fault or privity, or without the fault or neglect of its agents or servants. Article IV, rule 2(m) provides wastage in bulk or weight or any other loss or damage arising from the inherent defect, quality, or vice of the goods. Those representing cargo interests, who seek recovery from the carrier for their cargo loss/damage and an indemnity for general average and salvage liabilities, will work hard to prove that the vessel was causatively unseaworthy at the commencement of the voyage and refute evidence that the carrier exercised due diligence.

For interpretation of article IV, rule 2(b) in the *Lady M*, Simon LJ stated that:[11]

> The words, "fire, unless caused by the actual fault or privity of the carrie," is a phrase whose natural and ordinary meaning is clear. The words exclude the carrier from liability for fire however caused, provided it is not caused with the actual fault or privity of the carrier or in breach of its obligations set out in article III.1. The word "fire" contains no implicit qualification as to how the fire is started, whether accidentally or deliberately, negligently or otherwise. Nor is there any implicit qualification depending on who may be responsible for the fire. The only express qualification is the proviso in the second part of the clause, "unless caused by the actual fault or privity of the carrier." Unless the cause of the fire falls within the proviso, fire is an excepted peril.

This view of the ordinary meaning of article IV.2(b) gains support from a number of authoritative textbooks. In *Bills of Lading*,[12] the following is stated:

> This is an important exception given the ease with which fire can start on board ship and the potentially serious danger posed to cargo, vessel and crew that may result from a fire. Because of the nature of fire and the destruction that results, the causes of a fire are often difficult to determine except by inference. The basic scheme of the rule is that if the damage is caused by fire then the carrier is excepted from liability even if the fire has resulted from negligence on the part of the officers, crew, independent contractors or anyone else that would otherwise render the carrier liable. There are two qualifications to this basic rule. First, the carrier cannot rely on the exception at all if there is a causative breach of Article III rule 1 and, secondly, as set out in the proviso to Rule 2(b), the carrier cannot rely on the exception if the fire was caused by his actual fault or privity.

The editors of *Scrutton on Charterparties and Bills of Lading*[13] adopt a similar analysis of the article IV.2(b) exception:

> The shipowner does not enjoy the protection of these exceptions where the loss is caused by his negligence or that of his servants or agents save insofar as protection is given under subheadings (a) and (b).

---

10 Meltem Deniz Guner-Ozbek, *The Carriage of Dangerous Goods by Sea* at p. 176.

11 *The Lady M* [2019] 2 Lloyd's Rep.109 (C.A.), per Simon LJ at p. 43.

12 *Bills of Lading*, 3rd ed, Informa Law, 2021, para. 11.241.

13 *Scrutton on Charterparties and Bills of Lading*, 24th ed, Sweet & Maxwell, 2020 at para. 14–072, and the comment at para. 14–082 to similar effect.

According to the editors of *Carver on Bills of Lading*:[14]

> If the fire creates unseaworthiness operative during the period over which the ship must be seaworthy under the Rules, this exception does not apply for the loss is caused by unseaworthiness, which is not an accepted peril. . . . Beyond this, the carrier is only liable for loss or damage caused by fire if this occurs with "his actual fault or privity." The word "fault" must obviously cover deliberate and reckless conduct as well as negligence.

Finally, the editors of *Voyage Charters*:[15]

> Once the facts proved by the carrier are prima facie within the exception, the onus falls on the owner of the good to disprove its operation, for example, where appropriate by proof of negligence, although even the proof of negligence will not exclude the operation of sub-rules (a) and (b) according to their specific wording.

Reviewing the above authorities, Simon LJ further stated that:[16]

> It is plain that, if the carrier has failed to comply with its obligations under article III.1 to exercise due diligence before and at the commencement of the voyage (a) to make the ship seaworthy, or (b) to properly man the ship, it will not be able to rely on the fire exception if a negligent or deliberate act of the crew have caused the fire. However, where there has been no prior causative breach of the carrier's obligations under article III.1, its liability for loss by fire is excluded by article IV.2(b) unless caused by the actual fault or privity of the owner.

In conclusion, the Court of Appeal held that if the fire was set by the deliberate act of the chief engineer, provided it was caused without their actual fault or privity, the owners can rely on the article IV.2(b) defence. It is sufficient, in these circumstances, for us to say that, on the agreed and assumed facts, the fire was deliberately caused with intent to cause damage, and the owners were, therefore, exempt from liability under article IV.2(b).

This appeal confirmed the previous decision in the High Court that the defence under article IV.2(b) is available to an owner for fire on board a vessel, howsoever caused, unless by the actual fault or privity of the carrier.

Under a time charter, the correct approach should be to ask, first, whether by the terms of the charter the owners have consented to carry the cargo shipped (or proposed to be shipped, if the question is the legitimacy of the charterers' orders). If they have not, therein lies charterers' breach. If the owners have consented, but only on the basis that they will be given sufficient information about any particular cargo nominated by the charterers for safe shipment, carriage and discharge, the charterers may yet be in breach of their obligation to give all requisite instructions. It is, therefore, neither possible nor desirable to formulate as a rule of law that a certain degree or quality of notice concerning the characteristics of the cargo proposed to be shipped determines the issue of liability. All will depend on the precise terms of the charter and the full facts of each case.[17]

Moreover, where cargo carried pursuant to a time charter has caused damage to the ship, a debate about the nature or extent of the charterers' obligations concerning dangerous cargo may be sterile. The owners' most natural claim in those circumstances is for an indemnity against the consequences of having complied with the charterers' orders (here, the order to load the particular cargo). In such a claim, it is suggested that the burden is on

---

14 *Carver on Bills of Lading*, 4th ed, Sweet & Maxwell, 2017 at para. 9–215.
15 *Voyage Charters*, 4th ed, Informa Law, 2014 at para. 85.261.
16 *The Lady M*, Ibid at p. 117.
17 *Time Charters*, 7th ed, Informa Law, 2014 at para. 9.31.

the charterers to show that the damage resulted from a risk the owners had agreed to bear. The owners, therefore, will not need to prove whether the cargo was of a dangerous type or was an unusual cargo of a type not automatically classified as dangerous.[18]

So if owners never breach their overriding obligation to exercise due diligence to make the vessel seaworthy and fit to receive cargo, crews have taken precautions to take care of goods, and the charterers will not be entitled to place the vessel off-hire in these issues relating to coal cargoes catching fire. The owners were exempt from liability under article IV.2(b); this defence is available to an owner for fire on board a vessel, howsoever caused, unless by the actual fault or privity of the carrier.

5.2 Cotton caught on fire

In the *Apostolis*,[19] cargo was loaded on 28 December 1992, including into hold 5, but by 1400, loading had stopped for the day. The fire was first discovered at 2015, when smoke was seen coming from hold 5. Attempts were made to deal with it by those on board, and help was soon at hand from the local firefighting agencies. However, by about 2300, the fire had spread by heating the bulkhead between the two holds to hold 4. By about 0400 the following day, it had been largely extinguished.

All the cargo loaded into holds 4 and 5 were damaged either by the fire or water used to extinguish it. Replacement cargo was loaded, and the vessel finally sailed from Salonika to Brazil on 4 March 1993. AMJ contended that the fire was caused by welding carried out on the deck, which put the owners in breach of the Hague–Visby Rules and therefore liable for their losses. The owners argued that the most probable cause of the fire was a discarded cigarette, for which AMJ was liable, and they counterclaimed their losses. The evidence established that if welding was being carried out on deck above hold 5 during the afternoon of 28 December, then a spark from this activity was the most probable cause of the fire. If no such work was being carried out, then a discarded cigarette was the most probable cause. The onus was on AMJ to establish that the fire was caused by welding.[20]

In the first instance, the trial judge, Tuckey J, stated that AMJ had established that there was welding on 28 December, and the fire was caused by welding being carried out between holds 4 and 5. Tuckey J observed that if it was simply fire in the cargo itself which made the vessel unseaworthy, as might be the case with a fire caused by a discarded cigarette, then there could be no breach of article III, rule 1. The threat to cargo posed by the spark was associated with welding carried out to the ship; the hold was not fit and safe for the cargo, and the vessel was unseaworthy and the owners were in breach of article III, rule 1. Tuckey J concluded that the fire was caused by welding; hence, owners were liable to AMJ for breach of article III, rule 1 of the Hague–Visby Rules and/or they were liable for breach of article IV, rule 2 because the fire was caused by their actual fault or privity.

As Leggatt LJ pointed out in the Court of Appeal, to show a breach of article III, rule 1, AMJ must show that the carriers failed to make the ship seaworthy and that their loss or damage was caused by the breach, or in other words, that the fire was caused

18 Ibid, para. 9.32.

19 *The Apostolis* [1996] 1 Lloyd's Rep.475; [1997] 2 Lloyd's Rep.241 (C.A.).

20 Ibid, [1997] 2 Lloyd's Rep.241 (C.A.) at p. 241.

by unseaworthiness. AMJ had to contend that the unseaworthiness consisted of exposure of the cargo to the risk of fire from a spark entering the hold. But even if that was what occurred, it was not unseaworthiness which caused the fire but the fire which rendered the vessel unseaworthy.[21]

Leggatt LJ continued to state that nothing about the state of the ship rendered her unseaworthy. The owners were not in breach of article III, rule 1 merely because welding exposed the cargo to an ephemeral risk of ignition. The holds themselves were not intrinsically unsafe. In *Maxine*, the House of Lords found it unnecessary to decide whether the vessel was on fire before the cargo was loaded. It was a fire in the fabric of the vessel, namely, the cork lining of the hold, which rendered her unseaworthy.

Here the ship only became so on account of the fire in the cargo. It cannot even be said that the welding was taking place in order to render the ship seaworthy. The fire might as well have been caused by a discarded cigarette, which, as the judge accepted, could not be a breach of article III, rule 1.[22]

Leggatt LJ held that the judge's resolution of this point, which he did not find easy, was wrong. Even if the fire was caused, as he found, there was no breach of article III, rule 1, and the owners were not liable on that ground.[23]

Phillips LJ added:[24]

> The Judge was urged to find that the cargo was damaged by unseaworthiness on two alternative bases. First it was argued that, once the cargo caught fire, the fact of the burning cargo rendered holds Nos. 4 and 5 unfit for the preservation of the cargo in those holds and thus unseaworthy. The Judge rejected that contention, and I think that he was right to do so. For a ship to be unseaworthy, or more strictly uncargoworthy, there must be some attribute of the ship itself which threatens the safety of the cargo. If a hold is dirty, that is properly considered as an attribute of the ship. But the fact that a hold contains cargo which threatens damage to other cargo stowed in proximity is not an attribute of the ship and does not render the ship unseaworthy.

Phillips LJ found that a difficult decision, but it is plainly distinguishable from the present case, for in *Maxine* the structure of the ship was on fire, which made it necessary to scuttle the ship. In those circumstances, it is not surprising that it was conceded that the ship was rendered unseaworthy by the fire.[25]

Phillips LJ stated:[26]

> A ship will be unseaworthy if she is not in such a state as will preserve the cargo from the risk of damage from the necessary incidents of a ship's existence, whether at sea or in harbour. But a ship will not be unseaworthy simply because she or her cargo will be endangered if an act or activity occurs on board her which it is not necessary to perform while she is in that condition and which reasonable care requires shall not be performed while she is in that condition. If a repairer shoots a Cox gun bolt into a gas filled tank, so that the tank explodes, he does not thereby demonstrate that the ship is unseaworthy. Hatches have to be off while cargo is being loaded, and it will at that point be possible to envisage various activities capable of damaging the cargo while that condition prevails, but if such an activity is indulged in and the cargo is

21 Ibid, p. 244.
22 Ibid, p. 245.
23 Ibid.
24 Ibid, per Phillips LJ at p. 257.
25 Ibid.
26 Ibid.

> damaged, it does not follow that the vessel is unseaworthy or that the condition of the vessel is the cause of the damage. The cause of the damage in such a case is the activity.

The Court of Appeal held that the judge was correct to have found that welding was taking place near a gap in the hatch cover that enabled sparks to gain access to the cargo, and that a spark from the welding gained access and ignited the cargo; the conclusion should have been that the cause of the damage to the cargo was a fire caused by the act of welding, and not unseaworthiness.

As Phillips LJ observed in this case, for a ship to be unseaworthy, or, more strictly, uncargoworthy, there must be some attribute of the ship itself which threatens the safety of the cargo. If a hold is dirty, that is properly considered as an attribute of the ship. But the fact that a hold contains cargo which threatens damage to other cargo stowed in proximity is not an attribute of the ship and does not render the ship unseaworthy.[27]

The suggestion that there is an attribute threshold has been criticised by some commentators. For example, *Bills of Lading*[28] and *Carver on Charterparties*.[29] As stated in *Carver on Charterparties*: "a requirement that the cause of the damage must be an attribute of the ship itself rather than an extrinsic cause can be difficult to apply in practice and can lead to anomalies." It is therefore suggested that any such requirement should be confined to cargoworthiness and should, in any event, "be regarded as illustrative rather than prescriptive."

If there is an "attribute threshold," it is clear to the authorities that it must be widely and diversely drawn. Seaworthiness is not limited to physical defects in the vessel and her equipment. It extends to documentary matters, such as adequate and update charts,[30] crew,[31] vessel's system for maintenance,[32] or hot works and fire safety.[33]

5.3 Ventilation system

According to SOLAS Chapter II-2, "Construction – Fire protection, fire detection and fire extinction," the main inlets and outlets of all ventilation systems shall be capable of being closed from outside the spaces being ventilated. The means of closing shall be easily accessible as well as prominently and permanently marked and shall indicate whether the shut-off is open or closed. Power ventilation of accommodation spaces, service spaces, cargo spaces, control stations, and machinery spaces shall be capable of being stopped from an easily accessible position outside the space being served.

This position shall not be readily cut off in the event of a fire in the spaces served. In passenger ships carrying more than 36 passengers, power ventilation, except machinery space and cargo space ventilation and any alternative system which may be required under regulation 8.2, shall be fitted with controls so grouped that all fans may be stopped from either of two separate positions which shall be situated as far apart as practicable. Fans serving power ventilation systems to cargo spaces shall be capable of being stopped from a safe position

27 Ibid.
28 *Aikens and others, Bills of Lading*, 3rd ed, 2021 at para. 11.127.
29 *Carver on Charterparties*, 2nd ed, 2020 at para. 3.115.
30 *The CMA CGM Libra* [2021] UKSC 51.
31 *The Eurasian Dream* [2002] 1 Lloyd's Rep.719.
32 *The Devon* [2012] EWHC 3747 (Comm).
33 *The Maersk Karachi* [2019] EWHC 1099 (Comm).

outside such spaces. Machinery spaces of category A shall be adequately ventilated so as to ensure that when machinery or boilers therein are operating at full power in all weather conditions, including heavy weather, an adequate supply of air is maintained in the spaces for the safety and comfort of personnel and the operation of the machinery. Any other machinery space shall be adequately ventilated and appropriate for the purpose of that machinery space.

In addition to the requirements of regulation 5.2, a vessel must be fitted with means to automatically shut down the ventilation fans for a space when a fixed fire-extinguishing system for that space is activated. In addition to the requirements of regulation 5.2.2.3, a vessel must be fitted with means of control if the vessel is provided with any other equipment, such as hydraulic power systems, that could create a fire or any other danger in the space.

Fire damper, ventilation, emergency fire pump and its pipes, fire doors/openings in fire-resisting, fire detection and alarm system, fire drills, and major types and details of deficiencies are noted under the category of "fire safety." Many vessels are detained by PSC or MSA due to these detainable deficiencies.

Under article III, rule 2 of the Hague–Visby rules, incorporated into the charterparty, carrier has a duty properly and carefully to carry, keep, and care for the cargo. "Properly" means "in accordance with a sound system." It relates to the method chosen and agreed for performing the contract of carriage, which may thus include the duty of proceeding on the contractual voyage with reasonable despatch, at least where the cargo is perishable. Soundness does not require perfection but should be judged in the light of the knowledge that the carrier has or ought to have about the cargo to be carried and in the light of the accepted practices of prudent carriers. The significance of differentiating between "properly" and "carefully" would seem to be that the carrier is bound not only to adopt a sound system for handling, carrying, and caring for the goods as contracted but must also be careful in his application of that system. Thus, it is no defence to a carrier to argue that he adopted a sound system if his crew are negligent in operating it, and similarly, it is no defence if his crew have carefully applied a system of carriage which is not a proper one for the carriage in question.[34]

In the *Subro Valour*,[35] on 25 November 1987, the plaintiffs' cargo of 327.69 t of peas was shipped on board the vessel at Wivenhoe in England for carriage to and delivery at Oss in Holland. The cargo was shipped under a bill of lading dated 25 November, and it was common ground between the parties that the contract contained in or evidenced by the bill of lading incorporated the Hague–Visby Rules.

The vessel sailed from Wivenhoe at about 1400 hours on 26 November and reached the sea at 1535 hours. At about 2051 hours, the master smelled fumes. The fire spread to the accommodation. The master decided to anchor the vessel in order to put her head to the wind, in an attempt to direct the smoke and flames away from the cargo hold. In the event, the fire did not spread to the cargo. The master and crew were subsequently taken off by helicopter, and the vessel was taken in tow by salvors pursuant to LOF and towed to Brightlingsea, where she was berthed on 28 November at 1745 hours. Thereafter, the cargo was transhipped and taken to Oss in another vessel.

The plaintiffs contended that they were entitled to recover damages because they had suffered loss as a result of the fire on *Subro Valour*. They submitted that the fire was

34 See *Voyage Charters*, 4th ed at para. 85.117.
35 *The Subro Valour* [1995] 1 Lloyd's Rep.509.

caused by the unseaworthiness of the vessel at the commencement of the voyage, that the spread of the fire and the subsequent necessity to take salvage assistance was caused by the unseaworthiness at the commencement of the voyage, and that the alleged loss was caused by the unseaworthiness of the vessel in one or both of those aspects. The defendants admitted that if the vessel was unseaworthy at the commencement of the voyage, there was a breach of the contract of carriage, unless they proved that the unseaworthiness occurred notwithstanding the exercise of due diligence on the part of themselves, their servants, or their agents.[36]

Clarke J accepted the evidence of Dr Bound that this theory is as consistent with the fire patterns and the debris as either of the other theories. The only other possibility which was mentioned at all was that material might have fallen from the shelves during the voyage and caught fire by contact with a hot spot on the exhaust. There is, however, no evidence to support that as a possibility. Moreover, the material would have had to fall some little way in order to come into contact with the exhaust. I have therefore reached the conclusion that in all the circumstances, the fire was probably caused as a result of mechanical damage to the wiring or to its insulation, which led to the development of a high-resistance fault, which in turn caused ignition.[37]

Clarke J discussed the question of unseaworthiness and stated:[38]

> In my judgment it follows from that conclusion that the vessel was unseaworthy at the commencement of the voyage. There is no suggestion that mechanical damage to the insulation or wiring occurred after the voyage began. If it did, either the wiring or insulation on the one hand or the shelving or whatever caused the damage on the other, was in such a condition or position that mechanical damage could be caused during the voyage. No-one suggests or could suggest that conditions during the voyage were in any way unexpected or out of the ordinary. It follows that at the commencement of the voyage the vessel cannot have been fit in all respects to carry her cargo safely to its destination having regard to the ordinary perils which might be expected on the voyage. That is because either the wiring or its insulation were in such a condition at the commencement of the voyage that an electrical fire could be started or the conditions were such at that time that mechanical damage leading to a fire could occur. It follows that if (as I have held to be probable) the fire was electrical, the vessel was unseaworthy.

Clarke J observed that if the damage was caused by materials on the shelves, it must follow that the materials were not properly stowed or secured, because, having regard to the risk of fire from damage to wiring, they should have been so stowed and secured that they could not come into contact with the wires. The same is true if the damage was caused by the shelves themselves. The shelves should not have been constructed in such a place that they could damage the wiring. Lastly, if the damage occurred from some extraneous cause, again the exercise of proper care should have avoided it.[39]

Clarke J continued to hold that the defendants are unable to show that they exercised due diligence (by themselves, their servants, their agents, and their contractors) to avoid damage to the wiring and therefore to make the vessel seaworthy at the commencement of the voyage. It also follows that they are liable to the plaintiffs for the consequences of the fire.[40]

36 Ibid.
37 Ibid, per Clarke J at p. 515.
38 Ibid, p. 516.
39 Ibid, p. 517.
40 Ibid.

In these circumstances, it is not strictly necessary to consider whether due diligence was exercised if the fire was caused by the ignition of material left in the vicinity of the exhaust or of material falling off the shelving; in either case, it was contributed to by the fact that the exhaust was not properly lagged. It is sufficient to say that in none of those cases would the defendants have discharged the burden of proving the exercise of due diligence. If the material was left near the exhaust, it should not have been because of the risk of fire. If the material was not properly secured on the shelves, it should have been for the same reason. Finally, if the exhaust was not properly lagged, it should have been, again, for the same reason.[41]

The problem, as Clarke J viewed it, was that on the day of the fire, either the lever was missing or it was present and the master had not been told about it. Although, according to Captain Bowling, the lever had been present at some stage, it is, in my judgment, more likely than not that it was missing. In either event, the vessel was unseaworthy in that respect because the ability to close the ventilation to the engine room was an important facet of the firefighting capability of the vessel. Yet it was either not possible physically to close the flap because of the absence of the lever or not possible in practice because neither the master nor anyone else was apparently aware of the lever. That unseaworthiness existed at the commencement of the voyage. Moreover, the lever should have been in position, and the master should have been instructed as to its existence and purpose before the voyage began. It follows that the owners failed to exercise due diligence to make the vessel seaworthy in that respect.[42]

However, even if the master had been aware of the flaps and ordered them to be closed or closed them himself at a very early stage, it would, in my judgment, have been likely to take more than two minutes before the flaps and the engine room skylight were closed. The evidence is that after the master had become aware of the fire, he roused the mate, who in turn roused the others on board, including the master's wife. He then went to the upper deck and closed the skylight to the engine room. By that time, given the fact that the fire already had a significant hold, it is not, in my judgment, possible to say on the balance of probabilities that the fire would not have spread to the accommodation as it did. Nor is it possible to say on the balance of probabilities that if the flap had been operated, it would have had such an effect upon the state of the vessel that salvage services would not have been required or that transhipment would not have been necessary.[43]

Clarke J considered the aforementioned and concluded:[44]

> For those reasons I would hold that the plaintiffs had failed to prove that any of their loss was caused by any unseaworthiness of the vessel so far as her fire fighting capabilities were concerned. However, for the reasons which I have already given, the defendants are nevertheless liable because their breach of contract caused the fire.

It's suggested that a fire will fall within the exception unless "caused by the personal design or neglect of the Owner" or "unless caused by the actual fault or privity of the carrier." However, fire which results from failure to exercise due diligence to make the vessel seaworthy before and at the beginning of the voyage will not be covered. The

---

41 Ibid.
42 Ibid, p. 518.
43 Ibid.
44 Ibid.

shipowner was held unable to rely on its Hague Rules defence as such constituted a breach by the shipowner of its overriding obligation to exercise due diligence before and at the beginning of the voyage.[45]

For ventilation system, one was discussed by Andrew Henshaw QC in the *Santa Isabella*[46] recently. In this case, the vessel is a 2006-built geared bulk with natural ventilation holds that carried a cargo of 44,000 t of corn/maize from Topolobampo, Mexico, to Durban from 24 June to 1 August 2016. The defendant charterers alleged that the cargo and the delays at Durban and Richards Bay, caused by two of four, are (a) the vessel taking the Cape Horn route rather than the Panama Canal route from Topolobampo to Durban, (b) failure by the vessel to ventilate the cargo in accordance with a sound system.

Andrew Henshaw QC discussed the duties of the shipowner, to properly and carefully carry, keep, and care for the cargo under article III, rule 2 of the Hague–Visby Rules, and he said:[47]

> "Properly" means in accordance with a sound system. Soundness does not require perfection, but should be judged in the light of the knowledge which the carrier has or ought to have about the cargo to be carried and in the light of the accepted practices of prudent carriers. The significance of differentiating between "properly" and "carefully" is that the carrier is bound not only to adopt a sound system for handling, carrying and caring for the goods as contracted but must also be careful in his application of that system. Thus, it is no defence for a carrier to argue that he adopted a sound system if his crew are negligent in operating it and, similarly, it is no defence if his crew have carefully applied a system of carriage which is not a proper one for the carriage in question.

Andrew Henshaw QC observed that a cargo requires ventilation when the potential for condensation within the hold exists, namely, when the outside air dew point temperature is lower than the dew point temperature of the air inside the cargo hold. In these conditions, the inner steel surfaces of the cargo hold act as a condensation surface.

Both the dewpoint rule and the 3° rule operate on the basis that ventilation should occur whenever their respective criteria are met. Neither contains any in-built limitation to the effect that ventilation should occur only during the day. On the contrary, all the P&I bulletins produced in evidence make clear that, where the criteria are met, ventilation should occur at night. Andrew Henshaw QC accepted that the risk of a small quantity of rain/spray entering through the small aperture of the ventilators, for 20 minutes or so, must be set against the consequences of the holds going without necessary ventilation for a period of up to 17 hours.

Andrew Henshaw QC stated:[48]

> In my judgment this approaches matters in the wrong way, and is in any event incorrect. A sound system of ventilation for a hygroscopic cargo would involve the use of either the dew point rule or the three degree rule. That reflects the recommendations made in all the P&I club bulletins in evidence, and was not disputed by any witness (factual or expert) in this case. Neither rule makes any distinction between daytime or night-time ventilation; and for the reasons given earlier ventilation at night is generally likely to be even more necessary and effective than daytime ventilation. None of the P&I club bulletins gives any indication that ventilation is not

45 *The Maruinne* [1959] 2 Lloyd's Rep.105.
46 *The Santa Isabella* [2019] EWHC 3152 (Comm).
47 Ibid, per Andrew Henshaw QC at p. 107.
48 Ibid, p. 174.

> expected to occur at night: on the contrary, they are (so far as the evidence before me goes) unanimous in stating the contrary.

Andrew Henshaw QC observed that the likely outcome had there been proper ventilation when it was safe to do so (including ventilation at night, save when weather conditions made it unsafe) would have been 6 to 12 in of dried crust at the top of the cargo but no greater type or degree of level of cargo damage.

Ultimately, Andrew Henshaw QC found elsewhere in this judgment that Alianca was in breach of its duties to care for the cargo during the voyage and that but for those breaches, the cargo would have arrived with no more than 6–12 in of dried crust on the top of the stow and could have discharged at Durban and then at Richards Bay without lengthy delays. On that footing, the question of ventilation while she was lying at anchor off Durban would not have arisen. It is therefore not necessary to decide the extent, if any, of further damage caused to the remaining cargo discharged at Richards Bay by reason of inadequate ventilation at Durban.[49]

On the basis of the evidence as a whole, Andrew Henshaw QC concluded that the infestations resulted, on the balance of probabilities, from inadequate cleaning of the topsides following loading, and again following fumigation in Durban, and that the shipowner thereby breached its duty under article III, rule 2 properly and carefully to handle, keep, and care for the cargo and is not protected by rule 2(q) of article IV.[50]

As Andrew Henshaw QC found, the owners had failed to properly and carefully ventilate the cargo in accordance with a sound system. This failure was a breach of the owners' duty to care for the cargo, and this breach was the cause of damage to the cargo, which but for the breach would, on the balance of probabilities, have arrived with damage limited to 6–12 in of dried crust on the top of each stow. That, in turn, was the cause of the long delays in discharging at Durban. It was found that owners were also in breach of their duties properly to care for the cargo by failing properly to disinfest the vessel's topsides, that being on the balance of probabilities the likely cause of the insect infestations encountered at Durban and Richards Bay. The latter infestation was the cause of delay in discharging at Richards Bay.[51]

In this case, Andrew Henshaw QC stated, as a matter of common sense, that the arrival in a seriously damaged condition of a cargo loaded in apparent good order and condition calls for an explanation, and a want of care on the part of the shipowner is a possible inference.[52] Thus, if cargo is found damaged on discharge, the owners must show that they have a sound system for cargo in place, including ventilation and disinfection where necessary, and the system has been followed.

5.4 Dangerous cargo under deck

According to IM guidance, SOLAS, as amended, deals with various aspects of maritime safety and contains in Chapter VII the mandatory provisions governing the carriage of dangerous goods in packaged form. The carriage of dangerous goods in packaged

49 Ibid, p. 226.
50 Ibid, p. 239.
51 Ibid, p. 257.
52 Ibid, p. 52.

form shall comply with the relevant provisions of the International Maritime Dangerous Goods (IMDG) Code, which is considered an extension to the provisions of SOLAS Chapter VII.

Furthermore, the International Convention for the Prevention of Pollution from Ships, 1973, as modified by the Protocol of 1978 relating thereto (MARPOL), which contains in its Annex III mandatory provisions for the prevention of pollution by harmful substances carried by sea in packaged form, prohibits the carriage of harmful substances in ships except in accordance with the provisions of MARPOL Annex III, which are also extended in the IMDG Code.

The IMDG Code was developed as an international code for the maritime transport of dangerous goods in packaged form in order to enhance and harmonize the safe carriage of dangerous goods and to prevent pollution of the environment. The code sets out in detail the requirements applicable to each individual substance, material, or article, covering matters such as packing, container traffic, and stowage, with particular reference to the segregation of incompatible substances.

Since its introduction in 1965, the IMDG Code has undergone many changes, both in appearance and content, to keep pace with the ever-changing needs of the industry. Amendments which do not affect the principles upon which the code is based may be adopted by the Maritime Safety Committee alone. Thus, IMO can respond to transport developments in a reasonable time.

Amendments to the IMDG Code are made (E&T Group) on a two-year cycle; these mainly originated from two sources: proposals submitted directly to IMO by member governments and amendments required to take account of changes to the United Nations Recommendations on the Transport of Dangerous Goods, which sets the basic requirements for all the transport modes.

The code was initially adopted in 1965 as a recommendatory instrument. It was in 2002 that the General Assembly, at its seventeenth session, adopted by Resolution A.716(17) the IMDG Code and decided to give it a mandatory status under the umbrella of the SOLAS Convention, from 1 January 2004. However, some parts of the code remain recommendatory. Clear guidelines apply to the stowage and segregation of dangerous goods and, in some cases, may require particular commodities to be carried in completely separate holds. The interaction of two cargoes will not occur if the packaging of that cargo remains intact. However, the master must always consider the possible effect should the cargo escape for any reason and should not restrict his consideration to those cargoes, which are listed in the IMDG Code. Every dangerous cargo shipment shall be made in line with IMO policy and be accompanied by required documentation. Dangerous cargo with restricted/prohibited UN numbers shall not be accepted for shipment unless, under special circumstances, express permission is obtained from the company.

In the *Kapitan Sakharov*,[53] on 4 July 1993, *Kapitan Sakharov* was carrying laden containers of DSR and CYL on a short voyage from Khor Fakkan near the entrance to the Arabian Gulf to other ports in the Gulf. Shortly before midday, a container on deck containing dangerous cargo exploded, causing a fire on the deck which spread below, resulting in the sinking of the vessel shortly after midnight on the next day.

53 *The Kapitan Sakharov* [2000] 2 Lloyd's Rep.255 (C.A.).

It was common ground that the explosion resulted in the cracking open of hatch 3 and a fire which, despite vigorous firefighting by the ship's crew, spread down into hold 3 in the aft section, of which there were eight CYL tank containers of isopentane. It was a liquid more flammable than petrol, having a flash point well below 0°C and a boiling point of about 28°C. Ambient temperatures in the Gulf would have been well above that boiling point so that the isopentane would have been under pressure and any escape of it would have been in the form of vapour. The degree of risk of such vapour combusting and/or contributing to a fire in the hold depended on how well it was ventilated. There was no mechanical ventilation in the holds of *Kapitan Sakharov*.[54]

In the first instance, Clarke J ruled that the initial explosion occurred in undeclared and dangerous cargo in a DSR container stored on deck on hatch 3; the stowage of that cargo had rendered the vessel unseaworthy, though not because of any lack of due diligence by NSC; the explosion and resultant fire on deck caused damage to part of the ship and part of the cargo and were an effective cause of the sinking and loss of the vessel and most of the cargo. However, that would not have caused those further losses if NSC had not stowed CYL's isopentane below deck, and this stowage had rendered the vessel unseaworthy and was due to NSC's lack of due diligence. It contributed to the fire below deck and explosion of one or both of the diesel tanks and was a further effective cause of the loss of the vessel and most of the cargo.[55]

The plaintiffs appealed, and the defendants cross-appealed the issues for decision being: (1) whether the judge applied the correct test in finding that the cause of the explosion was undeclared and dangerous cargo of DSR stowed on deck and whether his finding, in any event, was supported by the evidence; (2) whether the judge was correct in finding that the vessel was unseaworthy by reason of NSC's stowage of CYL's isopentane below deck and, if so, that the unseaworthiness was caused by NSC's lack of due diligence; (3) if so, whether the judge was correct in holding that NSC's lack of due diligence excused DSR from liability to NSC under article IV, rule 6 of the Hague Rules and at common law for the total loss of the vessel; and (4) whether the judge was correct in holding that CYL's counterclaim under article III, rule 1 of the Hague Rules for its losses resulting from unseaworthiness of the vessel by reason of the initial explosion and fire and from the isopentane fire could only succeed as to the latter because the unseaworthiness resulting from the carriage of DSR's undeclared dangerous cargo on deck was not caused by any want of due diligence of NSC.[56]

Auld LJ, in giving judgment, observed that the international standards as to seaworthiness were those embodied in the SOLAS and, in this case, the USSR's, now the Russian Federation's, version of the International Maritime Dangerous Goods Code ("the IMDG Code"), given the initials "MOPOG." SOLAS and IMDG have been given effect to in the United Kingdom by regulations made under the Merchant Shipping Acts. SOLAS, in Chapter VII, regulation 6.3, provided that "dangerous goods in a packaged form which give off dangerous vapours shall be stowed in a mechanically ventilated space or on deck," and in IMDG, regulation 5, that class 3.1 liquids should be carried in a well-ventilated

54 Ibid, p. 255.
55 Ibid.
56 Ibid, p. 256.

space. MOPOG, the preamble of which stated that it complied with both SOLAS and IMDG, made a similar provision.[57]

Auld LJ agreed with the judge that the stowage of the tank containers of isopentane under the deck in the circumstance clearly contravened SOLAS, the IMDG, and MOPOG and was not permitted by the technical certificate. Even if there were room for another view on the question of construction of MOPOG and the technical certificate, the court may have greater latitude to interfere with a finding of fact on a question of foreign law, where expert evidence as to it is lacking than with other findings of fact. Auld LJ concluded that the judge correctly found that the stowage of the isopentane below deck rendered the vessel unseaworthy.[58]

At the first instance, the judge held that NSC was in breach of article III, rule 1 of the Hague Rules in failing to exercise due diligence to make the ship seaworthy in respect of the stowage of the isopentane below deck. Auld LJ accepted that the vessel was not reasonably fit to withstand the ordinary incidents of the voyage with it stowed under deck because it might itself catch fire or, if another fire broke out, it would be likely to exacerbate it. It follows that she was unseaworthy at the commencement of the voyage. Moreover, the plaintiffs failed to exercise due diligence to make the vessel seaworthy in that respect because the master and cargo officer permitted the isopentane to be stowed under the deck in circumstances in which, if they had exercised reasonable skill and care, they would not have done so. In all the circumstances, Auld LJ reached the conclusion that the plaintiffs were in breach of article III, rule 1 of the Hague Rules. In Auld LJ's judgment, the judge's holding that NSC had not exercised due diligence in this respect is unassailable, both on the expert evidence and as a matter of common sense on the strength of his findings of primary fact.[59]

The judge held that, as NSC's want of due diligence in failing to render the vessel seaworthy was an effective, albeit not the only, cause of its loss of the ship and most of the cargo, it could not recover damages for, or an indemnity in respect of, that loss against DSR under article IV, rule 6 or at common law. Auld LJ observed that the essential question was whether NSC's lack of due diligence in the stowage of the isopentane breach of contract causing unseaworthiness in the vessel was *an* effective cause of the fire in hold 3 and her loss.

Auld LJ continued to discuss and held that:[60]

> For all those reasons, I would: (1) dismiss NSC's appeal against the Judge's finding that it had failed to exercise due diligence to make the ship seaworthy in respect of the stowage of isopentane; (2) dismiss DSR's appeal against the Judge's finding that the initial explosion and fire occurred in one of its containers on the forepart of hatch 3; and (3) dismiss CYL's appeal against the Judge's finding that NSC exercised due diligence in respect of DSR's shipment of undeclared and dangerous cargo.

The Court of Appeal upheld the judgment of Clarke J to the effect that the carrier was able to claim an indemnity from DSR in respect of his liability for the on-deck containers, but not for the loss of the vessel and the other containers. His breach of article III, rule 1

57 Ibid, per Auld LJ at p. 264.
58 Ibid, p. 266.
59 Ibid, p. 268.
60 Ibid, p. 273.

was not causative of the initial explosion or the loss of the surrounding containers; those losses resulted from the shipment of the dangerous cargo. The latter head of loss resulted from a combination of the shipment of the dangerous cargo and the carrier's want of due diligence, neither being the dominant cause, but that was irrelevant as long as the carrier's breach was an effective cause of loss.[61] Just as Auld LJ pointed out, the carrier may not be liable for lack of due diligence which occurs before the cargo "comes into his orbit," just as the carrier may not be liable for lack of due diligence which occurs before the vessel "comes into his orbit."

Following this case, bad stowage which endangers a ship may render it unseaworthy. Bad stowage endangering a ship may take the form of stowing an otherwise-harmless cargo in a place which renders it dangerous, say, because of its weight and the effect of that on the stability of the ship or because of its nature, which may be adversely affected by the place of stowage, or simply because it is dangerous wherever and however it is stowed. Unseaworthiness is a physical state. The shipper's knowledge or ignorance of characteristics of the cargo which make it dangerous if stowed in the wrong place or anywhere on its ship cannot determine that state, but it is material to the question whether the carrier has exercised due diligence and, therefore, of his responsibility for the unseaworthiness. The carrier may nevertheless be liable if the defect or danger would be reasonably discoverable by the exercise of due diligence once the vessel or cargo has come within its control.

On the other hand, article III, rule 1 of the Hague Rules requires a carrier before and at the beginning of a voyage to exercise due diligence to make the ship seaworthy. Article IV, rule 6 of the rules renders the shipper of inflammable, explosive, or otherwise-dangerous goods, who gives no notice of their nature and dangerous character, liable to the carrier "for all damages and expenses directly or indirectly arising out of or resulting from their shipment." The shipper is so liable irrespective of its knowledge of the dangerous nature of the goods.[62]

5.5 Fire in engine room

In the *Star Sea*,[63] on 27 May 1990, the vessel sailed from Corinto in Nicaragua, bound for Zeebrugge, with a full cargo of bananas, mangoes, and coffee. On 29 May, as the ship approached the Panama Canal, a fire started in her engine room. It spread to other parts of the ship and was not finally put out for several days, by which time the ship had become a constructive total loss.

The plaintiffs claimed under the insurance policy, but the defendant underwriters denied liability, contending that the ship had been sent to sea in an unseaworthy state with the privity of the assured (s.39[5] of the Marine Insurance Act, 1906) and that this was the cause of most of the loss.

The underwriters alleged inter alia that the vessel was made unseaworthy by the cut pipe because the emergency fire pump was useless when the vessel was laden, by the ineffective sealing of the engine room, and by the fact that the master was incompetent in that he was unaware of the need to use the CO_2 system as soon as he realized that the

61 See *Voyage Charters*, 4th ed at para. 85.457.
62 *The Giannis NK* [1998] 1 Lloyd's Rep.337 (H.L.).
63 *The Star Sea* [1997] 1 Lloyd's Rep.3609 (C.A.); [2001] 1 Lloyd's Rep.389 (H.L.).

fire could not be fought in any other way and that for the system to be effective in the engine room, all the CO_2 had to be discharged at once. The underwriters also contended that they were not liable for any part of the claim because the plaintiffs had breached the duty of utmost good faith. Part of the underwriters' case on privity was based on what was learned from two earlier fires aboard *Centaurus* and *Kastora*. The breach of duty of utmost good faith related to what the plaintiffs said they learned from the *Kastora* fire in witness statements exchanged before trial and in a letter sent by their brokers to the underwriters in March 1994. There were also issues as to quantum and indemnity for salvage claims.[64]

At first instance, Tuckey J held that the defence under section 39(5) had been made out in that the assured had been privy to the vessel putting to sea in an unseaworthy condition, the defence under section 17 failed, and the submission that the assured was under a continuing duty of the utmost good faith to disclose to the insurers any information material to the claim and which might affect their decision to pay or defend the claim would be rejected. The Court of Appeal held that the defendants' appeal under section 17 would be dismissed; the claimants' appeal under section 39(5) would be allowed.

The judge found that the vessel was unseaworthy in a number of respects when she set sail from Corinto. These reflected the age of the vessel and a low standard of maintenance. But he found that the failure to put out the fire on the morning of the 29th was attributable to only two of them. The vessel was equipped with a CO_2 fire extinguishing system. This system worked on the principle of discharging a large quantity of CO_2 gas into the engine room so as to suffocate and thereby extinguish the fire by depriving it of free oxygen. For the system to be effective, a number of conditions have to be observed. It should be used as soon as possible before the fire has spread to other spaces. The engine room must first have been sealed, closing all the vents and other apertures through which CO_2 might escape or oxygen enter, thus prejudicing the suffocation of the fire.[65]

The judge further found that the failure to use the CO_2 earlier and the failure to use all four banks of bottles at once were attributable to the incompetence of the master in that he was ignorant of what was required for the successful use of the CO_2 system. He held that this disabling lack of knowledge on the part of the master amounted to unseaworthiness. (*Standard Oil Co. of New York v Clan Line Steamers*, (1923) 17 Ll.L.Rep.120; [1924] A.C. 100.) The judge found that the defective condition of the funnel dampers which made it impossible to shut them fully also amounted to unseaworthiness. On the hearing of the appeal, these findings were not challenged. The defendants also conceded that, for the purposes of making good the defence under s.39(5), it was necessary for them to establish that the assured was privy to both of these aspects of unseaworthiness.[66]

In this case, the plaintiffs admit that the cut pipe in the forepeak tank made the ship unseaworthy, because it meant that the emergency fire pump was useless when the ship was laden, as it was on 27 May 1990, when it left Corinto. It is also admitted that at that time, the engine was seized, so this is a further reason that the pump was useless. The expert metallurgical evidence was directed to establishing how long it would have taken for the engine to get into this state, given that the cause of seizure was seawater entering one of the engine's cylinders via its exhaust pipe. As the emergency fire pump was useless,

64 Ibid, [2001] 1 Lloyd's Rep.389 (H.L.) at p. 389.
65 Ibid, p. 394.
66 Ibid.

the distribution system was not put to the test. However, these defects were not disputed and are indicative of a lack of maintenance.

Fire is one of the greatest threats to ships at sea. The ship's firefighting ability and, therefore, its seaworthiness is crucially dependent upon the competence of its crew as the firefighters and, in particular, its master as their leader.

The CO_2 system was the most potent weapon in the firefighters' armoury. Knowledge of when and how it should be used was essential. The master's conduct demonstrates to my mind a massive ignorance of these essentials which can only be characterized as incompetence. The master's decision to discharge only half the CO_2 bottles was an incomprehensible mistake, which suggested that he did not have the required level of competence. The master had made an elementary mistake. Due to this incompetence, the court also held the vessel was unseaworthy at this point.

A ship is unseaworthy if it is not in a condition to encounter whatever perils of the sea a ship of that kind and laden in that way may be fairly expected to encounter on the voyage.[67]

5.6 C/E deliberately setting fire

In the *Lady M*,[68] the dispute arose out of a fire in the engine control room of the vessel during her loaded voyage from Taman, Russia, to Houston, USA. It was common ground that the fire was started by a member of the crew (C/E). As a result of the fire, the defendant owners (owners) engaged salvors and declared general average, and the vessel was towed to Las Palmas. The claimant cargo interests (Glencore) were claimed against the defendant owners (Owners) of the vessel. Part of Glencore's case was that the owners had failed to care for the cargo in breach of article III(2) of the rules. In response, the owners relied on the exceptions in articles IV(2)(b) and (q). Glencore asserted that neither of those exceptions was available to the owners because (1) the fire was caused by barratry and (2) neither of the exceptions was capable of applying in cases of barratry. On a trial of three preliminary issues formulated to test Glencore's case, it was assumed that (a) the fire was started by the deliberate act of the chief engineer and (b) the chief engineer was suffering from a personality disorder or mental illness.

Popplewell J referred to a number of authorities[69] on the correct approach to the construction of the Hague Rules. He summarized the material principles from those cases:[70]

> Because the Hague Rules are the outcome of international conferences and have an international currency, being applied by foreign courts, it is in the interests of uniformity that they should be construed on broad principles of interpretation which are generally accepted rather than rules of construction particular to English law. For the same reasons, their interpretation is not to be controlled by the English law cases which preceded the Rules, and the court should not pay

67 *Steel v State Lines S.S. Co.* [1877] 3 App. Cas. 72 at p. 77.

68 *The Lady M* [2019] 2 Lloyd's Rep.109 (C.A.).

69 *Stag Line v Foscolo, Mango & Co Ltd.* [1932] AC 328 per Lord Atkin at pp. 342–343 and Lord MacMillan at p. 350; *The Torenia* [1983] 2 Lloyd's Rep 210 per Hobhouse J at p. 219; *CMA CGM S.A. v Classica Shipping Co Ltd.* [2004] 1 Lloyd's Rep.460 per Longmore LJ at pp. 463–464; *The Jordan II* [2005] 1 Lloyd's Rep 57 per Lord Steyn at pp. 63–64; *The Giannis N.K.* [1998] AC 605 per Lord Lloyd at p. 615 and Lord Steyn at p. 623; *The Limnos* [2008] 2 Lloyd's Rep.166.

70 *The Lady M* [2017] EWHC 3348 (Comm); [2018] 1 Lloyd's Rep Plus 22.

> excessive regard to earlier decisions of English Courts in construing the international code. Where there are words or expressions which have received judicial interpretation as terms of art, the words may be presumed to have been used in the sense already judicially imputed to them; but the words have to be given their plain meaning, which should be given effect to without concern as to whether that involves altering the previous law.

Popplewell J held that: (1) the article IV(2)(b) was capable of applying to fires that were deliberately or barratrously started by the crew, and (2) he could not determine whether the chief engineer's conduct constituted barratry without further findings of fact as to the chief engineer's state of mind.

Simon LJ, in the Court of Appeal, discussed the ordinary meaning of the words in article IV.2(b), saying:[71]

> The words, "fire, unless caused by the actual fault or privity of the carrier," is a phrase whose natural and ordinary meaning is clear. The words exclude the carrier from liability for fire however caused, provided it is not caused with the actual fault or privity of the carrier or in breach of its obligations set out in article III.1. The word "fire" contains no implicit qualification as to how the fire is started, whether accidentally or deliberately, negligently or otherwise. Nor is there any implicit qualification depending on who may be responsible for the fire. The only express qualification is the proviso in the second part of the clause, "unless caused by the actual fault or privity of the carrier." Unless the cause of the fire falls within the proviso, fire is an excepted peril.

Simon LJ observed that this view of the ordinary meaning of article IV.2(b) gains support from a number of authoritative textbooks.[72] He ruled on issue 2 that:[73]

> It was common ground that an act of barratry occurs without the actual fault or privity of the carrier. However, Glencore's argument necessarily implies an additional qualification to the words, "Fire, unless caused by the actual fault or privity of the carrier, or the fault or neglect of the crew." I can see no proper basis for implying such words either as a matter of ordinary meaning nor on any of the supplementary arguments advanced by Glencore, and I see principled reasons for not doing so.

It followed that in this case, the issue of whether the conduct of the chief engineer in starting the fire constituted barratry is not determinative of whether the owners are exempt from liability for the fire under article IV.2(b) because it was agreed that the fire was caused deliberately by him with intent to cause damage. Article IV.2(b) exempts the owners from liability if the fire was caused deliberately or barratrously, subject only to (i) a causative breach of article III.1 or (ii) the actual fault or privity of the owners. The Court of Appeal dismissed Glencore's appeal on issue 2 (the fire exception) and allowed its appeal on issue 1 (whether the conduct of the chief engineer necessarily constituted barratry on the assumed facts).[74]

There was some discussion by Simon LJ of the Hague Rules and its history, context, object, and purpose for the relevance in examining the meaning of the words "fire, unless caused by the actual fault or privity of the carrier." The Court of Appeal also confirmed the previous decision in the High Court that the defence under article IV.2(b), which clearly excludes the carrier from liability for fire, however caused, provided it was not

71 Ibid, per Simon LJ [2019] 2 Lloyd's Rep.109 (C.A.) at pp. 43, 116.

72 *Bills of Lading*, 3rd ed at para. 11.241; *Scrutton on Charterparties and Bills of Lading*, 24th ed at para. 14–074; *Carver on Bills of Lading*, 4th ed at para. 9–215; *Voyage Charters*, 4th ed at para. 85.261.

73 *The Lady M*, sup., per Simon LJ at pp. 122, 100.

74 Ibid, p. 125.

caused with the actual fault or privity of the carrier or in breach of its obligations set out in article 3.1.

5.7 Unseaworthy when catching fire

As the law laid down in the *CMA CGM Libra*,[75] the vessel is unseaworthy before and at the beginning of the voyage. However, those defects that could be rectified quickly will not render the vessel unseaworthy; this view gains support from a number of authoritative textbooks.

According to the editors of *Carver on Charterparties*:[76]

> Defects that are capable of being quickly remedied on the passage do not render a ship unseaworthy.

Editors of *Carver on Bills of Lading*[77] to similar effect:

> Where a particular matter can be put right quickly and easily at sea, the ship need not be unseaworthy in sailing without its having been rectified.

Finally, the editor of *Scrutton on Charterparties and Bills of Lading*[78] put it this way:

> Nor does a defect that can be quickly remedied at sea necessarily make the ship unseaworthy.

It's also suggested that a vessel is not unseaworthy because, at the commencement of the voyage, there is something which may need a correction which can readily be made and the need for which has not been hidden.[79] In *Steel v State Line Steamship Co*,[80] Lord Blackburn distinguished between (i) a porthole left open on the orlop deck with cargo piled up high against it, where no one could see whether the porthole had been left open or not, in circumstances where it would require a great deal of time to remove the cargo, and (ii) a porthole left open in a cabin which could be shut at a moment's notice as soon as the sea became rough. In the latter case, the vessel would not be unfit to encounter the perils of the voyage because the matter could be set right within a few minutes, and "if they did not put it right after such a warning, that would be negligence on the part of the crew and not unseaworthiness of the ship."

In the *Maurienne*,[81] the vessel arrived at Halifax on Saturday, 31 January. It has been common ground that the appellants' cargo was loaded in no. 3 hold. The loading of this hold probably began on Tuesday, 3 February, and finished on Friday, 6 February. In the view which Their Lordships take, the precise times do not matter. The loading of all cargo was completed at about 8:15 on Friday evening. On the morning of Friday, it was found that three scupper pipes passing through no. 3 hold and discharging from the bath, toilet,

75 *The CMA CGM Libra* [2019] 1 Lloyd's Rep.595 (C.A.); [2021] UKSC 51.

76 *Carver on Charterparties*, 2nd ed at para. 3–122.

77 *Carver on Bills of Lading*, 4th ed at para. 9–015.

78 *Scrutton on Charterparties and Bills of Lading*, 24th ed at para. 7–025.

79 *The Northumberland* [1926] 24 Ll.L. Rep.446; [1927] 27 Ll.L. Rep.395 (H.L.); *Moore and Another v Lunn and Others* [1922] 11 Ll.L. Rep.86; [1923] 15 Ll.L. Rep.155; *Steel et al. v The State Line Steamship Company* (1877–78) L.R. 3 App. Cas.72; *International Packers London Ltd v Ocean SS Co.* [1955] 2 Lloyd's Rep.218; *The Aconcagua* [2010] 1 Lloyd's Rep.1 per Christopher Clarke J at p. 52.

80 *Steel v State Line Steamship Co.* [1877] LR 3 App. Cas. 72.

81 *The Maurienne* [1959] 2 Lloyd's Rep.105.

and galley sink were blocked by ice at the point at which they met the ship's side. The master instructed one of the officers to have these pipes thawed out. This work was done between 3:00 and 4:00 on Friday afternoon by an employee of a Halifax firm, Purdy Bros., who used an acetylene torch. There was cork insulation around the pipes. The heat of the acetylene torch acting on the cork started a fire. This was detected at about 11:30 p.m. Despite efforts to extinguish the fire, it spread, and at about 5:30 a.m. on Saturday, 7 February, the master was forced to order the scuttling of the ship, which resulted in the loss (inter alia) of the appellants' cargo.

On the pleadings, the appellants claimed for their goods: the respondents relied on the immunities under article IV, rule 1 and rule 2(a) and (b). They further submitted that they had performed their obligations under article III, rule 1. The appellants submitted that the respondents had not exercised due diligence to make the ship seaworthy within article III, rule 1; that the unseaworthiness so resulting caused the damage; and that, in these circumstances, the respondents could not rely on the immunities under article IV.

The district judge in admiralty found that the fire was due to the heat generated by the acetylene torch, and this is not now disputed. It had been contended by the appellants that the presence of ice made the ship unseaworthy. This was rejected by the learned judge, and this finding is not now disputed. The learned judge held that the warranty of seaworthiness was not a continuing warranty. He held that, on the evidence, the appellants' cargo had been loaded before the attempt to thaw the ice had begun and that the ship was seaworthy at the "loading stage." He further held that the question of seaworthiness for the voyage never arose as the ship never sailed. In these circumstances, the respondents were entitled to rely on article IV.[82]

The Exchequer Court, on appeal, held that the fourth officer and, possibly, the master and chief engineer were negligent in relation to the use of the acetylene torch. Cameron J held that the presence of ice did not make the ship unseaworthy. The learned judge held that the obligations under article III had been fully carried out before the thawing-out operations started. He further held that, on this basis, the fire arose from negligence in the management of the ship. The respondents were therefore entitled to the benefit of rule 2 (a) of article IV. The court considered various authorities on what constituted management. It was further held that the respondents could rely on rule 2(b) in that the negligence of the respondents' servants did not constitute actual fault or privity of the carrier.[83]

In the Supreme Court, the majority held that, on the evidence, the appellants' goods were not stowed until after the commencement of the fire. On the assumption that a plaintiff can only rely on unseaworthiness at the commencement of the loading and that, for this purpose, the commencement of the loading means the commencement of the loading of each shippers' parcel and not the commencement of loading any cargo, the appellants had therefore established a breach of article III, subject to due diligence. The Supreme Court held that the respondents had established due diligence.[84]

Lord Somervell of Harrow, in Judicial Committee of the Privy Council, giving the judgment, observed that in cases of fire, article III never comes into operation even though the fire makes the ship unseaworthy. All fires and all damage from a fire on this argument fall to be dealt with under article IV, rule 2(b). If this were right, there was, at any rate, a

82 Ibid, p. 112.
83 Ibid.
84 Ibid.

very strong case for saying that there was no fault or privity of the carrier within that rule, and the respondents would succeed.[85]

Lord Somervell of Harrow stated:[86]

> In their Lordships' opinion the point fails. Art. III, Rule 1, is an overriding obligation. If it is not fulfilled and the non-fulfilment causes the damage, the immunities of Art. IV cannot be relied on. This is the natural construction apart from the opening words of Art. IV, Rule 2. The fact that that Rule is made subject to the provision of Art. IV and Rule 1 is not so conditioned makes the point clear beyond argument.

It is important to remember that the Act of 1924 was the outcome of an international conference and that the rules in the schedule have an international currency. As these rules must come under the consideration of foreign courts, it is desirable in the interests of uniformity that their interpretation should not be rigidly controlled by domestic precedents of antecedent date, but rather that the language of the rules should be construed on broad principles of general acceptation.

In Their Lordships' opinion "before and at the beginning of the voyage" means the period from at least the beginning of the loading until the vessel starts on her voyage. The word "before" cannot, in their opinion, be read as meaning "at the commencement of the loading." If this had been intended, it would have been said. The question when precisely the period begins does not arise in this case, hence the insertion in the previous passage of the words "at least."[87]

In that view, the obligation to exercise due diligence to make the ship seaworthy continued over the whole of the period from the beginning of loading until the ship sank. There was a failure to exercise due diligence during that period. As a result, the ship became unseaworthy, and this unseaworthiness caused the damage to and loss of the appellants' goods. The appellants are therefore entitled to succeed.[88]

Their Lordships observed that the doctrine of stages had its anomalies, and some important matters were never elucidated by authority. When the warranty was absolute, it seems at any rate intelligible to restrict it to certain points of time. It would be surprising if a duty to exercise due diligence ceased as soon as loading began, only to reappear later shortly before the beginning of the voyage.[89] It followed that the shipowner will be unable to rely on its Hague Rules defence, as such constituted a breach by the shipowner of its overriding obligation to exercise due diligence before and at the beginning of the voyage.

5.8 Lack of due diligence

As noted in the *Maurienne*, *sup*., the obligations arising under article III, rule 1 are overriding. The due diligence required is due diligence in the work itself by the carrier and all persons, whether servants or agents or independent contractors whom he employs or engages in the task of making the ship seaworthy; the carrier does not, therefore, discharge the burden of proving that due diligence has been exercised by proof that he engaged

85 Ibid, per Lord Somervell of Harrow at p. 113.
86 Ibid.
87 Ibid.
88 Ibid.
89 Ibid, p. 114.

competent experts to perform and supervise the task of making the ship seaworthy. The statute imposes an inescapable personal obligation.[90]

In the *Eurasian Dream*,[91] a pure car carrier, on 23 July 1998, a fire started on deck 4 while she was in the port at Sharjah. The fire, which was not extinguished by the master and crew, eventually destroyed or damaged the vessel's cargo of new and second-hand vehicles and rendered the vessel itself a constructive total loss. The claimants, who were the relevant cargo interests, claimed against the defendant carrier in respect of destruction or damage to the vehicles.

The claimants' case was that the vessel was unseaworthy in many respects and that there was a wholesale failure by the vessel's technical managers, Univan Ship Management of Hong Kong (Univan), to exercise due diligence. The serious failings of Univan led to a ship and a crew unfitted for the foreseeable eventualities of the voyage. The negligence and incompetence of Univan's management resulted in an incompetent crew and an unseaworthy ship. The claimants alleged that the defendants were in breach of their obligations under article III, rule 1 of the Hague/Hague–Visby Rules. In their alternative case under article III, rule 2, the claimants argued that the evidence showed the fault or privity of Univan for the purposes of the fire exception. The claimants submitted that the vessel was unseaworthy in the vessel's equipment, the competence/efficiency of the master and crew, and the adequacy of the documentation supplied to the vessel.[92]

The parties helpfully provided a summary of the relevant legal principles which Cresswell J largely agreed. It was common ground that the bill of lading contracts in the present case incorporated either the Hague or Hague–Visby Rules. For the purposes of liability, nothing turns upon the distinction between the two sets of rules. And for the burden of proof, authorities are free to be summarized:

(1) The burden of proof is on the claimants to prove that the vessel was unseaworthy, pursuant to article III, rule 1, before and at the beginning of the voyage.
(2) The claimants must then also prove that the loss or damage was caused by that unseaworthiness.[93]
(3) If the claimants discharge the burden in respect of (1) and (2), the burden passes to the defendants to prove that they and those for whom they are responsible exercised due diligence to make the ship seaworthy in the relevant respects.[94]
    (a) If they fail to do so, the defendants are not entitled to rely upon the exceptions in article IV, rule 2, including the "fire" exception.
    (b) If the defendants are able to do so, they can rely upon the "fire" exception as a defence to breach of article III, rule 2, subject to the claimants proving that the loss or damage was "caused by the actual fault or privity of the carrier."[95]
(4) In relation to due diligence, proof of unseaworthiness fulfils the same function as *res ipsa loquitur* does in ordinary cases of negligence.[96]

90 *Scrutton on Charterparties and Bills of Lading*, 24th ed at para. 14–046.
91 *The Eurasian Dream* [2002] 1 Lloyd's Rep.719.
92 Ibid.
93 *The Europa* [1908], pp. 84, 97–98.
94 *The Toledo* [1995] 1 Lloyd's Rep.40 at p. 50.
95 *The Apostolis* [1996] 1 Lloyd's Rep.475 at p. 483.
96 *The Amstelslot* [1963] 2 Lloyd's Rep.223 at p. 235 per Lord Devlin; *The Fjord Wind* [2000] 2 Lloyd's Rep.191 at p. 205. In practical terms, the reasoning is: "a ship should not be unseaworthy if proper care is taken" (per Lord Justice Stuart-Smith).

Cresswell J discussed the duty to provide a seaworthy ship under article III, rule 1 and stated that the absolute duty at common law to provide a seaworthy ship is displaced by article III, rule 1 of the rules, which requires the carrier to exercise due diligence to provide a seaworthy ship "before and at the beginning of the voyage".[97]

Cresswell J accepted that the classic definition of *seaworthiness* is contained in the judgment of Scrutton LJ in *F. C. Bradley & Sons Ltd. v Federal Steam Navigation Co.*, approving a statement from Carver on *Carriage by Sea*:

> The ship must have that degree of fitness which an ordinary careful owner would require his vessel to have at the commencement of her voyage having regard to all the probable circumstances of it. Would a prudent owner have required that it (sc the defect) be made good before sending his ship to sea, had he known of it?[98]

Cresswell J also agreed that seaworthiness is not an absolute concept; it is relative to the nature of the ship, to the particular voyage, and even to the particular stage of the voyage on which the ship is engaged.[99] Seaworthiness must be judged by the standards and practices of the industry at the relevant time, at least so long as those standards and practices are reasonable.

Cresswell J summarized the components of the duty as follows:[100]

(1) The vessel must be in a suitable condition and suitably manned and equipped to meet the ordinary perils likely to be encountered while performing the services required of it. This aspect of the duty relates to the following matters:
  (a) The physical condition of the vessel and its equipment.
  (b) The competence/efficiency of the master and crew.
  (c) The adequacy of stores and documentation.
(2) The vessel must be cargoworthy in the sense that it is in a fit state to receive the specified cargo.

Cresswell J discussed the duty of due diligence, saying:[101]

> The duty of "due diligence" is an "inescapable personal obligation"; it is non-delegable. The carrier will therefore be responsible for negligence of those to whom it delegates due diligence. The question is whether unseaworthiness is due to any lack of diligence in those who have been implicated by the carrier in the work of keeping or making the vessel seaworthy. Such persons are the carriers' agents whose diligence or lack of it is attributable to the carrier. This principle is relevant in two respects: (1) the carrier under the bills of lading is liable for the want of due diligence by the owners or managers; (2) the carrier is liable for the want of due diligence of the master insofar as the carrier or the owners or managers have delegated to him their duties as to seaworthiness.
>
> The exercise of due diligence is equivalent to the exercise of reasonable care and skill: "Lack of due diligence is negligence; and what is in issue, in this case, is whether there was an error of judgment that amounted to professional negligence."

97 *The Maurienne* [1959] 2 Lloyd's Rep.105.

98 *F.C. Bradley & Sons Ltd. v Federal Steam Navigation Co.* [1926] 24 Ll.L. Rep.446 at p. 454.

99 *The Fjord Wind* [1999] 1 Lloyd's Rep.307, per Moore-Bick J at p. 315 (approved by Clarke LJ at [2000] 2 Lloyd's Rep.191 at p. 197.

100 *The Eurasian Dream* [2002] 1 Lloyd's Rep.719 per Cresswell J at p. 736.

101 Ibid, p. 737.

Cresswell J pointed out that the obligation under article III, rule 2 is to carry and care for the goods "properly and carefully." The rule imposes a duty to adopt a sound system and to exercise reasonable care in its operation. The exceptions under article IV, rule 2 may not be relied upon where the carrier is in breach of the "overriding obligation" to provide a seaworthy ship under article III, rule 1 and that breach is causative of the loss/damage.[102]

Cresswell J viewed that fire is one of the greatest threats to ships at sea. The ship's firefighting ability, and therefore its seaworthiness, is crucially dependent upon the competence of its crew as the firefighters and, in particular, the master as their leader. The CO_2 system is a potent weapon in the firefighters' armoury. Knowledge of when and how it should be used is essential.[103]

Cresswell J found that the vessel was not in a suitable condition and suitably manned and equipped. Although it is convenient to categorize the findings of unseaworthiness under three headings (the vessel's equipment, the competence/efficiency of the master and the crew, and the adequacy of the documentation supplied to the vessel).[104]

Cresswell J further found that the defendants have failed to prove that they and those for whom they are responsible exercised due diligence to make the ship seaworthy in the relevant respects. The defendants as a bill of lading carriers are liable for the want of due diligence by the owners/managers and for the want of due diligence of the master insofar as the first defendants or the owners or managers delegated to him their duties as to seaworthiness.[105]

The competence or efficiency of the master and crew is explained by Cresswell J in this case. It is not disputed that a ship may be rendered unseaworthy by the inefficiency of the master who commands her. Incompetence or inefficiency may consist of a "disabling want of skill" or a "disabling want of knowledge." Incompetence or inefficiency is a question of fact, which may be proved from one incident, and need not be demonstrated by reference to a series of acts. However, one mistake or even more than one mistake does not necessarily render a crew member incompetent.[106]

"Disabling want of skill" and "disabling lack of knowledge" equally render the master unfit and unqualified to command. It must be possible, in certain circumstances, to draw the inference from one incident that someone had a "disabling lack of knowledge." One mistake or even more than one mistake does not necessarily render a crew member incompetent. Anyone can make a mistake without the conclusion being drawn that he has either "a disabling want of skill" or a "disabling lack of knowledge."[107]

Turning to incompetence, as explained by Cresswell J in this case, it is to be distinguished from negligence and may derive from:

(a) An inherent lack of ability.
(b) A lack of adequate training or instruction, for example, lack of adequate firefighting training.

102 Ibid, p. 738.
103 Ibid, p. 739.
104 Ibid, p. 742.
105 Ibid, p. 744.
106 Ibid, p. 736.
107 *The Clan Gordon* [1923] 17 Ll.L. Rep.120 (H.L.).

(c) A lack of knowledge about a particular vessel and/or its systems.[108]
(d) A disinclination to perform the job properly.
(e) Physical or mental disability or incapacity (e.g. drunkenness, illness).[109]

It's followed that once an incompetent crew has been found, it is the owner's burden of proof to show that due diligence was exercised. The exercise of due diligence by a shipowner is equivalent to the exercise of reasonable care and skill. Lack of due diligence is negligence, and it is relevant to consider "what other skilled men do in comparable circumstances."[110] In other words, the standard, again, is what the reasonable, prudent shipowner would have done in the circumstances.[111] This includes the initial selection and appointment of crew[112] and the necessary specific instruction of the crew in relation to a specific vessel and/or her systems and/or voyage. The continuous supervision and training of the crew is an element of the shipowner's due diligence.[113]

5.9 Explosion

> In the MS *ER Hamburg*,[114] this is an appeal against a final declaratory arbitration award dated 1 March 2005. The dispute between the parties arose from an explosion on board a vessel owned by a German company (the owners) which was chartered by the owners' predecessors in title to a South American company (the charterers) by a charterparty on an amended New York Produce Exchange (1946) form. The explosion severely damaged the vessel, and the owners brought a claim against the charterers for loss of hire and loss and damage, which they contended had been caused by the loading of a container of calcium hypochlorite. The amount of the claim was some US$63 million. The charterers counterclaimed for some US$12 million.[115]
>
> https://vlex.co.uk/vid/compania-sud-american-vapores-805801377

Morison J observed that the question at issue is dependent upon the true construction of the charterparty. In the case, the question is not whether the owners were under a duty to intervene in the loading process but rather whether they owed that duty to the charterers; there is no authority which assists the charterers' case.

Morison J referred to *Court Line Ltd v Canadian Transport Co Ltd.*[116] In this case, Lord Atkin robustly rejected the "there is no foundation at all for this defence" defence, that the words "under the supervision of the captain" placed responsibility for stowage or to exercise due supervision over stowage upon the owners. The supervision of the stowage by the captain is, in any case, a matter of course; he has, in any event, to protect his ship from being made unseaworthy, and this could not be read as impacting on the duty owed by the owners to the charterers for stowage. The reservation of the right of the captain to supervise, a right which, in my opinion, would have existed even if not expressly reserved, has no effect whatever in relieving the charterers of their primary duty to stow safely.

108 *The Farrandoc* [1967] 2 Lloyd's Rep.276; *The Star Sea* [2001] 1 Lloyd's Rep.389 (H.L.) (operation of the CO_2 firefighting system).
109 *Moore v Lunn* [1923] 15 Ll.L. Rep.155; *Rio Tinto Co. v Seed Shipping Co.* [1926] 24 Ll.L. Rep.316.
110 *The Amstelslot* [1963] 2 Lloyd's Rep.223 (H.L.).
111 *The Garden City* [1982] 2 Lloyd's Rep.382.
112 *The Makedonia* [1962] 1 Lloyd's Rep.316.
113 *The Marion* [1984] 2 Lloyd's Rep.1.
114 *The MS ER Hamburg* [2006] 2 Lloyd's Rep.66.
115 Ibid, p. 67.
116 *Court Line Ltd v Canadian Transport Co Ltd.* [1940] 67 Ll.L. Rep.161.

Morison J commented that Lord Atkin is simply saying that a master is entitled to seek to protect his vessel from stowage which renders the vessel unsafe and that he would have that right whether or not the contract expressly conferred it on him. But there is clearly a difference between a right to supervise and requiring reloading. This case was dealing with damage to cargo caused by bad stowage, rather than damage to the vessel herself, where there was an unamended clause 8 and express incorporation of the Hague Rules. There is no suggestion at all that the question of the relationship between stowage and seaworthiness in a contract such as this was not in the minds of the members of the House, as Lord Wright's speech and the passage relating to safety in Lord Atkin's speech. A clear distinction was drawn between an entitlement to supervise on the one hand and a duty to do so (owed to the charterers) on the other. An owner might be liable under a bill of lading to a cargo owner if the stowage was such as to render the vessel unseaworthy and the owners were guilty of a lack of due diligence in "looking after" the vessel and the goods, but as Lord Wright explained, the effect of clause 8 was to transfer that responsibility to the charterers from whom the owners would be entitled to an indemnity.[117]

Turning to the first issue in this appeal, what is the proper interpretation of clause 8 of the charterparty, which places the responsibility for stowage on the charterers, in light of clause 24, which is expressly incorporated as a clause paramount of the Hague–Visby Rules? In other words, if the stowage was done in such a way as to render the vessel unseaworthy, are the owners or charterers responsible under the contract for the losses? Morision J concluded:[118]

> There was a clear distinction between the owners' entitlement to supervise, on the one hand, and a duty to do so – owed to the charterers – on the other. An owner might be liable under a bill of lading to a cargo owner if the stowage was such as to render the vessel unseaworthy and the owners were guilty of a lack of due diligence in looking after the vessel and the goods. The effect of the unamended clause 8 of the NYPE form was to transfer that responsibility to the charterers from whom the owners would be entitled to an indemnity. There was no authority which supported the charterers' argument that the owners had a duty to the charterers to intervene to avoid unseaworthiness.

And for the second issue, assuming as a fact that the bunkers were heated to a temperature above what was required to keep the fuel oil reasonably thin and that this was causative of the explosion, do owners have a defence to a claim for breach of article III, rule 2 by reason of article IV, rule 2? Morision J stated:[119]

> The arbitrators' decision was correct. The excessive heating of the bunker oil was clearly something done as part of the running of the ship not specifically related to the cargo. The heating of the bunker tank was to facilitate the transfer of oil from it to the engines. It was a single act which did not relate in any way to the care of the cargo, albeit it might have indirectly adversely affected the cargo.

There is another question. The duty under article III.1 was discussed in this case. As per Lord Keith in *Riverstone Meat Company Pty Ltd v Lancashire Shipping Co. Ltd*[120] on page 871:

117 *The MS ER Hamburg*, sup., per Morision J at p. 79.
118 Ibid.
119 Ibid, p. 82.
120 *Riverstone Meat Company Pty Ltd v Lancashire Shipping Co. Ltd* [1961] AC 807.

> The obligation is a statutory obligation imposed in defined contracts between the carrier and the shipper. There is nothing novel in a statutory obligation being held to be incapable of delegation so as to free the person bound of liability for breach of the obligation, and the reasons for this become, I think, more compelling where the obligation is made part of a contract between parties. We are not faced with a question in the realm of tort, or negligence. The obligation is a statutory contractual obligation. The novelty, if there is one, is that the statutory obligation is expressed in terms of an obligation to exercise due diligence, etc. There is nothing extravagant in saying that this is an inescapable personal obligation. The carrier cannot claim to have shed his obligation to exercise due diligence to make his ship seaworthy by selecting a firm of competent ship repairers to make his ship seaworthy. Their failure to use due diligence to do so is his failure. The question, as I see it, is not one of vicarious responsibility at all. It is a question of statutory obligation.

It followed that the owners will be responsible for loss and damage caused by personal want of due diligence on the part of the owners or their managers or their servants, which is established in the *CMA CGM Libra*[121] recently. In this landmark case, the Supreme Court concluded that, at 144–145:

> The carrier cannot escape from its responsibilities under Article III rule 1 of the Hague Rules by delegating them to its servants or agents qua navigators, or qua managers, or qua engineers or qua ship repairers. If the task of making the vessel seaworthy has been entrusted by the carrier to those servants or agents then (if relevant) they are acting qua carriers and under Article III Rule 1 of the Hague Rules the carrier is responsible for any causative failure by them to exercise due diligence.
>
> The carrier's obligation under the Hague Rules is not subject to a category-based distinction between a vessel's quality of seaworthiness or navigability and the crew's act of navigating. The crew's failure to navigate the ship safely is capable of constituting a lack of due diligence by the carrier. It makes no difference that the delegated task of making the vessel seaworthy involves navigation.

However, a number of cases have stressed the need for there to be an unbroken chain of causation between the charterers' order and the loss, damage, or liability – see, for example, the *Ann Stathatos*,[122] the *Athanasia Comninos*,[123] and the *Aconcagua*.[124] Causation in fact or "but for" causation is insufficient. As stated by Donaldson J in the *White Rose*:[125]

> It is necessary in every case to establish an unbroken chain of causation, although I would not accept as a generalization that "if some act of negligence intervenes or some marine casualty intervenes then I think the chain of causation is broken and the indemnity does not operate." A loss may well arise in the course of compliance with the time charterers' orders, but this fact does not, without more, establish that it was caused by and is in law a consequence of such compliance and, in the absence of proof of such causation, there is no right to indemnity.

In the *Ann Stathatos*,[126] an issue arises out of a series of explosions which occurred in June 1942, and as a result of which, she had to undergo certain repairs. At the time she was on time charter to the Minister of Transport. The immediate cause of the first explosion was the starting of a flame or spark in an explosive atmosphere consisting of gas emanating from a cargo of coal which, a few days before, the owners had loaded on the instructions of the

121 *The CMA CGM Libra* [2021] UKSC 51.
122 *The Ann Stathatos* [1950] 83 Ll.L. Rep.228.
123 *The Athanasia Comminos* [1990] 1 Lloyd's Rep.277.
124 *The Aconcagua* [2010] 1 Lloyd's Rep.1; [2011] 1 Lloyd's Rep.683 (C.A.).
125 *The White Rose* [1969] 2 Lloyd's Rep.52, per Donaldson J. at p. 59.
126 *The Ann Stathatos* [1950] 83 Ll.L. Rep.228.

charterer. The owners contend that the ship was not off-hire during the period of detention necessitated for her repair and, alternatively, that they are entitled to be indemnified by the charterer under clause 9 of the charterparty against the loss caused by her detention.

Devlin J (as he then was) viewed that express and apparently unambiguous words in one clause may have to be reduced in effect if they conflict with the express words of another clause, for the two clauses must be construed so that they may stand together; but if the conflict is only with an implication, it is the implication that must give way. Accordingly, the learned justice held that an order to load a particular cargo was an order as to the employment of the ship, and that the consequences of complying with such an order are within the scope of the indemnity provided by clause 9. In his judgment, an arbitrator's finding on causation, unless he can be shown to have misdirected himself on some principle of law or on some point of construction, or to have acted on insufficient evidence, is conclusive.

Therefore, the real question is whether the charterers' order was an effective cause of the owner having to bear risk or cost of a kind which he had not contractually agreed to bear. Like all questions of causation, this one is sensitive to the legal context in which it arises. It depends on the intended scope of the indemnity as a matter of construction, which is necessarily informed by its purpose.[127]

In the *Aconcagua*,[128] at about 0230 local time on 30 December 1998, an explosion took place in the no. 3 hold of the vessel when she was on passage off the coast of Ecuador. The fire which resulted was so great that the crew had to abandon the ship. Widespread damage was caused to the vessel and her cargo. The cause of the explosion was the self-ignition of 334 kegs of calcium hypochlorite, which were themselves loaded in a container. The container had been loaded at Busan, South Korea, and was due to be discharged at San Antonio in Chile. The charterers claimed an indemnity from the shippers under article IV, rule 6 of the Hague Rules. The charterers submitted that the calcium hypochlorite had, unknown to them, an abnormally high thermal instability, being prone to self-heat at ordinary carriage temperatures. They admitted that the stowage of the container next to the bunker tank was negligent and that the IMDG Code required the cargo to be stowed "away from" sources of heat. However, the charterers denied that the heating of the bunker tank was causative of the explosion. In any event, the vessel was not unseaworthy, and the negligent decision of the chief officer to heat a bunker tank adjacent to a cargo of calcium hypochlorite was "an act, neglect or default in the management of the vessel" for which the charterers were not responsible by virtue of article IV, rule 2(a) of the Hague Rules.

The shippers contended that the calcium hypochlorite was not abnormal or, at least, had not been shown to be so, that the heating of the bunker tank was a cause of the explosion, and that the bad stowage of the container and its contents amounted to unseaworthiness.

Clarke J observed that the carrier is bound before and at the beginning of the voyage to exercise due diligence to make the vessel seaworthy. In order for the carrier to be in breach, the vessel must be unseaworthy at the commencement of the voyage.[129]

---

127 *The Kos* [2012] UKSC 17; [2012] 2 Lloyd's Rep.292, 12.

128 *The Aconcagua* [2010] 1 Lloyd's Rep.1; [2011] 1 Lloyd's Rep.683 (C.A.).

129 Ibid, per Christopher Clarke J [2010] 1 Lloyd's Rep.1 at p. 52.

Clarke J viewed that bad stowage which endangers the safety of the ship and cannot readily be cured on the voyage cause unseaworthiness. Unseaworthiness is usually a physical state existing at the commencement of the voyage which endangers the safety of the vessel. That state existed in that case because isopentane with a flash point well below 0°C and a boiling point of about 28°C was a source of immediate danger in a voyage in July in the Arabian Gulf. The proximity of the container to no. 3 FFOTS does not, by itself, constitute a dangerous physical state. But there can be unseaworthiness, not classifiable as a physical state, for example, where there are incompetent officers or crew, which is not here alleged.[130]

Clarke J ruled that the vessel was only potentially in danger if the no. 3 FFOTS was heated on the voyage to San Antonio. If no such heating had taken place, the container would, so far as anything concerning the vessel was concerned, be entirely safe. In those circumstances, the vessel cannot be treated as unseaworthy at the commencement of the voyage, unless such heating was bound to occur because the no. 3 FFOTS had to be used on the voyage to San Antonio, or if such heating was pre-programmed to occur, or if the crew were incompetent in the sense that they were so ill-trained that they did not know they had to protect heat-sensitive cargoes.[131]

In the case, the vessel did not have to use the no. 3 FFO tanks on the voyage from Busan to San Antonio. She had not used them during the voyage from Busan to Los Angeles. At Los Angeles, she had bunkered, and all tanks were available for use on the next leg of the voyage to San Antonio. The vessel bunkered no. 2S, nos. 3AFOT (P&S), and nos. 4P and 4S and, in addition, had available no. 3 FFOT P. In Clarke J's view, whether or not those tanks were used would depend on an operational decision made during the voyage. The operative fault lay not in the stowage of the container but in the decision to use and heat no. 3 FFOTS and the failure of the chief officer and the chief engineer, in deciding which bunkers to use on the leg out from Los Angeles, to appreciate that a cargo described as one to be stowed away from sources of heat ought not to be heated by the bunker tank around it and that bunkers from other tanks should be used.

Clarke J stated that a vessel may be unseaworthy if there is no system in operation to deal with the ordinary incidents of a voyage, including the need for the cargo to be stowed in a way that does not endanger the ship. To heat no. 3 FFOTS was negligence, but not unseaworthiness. The obligation to take care to make the vessel seaworthy does not mean that the ship must be immune from the negligence of her crew.[132]

In summary, Clarke J concluded:[133]

(a) The CH shipped on board Aconcagua was of a dangerous nature of which CSAV did not, nor ought it to have had knowledge;
(b) Sinochem, on whom lies the burden of proof, has not established that the heating of No. 3 FFOTS was a cause of the explosion. The likelihood is that it was not;
(c) The heating of the No 3 FFOTS did not constitute or result fromunseaworthiness;
(d) The heating constituted an act, neglect or default in the management of the vessel, which is an excepted peril;

130 Ibid.
131 Ibid, p. 53.
132 Ibid.
133 Ibid, p. 54.

(e) Accordingly, even if the heating had been causative, CSAV would still be entitled to an indemnity under article IV, rule 6.

It was held in this case that the heating of the bunker tank did not constitute or result from unseaworthiness. The vessel could not be treated as unseaworthy at the commencement of the voyage unless the heating of the bunker tank was bound to occur, which, on the facts of the present case, it was not. Whether or not that particular bunker tank was used would depend on an operational decision made during the voyage. The operative fault lay not in the stowage of the container in the position it was stowed but in the negligence of the crew in using and heating the relevant bunker tank. To heat the bunker tank around hold no. 3 was negligence, but not unseaworthiness. The obligation to take care to make the vessel seaworthy did not mean that the ship had to be immune from the negligence of her crew, which was upheld in the Court of Appeal.[134]

A commonly seaworthiness applied test is whether a prudent shipowner, if he had known of the defect, would have sent the ship to sea in that condition.[135] Another is to ask whether the vessel was, in all respects, fit to carry her cargo safely to her destination having regard to the ordinary perils to which such cargo would be exposed on the voyage.[136] That formulation is not, however, to be interpreted as a warranty that the vessel will successfully overcome all ordinary perils. The ship must have that degree of fitness that an ordinary careful owner would require his vessel to have at the commencement of her voyage, having regard to all the probable consequences of it.[137] Furthermore, a master or other responsible officer should possess when engaged upon the carriage of particular cargo.[138]

The implied obligation not to carry dangerous cargo without informing the carrier extends beyond the case of common carriage to the case of carriage in pursuance of statutory duty. In case damage is due to the misdeclaration of goods, the shipper is typically held liable for all damages. This includes reimbursing the shipping company for all damage to the ship and paying other cargo owners whose goods were damaged or destroyed. The charterers will be liable for the shipper's misdeclaration under charterparty chain. Against the background of cargo misdeclaration, one might legitimately ask that if a vessel is rendered unseaworthy at the commencement of the voyage by misdeclared cargo, might a carrier's failure to have any adequate firefighting systems to put out fire amount to a failure to exercise due diligence within the meaning of article IV, rule 1, the same as causation issue?

134 *The Aconcagua*, sup. [2011] 1 Lloyd's Rep.683 (C.A.).
135 *The Beuersstraat* [1962] 1 Lloyd's Rep.180.
136 *The Kriti Rex* [1996] 2 Lloyd's Rep.171.
137 *The Northumberland* [1926] 24 Ll.L. Rep.446; [1927] 27 Ll.L. Rep.395 (H.L.).
138 *The Athanasia Comninos and Georges Chr.Lemos* [1990] 1 Lloyd's Rep.277.

CHAPTER 6

Crew and spare parts

6.1 Introduction

Crew manning is also another important factor related to the seaworthiness of a ship. If the captain or crew is incompetent, this may render the ship unseaworthy.[1] In fact, most marine accidents can be traced back to human error in some way. In the reported cases, it is found that human factors account for a large proportion of marine accidents. This incompetence of the crew may include a lack of skills or a lack of relevant knowledge. For example, the stability of the ship is insufficient,[2] or its ballast and fuel oil system[3] or fire extinguishing system,[4] or simply the number of personnel is insufficient. In addition, crews confirmed that skills and knowledge may also render the ship unseaworthy.[5] Of course, shipowners use ordinary standards of care in selecting the right captain, and the captain need not be in perfect health. Thus, in order to avoid damage or loss of cargo due to accidents, shipowners must ensure that their ships are equipped with a sufficient number of trained and qualified crews.

Shipowners are obliged to ensure that their crews are aware of the ship's specifications or any special requirements, because if management requires a particular knowledge about its particularity, the crew on board is not informed of that knowledge or operational considerations, then it may not be possible to steer and manoeuvre the vessel safely, possibly putting the vessel at risk.[6] A vessel which requires special precautions of an unusual character to be taken in the maintenance of sufficient water ballast to ensure conditions of stability, which would not be known to a captain of ordinary skill and experience, and which have not been brought to his notice, although they had been specifically indicated to the shipowners in instructions sent to them from the shipbuilders, is not manned so as to be seaworthy, and that there was a duty on the owners to have brought such instruction to the notice of the captain. In addition, it is important for the shipowner to know how the crew member is manning to perform in a given situation and how he will handle the emergencies that may arise during the voyage, as competency includes the ability to deal with emergencies; therefore, various emergency drills on board are essential.[7]

1 *The Hong Kong Fir* [1961] 2 Lloyd's Rep.478 (C.A.); *The Makedonia* [1962] 1 Lloyd's Rep.316.
2 *Standard Oil v Clan Line* [1924] A.C. 100 (failure to furnish the master with special information as to the type of the ship and her proper method of stowage, as supplied by the builders to the owner).
3 *The Makedonia* [1962] 1 Lloyd's Rep.316.
4 *The Star Sea* [1997] 1 Lloyd's Rep.360; [2001] 1 Lloyd's Rep.389.
5 *The Heinz Horn* [1970] 1 Lloyd's Rep.191 (US 5th Circuit CA).
6 *The Farrandoc* [1967] 1 Lloyd's Rep.232; *The Eurasian Dream* [2002] 1 Lloyd's Rep.719.
7 Roger White, The Human Factor in Unseaworthiness Claims [1996] L.M.C.L.Q.

DOI: 10.4324/9781003279938-6

Furthermore, the shipowner must pay attention to the conduct of the captain or chief engineer on board, as the captain is impossible to control the ship; for example, he is regularly drunk and cannot perform his duties.[8] The test is an objective one, directed to ascertaining what an ordinarily competent fishing boat skipper might reasonably be expected to do in the same circumstances.[9]

A ship may be rendered unseaworthy by the inefficiency of the master who commands her. Disabling want of skill and disabling want of knowledge each equally renders the master unfit and unqualified to command and therefore makes the ship he commands unseaworthy.[10] Similarly, a properly qualified and generally competent master may lack sufficient knowledge of one particular skill or technique, and this may also amount to unseaworthiness.[11]

Under minimum manning requirements, shipowners must also employ a sufficient number of crew members on board to be able to provide the required services and to ensure that there are sufficient crew members to carry out emergency procedures in an emergency situation.[12] Therefore, sailing without adequate crews may render the ship unseaworthy, and the owner will therefore put them in breach of his obligation to provide a seaworthy ship.[13]

6.2 Ballast system lack of instruction

The requirement of proper manning is expressly included in a particular clause, but this does no more than reflecting an essential element in the concept of seaworthiness under the general law. The vessel must have an adequate number of persons employed to serve on board to perform functions for which they are qualified and, in fact, competent and efficient. Thus, however well qualified a vessel's master or chief engineer, if they are drunkards or too ill or too institutionally lazy, or otherwise disinclined, to perform their functions, then the vessel is unseaworthy. With the increasing risk of piratical attacks off the east coast of Africa, for such voyages, there will be a requirement for suitable training in pirate resistance methods and even possibly a measure of reasonable courage to do such things as man water cannon to repel armed boarders. Without sufficiently trained and ordinarily courageous crew, a vessel on a voyage across the Indian Ocean might well be unseaworthy.[14]

8 *Moore and Another v Lunn and Others* [1923] 15 Ll.L. Rep.155. Bankes LJ stated at p. 156 "I think that the learned Judge has found, and in my opinion rightly found, that she was not seaworthy in that respect, and for the reason that the captain and the chief engineer, at any rate, from the time the vessel ar rived in Mobile in the previous September, had both of them been what I may call habitual drunkards." *The Makedonia* [1962] 1 Lloyd's Rep.316 at p. 336.

9 *The Roberta* [1938] 60 Ll.L. Rep.84, per Greer LJ at p. 86. Also the test was mentioned in *The Hongkong Fir*, sup. at p. 168, the test would apply in case of the Human Seaworthiness "Would a reasonably prudent owner, knowing the relevant facts, have allowed this vessel to put to sea with this engine-room staff" by Salmon J; and *The Talisman* [1989] 1 Lloyd's Rep.535 at p. 539.

10 *Standard Oil Company of New York v Clan Line Steamers, Ltd.* [1924] A.C. 100, pp. 120–121; *The Farrandoc* [1967] 1 Lloyd's Rep.232.

11 *The Eurasian Dream* [2002] 1 Lloyd's Rep.719; *The Star Sea* [2001] 1 Lloyd's Rep.389.

12 *Burnard & Alger, Ltd. v Player & Co.* [1928] 31 Ll.L. Rep.281. The court found that the vessel was unseaworthy due to both causes and that the absence of one of the shipmates made a difference which led to such a result, p. 248.

13 *The Hongkong Fir* [1961] 1 Lloyd's Rep.159; [1961] 2 Lloyd's Rep.478 (C.A.); *Burnard & Alger, Ltd. v Player & Co.* [1928] 31 Ll.L. Rep.281.

14 *Voyage Charters*, 4th ed at para. 11.34.

However, even an adequate and efficient crew may lack certain specific knowledge as to the characteristics of the ship or cargo and thus render the vessel unseaworthy. In the *Clan Gordon*,[15] at the time of the occurrence, the vessel, a turret-built ship, sailed with two of her ballast tanks full of water while she was loaded down to her marks. Two days out, the captain, for the purpose of trimming the vessel more by the stern, thus giving her more freeboard and obtaining more speed, ordered the water to be pumped out of the tanks. When they were nearly empty, the captain ordered the helm to be put hard-a-port, with the object of getting bearings on south-westerly courses, and on the order being carried out, the ship heeled over and gradually turned turtle, becoming a total loss with her whole cargo.

The owners pleaded the incorporation in the charterparty of a section of the Harter Act of the United States, which provides that in the event of all due diligence being used to make the vessel seaworthy and properly manned, there should be no liability for damage or loss resulting from faults or errors in the navigation or management of the vessel. The Standard Oil Company contended that the vessel was unseaworthy when she left New York in that she was insufficiently stable, and that the captain had not been furnished with instructions for loading sent by the builders to the owners.

Viscount Haldane viewed that only scientific calculation could show the absolute character of a requirement which, if not observed, would render the ship unseaworthy. The master had not been instructed as to its special significance in the case of a turret ship like the *Clan Gordon*. He could not divine it, nor could the ordinary experience of a master not informed of the special peril due to abnormal construction be relied on to disclose it. The master did not know the unusual risk he was called on to undertake. The fault of this absence of knowledge lay not with him but with the owners, whose duty it was to have instructed him that while the vessel was seaworthy, it was only conditionally seaworthy. The breach of the condition was therefore an occurrence for which they were personally at fault.[16]

Viscount Haldane observed that it is not in serious dispute that the vessel was defective in righting power and, therefore, unseaworthy when loaded unballasted down to her marks with a homogeneous cargo. Viscount Haldane stated that the vessel was unseaworthy in that she could not safely undertake a voyage with a cargo of an approximately homogeneous character unless she had, and retained, at least 290 t of water in her lower tanks. That this was her indisputable condition for safety is not the less true because she, and vessels resembling her in shape and construction, had successfully made a certain number of voyages with a full cargo and without this minimum ballast required. Viscount Haldane draws the inference that the ship was inherently unseaworthy in certain not improbable conditions unless special precautions were taken, which it was the duty of the owners to enjoin, as is required by the structure of their ship.[17]

Lord Atkinson added and concluded:[18]

> I think, that a ship may be rendered unseaworthy by the inefficiency of the master who commands her. Does not that principle apply where the master's inefficiency consists, whatever his general efficiency may be, in his ignorance as to how his ship may, owing to the peculiarities of her structure, behave in circumstances likely to be met with on an ordinary ocean voyage? There

15 *The Clan Gordon* [1922] 13 L.l.L. Rep.597; [1923] 17 L.l.L. Rep.120 (H.L.).
16 Ibid, per Viscount Haldane [1923] 17 L.l.L. Rep.120 (H.L.) at p. 120.
17 Ibid, p. 123.
18 Ibid, per Lord Atkinson at p. 125.

> cannot be any difference in principle, I think, between disabling want of skill and disabling want of knowledge. Each equally renders the master unfit and unqualified to command and therefore makes the ship he commands unseaworthy. And the owner who withholds from the master the necessary information should, in all reason, be as responsible for the result of the master's ignorance as if he deprived the latter of the general skill and efficiency he presumably possessed.

Their Lordship thought that if any want of due diligence by the owners was here proved to have been either the sole or a contributory cause of the error of the captain, the defendants could not escape liability in respect of the exceptions from liability contained in the Harter Act and the bill of lading. In that view, it seemed unnecessary to determine whether ignorance, error, or a foolish resolution in the mind of the captain, when the vessel weighed anchor, rendered the vessel technically unseaworthy.

Thus, it was the duty of the owners, whose business to make their ship seaworthy it was, to have the master instructed as to all defects in seaworthiness during the voyage arising from inherent causes that were not obvious and of which his merely practical knowledge could not be relied on to inform him. These instructions may be open to criticism in detail.

Their Lordship ruled that there was a duty on the respondents to bring the instructions to the notice of the captain of the vessel and that the respondents have failed to prove that they used due diligence. There is no doubt that if there was a duty on the respondents to bring the instructions to the notice of the captain, the vessel was not seaworthy and that the loss resulted from her unseaworthiness.[19]

6.3 Stevedores stealing storm vale cover

There are numerous cases reported that when the vessels stay at anchorage, thieves climb to the ship along the anchor chain to steal the ship's spares. In particular, the materials and spare parts in the forepeak cabin, and even the fire hoses, fire hydrants, and mooring ropes. If the ship lacks these spare parts, such as the fire hoses and fire hydrant, the shipowner will be held responsible for cargo damage if a fire occurred in a cargo hold which could not be extinguished, or if storm vale cover was stolen, seawater also will cause cargo damage.

In the *Chyebassa*,[20] the plaintiffs' goods were shipped from Calcutta to Rotterdam on the defendants' vessel under bills of lading incorporating Hague Rules, and goods were delivered damaged by seawater owing to shipowners' stevedores stealing storm valve cover plate during unloading and loading of other cargo at Port Sudan. Plaintiffs claimed against shipowners, alleging that shipowners were liable under article III, rule 1 and 2. It was agreed that *Chyebassa*'s officers and crew were not negligent, that she was seaworthy when she left Calcutta but was unseaworthy from the time the storm valve cover plate was removed at Port Sudan. Shipowners contended that they were protected from liability by article IV, rules 1 and 2.

McNair J referred to his own judgment in the *Hector*,[21] a case under the Australian Sea-Carriage of Goods Act, 1924, concerning damage to cargo by the entry of seawater through the hatches, in which McNair J used this language:[22]

---

19 Ibid, per Lord Parmoor at p. 131.
20 *The Chyebassa* [1966] 1 Lloyd's Rep.450.
21 *The Hector* [1955] 2 Lloyd's Rep.18.
22 Ibid, per McNair J at p. 236.

> The obligation imposed by Art. III, r. 2, like the obligation imposed by Art. III, r. 1, to exercise due diligence to make the ship seaworthy, is an obligation imposed upon the shipowner himself which he cannot escape on proof that he employed a competent independent contractor who was in fact negligent.

McNair J observed that though it was agreed that the vessel became unseaworthy at Port Sudan when the cover plate was removed and that the ship's officers were not negligent in failing to ascertain that the cover plate had been removed, he has formed a clear opinion and so holds that article IV, rule 1 only applies to the obligation to exercise due diligence to secure initial seaworthiness "before and at the beginning of the voyage." See the words "in accordance with the provisions of paragraph 1 of Article III," which occur at the end of the first sentence of article IV, rule 1. Except that by the rules the absolute obligation to secure seaworthiness at this stage is altered to an obligation to exercise due diligence to secure seaworthiness, the rules do not, so far as is material for present purposes, alter the position as it existed before the act at common law.[23]

McNair J pointed out that the felonious act of the stevedores in removing the cover plate was not an act done in the navigation of the ship, and also, it was not an act done in the management of the ship. The effective cause of the admission of seawater was the act of the thieves employed by the shipowners in the performance of their obligation to discharge and load. In common law, the shipowner was always responsible for the loss by theft by persons in the ship's service. The basic principle is that it is only by clear and explicit language that the shipowner can protect himself in respect of damage to cargo caused, or contributed to, by thieves in the ship's service.[24]

McNair J held the act or default which caused or contributed to the damage to the plaintiffs' goods was the act or default of a member of the crew or a stevedore who was on board the ship as a result of the engagement of his principal by the shipowner for the performance of the shipowner's obligation to discharge or load goods generally. McNair J ruled that the defendants have failed to prove that neither the fault nor neglect of their agents or servants caused the damage to the plaintiffs' goods, still less that it did not contribute to that damage.[25]

It was held by the court that under article III, rule 2, shipowners were responsible for the action of every person whom they employed or who was employed by anyone employed by them to perform the obligation so imposed upon them for the purpose of the voyage; article IV, rule 1 only applied to the obligation to exercise due diligence to secure initial seaworthiness at the beginning of the voyage. A felonious act of stevedores was not an act done in the management of ship within article IV, rule 2. The cause of the admission of seawater was the act of the thieves employed by shipowners in performance of their obligation to discharge and load, and it was only by clear and explicit language that shipowners could protect themselves in respect of damage to cargo caused or contributed to by thieves in ship's service.[26]

It followed that it was impossible to put any reasonable construction upon the statute except by regarding the servant of the persons who are employed by the shipowner in order

---

23 *The Chyebassa*, sup., per McNair J at p. 457.
24 Ibid, p. 458.
25 Ibid, p. 460.
26 Ibid, p. 450.

to fulfil his statutory obligation to discharge the vessel as being the agent of the shipowner himself for that purpose. There was a statutory obligation on the ship to discharge, and they performed that duty by entering into a contract with the master stevedore, who, for that purpose, was their agent in performing their statutory duty; that in itself would be sufficient to support the matter, because it is plain that the master stevedore, according to law, would be responsible for the tortious acts of his servants done in the scope of their employment.[27]

But by no means everyone who gives orders to the ship, the charterers will be not liable if port authorities,[28] bunker supplier,[29] shipper,[30] or receiver[31] are not their agent. As Lord Sumption commented, strictly speaking, an "agent" is a person authorised by the principal to perform some act on his behalf.[32]

6.4 Giving the stern order too late

According to authorities as explained previously, a seaworthy vessel is one that fits to meet and undergo the perils of the sea and other incidental risks, to which, of necessity, she must be exposed in the course of the voyage.[33] Under a time charter, if a vessel's lack of a deratisation certificate prevented a good delivery to charterers, without that document, the ship could not sail to her next port. The owners will breach an express undertaking of seaworthiness and that seaworthiness required that the ship possess the documents necessary to enable her to sail.[34]

In western Australia ports, especially in Port Hedland, once there are problems with the vessel's main engine, propulsion mechanism, steering system, mooring system, navigation equipment, also crew, all should be rectified before the vessel can be accepted in the line-up to berth or leave there. Shipowners should surrender root cause analysis (RCA), corrective and preventive measures, and all other necessary documents. In the port authority view, RCA is the process of discovering the root causes of problems in order to identify appropriate solutions; it is much more effective to systematically prevent and solve underlying issues rather than just treating *ad hoc* symptoms and putting out fires.

In the *Aliakmon Progress*,[35] the vessel was delivered on 24 February 1977. While approaching her berth at the Icelandic port of Reydharfjordhur, the vessel heavily struck the quayside, seriously damaging her stem plating, forepeak, and no. 1 collision bulkhead. Defendant's case is that the master must have been incompetent, seeing that he rammed the quayside twice. But there is nothing in the affidavit suggesting the incompetence of the master. The affidavit only says:

> This must have been either because the engine room crew were inattentive or because the engines/controls were in such a poor state that the order could not be executed. In any event the astern order was given too late to have any effect.

27 *Hourani v T. & J. Harrison* [1927] 28 Ll.L. Rep.120, per Atkin LJ at p. 126.
28 *The Isabelle* [1984] 1 Lloyd's Rep.366 (C.A.).
29 *The Mediolanum* [1984] 1 Lloyd's Rep.136 (C.A.).
30 *The Arctic Trader* [1996] 2 Lloyd's Rep.449 (C.A.).
31 *The Goodpal* [2000] 1 Lloyd's Rep.638.
32 *The Global Santosh* [2016] UKSC 20.
33 S. Baughen, *Shipping Law*, 7th ed at p. 81.
34 *The Madeleine* [1967] 2 Lloyd's Rep.224.
35 *The Aliakmon Progress* [1978] 2 Lloyd's Rep.499 (C.A.).

Lord Denning MR observed that it is pretty plain that the cause of the incident was giving the astern order too late and not that there was anything wrong with the engines. So unseaworthiness goes out of the case.[36]

Geoffrey Lane LJ added that the counsel who then appeared for the second defendants conceded that no question of unseaworthiness arose, and the applicability of the Hague Rules was the point which was primarily argued; but here Mr Macdonald rightly conceded that the Hague Rules had applied and was faced with the problem of arguing unseaworthiness which had already been conceded against him.[37]

In the Court of Appeal's view, there was nothing in the affidavit which suggested that the master was incompetent, but it was plain that the cause of the incident was giving the astern order too late and not that there was anything wrong with the engines, and the defence of unseaworthiness failed.

The Court of Appeal held that since the provisions of the Hague Rules applied, the owners were not responsible for any act, neglect, or default of the master, mariner, pilot, or servant in the navigation or management of the ship, and if the incident at the Icelandic port was caused by the negligence of the master, the owners were not liable.[38]

The Court of Appeal also ruled that the cross-claim for consequential damage in that the vessel had lost her previous arrangements for cargo and had to wait a long time before she could get a cargo of cement were inadmissible because they arose out of the alleged negligence of the master, and this was excluded by the Hague Rules.[39]

But as Cresswell J said in the *Eurasian Dream*,[40] that an incompetent crew member is not able – that is, does not possess the necessary skill/knowledge – to carry out the particular task or duty (extinguish the fire), such as the crew were improperly or inadequately trained in firefighting or lacked firefighting knowledge, the crew were not drilled, the crew failed to supervise the stevedores properly, the master and members of the crew failed to muster, etc. will make the vessel unseaworthy.[41]

6.5 Deviation

Under a time charter, the owners promise to provide the charterers with the services of the chartered ship. To that end, under clause 8 of the New York Produce form, the owners promise that (1) the master will follow the charterers' orders as to how the ship is to be employed (an undertaking considered in the next chapter), (2) the voyages that the ship undertakes will be performed with "the utmost despatch," and (3) the master will ensure that his crew provide "all customary assistance" with the ship's trading.[42] It followed that after delivery, or putting the ship at the charterers' disposal, the vessel should obey charterers' legitimate orders. The delivery of the chartered vessel to the charterers is a significant stage in a time charter, "placing the services of the chartered vessel's master,

36 Ibid, per Lord Denning MR at p. 501.
37 Ibid, per Geoffrey Lane LJ at p. 501.
38 Ibid.
39 Ibid.
40 *The Eurasian Dream* [2002] 1 Lloyd's Rep.719.
41 Ibid, per Cresswell J at pp. 42–743.
42 *Time Charters*, 7th ed at para. 18.1.

officers and crews at the Charterers' disposal, so that the charterers may give orders as to the employment of the vessel."[43]

The vessels are designed and built to be able to sail safely in heavy weather. The classification society rules require, as does clause 1 of the NYPE form, the maintenance of these safety standards. It is no excuse for the owners to say that the shortest route would (even if it be the case) take the vessel through the heavy weather that she is designed to be able to encounter.[44] So if there was no evidence that any other route was a usual route, the master must choose the shortest route. It is the duty of a ship, at any rate, when sailing upon an ocean voyage from one port to another, to take the usual route between those two ports. If no evidence is given, that route is presumed to be the direct geographical route, but it may be modified in many cases for navigational or other reasons, and evidence may always be given to show what the usual route is unless a specific route is prescribed by the charterparty or bill of lading.[45] Thus, the obligation to proceed with reasonable despatch means taking the shortest and quickest route to the destination port unless there is another route which is the usual route. If the master adopts a route that differs from the contract route, as opposed to a departure from that route as a result of a navigational error or an involuntary departure caused by wind or currents, which will amount to a deviation, the owners will be liable for damage if without reasonable ground.[46]

In the *Marjorie Seed*,[47] on 25 December 1924, the vessel left Rothesay Dock to proceed down the Clyde and thence to a port in Spain, carrying a cargo of coal. Some hour and a half or two hours after sunset, the *Marjorie Seed* struck a rock on the coast of Ayr off Troon. The probability is that the rock is the one marked on the chart under the name Troon Rock. The cargo and the ship were totally destroyed, was declared as total loss. The plaintiffs contended that the vessel was unseaworthy, owing to the fact that the master was so ill and mentally affected as to be unfit to navigate her, with the result that she grounded on the rocks between Lady Island and Troon Harbour.

Roche J commented that the master was a competent man. There is no doubt that he was guilty of a lapse on the night in question, which was very serious in its consequences, both to the owner of the ship and cargo and to their underwriters, and a very serious thing in its effect upon his own career, which has doubtless been brought to an end as regards any question of his commanding a ship in the future. The whole question is whether his action was an error of judgment or an act of negligence, as it was at the lowest, or whether it was an act which indicated incompetence or unfitness to command so as to constitute the vessel, which was commanded by such a commander, unseaworthy and unfit for the voyage, and whether the position at which the ship had arrived at the time when she was lost was such as to indicate that there was a deviation, within the meaning of the authorities, from the voyage, or whether there was merely such a mistake or error in following the route contemplated by the charterparty as not to amount to deviation.[48]

Roche J held that the master was neither incompetent nor unfit to command this ship. He was satisfied that, had he been in a better state of health and wakefulness on that day, the

43 *Charterparties Law, Practice and Emerging Legal Issues*, 2018 at p. 68.
44 *The Hill Harmony* [2001] 1 Lloyd's Rep.147 (H.L.) per Lord Hobhouse at p. 157.
45 *The Indian City* [1939] 64 Ll.L. Rep.229 (H.L.) per Lord Porter at p. 241.
46 *The Santa Isabella* [2019] EWHC 3152 (Comm).
47 *The Marjorie Seed* [1926] 24 Ll.L. Rep.316.
48 Ibid, per Roche J at p. 318.

master was quite competent, that is to say, quite able to have adequately deduced from the chart what the proper course was, to have properly laid it off and to have given adequate and proper directions as to how the ship should be navigated. Under those circumstances, Roche J stated that he was a competent master, notwithstanding the terrible and unfortunate error or mistake of which he was guilty on that afternoon.[49]

Roche J observed that a mere departure or failure to follow the contract voyage or route is not necessarily a deviation, or every stranding which occurred in the course of a voyage would be a deviation, because the voyage contracted for is in no case one which essentially involves the necessity of stranding. It is a change of voyage, a radical breach of the contract, that is required to, and essentially does, constitute a deviation.[50]

Roche J was satisfied, as a fact, that the master never intended to leave the route of the voyage, that is to say, the route of the voyage from Glasgow to Huelva. What the master did was to make a mistake as to the compass course which was necessary to take him from the terminus a quo to the terminus ad quem. To use an analogy, although analogies are misleading, the master did not adopt another road instead of the road that he had agreed to take, but he got himself into the ditch at the side of the road which he was intending to follow. He was not on another route; he was on the existing route, although he was out of the proper part of the route which he ought to have followed. Roche J stated that there was no substitution or change of route which is necessary to constitute a deviation.[51]

Roche J viewed that it was unnecessary to go into the question as to whether the deviation was justified or what was the motive from the findings of fact so occurred.

Roche J ruled that the onus is upon the plaintiffs to prove unseaworthiness. They have failed to show the ship was unseaworthy in respect of her master. Note in this case: the master acted, constituted unseaworthiness or breach of the contract or warranty that the ship should start commanded by a proper and competent commander. There is no doubt that there is such a warranty or contract as that. It was laid down and had been reaffirmed by the House of Lords in the case of the *Clan Gordon*.[52]

The legal consequences of a deviation, as editors of *Bills of Lading*,[53] are summarized: First, deviation effectively reverses the burden of proof on causation, and a shipowner will only escape liability for a loss whilst deviating if he can show that the loss would have happened anyway. The second and related consequence is that the carrier may lose the protection of all clauses exempting him from the liability he has under the contract. A deviating carrier also loses his rights under the contract, including the rights to contractual freight, or demurrage.

The particular significance attached to a deviation flows from the characterisation of the voyage to be undertaken under a voyage charterparty, not merely as a promissory obligation arising under the contract, but as an essential part of the definition of the maritime adventure that is the subject of the contract.[54] It is a fundamental condition that in the absence of express liberties, the ship shall proceed by the ordinary and customary route. Any deviation changes the adventure. It has also the serious consequences that it

49 Ibid, p. 320.
50 Ibid.
51 Ibid, p. 321.
52 *The Clan Gordon* [1924] 17 L.l.L. Rep.120 (H.L.).
53 *Bills of Lading*, 3rd ed at para. 11.313–11.315.
54 *Carver on Charterparties*, 2nd ed at para. 4–328.

vitiates the goods owners' insurance.[55] The cases show that for a long series of years, the courts have held that a deviation is such a serious matter and changes the character of the contemplated voyage so essentially that a shipowner who has been guilty of a deviation cannot be considered as having performed his part of the bill of lading contract, but something fundamentally different, and therefore he cannot claim the benefit of stipulations in his favour contained in the bill of lading.[56]

6.6 Incompetent second engineer

The shipowner is obliged to man the ship with a competent crew, selecting, equipping, and training the master and crew, providing concerning plans and necessary instructions, and taking into account the length and circumstances of the voyage.[57]

In the *Farrandoc*,[58] the wheat was loaded on the vessel at Kingston on 26 November 1962, and a portion of it, stowed in no. 2 hold, was found to be wetted when it was being unloaded in Montreal on the morning of 28 November 1962. At Montreal, second engineer, H., opened a wrong valve during pumping operations, and water entered the hold, damaging cargo. Plaintiff claimed against the defendant, who denied liability, contending that damage was due to an error in the management of the ship within article IV, rule 2(a) of Canadian Water Carriage of Goods Act, 1936. Plaintiff alleged that H. was incompetent, that defendant failed to inquire into his competence, reliability, or familiarity with the vessel's engine room piping and machinery, and that defendant had no plan of engine room piping on the vessel and took no precautions to prevent error such as was committed. There was evidence that H. was engaged on the day the vessel sailed from Kingston, that no inquiries were made as to his experience or to his familiarity with the type of engine room machinery and piping on the vessel, and that the vessel's piping was not usual.

Thurlow J, in Canada Exchequer Court, viewed that the appellant would be liable on the basis of the breach of its obligation under article III, rule 2, which is to be inferred from the fact of the wheat having become wetted and its failure to prove that the cause of the loss was one for which it was not responsible under the rules. Considering that there was no evidence to the contrary, Thurlow J agreed that the second engineer was not competent to be in charge of the engine room on such a ship and that there was no plan of the engine room piping available for his use and that in these respects the vessel was not properly manned and equipped and was, to that extent, unseaworthy.[59]

It is well established, however, that before such a defence becomes available to the shipowners, the latter must have established either that the vessel was seaworthy or that it (the shipowners) exercised due diligence to make the ship seaworthy for the voyage and to secure that the ship was properly manned, equipped, and supplied. Unless, therefore, the

55 *The Tregenna* [1936] 55 L.l.L. Rep.159 (H.L.).

56 *Joseph Thorley & Co. v Orchis Steamship Company* [1907] 1 K.B. 660.

57 *The Roberta* [1938] 60 L.l.L. Rep.84; *The Hong Kong Fir* [1961] 2 Lloyd's Rep.478 (C.A.); *The Makedonia* [1962] 1 Lloyd's Rep.316; *The Heinz Horn* [1970] 1 Lloyd's Rep.191; *The Star Sea* [2001] 1 Lloyd's Rep.389 (H.L.); *The Eurasian Dream* [2002] 1 Lloyd's Rep.719.

58 *The Farrandoc* [1967] 2 Lloyd's Rep.276.

59 Ibid, per Thurlow J at p. 280.

defendant has discharged this burden of proof, the immunity provided by the said article of the Water Carriage of Goods Act does not apply in the defendant's favour.

In Thurlow J's view, the question therefore which the court is required to determine is whether the defendant was successful in proving it had exercised due diligence to make the ship seaworthy and to secure that the ship was properly manned, equipped, and supplied for the voyage.

The question of seaworthiness and that in the context of what the impugned paragraph means is simply that there were two ways of discharging the onus of proof of the exercise of due diligence, (1) to prove that the ship was in fact seaworthy, which would necessarily destroy any case based on unseaworthiness and render proof of the exercise of due diligence unnecessary, or (2) to prove the exercise of due diligence. Thurlow J ruled that the vessel was unseaworthy in not being properly manned and equipped in the respects mentioned.[60]

Considering reasons that the second engineer was not competent in that he did not know the engine room piping system and the peculiarities of the ship and there was no plan of the engine room piping system available to the ship's personnel from which the engineer might have instructed himself, Thurlow J observed that this unseaworthiness was a cause of the respondent's loss.

Turning to section 3 of the Water Carriage of Goods Act relieves the carrier of any implied absolute undertaking to provide a seaworthy ship, in place of any such undertaking article III, rule 1, and rule 2 of article III. In Thurlow J's view, the result of these provisions is that the carrier is liable for loss or damage to cargo caused by unseaworthiness or improper manning or equipping of the ship only if he has failed to exercise due diligence to make the ship seaworthy and to secure that she was properly manned and equipped and such failure has been a cause of the loss or damage. But the onus is upon him to satisfy the court that due diligence was exercised.[61]

Thurlow J agreed, as the learned trial judge held, that the appellant had failed to exercise due diligence to make the ship seaworthy for the voyage in that the appellant had not taken sufficient care to assure itself of the experience, competence, and reliability of the second engineer and did not equip the vessel with and make available to the ship's personnel a plan of the engine room piping system. In reaching this conclusion, the learned trial judge referred to the apparent fact that the second engineer had been engaged solely on the basis of his holding a second engineer's certificate and that no evidence had been given that any inquiry had been made as to his previous experience or record or whether he was familiar with the type of engine room machinery and piping on board the vessel.[62]

In this case, the second engineer, in fact, held a certificate, but there is no evidence of any inquiry having been made either of the second engineer or of anyone else to ascertain the extent of his knowledge or experience or suitability for the post. What the rule requires is that the carrier sees that the ship is properly manned and equipped so far as the exercise of due diligence can serve to secure it. A person taking reasonable care for his own ship or cargo or seeking to discharge this obligation even when told that the person to be employed in a position involving responsibility held a qualifying certificate would scarcely fail to make further inquiries as to his ability and experience. Even after making such inquiries,

60 Ibid, p. 280.
61 Ibid, p. 281.
62 Ibid.

he would inquire how far the man's experience fitted him for service in the particular ship and take steps to see that the man was adequately instructed with respect to any features of the particular ship with which it was necessary for him to be familiar to properly discharge the duties of his position and to avoid damage to the ship and her cargo. Here it was not established that any such inquiries were made or that any sufficient steps were taken to ensure that a second engineer would be adequately instructed.[63]

Noel J observed that it was sufficient to establish that the ship was unseaworthy or was not properly manned, and it, therefore, became incumbent upon the defendant to establish that it had exercised due diligence to make her seaworthy for the voyage. In most cases, the shipowner, in the process of establishing, as he must do, the cause of the damage or loss and that he falls within the exception which gives him immunity (on the basis that one who claims an exception or exemption must also establish that he falls within its conditions), will, particularly in the case of an error of navigation or an error in the management of the ship, at the same time establish facts which disclose that his ship was unseaworthy (within its extensive meaning under article III of the Water Carriage of Goods Act), and this appears to be what happened in the present case.[64]

It followed that in this case, lack of a plan of the piping on the vessel could also be considered as a lack of due diligence. The safety of the ship and cargo would have required that every member of the crew (and particularly, in this case, the second engineer, who was responsible for the engine room) likely to use this coffer-dam valve should, before the voyage had commenced, have been fully instructed as to its proper use and fully informed as to the danger to be avoided, as the best-equipped ship may become unseaworthy if her crew or those in charge of her appliances are unacquainted with their purpose and proper use. It, therefore, follows that this ship, equipped as she was, by the second engineer, in charge of the engine room, ignorant as he was of the existence of the coffer dam, was in fact improperly manned, and the defendant has failed to show that due diligence was exercised to man her properly.

The carrier is liable for loss or damage to cargo caused by unseaworthiness or improper manning or equipping of the ship only if he has failed to exercise due diligence to make the ship seaworthy and to secure that she was properly manned and equipped and such failure has been a cause of the loss or damage. But the onus is upon him to satisfy the court that due diligence was exercised, as article III, rule 1 of the Hague Rules, to provide a seaworthy ship, is an overriding obligation.[65]

6.7 Inefficiency of crew

It's settled law that shipowners should be bound before and at the beginning of the voyage to exercise due diligence to make the ship seaworthy. The owners will not be protected where it has failed to exercise due diligence to engage a competent crew.[66] *Due diligence* means the exercise of reasonable skill and care.[67] The standard equates to the duty of care

63 Ibid, p. 282.
64 Ibid, per Noel J at p. 285.
65 *The Maruinne* [1959] 2 Lloyd's Rep.105 (H.L.).
66 *The Roberta* [1938] 60 Ll.L. Rep.84; *The Hongkong Fir* [1961] 2 Lloyd's Rep.478 (C.A.).
67 *The Fiord Wind* [2000] 2 Lloyd's Rep.191; *The Cape Bonny* [2018] 1 Lloyd's Rep.356 (C.A.).

at common law so that the absence of due diligence is equivalent to negligence at common law.[68] The shipowners also need to provide specific instruction to the master and crew as to how to carry cargoes of the type in question, and thereafter operate a continuous system of supervision, including regular or random checks of the ship by marine superintendents, including checking the contents of chartrooms or ventilation system.[69] An adequate and efficient crew may lack certain specific knowledge as to the characteristics of the ship or cargo and thus render the vessel unseaworthy.[70]

In the *Makedonia*,[71] in the course of the voyage from western Canadian ports to the United Kingdom, the vessel broke down in mid-Atlantic, about 870 mi to the southward and westward of the Azores. It is alleged that she broke down as a result of two causes, firstly, contamination of oil fuel and the lack of feedwater, that is, fresh water, for the boilers. As a result of this breakdown, she was entirely immobilized and had to take salvage assistance under Lloyd's Standard Form of Salvage Agreement to the Azores, for which an award of £44,000 was made against the ship and the cargo. Contended by plaintiffs that under article III, if the vessel was unseaworthy on leaving bunkering port owing to defective bunkers or contamination of fuel oil, shipowners were responsible for a lack of due diligence on part of the ship's engineers at the beginning of that stage and were precluded from exemptions in article IV(2).

Hewson J viewed section 3 of the Canadian Act of 1936, which provides that there shall not be implied in any contract for the carriage of goods by water to which the rules apply any absolute undertaking of the carrier of the goods to provide a seaworthy ship.[72]

Hewson J considered that it is not disputed that a ship may be rendered unseaworthy by the inefficiency of the master who commands her. Does not that principle apply where the master's inefficiency consists, whatever his general efficiency may be, in his ignorance as to how his ship may, owing to the peculiarities of her structure, behave in circumstances likely to be met with on an ordinary ocean voyage? Hewson J observed that there cannot be any difference in principle between disabling want of skill and disabling want of knowledge. Each equally renders the master unfit and unqualified to command and therefore makes the ship he commands unseaworthy. And the owner who withholds from the master the necessary information should, in all reason, be as responsible for the result of the master's ignorance as if he deprived the latter of the general skill and efficiency he presumably possessed.[73]

Turning to liability for the under-deck cargo, Hewson J observed that the Hague Rules apply. He found that the ship was unseaworthy through improper manning and lack of a proper plan of the ballast and fuel system and that the salvage, the burning of the cargo, and

68 *The Amstelslot* [1963] 2 Lloyd's Rep.223 (H.L.); *The Muncaster Castle* [1961] A.C. 807 at p. 871, per Lord Keith. See also, e.g. *G.E. Dobell & Co v The Steamship Rossmore Co Ltd.* [1895] 2 Q.B. 408 (shipowner responsible for carpenter's negligence in closing porthole in a manner which allowed water ingress); *Northumbrian Shipping Co Ltd v E. Timm & Son Ltd.* [1939] A.C. 397 (shipowner responsible for the negligence of its employee in failing to take on sufficient bunkers); *The Kamsar Voyager* [2002] 2 Lloyd's Rep.57 (shipowner held responsible for the error of engine manufacturer in supply a spare piston of the wrong dimensions).

69 *The Clan Gordon* [1923] 17 L.l.L. Rep.120 (H.L.).

70 *The Santa Isabella* [2019] EWHC 3152 (Comm); *The Eurasian Dream* [2002] 1 Lloyd's Rep.719.

71 *The Makedonia* [1962] 1 Lloyd's Rep.316.

72 Ibid, per Hewson J at p. 328.

73 Ibid, p. 335.

the port of refuge expenses were all occasioned by this unseaworthiness and the carriers are in default.[74]

The court held that the shipowners had failed to prove that they had exercised proper care in the appointment of ship's engineers, and the ship's engineers were inefficient at the commencement of voyage, and the shipowners also had failed to exercise due diligence before and at beginning of the voyage properly to man their vessel. The court further concluded that the vessel was unseaworthy in that she was improperly manned and the shipowners had failed to provide a plan of ballast and fuel system; that salvage, burning of cargo, and port of refuge expenses were all occasioned by this unseaworthiness; and that shipowners were in default.[75]

It followed that, in this case, the shipowner is obliged to man the ship with a competent crew, taking into account the length and circumstances of the voyage. And under article III, the obligation of shipowners was to exercise due diligence before and at beginning of sailing from the loading port to have the vessel adequately bunkered for the first stage and to arrange for adequate bunkers at intermediate ports so that voyage could be performed; that that obligation as to bunkering included the provision of feedwater; and that shipowners performed that obligation, the equipment and machinery were satisfactory, and the immediate cause of the breakdown was lack of burnable fuel oil, owing to the inefficiency of the ship's engineers, and the breakdown caused all loss sustained by the plaintiffs.

6.8 Insufficiency of crew

The most important effect of incorporating COGSA in the charter is that the implied warranty of seaworthiness is modified and reduced from an absolute warranty to an undertaking by the owner to exercise due diligence to make the ship seaworthy.[76] However, the shipowners still should employ an adequate number of crew; if they are not able to provide the required service in emergency[77] or sail without a sufficient number of crew, the vessel will be unseaworthy and the shipowners will put them in breach to provide a seaworthy vessel.[78]

In the *Taycraig*,[79] the vessel carried a cargo of potash of salts and other potash products shipped at Antwerp for carriage to Plymouth. The voyage took place just after Christmas 1927. The damage complained of was caused by the hatchway becoming uncovered in the course of the voyage and a large quantity of water entering the hold and thereby damaging the cargo to the extent of more than half its value. The plaintiffs contended that the damage in question was occasioned either by the unseaworthiness of the vessel or by the negligence of the master and crew.

The unseaworthiness complained of is in the matter of the proper wedging of the battens which secured the tarpaulin over the hatchway in question, no. 1, and it is further complained that the vessel was unseaworthy in that it was not properly manned, and it is

74 Ibid, p. 338.
75 Ibid, p. 317.
76 *Time Charters*, 7th ed at para. 3A.24.
77 *The Taycraig* [1928] 31 Ll.L. Rep.281; *The Heinz Horn* [1970] 1 Lloyd's Rep.191.
78 *The Hongkong Fir* [1961] 2 Lloyd's Rep.478 (C.A.).
79 *The Taycraig* [1928] 31 Ll.L. Rep.281.

said that the tarpaulins were not properly wedged and secured by the battens because there was not a proper complement on board the ship.

Roche J, in giving judgment, was not concerned with what number constitutes a sufficient crew to make the vessel seaworthy, but he decided that it is not seaworthy if it sails on this voyage in wintry weather without a second officer competent to navigate the ship, and an officer or man competent to attend to the wedges on a voyage such as this. Roche J held that that constituted the vessel unseaworthy.[80]

Therefore, Roche J held that whether or not the vessel had sailed on her voyage when she left the quay, although she remained in the dock, she started on a different stage of the voyage when she left the dock. Inasmuch as she started on that stage without the mate, she was not seaworthy, and the shipowner was in breach of his warranty in that regard.[81]

On those grounds, Roche J held that the defence of the exceptions fails, and it fails because the peril of the sea and the accident of navigation, that is, the entrance of water, were due to non-attention to the adequate tightening of the wedges which held the battens which held the tarpaulin in place over the hatches of the ship, and that was so connected with the absence of the mate as to prevent the shipowner, who is in breach in the matter of seaworthiness of his obligation in that regard, from relying on the exception.

Roche J pointed out that the implied undertaking of the shipowner that the vessel shall be seaworthy when she starts on the voyage in question, or any of the stages of the voyage, is not present and operative. Roche J concluded that the absence of the mate made all the difference, and that absence constituted unseaworthiness.[82]

In the *Heinz Horn*,[83] on her first voyage, the vessel loaded bananas at Puerto Bolivar on 10 June 1962. Cargo was consigned to the second defendant, and the vessel was directed to Mobile. The master left the vessel at Panama Canal due to illness, and the chief mate became an acting master. He and the second mate were the only officers on board, whereas the normal complement of officers was a master and three mates. The vessel was discharged at Mobile on 22 June. Many bananas were found to be ripe and of no use. The vessel was to sail from Mobile on orders of the first defendant, but no orders were issued until 29 June. During the period from 22 June to 29 June, the vessel went for one day into the dry dock for inspection. Defendants refused to pay the hire for the remaining six days. Upon arrival at Puerto Bolivar for the second voyage, the vessel stood by for two days, awaiting bananas for loading, since they were not available due to the vessel's delay in leaving Mobile. Defendants refused to pay hire for this period of two days. On her fourth voyage, she loaded bananas at Guayaquil, Ecuador, on 2 and 3 September. On her arrival at Mobile on 11 September, many bananas were found to be ripe. On 21 September the first defendant notified the plaintiff that it was best to cancel charterparties, and this was done.

Circuit Judge Rives observed that maritime law infers a general warranty of seaworthiness from a charterparty agreement even where such warranty is not expressly made. The term "seaworthiness" is read to mean, *inter alia*, fitness for the use anticipated. A similar warranty of seaworthiness at one time was read into contracts of carriage or

80 Ibid, per Roche J at p. 284.
81 Ibid.
82 Ibid.
83 *The Heinz Horn* [1970] 1 Lloyd's Rep.191.

bills of lading. The Carriage of Goods by Sea Act of 1936 (COGSA), *et seq.*, abolished that general warranty with regard to the carrier–shipper relationship governed by bills of lading. Instead, the carrier is statutorily obligated to use due diligence to make the vessel seaworthy. Such obligation is either met or not met when the vessel "breaks ground" on the voyage.[84]

Rivers CtJ pointed out, as was the situation here, that the owner and the charterer sometimes choose to incorporate COGSA into the charterparty. Such a practice serves to cut the general seaworthiness warranty "down to COGSA dimensions," that is, to the level of due diligence. Rivers CtJ concluded that the ship was unseaworthy with respect to its crew.[85]

Faced with such evidence, Rivers CtJ conclude that the vessel was not seaworthy with regard to its personnel. The owner bore the burden of proving the exercise of due diligence to make the vessel seaworthy, and the owner failed to exercise due diligence to make the vessel seaworthy at the start of the voyage by not ensuring that adequate and competent personnel would remain on board through the voyage.[86]

Under the Harter Act, the owner whose diligence in providing a seaworthy vessel is found deficient is liable for damage to cargo without causal relation between the defect and the disaster. However, with calls for such causal relation as a prerequisite to a finding of liability unseaworthiness or of failure to use due diligence to make the vessel seaworthy, as well as of failure properly to operate the refrigeration mechanism, the District Court inferred the last explanation as to the source of trouble, rather than the condition of the equipment.

In conclusion, Rivers CtJ stated that *seaworthiness* is a relative term, depending on its application to the type of vessel and the character of the voyage. The general rule is that the ship must be staunch and strong and well equipped for the intended voyage. And she must also be provided with a crew, adequate in number and competent for the voyage with reference to its length and other particulars, and have a competent and skilled master of sound judgment and discretion.[87]

It followed that where the crew is incompetent or insufficient to manage the ship, the vessel would be unseaworthy.[88] On the other hand, a ship may be rendered unseaworthy by the inefficiency of the master who commands her/And the owner whom withholds from the master the necessary information should, in all reason, be as responsible for the result of the master's ignorance as if the deprived the latter of the general skill and efficiency he presumably possessed.[89] Seaworthiness of a vessel, therefore, embraces all matters that affect a vessel's ability to perform properly the contractual voyage. The expression covers not only the physical characteristics of a ship, such as her shell plating, but also other matters, such as her equipment and crew and documentation for the intended voyage.[90]

---

84 Ibid, per Rivers, CtJ at p. 195.
85 Ibid, p. 197.
86 Ibid.
87 Ibid.
88 *The Makedonia* [1962] 1 Lloyd's Rep.316.
89 *The Clan Gordon* [1923] 17 Ll.L. Rep.120 (H.L.).
90 *Bills of Lading*, 3rd ed at para. 11.102.

6.9 Negligence of engineer

A vessel that does not have a sufficient, efficient, and competent crew is unseaworthy.[91] However, negligence by the master or crew will not itself justify a finding of incompetency.[92] To be negligent, a crew must fall below the expected standard of care as required by his level. The common definition of *negligence* could be found in *Blyth v Birmingham Waterworks*:[93]

> Negligence is the omission to do something which a reasonable man, guided upon those considerations which ordinarily regulate the conduct of human affairs, would do, or doing something which a prudent and reasonable man would not do.

However, negligence of the crew may also justify a finding of incompetency, where the shipowners will be liable for the damage. In the *Roberta*,[94] the proceedings arose from a claim by various owners of cargo carried by the vessel from Dordrecht to Horseferry Wharf, London, in January 1936, which was alleged to have been seriously damaged by water, against the first defendants, the owners of the vessel, and against the second defendants, Walford Lines Ltd., time charterers of the vessel.

His Lordship found definitely that it was impossible on the evidence to decide whether or not the ship was seaworthy when she sailed. Clause 2 of the charterparty provided: "Owners to maintain her in a thoroughly efficient state in hull and machinery during service." There was no proof of inefficiency under this clause to secure the protection of clause 12 of the charterparty; plaintiffs had to prove (1) that the ship was unseaworthy, (2) that the damage was caused by that unseaworthiness, and (3) that there was a lack of due diligence by the owner or his manager resulting in the ship being so unseaworthy. Counsel submitted that Walford Lines had failed to prove one of them.

Langton J, in giving judgment, found that the plaintiffs were entitled to succeed against the carrier because the carrier had been guilty of a lack of due diligence in making the steamer seaworthy. Indeed, the contract between the plaintiffs and the carrier – in this case the second defendants – was a narrower contract. It was a contract to be construed according to Dutch law, and as I understand the Dutch law, their view of this lack of due diligence is rather narrower than the English view of lack of due diligence. As the English law in a matter of this kind is, stated somewhat more broadly, that the vessel was undermanned, the vessel was not properly equipped in the matter of crew; as in this case the selection of the crew – the complement of the men – rested entirely with the owner himself, it would follow as a natural consequence of finding that the vessel was undermanned, and that the owner was lacking in due diligence, as he had not got together a good, proper, and competent crew.[95]

Looking at it again broadly, Langton J is satisfied that an ordinarily competent and trustworthy man would have seen it and noticed it. If, on the other hand, he left it open, then he left it open because he was an incompetent and untrustworthy man. Therefore, upon either consideration, it seems to be fair and right to hold that the plaintiffs should

---

91 *The Hong Kong Fir* [1961] 2 Lloyd's Rep.478 (C.A.); *The Makedonia* [1962] 1 Lloyd's Rep.316; *The Eurasian Dream* [2002] 1 Lloyd's Rep.719.

92 *The Isla Fernandina* [2000] 2 Lloyd's Rep.15.

93 *Blyth v Birmingham Waterworks* [1856] 11 Ex R 781.

94 *The Roberta* [1937] 58 Ll.L. Rep.231; [1938] 60 Ll.L. Rep.84 (C.A.).

95 Ibid, per Langton J [1937] 58 Ll.L. Rep.231 at p. 235.

succeed in this case because the owner failed to provide a competent and trustworthy man and was himself guilty of a want of due diligence in making the vessel seaworthy and fitted for the voyage.[96]

In the Court of Appeal, Greer LJ pointed out that it could not be suggested that if the charterer had put his own goods on board and those goods had been delivered damaged, there would not be an onus upon the shipowner to account in some way for the damage; he would be a bailee of those goods, receiving them in good order and delivering them in bad order, and he would be called upon to give some explanation to account for the fact that they were delivered in bad order. Greer LJ agreed with the learned judge that the question of the onus is a question of English law, and also agreed with him that the onus rests upon the defendant shipowner to bring himself within one of the exceptions.[97]

Greer LJ observed that even if the onus was not upon the shipowner but was upon the charterer, the charterer has sufficiently discharged that onus. It seems to me quite clear – it has not been disputed in the action, and it cannot be disputed – that this engineer, by some oversight, left what has been called cock "F" open when it ought to have been closed; he was the sole person in charge of it, and it was his regular duty during the voyage to examine some other cocks which were within a few yards of this particular cock. That indicates to my mind that if he is a man who was so frequently in the presence of a cock which was within his own knowledge and in respect of which he must have known he had done something with regard to it, he should have discovered that something ought to have been remedied and the cock put in a position in which no more water was let into the vessel. Greer LJ thought that it was affirmatively established, by reason of all the facts in the case, that he was a man who was incompetent to be the engineer of this small vessel, whether he had or had not been negligent.[98]

Greer LJ concluded that the shipowner had failed to discharge the onus of showing that the damage was not caused by want of due diligence on his part; the evidence showed that the damage was due to the incompetence of the engineer, who was engaged by the owner without any knowledge of his capabilities and without any real inquiry being made.[99]

In this case, the water entered the vessel either because the cock was left open or because it was a deficient cock. Langton J held that the ship was unseaworthy either because she had an incompetent engineer or because she had a defective cock, which was upheld by the Court of Appeal.

6.10 A negligent of lookout

According to COLREGS, every vessel shall, at all times, maintain a proper lookout by sight and hearing as well as by all available means appropriate in the prevailing circumstances and conditions so as to make a full appraisal of the situation and of the risk of collision. See Convention on the International Regulations for Preventing.[100] Every vessel shall take

96 Ibid, p. 236.
97 Ibid, per Greer LJ [1938] 60 Ll.L. Rep.84 (C.A.) at p. 85.
98 Ibid, p. 86.
99 Ibid.
100 *Convention on the International Regulations for Preventing Collisions at Sea*, 1972, Rule 5-Look-Out.

all available means to avoid a collision. Even if the vessel stays at anchorage, the crew can still take many measures, such as slipping her anchor to avoid a collision. A vessel at anchor is not justified under all circumstances in holding on when, by slipping, she could avoid a collision. If she could have avoided the breakwater by slipping from her anchor and getting underway, she did not slip in time, went ashore, and damaged the breakwater. It was held that she was liable for the damage because of her negligence in not slipping in time.[101]

Good seamanship involves competence in, and proper monitoring of, radar at all times.[102] In the *Lady Gwendolen*,[103] the failure of the master of a vessel in the Mersey to monitor his radar while proceeding at high speed in the fog was not surprisingly admitted to being negligent, as was the failure of the owners to press upon the master the necessity to keep such a lookout. In *Samco Europe (Owners) v MSC Prestige (Owners)*,[104] the second officer of one vessel involved in the collision was found to have failed actively to monitor the echo of the other until a late stage; this was regarded as relevant to the fault of the vessel concerned.

A lookout should check the proper working of the ship's navigational equipment. In the *Staffordshire*,[105] at p. 145, Willmer J said:

> Where, in my judgment, she was at fault, was in having a very bad lookout, and a bad lookout in every possible sense of the term. It seems to me that it comes within the term "bad lookout" when I say that she was at fault for failing to take proper precautions to meet the situation in the event of the compass breaking down again, as it in fact did. It was, in my judgment, bad lookout on the part of this young third officer in failing to appreciate, long before he did appreciate it, what was happening, namely, that this vessel was falling off to starboard, and in failing to appreciate what the probable cause of the falling off was. It was bad lookout on the part of the quartermaster, when he knew perfectly well that the compass had stuck again, not to report the matter at once to the officer in charge. It was bad lookout on the part of the officer to take no steps himself, whether by going to the standard compass or otherwise, to check up on what was happening and what was the course of his vessel.

A poor lookout has contributed to many collisions. In the *Jia Li Hai*,[106] On 6 December 2013, a collision occurred off China involving the claimant's vessel. The claimant brought an action and joined the cargo insurer, AIG Insurance Hong Kong Ltd, as the second defendant. The second defendant had provided a general average guarantee on surrender by the claimant of its lien on the cargo securing a general average contribution.

The claimant's claim was met with an allegation of unseaworthiness from the second defendant, who focused on the vessel's systems, including systems for implementation of required procedures. The second defendant relied on a report of the Ningbo Maritime Safety Administration Authority of China which concluded that there had been a negligent lookout, a failure to proceed at a safe speed, and negligence in taking precautions. The second defendant contended that for a vessel to be seaworthy, she, her equipment, and her systems

101 *Marsden and Gault on Collisions*, 15th ed, Sweet & Maxwell at para. 5–057.
102 *The St Louis* [1986] 2 Lloyd's Rep.125; *The Antares II and The Victory* [1996] 2 Lloyd's Rep.482.
103 *The Lady Gwendolen* [1965] at p. 294.
104 *Samco Europe (Owners) v MSC Prestige (Owners)* [2001] EWHC 1580(Admlty).
105 *The Staffordshire* [1948] 81 Ll.L. Rep.141.
106 *The Jia Li Hai* [2018] 1 Lloyd's Rep.396.

had to be reasonably fit to withstand the perils which might foreseeably be encountered on the voyage and to keep the cargo reasonably safe from those perils. The factual foundation for the unseaworthiness allegation as pleaded in the defence and counterclaim was that "the vessel had no or no adequate passage planning, bridge management and/or safety management systems in operation to deal with the ordinary incidents of the voyage." The claimant applied to strike out the unseaworthiness allegations, alternatively for summary judgment, in its favour.[107]

Robin Knowles J considered it is for the second defendant to show some foundation for allegations that it has pleaded in its defence, supported by a statement of truth. It can, in the present case, perhaps show that systems were breached on this occasion, but it cannot show inadequate systems or inadequate arrangements for the implementation of those systems.[108]

Robin Knowles J concluded that the second defendant had no real prospect of success in the relevant respects and had pleaded a defence without foundation. Waiting for disclosure was not a proper or sufficient reason for allowing the matter to proceed to trial on those aspects of the case. Summary judgment would be given, dismissing the pleaded assertions of unseaworthiness.[109]

In this case, Robin Knowles J also discussed the burden of proof, which, according to editors of *Scrutton on Charterparties*:[110]

> The burden of proving unseaworthiness rests upon the party who asserts it and the party intending to rely upon unseaworthiness must plead it with sufficient particularity. But where a ship, shortly after leaving port and without any apparent reason sinks or leaks, the mere facts afford prima facie evidence of unseaworthiness, which must be rebutted.

The shipowners will be blamed if their crew fails to have proper lookouts. Where a crew is incompetent and commits a negligent act, such as the master navigating erroneously[111] or the crew opening the wrong valve and flooding the cargo instead of a ballast tank,[112] the proof follows the same order as in any other claim. The carrier proves the cause of the loss and then proves that due diligence was exercised in the employment and training of the party concerned, for example, the crew was carefully selected at the time of hiring and properly trained in the performance of his duties. The cargo claimant then attempts to prove that the officer in question was incompetent and that due diligence was not exercised in his employment and/or training.[113]

Thus, in effect, both parties make proof of seaworthiness and due diligence to the best of their ability, but the initial and major burden of proof is on the carrier. That burden was described by Cresswell J in the *Eurasian Dream*.[114] He observed that the burden of proof is on the claimants to prove that the vessel was unseaworthy, pursuant to article III, rule 1, before and at the beginning of the voyage. The claimants must then also prove that the loss or damage was caused by that unseaworthiness.

---

107 Ibid.

108 *The Jia Li Hai*, per Robin Knowles J at p. 398.

109 Ibid.

110 *Scrutton on Charterparties and Bills of Lading*, 24th ed at para. 7–030.

111 *The Eurybates* [1981] AMC 2350.

112 *The Farrandoc* [1967] 2 Lloyd's Rep.276.

113 William Tetley, *Marine Cargo Claims*, 4th ed, Chapter 15.

114 *The Eurasian Dream* [2002] 1 Lloyd's Rep.719.

Cresswell J also reviewed the authorities and identified the following basic categories of deficiency in this area which could amount to unseaworthiness:[115]

(1) A disabling want of skill or a disabling want of knowledge on the part of the master, which is a question of fact that may be proved from one incident and need not be demonstrated by a series of acts.
(2) Incompetence going beyond negligence which may derive from
    (a) an inherent lack of ability,
    (b) a lack of adequate training or instruction,
    (c) a lack of knowledge about a particular vessel or its systems,
    (d) a disinclination to perform the job properly, and
    (e) physical or mental disability or incapacity, for example, drunkenness, illness, or as is commonly alleged, fatigue.

It follows that the shipowners, to satisfy the requirements of seaworthiness, must employ competent crews. The shipowners also should pay keen attention to training and knowledge of management of the vessel; the crews should be able to resolve the problem that may arise during the voyage.

6.11 Non-delegable obligation

The exercise of due diligence is equivalent to the exercise of reasonable care and skill. Lack of due diligence is negligence, and in this case, there were numerous failures and errors of judgment that amounted to professional negligence. Carriers are liable for the want of due diligence by the owners/managers and for the want of due diligence of the master insofar as the owners or managers delegated to him their duties as to seaworthiness.[116]

By virtue of article III, rule 1 of the Hague Rules, a carrier is under a non-delegable duty to use due diligence to make the vessel seaworthy before and at the start of the voyage. Subject to the defence of having used due diligence, the carrier is liable for any acts or omissions of independent sub-contractors that have resulted in the ship being unseaworthy.[117] However, the carrier's non-delegable duty under article III, rule 1 attached when the vessel came into its "orbit," or under its ownership, possession, or control.[118]

In the *Muncaster Castle*,[119] plaintiffs' 150 cases of ox tongues were stored in the aft part of no. 5 lower hold of the defendants' vessel, from Australia to London, under a bill of lading subject to Australian Sea. Heavy weather was encountered on the homeward voyage. Seawater damage was discovered to the cargo hold during discharge in London. Cargo owners alleged that the vessel was unseaworthy in some inspection covers due to faulty hardening up of nuts. Shipowners contended that they had exercised due diligence to make the vessel seaworthy.

The point at issue was whether, where loss or damage had resulted from the unseaworthiness of his ship, the carrier was entitled to the immunity conferred on him by

115 Ibid, per Cresswell J at p. 737.
116 *The Eurasian Dream* [2002] 1 Lloyd's Rep.719, per Cresswell J at p. 744.
117 *Bills of Lading*, 3rd ed at para. 10.32.
118 *The Happy Ranger* [2006] 1 Lloyd's Rep.649, per Gloster J at p. 656.
119 *The Muncaster Castle* [1961] 1 Lloyd's Rep.57 (H.L.).

article IV, rule 1 of the Australian Sea-Carriage of Goods Act, 1924, if the unseaworthiness had resulted from the negligence of a workman employed by a competent ship repairer engaged by the carrier, the result of whose negligence would not be discoverable by appropriate surveys and inspections carried out in accordance with ordinary prudent practice.[120]

In the first instance, the court held that the most probable cause of the water entering the hold was the negligent failure by the ship repairers' fitter properly to harden up the nuts on the inspection covers over the storm valves, that shipowners' surveyor was not negligent in failing to detect that bad workmanship, and that shipowners had discharged the burden of proving that they exercised due diligence.

The appeal by cargo owners was that shipowners were under a duty to exercise due diligence and that they were liable if they failed to perform their duty or if there was a failure on the part of anyone to whom the performance of the duty was delegated.

The Court of Appeal held that the unseaworthiness was due to the fault of the ship repairers' fitter; that there was no fault on the part of shipowners' managers' marine superintendent; that shipowners exercised due diligence in arranging for a survey to be carried out and, having regard to the technical nature of the work, exercised due diligence by entrusting the vessel to a competent firm of ship repairers; that the act was in the performance of, and not a delegation of, their obligation to exercise due diligence; and that, therefore, cargo owners' appeal would be dismissed.[121]

Viscount Simonds observed that the question, then, is whether the respondents discharged this burden, and it is conceded that they did, unless they are to be held responsible for the negligence of the fitter. Its solution depends on the meaning of the words occurring in article III, rule 1, and repeated in article IV, rule 1, "due diligence to make the ship seaworthy." To ascertain their meaning, it is, in my opinion, necessary to pay particular regard to their history, origin, and context, and as I think the courts later have not paid sufficient regard to this aspect of the case, I must deal with it at some length. The Hague Rules, as is well known, were the result of the Conferences on Maritime Law held in Brussels in 1922 and 1923. Their aim was broadly to standardize within certain limits the rights of every holder of a bill of lading against the shipowner, prescribing a minimum for the responsibilities and liabilities to be undertaken by the latter. To guide them, the framers of the rules had, among other precedents, the American Harter Act, 1893, the Australian Sea-Carriage of Goods Act, 1904, the Canadian Water Carriage of Goods Act, 1910, and though they had no British Act as a model, they had decisions of the English courts in which the language of the Harter Act had fallen to be construed by virtue of its provisions being embodied in bills of lading. In all these acts, the relevant words "exercise due diligence to make the ship seaworthy" are to be found. It was in these circumstances that these words were adopted in the Hague Rules.[122]

Viscount Simonds stated that the shipowners were not entitled to exemption for the negligence of an independent contractor in respect of work upon the vessel. Viscount Simonds concluded:[123]

120 Ibid, p. 59.
121 Ibid, p. 67.
122 Ibid, per Viscount Simonds at p. 67.
123 Ibid, p. 73.

> I will end by categorically repelling the second and third formal reasons in the respondents' case. They did not, on the facts of the case, by entrusting the vessel to reputable ship-repairers, perform their duty to exercise due diligence. They were vicariously liable for negligence of a servant of an independent contractor, namely, the fitter.

Lord Merriman agreed with the conclusion reached by Willmer LJ that insofar as the shipowner can be said to delegate to the repairers at all, he delegates the performance of the actual job of doing the repairs and making the ship seaworthy. The authorities already quoted make it clear that what is required is due diligence in the work itself, and that this is the personal responsibility of the shipowner.[124]

Lord Radcliffe pointed out that it was impossible to transfer these considerations, which are apposite to the building of ships, to the case of the survey and repair of a ship which is already in the service of a carrier. There, the duty to have the necessary work done is directly upon the carrier from whatever moment of time is chosen as the date when the duty attaches, and whatever is done is necessarily done by agents on his behalf. Any faults of such agents, therefore, are attributable to him, provided only that they are employed upon the work.[125]

Lord Keith of Avonholm observed that the obligation is a statutory obligation imposed in defined contracts between the carrier and the shipper. There is nothing novel in a statutory obligation being held to be incapable of delegation so as to free the person bound of liability for breach of the obligation and the reasons for this to become more compelling where the obligation is made part of a contract between parties. Sub-contractors are brought on to the ship by the repairers to enable them to perform the work which they contracted to do. Their failure must also be the failure of the carrier on whom the statutory duty rests, unless in some very exceptional circumstances their employment can be said to be without any authority, express or implied, of the carrier, a case which can be considered if ever it arises.[126]

Lord Keith concluded:[127]

> The Hague Rules abolished the absolute warranty of seaworthiness. They substituted a lower measure of obligation. The old law no doubt worked hardly on shipowners and charterers, in the absence of exception or exclusion. The change in the law, not confined entirely to England, operated to afford relief to shipowners, as well as some protection to shippers. It would, however, be a most sweeping change if it had the result of providing carriers with a simple escape from their new obligation to exercise due diligence to make a ship seaworthy. If this were the plain effect of the statute, *cadit quaestio*. But *in dubio* the Courts should, in a change of the suggested dimensions, lean the other way. The language of the Hague Rules does not lead to the result contended for by the respondents. The carrier will have some relief which, weighed in the scales, is not inconsiderable when contrasted with his previous common-law position. He will be protected against latent defects, in the strict sense, in work done on his ship, that is to say, defects not due to any negligent workmanship of repairers or others employed by the repairers and against defects making for unseaworthiness in the ship, however caused, before it became his ship, if these could not be discovered by him, or competent experts employed by him, by the exercise of due diligence.

124 Ibid, per Lord Merriman at p. 80.
125 Ibid, per Lord Radcliffe at p. 85.
126 Ibid, per Lord Keith at p. 87.
127 Ibid.

Their Lordships held that the words "exercise due diligence to make the ship seaworthy" in the Hague Rules were adopted from the American Harter Act, 1893, and similar British Commonwealth statutes; that those words should be given the meaning attributed to them prior to the Hague Rules; that, accordingly, a carrier was responsible to the cargo owner unless due diligence in the work had been shown by every person to whom any part of the necessary work had been entrusted, no matter whether he was the carrier's servant, agent, or independent contractor; and that, therefore, shipowners were liable for the negligence of ship repairers' fitter.

On the other hand, it was held by Lord Radcliffe that the carrier's responsibility for the work itself does not begin until the ship comes into his orbit, and it begins then as a responsibility to make sure by careful and skilled inspection that what he is taking into his service is in a fit condition for the purpose and, if there is anything lacking that is fairly discoverable, to put it right.[128]

Therefore, a shipowner may not be responsible for the omissions of the shipbuilder as his contractor but may be responsible for the omission of an inspector supervising the building. The carrier may delegate the performance of the task of making his vessel seaworthy, but he cannot cast off his liability for negligence in that performance. The carrier's duty to exercise due diligence is thus non-delegable; it is a duty of due diligence by whomsoever carries out the work of maintaining or repairing the ship to a standard of seaworthiness, whether employees of the carrier or independent contractors. This is so even when the work requires special skill which the carrier cannot reasonably be expected himself to possess, and even where the failure to exercise the necessary skill and care would not be apparent to the carrier. The carrier cannot discharge the duty simply by employing competent persons to do and supervise whatever has to be done. If any servant or agent fails to exercise the proper skill and care, then the carrier is liable for the loss and damage resulting from the vessel's consequent unseaworthiness.[129]

Recently, in the landmark case the *CMA CGM Libra*,[130] the Supreme Court concluded that the carrier cannot escape from its responsibilities under article III, rule 1 of the Hague Rules by delegating them to its servants or agents qua navigators, or qua managers, or qua engineers, or qua ship repairers. If the task of making the vessel seaworthy has been entrusted by the carrier to those servants or agents, then (if relevant) they are acting qua carriers, and under article III, rule 1 of the Hague Rules, the carrier is responsible for any causative failure by them to exercise due diligence. The carrier's obligation under the Hague Rules is not subject to a category-based distinction between a vessel's quality of seaworthiness or navigability and the crew's act of navigating. The crew's failure to navigate the ship safely is capable of constituting a lack of due diligence by the carrier. It makes no difference that the delegated task of making the vessel seaworthy involves navigation.[131]

It follows that the shipowner's duty to make the ship seaworthy could not be delegated.

128 Ibid, per Lord Radcliffe at p. 85.

129 *Voyage Charters*, 4th ed at pp. 85, 99.

130 Ibid, p. 87.

131 Ibid, pp. 144–145.

6.12 Crew incompetent

Unequivocally, seafaring is a strenuous occupation, and seafarers are exposed to an increased number of work-related stressors: fatigue, long hours, monotony, noise, vibration, temperature changes, a multinational environment, limited recreation, isolation, and long periods away from home. To reduce those marine accidents caused by a mistake made by a crew, the crew should be repatriated timely once completing his employment contract. In other words: "Factors that may produce an imbalance between work demands and personal resources leading to a decline in physical and psychological health and an increased risk for accidents and injuries."

Sometimes, no crew incompetence issues on previous consecutive voyages arise on one of the subsequent voyages. This is similar to the safe port issue. For example, in the *Terneuzen*,[132] the charterer arranged the vessel to load cargoes at Leningrad under consecutive voyage charter, but on a certain voyage, the vessel was aground at the berth. Although the previous voyage was safe, the Court of Appeal still ruled that the charterer was responsible for unsafe berths. The incompetence of the crew is sometimes just a matter of luck, as Mustill J said in the *Mary Lou*,[133] that care and safety are not necessarily the opposite sides of the same coin. A third possibility must be taken into account, namely, that the casualty was the result of simple bad luck.

In the *Saxonstar*,[134] the voyage charter of the vessel chartered it for as many consecutive voyages as the vessel could perform within a period of 18 months. For the delays on voyages due to breakdown of engine room machinery, the charterers claimed for damages. It was alleged that owing to unseaworthiness, a reduced number of voyages was completed within the charter period. The learned umpire found that breakdowns were in general due to incompetence of engine room staff and that vessel was thereby unseaworthy. The owners had exercised due diligence in the appointment of such staff. The learned umpire further found that on one particular voyage, the vessel was not seaworthy; the damage to the machinery found at Recife was caused by the unseaworthiness of the vessel at the start of the voyage from Curaçao, which unseaworthiness was, in its turn, caused by the incompetence of the engine room staff, the defects thus caused not having been fully repaired at San Juan. When she left Buenos Aires on 5 October, she was seaworthy in respect of her machinery, but unseaworthy in that her engine room staff were incompetent; but due diligence had been exercised by her owners in that respect, and all reasonable and proper steps had been taken to put her in a seaworthy condition both as regards machinery and engine room staff. The damage to the machinery which occurred between Buenos Aires and Curaçao was also caused by the incompetence of the engine room staff.

The question is whether owners are in breach of the charterparty in respect of unseaworthiness which they had exercised due diligence to prevent.

It was held by Devlin J (as he then was) that, at first instance,[135] the plain object of clause 52 of the charterparty was to incorporate the Paramount Clause, and that adopting the principle "*Falsa demonstratio non nocet*," the Paramount Clause should be corrected to read, "This *charter-party* shall have effect subject to" the Act of 1936, notwithstanding

---

132 *The Terneuzen* [1935] 52 Ll.L. Rep.141 (C.A.).

133 *The Mary Lou* [1981] 2 Lloyd's Rep.272.

134 *The Saxon Star* [1957] 1 Lloyd's Rep.79; [1957] 1 Lloyd's Rep.271 (C.A.); [1958] 1 Lloyd's Rep.73 (H.L.).

135 Ibid, per Devlin J [1957] 1 Lloyd's Rep.79 at p. 80.

section 5 of the act, and that accordingly the rights and liabilities of the parties were governed by the provisions of the Act of 1936, but that such provisions applied only to cargo-carrying voyages and not to non-cargo-carrying voyages, which remained governed by the express and absolute warranty of seaworthiness contained in clause 1 of the charterparty.

In the Court of Appeal, Lord Denning MR found that the owners were clearly in breach of the charterparty on any one or more of the following grounds:[136]

(1) The owners were under an express or, alternatively, an implied obligation to ensure that the vessel was in seaworthy condition at the beginning of each successive voyage. In fact, this vessel was not seaworthy at any of those points because she was not manned by a competent engine room staff.

(2) The owners were under an express obligation to maintain the vessel in a seaworthy condition during each of the successive voyages, perils of the sea excepted. Their obligation was an absolute obligation to ensure that the vessel was, throughout, in a seaworthy condition, save only when the vessel was rendered unseaworthy by perils of the sea, or perhaps by any of the excepted perils in clause 9. The introduction of the exception "perils of the sea" would be meaningless unless the obligation to maintain was an absolute obligation to ensure that the vessel remained efficient. This obligation to maintain was broken by the fact that the machinery broke down on the voyages from Baltimore to Curaçao, from Curaçao to Recife, and from Buenos Aires to Curaçao. None of those breakdowns was due to perils of the sea, but to the incompetence of the engine room staff.

(3) The owners were under a duty to carry out their part of the contract with reasonable care and skill. They failed in that duty by the incompetence and consequent negligence of the engine room staff.

(4) The owners were under an express, or, alternatively, an implied, obligation to sail and proceed with all convenient dispatch to the nominated port of loading for each successive voyage and to proceed upon and complete such voyage with all reasonable dispatch. They broke this obligation by the delays which took place unless they can show some just cause or excuse for them.

Lord Denning MR concluded that:[137]

> This all leads me to the conclusion that this Paramount Clause cannot sensibly be applied to this charter-party. It must be rejected as insensible in this setting. I would emphasize the setting. This is an attempt by the shipowner to escape from liability which otherwise would be imposed upon him by his contract and by the law. We have repeatedly refused to allow a party to a contract to escape from his just liability under it by reason of an exempting clause, unless he does so by words which are perfectly clear, effective and precise.

According to Parker LJ:[138]

> This is not a time charter but a charter for successive voyages. In these circumstances, I think that the obligation to provide a seaworthy vessel applies at the commencement of each of the charter-party voyages. I agree with the umpire on this point. Even if I am wrong in the above, I think that the obligation to maintain in Clause 1, which extends over the whole period of the

136 Ibid, per Lord Denning MR [1957] 1 Lloyd's Rep.271 (C.A.) at p. 276.
137 Ibid, p. 278.
138 Ibid, p. 280.

> charter, amounts to an undertaking that the vessel would remain tight, staunch and strong and in every way fitted for the successive voyages, "perils of the sea excepted." The nature of the obligation to maintain must depend on the exact words used.

Parker LJ continued:[139]

> In its present form it can, I think, only be read as a continuing warranty of seaworthiness. Whether it is also subject to the exceptions in Clause 9 it is unnecessary to determine, since in the circumstances of the case they do not apply. I think that the effect of Clause 43 is to make the express provision in Clause 1, that the vessel should proceed to the first port of loading with all convenient dispatch, applicable to each charter-party voyage. In other words, the charterers are entitled to the use of the vessel for as many consecutive voyages for which the vessel can tender, the owners performing their obligations in regard to convenient dispatch subject to the express exceptions. Subject to the express exceptions, I think that it is an implied term of the charter-party that the owners and their servants will exercise reasonable skill and care.

There is no unseaworthiness issued in the House of Lords.

In this case, the Court of Appeal held that the shipowners are liable, unless expressly exempted, for failure to carry out the contract by reason of lack of reasonable care and skill of the master and crew; although, apparently, due diligence and care were taken by the shipowners, a competent engine room staff was never established, even though the members were changed, and the incompetence or negligence of one or more of the engineer officers was largely responsible for the breakdowns of the engines and the consequent delays.

Although the maintenance clause in the New York Produce form imposes only an obligation to exercise reasonable diligence to maintain the ship, other forms of maintenance clause may be so worded that the obligation is absolute, subject to any applicable exceptions. It was held by the Court of Appeal that an absolute obligation was created by a clause reading, "Being tight, staunch and strong, and every way fitted for the voyage, and to be maintained in such condition during the voyage, perils of the sea excepted." This maintenance provision had been included as part of the initial warranty of seaworthiness; it also contained its own exception of perils of the sea, which would not have been necessary if it was intended to impose an obligation that was less than absolute. It follows that the nature of the obligation to maintain must depend on the exact words used.[140]

6.13 Absence of the glass panel

The equipment on board is generally posted with a warning to remind crews to pay attention and to avoid any misoperation, like if missing cover in front of those equipment may cause accidents. In the *Lendoudis Evangelos II*,[141] on 7 March, while en route to Quebec, the vessel suffered a complete electrical failure which resulted in the stoppage of the main engine. Following the electrical blackout, the crew dropped the anchor, but despite this action, the vessel grounded in the St. Lawrence River and sustained serious bottom damage.

The power failure occurred because a member of the crew moved the control lever of the fuel tank's emergency shut-off system 180°. As a consequence, the quick-closing

139 Ibid.
140 *Time Charters*, 7th ed at para. 11.10.
141 *The Lendoudis Evangelos II* [2001] 2 Lloyd's Rep.304.

outlet valve of the generator daily service tank, in use at that time, supplying the generator engines with diesel oil by gravity, closed, causing both the nos. 2 and 3 generator engines to stop.

It is common ground that (i) the crew member could not have activated the emergency shut-off system accidentally, (ii) on a balance of probabilities the person concerned did not intend to cause any damage to the ship. The shipowners declared general average. The defendants deny liability for GA on the basis that the casualty was caused by the claimants' actionable fault.

Cresswell J pointed out that the burden of proving that the ship was not seaworthy and that unseaworthiness caused or contributed to the loss or damage complained of lies on the defendants. Once the defendants have proved these matters, the burden lies on the claimants to prove that the unseaworthiness was not caused by want of due diligence on the part of the claimants, their servants, or their agents.[142]

The classic definition of seaworthiness/unseaworthiness is that of Mr Carver in the passage approved by Scrutton LJ in the *Northumberland*,[143] at p. 454:

> The ship must have that degree of fitness which an ordinary careful owner would require his vessel to have at the commencement of her voyage having regard to all the probable consequences of it. Would a prudent owner have required that it should be made good before sending his ship to sea, had he known of it?

A reasonable difference of opinion does not amount to want of due diligence.[144] The doctrine of seaworthiness does not demand protection against a unique case which, if it occurred, would be against not only the probabilities but also against general experience.[145] Cresswell J considered that such a unique case would be entirely discounted by a prudent shipowner. Seaworthiness must be judged by the standards and practices of the industry at the relevant time, at least so long as those standards and practices are reasonable. The undertaking of seaworthiness is an innominate term. Cresswell J observed that whether a vessel is seaworthy is a question of fact.[146]

Turning to the issue of whether the fact that there was no glass panel in the front of the control box rendered the vessel unseaworthy, Cresswell J noted that must be judged through the spectacles of 1990. There was no class requirement for any form of guard. Care must be taken, however, not to place too much emphasis on this point. It is, however, to be noted that no published material from any industry or other source was placed before the court which mentioned the need for, or desirability of, any particular form of protection. Cresswell J pointed out that the primary requirement in regard to the remote operating panel was accessibility and ease of operation in case of an emergency, particularly fire (with safeguards to prevent accidental operation). These requirements were met in the present case. The activation of the emergency shut-off device was a grossly irresponsible act by an unknown member of the crew. The experts (drawing on wide experience) had never heard of a similar incident. To this extent, the incident was unprecedented.[147]

142 Ibid, per Cresswell J at p. 306.
143 *The Northumberland* [1926] 24 Ll.L. Rep.446 (C.A.).
144 *The Amstelslot* [1963] 2 Lloyd's Rep.223 (H.L.).
145 *The Liepaya* [1999] 1 Lloyd's Rep.649.
146 *The Lendoudis Evangelos II*, sup., per Cresswell J at p. 306.
147 Ibid, p. 311.

In Cresswell J's view, a prudent owner would have been entitled to take the view in 1990 (a) that the primary requirement was accessibility and ease of operation in case of emergency, particularly fire, and (b) that there would be greater accessibility and ease of operation in case of fire if there was no glass in front of the box. Such a view in 1990 would have been respectable, responsible, and reasonable. It would have had a logical basis. It would have involved weighing comparative risks. In all the circumstances, Cresswell J found that the ship was seaworthy at the material time.[148]

Cresswell J considered the activation of the emergency shut-off device a grossly irresponsible act by an unknown member of the crew. There is no evidence as to the reason for this grossly irresponsible act. It is a matter of speculation whether the unknown crew member would or would not have been deterred from acting as he did if the glass panel had been in place (whether the door was locked or unlocked). As there is no evidence as to the reason for the grossly irresponsible act, Cresswell J was not prepared to say that the defendants have proved on a balance of probabilities that the unknown crew member would have been deterred by a pane of glass.[149]

In this case, the court held that it would not naturally have occurred to any marine engineer to consider the vessel unseaworthy (in any sense) simply because of the absence of a glass panel in the door of the box housing her emergency fuel shut-off valve. As to due diligence, Cresswell J viewed that a reasonable difference of opinion does not amount to a want of due diligence.[150] It followed that, in this case, the vessel was not unseaworthy by reason of the absence of the glass panel.

6.14 Overloading the vessel

It is important to distinguish between the negligence of crews and the incompetency of crews. If the shipowner did not fulfil their obligation to employ competent crews, they will be liable for damages, as the obligation to provide a seaworthy vessel is an overriding obligation under the Hague/Hague–Visby Rules.[151] However, if loss or damages result from the negligence of crews but do not relate to seaworthiness, the shipowners will not be responsible under article IV, rule 2.

In the *Aquacharm*,[152] the vessel was delivered on 11 October and proceeded to Baltimore to load a cargo of coal for Japan up to the draught permitted by the Panama Canal Company of 39 ft, 6 in TWF (tropical fresh water). The vessel left Baltimore with 43,000 t of coal on 8 November, but when she arrived at the entrance to the Panama Canal, she was refused entry on the ground that she exceeded the permitted draught. After considerable delay, 636 t of coal were discharged into another vessel, the vessel going through the canal. The 635 t were then reloaded at the other end.

The charterers refused to pay hire and contended that the vessel had been off-hire, and the owners claimed that they were entitled to recover the hire.

At first instance, Lloyd J viewed that the concept of "seaworthiness" has, of course, been extended far beyond its original meaning of fitness to withstand the ordinary perils

148 Ibid.
149 Ibid, p. 312.
150 Ibid, p. 309.
151 *The Maruinne* [1959] 2 Lloyd's Rep.105.
152 *The Aquacharm* [1980] 2 Lloyd's Rep.237; [1982] 1 Lloyd's Rep.7 (C.A.).

of a sea voyage, or in a phrase, "worthiness to go to sea." Clearly, "seaworthy" has its ordinary extended meaning in section 2 of the Carriage of Goods by Sea Act, 1924, and "unseaworthy" has its ordinary extended meaning in the second paragraph of article 4, rule 1. It cannot have been intended that the word should bear a different and narrower meaning in article 3, rule 1(a). Lloyd J stated:[153]

> I am not prepared to extend the concept of unseaworthiness to cover such a case, and certainly I am not prepared to say that this vessel was unseaworthy for the particular voyage which involved a passage through the Panama Canal because she was an inch or two over her permitted draught of 39 ft. 6 in. when she arrived at the entrance to the canal. Moreover, the master was in this difficulty that if the vessel had loaded to less than her permitted draught the charterers could, if so minded, have complained that cargo had been unnecessarily shut out. For those reasons I agree with the umpire that the vessel was not unseaworthy.

In the Court of Appeal, Lord Denning MR considered the question of whether the charterers can recover damages from the owners; the answer depended on whether the vessel was seaworthy or not when she left Baltimore for her trip through the Panama Canal to Japan. If she was unseaworthy, the shipowners would be liable. The shipowners would not be able to prove that they exercised due diligence, and they would be liable under articles III (1)(a) and IV of the Hague Rules. If she was seaworthy, the shipowners would not be liable. They would be exempted from liability by reason of article IV (2)(a), because the loss arose from the neglect of the master in the "management" of the ship.[154]

Both the umpire and the judge found that this vessel was seaworthy. Lord Denning MR observed that the word "seaworthy" in the Hague Rules is used in its ordinary meaning and not in any extended or unnatural meaning. It means that the vessel – with her master and crew – is herself fit to encounter the perils of the voyage and also that she is fit to carry the cargo safely on that voyage. This vessel was so fit. It may be that she had to be lightened to pass through the Panama Canal, but that did not make her unfit. As the judge said, there is no case in which a ship has been held to be unseaworthy merely because she has to lighten in order to get into port. So also if she has to lighten in order to get through the canal.[155]

Griffiths LJ considered that there are two aspects of seaworthiness. The first requires that the ship, her crew, and her equipment shall be, in all respects, sound and able to encounter and withstand the ordinary perils of the sea during the contemplated voyage. The second requires that the ship shall be suitable to carry the contracted cargo.[156]

Griffiths LJ ruled that the vessel, at all times, fulfilled the first requirements of seaworthiness; there is no suggestion that her draught was such as to put her at risk in a heavy sea or to render her in any way unsafe to sail in. In Griffiths LJ's view, the vessel also fulfilled the second requirement; she was a suitable vessel to carry a cargo of coal. The reason she could not enter the Panama Canal was not that she was unsuitable to carry a cargo of coal but because the master had loaded the coal so that the vessel was down by the head when she arrived at the canal and possibly had loaded too much coal. The vessel was delayed because of bad stowage, not because she was unseaworthy. Therefore,

153 Ibid, per Lloyd J [1980] 2 Lloyd's Rep.237 at p. 241.
154 Ibid, per Lord Denning MR [1982] 1 Lloyd's Rep.7 (C.A.) at p. 9.
155 Ibid.
156 Ibid, per Griffiths LJ at p. 11.

the alternative way in which the charterers seek to escape liability for the hire during the period of delay also fails.[157]

It followed that the vessel was, at all times, seaworthy, delayed by bad stowage, and not because she was unseaworthy. It was also suggested that when considering whether a ship is seaworthy or not in relation to the apparatus which can be worked on the voyage and produce the desired result if worked, then one cannot say that the ship is unseaworthy because it was not worked.[158] However, a vessel is unseaworthy if she lacks the proper documents[159] or she was doomed to undergo fumigation at an intermediate port of call.[160]

6.15 Uncertificated officer and manning the vessel

According to editors of *Marsden and Gault on Collisions at Sea*,[161] the duty to stand by continues and the cases remain of value as illustrations of what amounts to compliance. Failure to observe this duty remains a criminal offence and might result in the cancellation or suspension of a certificate of competence if the person in charge of the vessel is a certificated officer.[162] Breach of duty by a certified officer may result in an inquiry into his conduct being held and his certificate being cancelled or suspended.[163] A certificate of competency may be cancelled or suspended if the holder of the certificate is unfit to discharge his duties whether by reason of incompetency or misconduct or for any other reason. The standards of competence and other conditions to be satisfied for particular certificates are laid down by regulations made by the Secretary of State. Unfitness to discharge duties imports a state or condition of unfitness. It implies a certain element of duration. It is not the same thing as isolated neglect or default, although serious negligence in the discharge of an officer's duties is now a ground for cancellation or suspension of a certificate. Incompetence means a lack of the capacity or qualifications required by a holder of a certificate. Where a deficiency in technical qualifications is established, it necessarily continues until, by further experience or training, the deficiency has been overcome. Incompetency may result from an absence of the moral qualifications required by the holder of a certificate without any blame attached to the officer concerned.[164]

In the *Empire Jamaica*,[165] owners of the vessel claimed to limit their liability in respect of damage arising from a collision between the vessel and the Dutch motor vessel *Garoet* in the Java Sea on 1 September 1951. The defendants, N. V. Koninklijke Rotterdamsche Lloyd (owners of the *Garoet*), and the owners of cargo laden in that ship contested the claim, alleging that the plaintiffs negligently allowed the ship to sail with an uncertificated second officer, who was in charge of navigation, during darkness, when the collision occurred.

157 Ibid.
158 *The Northumberland* [1925] 22 Ll.L. Rep.424.
159 *The Madeleine* [1967] 2 Lloyd's Rep.224.
160 *Ciampa v British India Steam Navigation Co. Ltd.* [1915] 2 K.B. 774.
161 *Marsden and Gault on Collisions at Sea*, 15th ed, 2021.
162 Ibid, para. 6–072.
163 Ibid, para. 6–078.
164 Ibid, para. 20–043.
165 *The Empire Jamaica* [1955] 2 Lloyd's Rep.109; [1956] 2 Lloyd's Rep.119 (H.L.).

The plaintiffs' case was that on 1 September 1951, there was a collision between the vessel and the *Garoet* in the Java Sea, in which both vessels and the *Garoet*'s cargo were damaged. There was no loss of life or personal injury. The plaintiffs admitted that the collision and damage were caused by the improper navigation or management of the vessel by their servants but claimed that the collision occurred without the plaintiffs' actual fault or privity.

The defendants' case rested entirely upon the plea that the vessel was unseaworthy because she did not comply with the Hongkong Merchant Shipping Ordinance as to certificates. The vessel was unseaworthy because of undermanning or defective manning. The court was invited to infer that unseaworthiness was the cause of the collision.

It was held by Willmer J at first instance that the plaintiffs have satisfied that, having supplied the ship with an officer whose competence (apart from his having no certificate) is not otherwise challenged, they cannot be held to be guilty of fault or privity in relation to this collision, notwithstanding the fact that the particular officer who was on duty on the bridge at the time of the collision, and whose negligence brought it about, was not the possessor of a certificate.[166]

In the Court of Appeal, Parker LJ put it this way:[167]

> The real question, to my mind, is whether the plaintiffs have proved that they were not privy to sending a ship to sea improperly manned. So far as the facts of this case are concerned, the issue can be further narrowed to this: have they shown that, as owners, they were entitled to believe, and did believe, that Sinon was competent to act as second mate? It was, I think, at one time suggested that to limit their liability the owners must go further and show that Sinon was in fact competent to act as second mate, but that, I think, is putting the onus too high. As I have said, I think the issue must be whether they were entitled to believe that he was competent, since only if they were not so entitled could they be said to be at fault.

In the judgment of Lord Morton of Henryton, he was satisfied that if the respondents were in breach of the ordinance in shipping Mr Sinon as the second mate without obtaining an exemption, under Regulation 19A, from the provisions of section 4 (3) (c), that breach had no causal connection whatsoever with the collision.[168]

Lord Merriman observed that the effect of the following judgments is that in the circumstances of the case, namely, the recognized shortage of certificated officers and the practice of the Marine Department of Hongkong, it has been established that the requirement of section 4(3) of the ordinance had been substantially complied with, or at least that the provision made by the employment of Mr Sinon as the second mate had been proved to be as effective as actual compliance with the requirement that the second mate should be duly certificated.[169]

Lord Cohen concluded:

> As I read his affidavit, apart altogether from the question of exemption under Regulation 19A of the Amending Regulations, owing to the shortage of British certificated officers in Hongkong it was the general practice of his department to sign on uncertificated men described in the article as "boatswain" or "chief boatswain" or as "mate" and not to require

166 Ibid, per Willmer J [1955] 1 Lloyd's Rep.50 at p. 53.
167 Ibid, per Parker LJ [1955] 2 Lloyd's Rep.109 (C.A.) at p. 118.
168 Ibid, per Lord Morton of Henryton [1956] 2 Lloyd's Rep.119 (H.L.) at p. 125.
169 Ibid, per Lord Merriman at p. 127.

owners to comply with Sect. 4 (3) © but only with Sect. 4 (3) (b). The articles of the *Empire Jamaica* conformed to this practice, and in these circumstances I do not think it can be said that the fact that Sinon was not certificated was a contributory cause of the collision.

On the other hand, Lord Goddard observed that an uncertificated man might well be competent, while a certificated officer might be incompetent. The vessel might be seaworthy in respect of her machinery, but unseaworthy in that her engine room staff were incompetent; the loss or damages might well be caused by the incompetence of the engine room staff.[170]

In the *Mountoswald*,[171] the vessel owned by the defendants left Baltimore on 20 February 1912 on a voyage to Hamburg. She carried a cargo of grain and a small general cargo under the deck, and upon the deck a number of heavy logs. She proceeded down the river on which Baltimore stands and through the bay as far as what is called the Capes. When she arrived at the Capes, she dropped her pilot on 22 February, having occupied two days in getting from Baltimore. On the way down from Baltimore to the Capes, she encountered ice, and as a result of striking the ice, she got a leak in the forepeak. She dropped the pilot on 22 February and was never heard of again.

The plaintiffs' case was that the vessel was unseaworthy because her no. 2 tank was bad, because of the engineer and the master, because the vessel went to sea with her deck cargo unlashed, and because of the condition of her forepeak. Secondly, it was not necessarily his case that the vessel was unseaworthy. Plaintiffs submitted that the owners did not exercise due diligence to make her seaworthy.

The defendant's case was that the Harter Act made null and void stipulations of a certain class, but the act had got nothing to say to a stipulation providing that there would be no liability for unseaworthiness if the owners had exercised due diligence to make the ship seaworthy. He further submitted that if his facts were right, the plaintiffs could make no case against the defendants for unseaworthiness because it would appear that the owners did all that was possible to make it seaworthy. Neither could they make any case against the defendants for negligent navigation on the voyage, because if the owners exercised due diligence, liability for negligence would not arise. His submissions were (1) that there was no ground for holding that the vessel was unseaworthy at all and (2) that even if the statement was well-founded, the effect of clause 3 of the Harter Act was not to make liability because of unseaworthiness, provided that the owners had exercised due diligence.[172]

It was held by Bailhache J that it is quite clear that if a vessel is to be seaworthy for an ocean voyage, and particularly for a North Atlantic voyage in the winter, it is essential that a deck cargo of logs should be securely lashed. If they are not, they are a danger not only to the life and limbs of the sailors but also to the structure of the ship. They may get loose and carry away ventilators and things of that sort. A vessel which has not got these logs securely lashed is not seaworthy for an ocean voyage. Again, it is quite clear that a vessel proceeding to sea with her forepeak full of water and with only hand pumps which cannot keep the water down

170 *The Saxonstar* [1958] 1 Lloyd's Rep.73 (H.L.).
171 *The Makedonia* [1962] 1 Lloyd's Rep.316.
172 Ibid, p. 88.

was not, at that time, seaworthy. She was therefore unseaworthy in at least two respects – the deck logs had not been lashed, and the forepeak was badly leaking.[173]

Baihache J considered that this voyage was, in fact, a voyage in stages. The first stage was the passage from Baltimore to the Capes at Chesapeake, and the second stage from Chesapeake to Hamburg, and though it is true that when a voyage is one and indivisible the warranty of seaworthiness attaches at the commencement and not afterwards, it is also true that when a voyage is in stages, the warranty of seaworthiness attaches at the commencement of each stage and it is necessary that the vessel should be seaworthy for the stage she is about to embark upon.[174]

Baihache J ruled that the voyage was treated as a voyage in stages, and being a voyage in stages, it is quite clear that when she left Chesapeake Capes, she was not seaworthy for an open-sea voyage; and if you treat it as a voyage in stages, she was not only not seaworthy for the reason of the logs but was also not seaworthy by reason of the fact that she had sprung the leak in the forepeak.[175]

Turning to the question of whether or not the owners had exercised due diligence to make the ship seaworthy and to have her properly equipped and manned, Baihache J pointed out that as to the first engineer, they had no reason to suspect him. The first engineer had undoubtedly given way to drink, and very seriously. Whether his drinking habits had anything to do with the loss of the vessel, the failure to lash the logs was certainly the fault of the master, owing to his drinking, and his failure to put into a port of refuge when he found the forepeak leaking was due to the state of mind he had gotten into by his drinking habits. Baihache J viewed that he was able to say that the vessel was unseaworthy because of the stranding at Mobile and the temporary repair to the ballast tank, but it is clear if that repair did not hold, the vessel would not be seaworthy. As far as the manning of the ship was concerned, Baihache J concluded that the defendants did not fail in due diligence.[176]

It's suggested that due diligence is the diligence of the reasonably prudent carrier and that the relevant acts or omissions must not be judged in light of hindsight.[177] As the test, whether it had shown that it, its servants, its agents, or its independent contractors had exercised all reasonable skill and care to ensure that the vessel was seaworthy at the commencement of its voyage, namely, reasonably fit to encounter the ordinary incidents of the voyage.[178] Further approach to due diligence in relation to seaworthiness could be found in the *Muncaster Castle*.[179]

6.16 Meaning of ship management

The Hague/Hague–Visby Rules provide the carrier, in article IV, rule 2, with protection from liability for loss or damage arising or resulting from act, default, or negligence of his

173 Ibid, per Baihache J at pp. 91–92.
174 Ibid, p. 92.
175 Ibid.
176 Ibid, p. 93.
177 *The Subro Valour* [1995] 1 Lloyd's Rep.509 at p. 516.
178 *The Kapitan Sakharov* [2000] 2 Lloyd's Rep.255 (C.A.) at p. 266. See also the *Eurasian Dream* [2002] 1 Lloyd's Rep.719.
179 *The Muncaster Castle* [1961] 1 Lloyd's Rep.57 (H.L.).

servants of the carrier in the navigation or management of the ship or caused by fire not resulting from his own actual fault or privity.

The definition of ship management was considered in the *Canadian Highlander*.[180]

In this case, a large number of tinplates was shipped at Swansea in the defendants' vessel for carriage to Vancouver. They were shipped in good condition but arrived in Vancouver seriously damaged by fresh water, of which, judging by the extent of the damage, a large quantity must have entered the hold in which they were stowed. At the trial, two theories were put forward to explain this freshwater damage. The shipowners alleged that the water came from the unseasoned timber of the boxes in which the tinplates were packed. The judge was not satisfied with this and found that the boxes were "good average normal boxes." The cargo owners alleged that the fresh water causing the damage was rain entering through the shelter deck and tween deck hatches of hold no. 5, left open by the negligence of the ship's officers and their deputies while it was raining. The question, therefore, is whether the facts found by the judge amount to "neglect or default of the servants of the carrier in the management of the ship."

In the Court of Appeal, Scrutton LJ observed that the words to be considered occur in a statutory contract between shipowner and cargo owner relating to the carriage of goods in a ship. The cargo owner has no interest in any empty ship or in its management. The shipowner undertakes to use due diligence to provide a ship fit for the carriage of goods, including proper propelling and pumping machinery and, where the cargo requires it, proper refrigerating and ventilating appliances, and in such a proper ship properly to carry and deliver cargo, and he exempts himself from liability for negligent management of such a ship by his servants.[181]

Scrutton LJ considered that for "management of the ship," this meaning would cover bad stowage and the management of the crew and stevedores. But without going as far as this, "management of the ship" must include "management of part of the ship" which incidentally damages some of the cargo, and if it is necessary that the management should be primarily intended to keep the ship fit, that condition is fulfilled when the management of part of the ship, the hatches, is for the purpose of repairing damage to the ship herself in the course of her contract voyage.[182]

In Greer LJ's judgment, the reasonable interpretation to put on the rules is that there is a paramount duty imposed safely to carry and take care of the cargo and that the performance of this duty is only excused if the damage to the cargo is the indirect result of an act or neglect, which can be described as either (1) negligence in caring for the safety of the ship, (2) failure to take care to prevent damage to the ship or some part of the ship, or (3) failure in the management of some operation connected with the movement or stability of the ship, or otherwise for ship's purposes. It was worth noting that article IV (2)(a) is not directed to acts, neglects, or defaults in the course of management of the ship but acts, neglects, or defaults in the management of the ship.[183] Greer LJ concluded that if the cause of the damage is solely, or even primarily, a neglect to take reasonable care of the cargo, the ship is liable, but if the cause of the damage is a neglect to take reasonable care of the

180 *The Canadian Highlander* [1927] 29 Ll.L. Rep.190; [1928] 32 Ll.L. Rep.91 (H.L.).
181 Ibid, per Scrutton LJ [1927] 29 Ll.L. Rep.190 (C.A.) at p. 191.
182 Ibid, p. 192.
183 Ibid, p. 197.

ship, or some part of it, as distinct from the cargo, the ship is relieved from liability, for if the negligence is not negligence towards the ship but only negligent failure to use the apparatus of the ship for the protection of the cargo, the ship is not so relieved.[184]

In the House of Lords, Lord Chancellor (Lord Hailsham) stated:[185]

> It is clear that the tinplates were not safely and properly cared for or carried; and it is for the respondents then to prove that they are protected from liability by the provisions of Art. IV, and that the damage was occasioned through the neglect or default of their servants in the management of the ship. In my judgment they have not even shown that the persons who were negligent *were* their servants; but even if it can be assumed that the negligence in dealing with the tarpaulins was by members of the crew, such negligence was not negligence in the management of the ship, and therefore is not negligence with regard to which Art. IV, Rule 2 (a), affords, any protection.

Viscount Sumner pointed out that the intention of this legislation in dealing with the liability of a shipowner as a carrier of goods by sea undoubtedly was to replace a conventional contract, in which it was constantly attempted, often with much success, to relieve the carrier from every kind of liability, by a legislative bargain, under which he should be permitted to limit his obligation to take good care of the cargo by an exception, among others, relating to navigation and management of the ship. Obviously, his position was to be one of restricted exemption.[186]

Viscount Sumner ruled:[187]

> If management of the ship includes any part of the ship or any operation with regard to the ship as a whole, which is carried out for ship's purposes and not merely in relation to cargo, I think that the shipowner's position would be certainly no less favourable than it was before under voluntary bills of lading, and probably more so; for on this construction the obligation of Art. III (2) to take care of the cargo is practically eviscerated and its business efficacy is frustrated. In every set of circumstances, of common occurrence at any rate, the shipowner would be relieved. Considering the provisions of the Act of 1924 and the circumstances in which it was passed, such an interpretation is admissible only if the words used are clear to that effect; and to my mind they are not.

Their Lordships approved the judgment of Greer LJ in the Court of Appeal. The intention of this legislation in dealing with the liability of a shipowner as a carrier of goods by sea undoubtedly was to replace a conventional contract, in which it was constantly attempted, often with much success, to relieve the carrier from every kind of liability, by a legislative bargain, under which he should be permitted to limit his obligation to take good care of the cargo by an exception, among others, relating to navigation and management of the ship.[188]

It follows that the management referred to is therefore of the whole vessel, as is the navigation, not of a particular part of it. If the navigation is of the entire ship, so must the management.[189]

The meaning of management of the ship was also considered in the *Dramatist and Spectator*.[190] The dispute is between a bill of lading owner and the shipowners. The bill

184 Ibid, p. 200.
185 Ibid, per Lord Hailsham [1928] 32 Ll.L. Rep.91 (H.L.) at p. 95.
186 Ibid, per Viscount Sumner at p. 96.
187 Ibid.
188 Ibid.
189 *Carver on Bills of Lading*, 4th ed at pp. 9–212.
190 *The Dramatist and Spectator* [1927] 28 Ll.L. Rep.120 (C.A.).

of lading holder is complaining about the loss of certain goods during a voyage. The fact, as proved before the learned judge, was that in the case of both vessels, goods had been consigned by the bill of lading holder from this country to ports in Mexico, and at one port the cargo, or portions of the cargo, had been stolen by the men employed by the stevedores in the discharge of the goods, and the shipowners contended that under the terms of the bill of lading, they were exempt from liability.

Bankes LJ, in giving judgment, said:[191]

> I think that, as an ordinary rule of construction of this language, when you find in the first place the legislature imposing this particular statutory duty upon the shipowner in reference, among other things, to the discharge of the goods carried, and then when it comes to enumerate the exceptions it has no exception dealing specifically with the goods, but it has an exception dealing with the ship and the management of the ship as it may affect the goods, in order to bring any particular matter within the exception it must be something which can be said to be in the management of the ship.

Bankes LJ observed that the more one looked into the authorities, the more authority one finds for the proposition that such an act as this, a mere discharging of the cargo, cannot properly be said to come within the expression "management of the ship," as used in article IV of the Carriage of Goods by Sea Act, or in the Harter Act.[192]

Atkin LJ considered that:[193]

> [T]he stevedores brought in were employed by the ship for the purpose of discharging the cargo, and that which was done was not a defect in the ship or a defect in the management of the ship as defined, but merely a default of a person dealing with a particular case of cargo, and in my view it is clearly not within the meaning of the words "management of the ship" as defined by the authorities.

According to Atkin LJ's view, there was a statutory obligation on the ship to discharge, and they performed that duty by entering into a contract with the master stevedore, who, for that purpose, was their agent in performing their statutory duty; and to my mind, that in itself would be sufficient to support the matter, because it was plain that the master stevedore, according to our law, would be responsible for the tortious acts of his servants done in the scope of their employment. But quite apart from that, the servants of the stevedore, for this purpose, are also the agents of the ship.[194] The stevedores brought in were employed by the ship for the purpose of discharging the cargo, and that which was done was not a defect in the ship or a defect in the management of the ship as defined but merely a default of a person dealing with a particular case of cargo. It is clearly not within the meaning of the words "management of the ship" as defined by the authorities.

More recently, in the *Iron Gippsland*,[195] throughout the passage the cargo was contaminated via the inert gas system, and its flashpoint was reduced to an unacceptable level for use as cutter stock. Carruthers J observed that it was true that inert gas systems were installed on tankers fundamentally for the protection of the vessel. However, the purpose of the inert gas system is primarily to manage the cargo, not only for the protection of the cargo, but also for

191 Ibid, per Bankes LJ at p. 122.
192 Ibid.
193 Ibid, per Atkin LJ at p. 126.
194 Ibid.
195 *The Iron Gippsland* [1994] 1 Lloyd's Rep.335.

the ultimate protection of the vessel from adverse consequences associated with that cargo. Thus, essentially, the inert gas system is concerned with the management of the cargo, and in my view, damage occasioned to cargo by mismanagement of the inert gas system cannot be categorized as neglect or fault in the management of the ship.[196]

Next, in the *Aconcagua*,[197] the court held that the heating of the cargo was, however, an "act, neglect or default in the management of the ship." The risk of loss arising therefrom was, therefore, an excepted peril, and the charterers were under no liability in respect of it. In the *Eternity*,[198] the court held that any failure to operate or maintain properly those parts of the IGS available for the purpose of avoiding contamination of cargo could not be categorised as neglect or default in the management of the ship. The separation valves had two purposes: one being the avoidance of contamination, the other facilitating gas freeing. The cause of the damage in the present case was primarily a failure to care for the cargo.

It's common ground that one of the most important exculpatory exceptions available to the carrier is an error in the navigation or management of the ship; in order to bring any particular matter within the exception, it must be something which definitely is said to be in the management of the ship. On the other hand, such as failure properly to use locking bars retaining hatch cover tarpaulins and tend wedges when at sea may amount to an error in the management of the vessel.[199]

6.17 Repudiation of a time charter for crew unseaworthiness

Under article III, rule 1, the carrier shall be bound before and at the beginning of the voyage to exercise due diligence to make the ship seaworthy, to properly man, equip, and supply the ship. The ship shall be seaworthy for the particular voyage and cargoworthy for the cargo to be carried. The carrier will be liable for loss or damage to the cargoes if it results from the ship's unseaworthiness, or uncargoworthiness. However, the seaworthiness term is not a condition but an intermediate term. The innocent party could not bring the charter to end, unless the breach deprives the innocent party of "substantially the whole benefit" of the contract.

In the *Hong Kong Fir*,[200] the vessel was under a time charter. It would be seen that between Liverpool and Osaka, she was at sea for about 812 weeks, off-hire for about 5 weeks, and had £21,400 spent upon her for repairs. While at Osaka, a further period of about 15 weeks and an expenditure of £37,500 were required to make her ready for sea. Repudiation of the charter was made by the charterers.

The owners claimed damages for wrongful repudiation of the contract. The charterers' defence was that they were entitled to throw up the charter because of breaches of the charter on the part of the owners. The charterers contended that any of these breaches would *per se* entitle them to throw up the charter. Alternatively, they said that they were so entitled to the failure of the owners to remedy the breaches (a) within a reasonable time or (b) within what has been referred to an argument as "a frustrating time" that they

196 Ibid, p. 358.
197 *The Aconcagua* [2010] 1 Lloyd's Rep.1.
198 *The Eternity* [2009] 1 Lloyd's Rep.107.
199 *The Hector* [1955] 2 Lloyd's Rep.218.
200 *The Hong Kong Fir* [1961] 1 Lloyd's Rep.159; [1961] 2 Lloyd's Rep.478 (C.A.).

contended that the breaches were such that the delay involved in remedying them frustrated the commercial purpose of the charter.

It was held by Salmon J, at first instance, that the machinery was in a reasonably good condition at Liverpool, but by reason of its age, it needed to be maintained by an experienced, competent, careful, and adequate engine room staff. Salmon J found that the engine room staff of this vessel was incompetent and insufficient in numbers. Accordingly, the owners were in breach of their obligation under clause 1 of the charter. There is no escape for them under clause 13, since for the reasons the breach was caused by want of due diligence on their part. Salmon J further found that the owners were also in breach of their obligation under clause 3 of the charter to maintain the vessel in a thoroughly efficient state.[201]

Salmon J stated:[202]

> However this may be, the authorities which I have reviewed, and by which I am bound in my judgment, clearly establish that unseaworthiness by itself gives the charterers no right to rescind, and I, accordingly, so hold. *A fortiori* a breach of the condition to maintain the vessel in a thoroughly efficient state cannot by itself entitle the charterers to rescind.

It followed that the charterers had no legal right to repudiate the charterparty. They would, however, be entitled to such damage as they suffered by reason of delay caused by the owners' breaches of the charterparty.

It was held by Sellers LJ in the Court of Appeal that by clause 1 of the charterparty, the shipowners contracted to deliver the vessel at Liverpool, "*she being in every way fitted for ordinary cargo service*." She was not fit for ordinary cargo service when delivered because the engine room staff was incompetent and inadequate, and this became apparent as the voyage proceeded. It is commonplace language to say that the vessel was unseaworthy by reason of this inefficiency in the engine room.[203]

Sellers LJ observed:[204]

> It would be unthinkable that all the relatively trivial matters which have been held to be unseaworthiness could be regarded as conditions of the contract or conditions precedent to a charterer's liability and justify in themselves a cancellation or refusal to perform on the part of the charterer.

Sellers LJ considered that if the shipowners had refused or failed so to do, their conduct and not the unseaworthiness would have amounted to a repudiation of the charterparty and entitled the charterers to accept it and treat the contract as at an end.

Diplock LJ (as he then was) observed that the shipowner's undertaking to tender a seaworthy ship has, as a result of numerous decisions as to what can amount to "unseaworthiness," become one of the most complex of contractual undertakings. It embraced obligations with respect to every part of the hull and machinery, stores and equipment, and the crew itself. It could be broken by the presence of trivial defects easily and rapidly remediable as well as by defects which must inevitably result in a total loss of the vessel.[205]

201 Ibid, per Salmon J [1961] 1 Lloyd's Rep.159 at p. 171.
202 Ibid, p. 173.
203 Ibid, per Sellers LJ [1961] 2 Lloyd's Rep.478 (C.A.) at p. 486.
204 Ibid.
205 Ibid, per Diplock LJ at p. 486.

Diplock LJ described:[206]

> No doubt there are many simple contractual undertakings, sometimes express, but more often because of their very simplicity ("It goes without saying") to be implied, of which it can be predicated that every breach of such an undertaking must give rise to an event which will deprive the party not in default of substantially the whole benefit which it was intended that he should obtain from the contract. And such a stipulation, unless the parties have agreed that breach of it shall not entitle the non-defaulting party to treat the contract as repudiated, is a "condition." So, too, there may be other simple contractual undertakings of which it can be predicated that no breach can give rise to an event which will deprive the party not in default of substantially the whole benefit which it was intended that he should obtain from the contract; and such a stipulation, unless the parties have agreed that breach of it shall entitle the non-defaulting party to treat the contract as repudiated, is a "warranty."

In Diplock LJ's view, either solved or soluble by debating whether the shipowner's express or implied undertaking to tender a seaworthy ship was a "condition" or a "warranty." It was, like so many other contractual terms, an undertaking, one breach of which may give rise to an event which relieves the charterer of further performance of his undertakings if he so elects, and another breach of which may not give rise to such an event but entitle him only to monetary compensation in the form of damages.[207]

Diplock LJ observed that in many hundreds of previous cases about the shipowner's undertaking to deliver a seaworthy ship, there is none where it was found profitable to discuss in the judgments the question whether that undertaking was a "condition" or a "warranty," for the true answer was that it was neither but one of that large class of contractual undertakings, one breach of which may have the same effect as that ascribed to a breach of "condition" under the Sale of Goods Act, and a different breach of which may have only the same effect as that ascribed to a breach of "warranty" under that act.[208] As to the Baltime 1939 charter clause 13, the "due diligence" clause, Diplock LJ viewed, that exempted the shipowners from responsibility for delay or loss or damage to goods on board due to unseaworthiness, unless such delay or loss or damage has been caused by want of due diligence of the owners in making the vessel seaworthy and fitted for the voyage, was in itself sufficient to show that the mere occurrence of the events that the vessel was, in some respect, unseaworthy would not deprive the charterer of the whole benefit which it was the intention of the parties he should obtain from the performance of his obligations under the contract.[209]

Of such undertakings, all that can be predicated is that some breaches will and others will not give rise to an event which will deprive the party not in default of substantially the whole benefit which it was intended that he should obtain from the contract, and the legal consequences of a breach of such an undertaking, unless provided for expressly in the contract, depend upon the nature of the event to which the breach gives rise and does not follow automatically from a prior classification of the undertaking as a "condition" or a "warranty."

The question then arises as to how serious in such a case the consequences of the breach must be to entitle discharge. The leading judgment of Diplock LJ in this case requires that

206 Ibid, p. 493.
207 Ibid, p. 494.
208 Ibid.
209 Ibid, p. 495.

the breach deprive the innocent party of "substantially the whole benefit" of the contract.[210] Where the time of performance is not of the essence, a delay in performance will nevertheless constitute a repudiation, where the continued failure of performance either deprives the innocent party of substantially the whole benefit intended to be obtained from performance, and thereby goes to the root of the contract, or amounts to a renunciation in that the guilty party's conduct evinces, in all the circumstances, an intention never to perform the contract at all or only in a manner substantially inconsistent with the contract so as to produce a fundamental deprivation of benefit.[211]

It follows that undertaking of seaworthiness mostly will not be a condition, but if a refusal or failure on the part of the shipowners to rectify the deficiency may show an intention no longer to be bound by the charter, the charterers may bring the charter to an end. It was held by Mustill J (as he then was) at first instance and the Court of Appeal in the *Hermosa*,[212] on the findings, that there was a breach of the initial warranty of seaworthiness or of the obligation to make the vessel seaworthy, and the deficiencies which constituted or evidenced this breach had not been put right by the time the charter was cancelled; the sub-charterers were not justified in treating the charter as discharged by reason of the ship's unseaworthiness, because the remaining defects were capable of being put right within a relatively short time and thereafter the sub- charter would still have had 16 to 20 months to run.

On the other hand, as in the *Yuri Maru*,[213] at first instance, Greer J found that the vessel was unseaworthy and that there was a failure to take reasonable steps within a reasonable time to put her into an efficient state. It was held by the Court of Appeal that the unseaworthiness of the ship had prevented the performance of the contract for such time as to frustrate the charter and that the charterers were entitled to act as they did. Bankes LJ put it in this way:[214]

> I think it is impossible to contend that, in a case like this of a time-charter, the charterer, simply because the vessel is off-hire, is bound to wait an interminable time (if I may use that expression) without getting his vessel, and yet have no right to terminate the contract under circumstances which make it not only absolutely impossible for him to use the vessel, but quite conclusively certain that he never will be able to make use of it for the purpose contemplated by both parties at the time they entered into the contract.

Therefore, the unseaworthiness of the ship at the time of delivery causes, or is likely to cause, a delay that will frustrate the commercial object of the charter, and the charterers may treat the contract as discharged. However, there is an express warranty of seaworthiness, and unless the ship is timeously delivered in a seaworthy condition, such as the necessary certificate from the port health authority, the charterers may have the right to cancel.[215]

To interpret this kind of charter, the only general rule that can be laid down is that one must consider the particular wording of the particular term in each case.

210 Also see discussion in *The Spar Capella* [2016] 2 Lloyd's Rep.447 (C.A.).
211 *Scrutton on Charterparties and Bills of Lading*, 24th ed at pp. 2–126.
212 *The Hermosa* [1980] 1 Lloyd's Rep.638; [1982] 1 Lloyd's Rep.570 (C.A.).
213 *The Yuri Maru* [1923] 17 Ll.L. Rep.78; [1924] 18 Ll.L. Rep.333 (C.A.).
214 Ibid, per Bankes LJ [1924] 18 Ll.L. Rep.333 (C.A.) at p. 335.
215 *The Madeleine* [1967] 2 Lloyd's Rep.224.

CHAPTER 7

Vessel's certificates and documents

7.1 Introduction

As discussed previously, for a vessel to be seaworthy, she "*must have that degree of fitness which an ordinary, careful and prudent owner would require his vessel to have, having regard to all the probable circumstances of the voyage.*"[1] The requirement of fitness under time charter that the ship be fit for the charter service imposes on owners an obligation to ensure that the ship is seaworthy on delivery. The words "in every way fitted for ordinary cargo service" constituted an express warranty of seaworthiness. If there was an express warranty of seaworthiness in charter, and unless the ship was timeously delivered in a seaworthy condition, including the necessary certificate from the port health authority, the charterers are entitled to claim damage against the owners for their breach.[2]

However, even in the absence of an express term that the ship is fixed for the service, a warranty that the ship is seaworthy on delivery would be implied in a time charter. So basic is this obligation in a charterparty that unless there is an express clause of exclusion, it will be implied.[3] Such fitness not only covers the physical condition of the vessel but also extends to documents, appropriate charts or passage plan,[4] navigational aids,[5] certificate,[6] or documentation[7] required for the vessel to be able to complete the voyage but to be justified in fact.

The master should be aware of IMO and flag state requirements to be observed, SOLAS and MARPOL, also vessel's class to comply, etc.[8] The vessel, in order to comply with ISM Code/SMS, etc., must be with valid certificates or documents on board; otherwise, the vessel might not be allowed to enter or leave the port. The vessel might be unseaworthy if the shipowners fail to exercise due diligence to maintain the vessel or if no system is in place for properly monitoring the vessel.[9]

In conclusion, the shipowner must provide the ship with all necessary documents for the voyage, namely, those validly required by the law of the vessel's flag or by the laws,

1 *McFadden v Blue Star Line* [1905] 1 K.B. 697. per Channell J.
2 *The Madeleine* [1967] 2 Lloyd's Rep.224.
3 *The Hong Kong Fir* [1961] 2 Lloyd's Rep.478 (C.A.).
4 *The CMA CGM Libra* [2020] EWCA Civ 293; [2021] UKSC 51.
5 *The Marion* [1984] 2 Lloyd's Rep.1 (H.L.); The Isla Fernandina [2000] 2 Lloyd's Rep.15.
6 *The Madeleine* [1967] 2 Lloyd's Rep.224.
7 *The Makedonia* [1962] 1 Lloyd's Rep.316; *The Derby* [1985] 2 Lloyd's Rep.325 (C.A.); *The Silver Constellation* [2008] 2 Lloyd's Rep.440.
8 *The Torepo* [2002] 2 Lloyd's Rep.535.
9 *The Devon* [2012] EWHC 3747 (Comm).

DOI: 10.4324/9781003279938-7

regulations, or lawful administrative practices of governmental or local authorities at the vessel's ports of call, where known.[10]

7.2 Embargo

An embargo is a government order that restricts commerce with a specified country or the exchange of specific goods. An embargo is usually created as a result of unfavourable political or economic circumstances between nations. It is designed to isolate a country and create difficulties for its governing body, forcing it to act on the issue that led to the embargo.

In the *Nizeti*,[11] an issue arose out of the failure of the shipowners to load a cargo of wheat in the *Nizeti* at Lattakia, Syria, in May/June 1956. The charterers claimed damages for breach of contract by the shipowners, who counterclaimed damages for the loss which they had sustained as the result of the cargo not being loaded. The vessel was unable to obtain free pratique when she arrived at Lattakia. Later, the Syrian government put an embargo on the exporting of grain to Algeria, and as a result, the vessel sailed from Lattakia without her cargo.

The charterers contended that the defect was one which put the owners in breach of their implied warranty of seaworthiness and, alternatively, in breach of their implied warranty that the ship shall commence and carry out the voyage contracted for with reasonable diligence, these two undertakings being implied in all contracts of carriage by sea in the absence of express stipulation to the contrary.

At first instance, the learned judge rejected these submissions but held that since it lay solely within the power of the owners and outside the power of the charterers to obtain the permission to load, a term must be implied in the charterparty to give business efficacy to the contract that the shipowners would at least exercise reasonable diligence to obtain the permission. He further held that, since the owners knew and the charterers neither knew nor ought to have known at the date of the charterparty that permission might be needed, there was an implied warranty by the shipowners not only that they would use due diligence to obtain.[12]

In the Court of Appeal, Hodson LJ observed that so far as seaworthiness is concerned, the contention is that this is a case of a vessel suffering from a fault not found in normal vessels, analogous to a defective boiler which made her unfit for the voyage. It cannot be said on the facts of this case that the voyage was foredoomed to failure by reason of any lack of seaworthiness. In any event, this warranty would not avail the charterers since there was no express warranty, and the implied warranty according to the authorities attaches not on the approach voyage but when the vessel sailed with her cargo.[13]

Hodson LJ stated that there was no business necessity for such an additional warranty as that implied by the learned judge. The obligation "expected ready to load" is sufficient for business efficacy. The implied warranties had stood for many years, and it must be rarely necessary for any further implication to be made. He found that it was the embargo which frustrated the contract between the parties and there was no breach by the owners.[14]

---

10 *Scrutton on Charterparties and Bills of Lading*, 24th ed at pp. 7–028.
11 *The Nizeti* [1958] 2 Lloyd's Rep.502; [1960] 1 Lloyd's Rep.132 (C.A.).
12 Ibid, per Diplock (as the then was) [1958] 2 Lloyd's Rep.502.
13 Ibid, per Hodson LJ [1960] 1 Lloyd's Rep.132 (C.A.).
14 Ibid, p. 138.

Ormerod LJ pointed out that there was no express warranty of seaworthiness in the charterparty. In the circumstances, there was an implied warranty of seaworthiness and, in addition, an implied warranty that the ship would commence and carry out the voyage contracted for with reasonable diligence. Ormerod LJ stated:[15]

> In the absence of express warranty of seaworthiness, there is an implied warranty which does not come into operation until the vessel starts loading. Seaworthiness, of course, means more than that the ship is "tight staunch and strong." It means that she must be fitted with everything necessary for the intended voyage and to carry the specified cargo or cargoes.

It was held by Gorman J that there is no express warranty of seaworthiness or fitness for the contemplated voyage. The implied warranty of seaworthiness does not arise until the vessel sails with her cargo and not on the approach voyage. In this case, this time was never reached, and the implied warranty of seaworthiness never attached to the vessel. Gorman J found that there was no breach of contract under the charterparty by owners.[16]

According to Hodson, it cannot be said on the facts of this case that, as in *Ciampa and Others v British India Steam Navigation Company Ltd*,[17] sup., the voyage was foredoomed to failure by reason of any lack of seaworthiness. In any event, this warranty would not avail the charterers since there is no express warranty and the implied warranty according to the authorities attaches not on the approach voyage but when the vessel sails with her cargo. The time of sailing with the cargo was never reached.[18]

It follows that the implied warranty of seaworthiness did not operate until a vessel sailed with her cargo; however, at the commencement of loading, the ship must be fit to receive her cargo and fit as a ship for the ordinary perils of lying afloat in harbour while receiving her cargo but need not be fit for sailing. At the completion of each stage, she must have the degree of fitness which is required for the next stage.

At present, most charters included express seaworthiness terms or fitness; implied warranty of seaworthiness is no more a matter. Of course, after an accident relating to seaworthiness, the shipowner has to prove that they have exercised due diligence to make the ship seaworthy; if the shipowners fail to prove, they will be liable for damage, as to make the ship seaworthy is an overriding obligation under article III, rule 1.[19]

7.3 Swedish measurement certificate

In 2016, due to an outbreak of the Zika virus such as in Brazil and Singapore, there were regulations that required vessels to call Brazil or Singapore to obtain a mosquito eradication certificate before calling Chinese ports. The certificate shall prove that the vessel was disinfected against mosquitoes before departure. If the vessel departed from those epidemic areas with no valid disinfection certificate, the local CIQ would carry out disinfection treatment before berthing.

---

15 Ibid, per Ormerod LJ at p. 139.

16 Ibid, per Gorman J at pp. 140–141.

17 *Ciampa and Others v British India Steam Navigation Company, Ltd.* [1915] 2 K.B. 774.

18 See *Cohn v Davidson and Another* [1877] 2 Q.B.D. 455, and *Scrutton LJ's judgment in A. E. Reed & Co., Ltd. v Page, Son & East, Ltd., and Another* [1927] 27 Ll.L. Rep.114 at p. 119, as to various stages of a voyage.

19 *The Maurienne* [1959] 2 Lloyd's Rep.105 (P.C.); *The Good Friend* [1984] 2 Lloyd's Rep.586 at pp. 588, 593; *The Happy Ranger* [2002] 2 Lloyd's Rep.357 at p. 364 (C.A.).

However, the situation has become worse in the recent days. According to the Command Centre of COVID-19 Control and Prevention, measures are to be further strengthened for preventing and controlling the spread of COVID-19 from crews of international vessels calling at Chinese ports. In addition to the requirement to change crews before entering Chinese waters is at least 14 days' or 21 days' or 28 days' isolation at anchorage since the last day of departure from international ports. On the other hand, before clear import formalities, an agent should also submit a document showing negative result of the test. If failure to comply with the aforementioned measures will cause delays to the vessel and cargo operations – in other words, if crews have no negative nucleic acid testing (NAT) certificate in hand – it may make the vessel unseaworthy.

However, unlike the deratting certificate,[20] some other certificates will not make the vessel unseaworthy. In the *Pencarrow*,[21] the charterers contended that the vessel set out from this country without a Swedish measurement certificate, with the result that as she went to Stockholm, one had to be provided and paid for by the charterers. They, therefore, claimed that that was a liability of the owners, upon the principle for which there was authority, that a ship, in order to be seaworthy and fit for the voyage, had to be provided with the necessary documents to enable her to enter the ports to which she was going.

With regard to the measurement certificate, the charterers further contended that the shipowners must pay for it upon the ground that without it, the ship was not "in every way fitted" for a Baltic round voyage. The failure of the ship to provide this document was a breach of the implied warranty of seaworthiness. In their submission, these general words could not be relied upon by the owners or be construed as covering the expenses incurred by the charterers, because of the failure of the owners to provide a seaworthy ship or a ship "in every way fitted for ordinary cargo service" for one Baltic round voyage.

The umpire had found that none of the damage suffered by the steamer was fair wear and tear within the meaning of the exception in clause 7 of the charterparty, that the respondents were liable to the claimants for the damage, and that when the steamer was delivered to the respondents, she was, in every respect, seaworthy and fitted to carry coal or coke cargo from England to the Baltic.[22]

Acton J, in giving judgment, said that the first point that is raised is a contention of the charterers based upon clause 1 of the charterparty that "the ship without a Swedish certificate of measurement was not in every way fitted for the Baltic round and was not seaworthy," and there was, therefore, a breach of the implied warranty of seaworthiness. In other words, it is said that the document was necessary to render the vessel seaworthy and fitted for a Baltic round.[23]

Acton J observed that there is nothing in the present case to indicate that this certificate of Swedish measurement was a document "which owners or captains usually procure," or such as are usually issued to and carried by ships sailing from this country for a Baltic round, or that the ship was either prevented from or delayed in entering the port of Stockholm because she had no such certificate at the commencement of the voyage, or indeed that the

20 *The Madeleine* [1967] 2 Lloyd's Rep.224.
21 *The Pencarrow* [1933] 45 Ll.L. Rep.190.
22 Ibid, p. 191.
23 Ibid, per Acton J at p. 192.

owners customarily obtained or could obtain such a certificate, either before the time the vessel sailed from the Tyne or between that time and the arrival of the ship at Stockholm.[24]

Acton J affirmed the award that the vessel was not unseaworthy by reason of her having no Swedish measurement certificate and that the cost of procuring that certificate fell upon the charterers.

For the requirement that the ship is fit for, or "fitted for," as in this case, clause 1 of the charterparty provided: "*[I]n every way fitted for ordinary cargo service*." The charter service imposes on the owners an obligation to ensure that the ship is seaworthy on delivery. It constituted an express warranty of seaworthiness, and this warranty required the provision of a sufficient and competent crew to operate the vessel for the purposes of the charter service;[25] it entailed not only that the ship is seaworthy but also that it is properly equipped, certified, and authorised to perform the service. To discharge their obligations under this charterparty, the owners were bound to provide a vessel which was physically fit to encounter all such perils as would be reasonably foreseeable on any voyage the charterers could legitimately require the ship to make and to carry safely to its destination any cargo which the charterers could properly specify; they had to man the ship with a master and a crew competent and sufficient for the purposes of any such voyages. The owners had to ensure that the ship was furnished with all such plant, tackle, and equipment as might be reasonably necessary for those purposes, all in good mechanical order, and with all appropriate navigational aids, such, for example, as charts.[26]

7.4 Up-to-date charts

The working charts are all the charts of the area at which the vessel is being navigated or shortly before the collision. The projected course of the ship will often be laid off on the chart as part of the passage-planning process. The actual positions of the ship may also be recorded on the chart at intervals so that the vessel's progress can be monitored and the speed or course can be adjusted to keep her on her projected course. The first action of the officer of the watch after his ship has been in a collision will usually be to check and record his position at the collision. An analysis of the markings on a working chart can be difficult, particularly in a case where the chart is not new and contains erased markings from earlier voyages.[27]

The requirements for voyage/passage planning are contained within SOLAS Chapter 5, "Safety of Navigation, IMO Res. A.893(21)," and the STCW, Section A-VIII/2, Part 2. The scope of the obligation imposed upon a shipowner by article III, rule 1 of the Hague/Hague–Visby Rules is to exercise due diligence to make the vessel seaworthy before and at the beginning of the voyage. As the Supreme Court handed down judgment on 10 November 2021 in the *CMA CGM Libra*,[28] defects in the vessel's passage plan and the relevant working chart will render the vessel unseaworthy.

24 Ibid, p. 193.
25 *The Madeleine* [1967] 1 Lloyd's Rep.224; *The Hong Kong Fir* [1961] 2 Lloyd's Rep.478 (C.A.).
26 *The Derby* [1985] 2 Lloyd's Rep.325 (C.A.).
27 *Marsden and Gault on Collisions at Sea*, 15th ed at pp. 16–223.
28 *The CMA CGM Libra* [2021] UKSC 51.

The owners must provide the ship with all necessary documents for the voyage.[29] A deficiency in documentation, including navigational charts, certificates bearing on seaworthiness, and certain other documents, may render a vessel unseaworthy.[30]

In the *Marion*,[31] the case concerns limitation of liability under the Merchant Shipping Act 1984 rather than a seaworthiness case. The plaintiffs admitted that the damage was caused partly by the negligence of one of their servants in that the reason the vessel anchored so close to the pipeline was that her master was unaware of its existence because he was navigating with the aid of a chart which had been published in 1953 and printed with small corrections up to 1959 but not corrected up to date. If he had looked at an up-to-date chart of the area, he would have seen marked thereon the position of the pipeline, and such a chart was available in the vessel's chartroom.

One of the questions for the decision of the court was, What action should have been taken by FMSL as reasonably prudent ship managers to ensure that the vessel was supplied with up-to-date charts? It's held by Lord Brandon in the House of Lords that it was the duty of the managing director to ensure that an adequate degree of supervision of the master of *Marion*, so far as the obtaining and keeping of up-to-date charts were concerned, was exercised either by himself or by his subordinate managerial staff, each of whom was fully qualified to exercise such supervision; insofar as the managing director failed to perform his duty in this respect, such failure constituted in law actual fault of the plaintiffs.[32]

Lord Brandon concluded there were therefore two actual faults of the plaintiffs. The first one is the managing director's failure to have a proper system of supervision in relation to charts, and the second one is the failure to give subordinate managerial staff instructions with regard to the matters of which they were required to be kept informed.[33]

According to Lord Brandon, the likelihood was, in either case, that captain would either have been persuaded by FMSL to abandon his propensity for navigating with obsolete charts or, if he proved to be incapable of reform in that respect, that he would have been relieved of his command. In these circumstances, it was impossible for the appellants to establish that the two actual faults of the appellants did not contribute to the damage to the pipeline.[34]

It's noted that, as Sheen J pointed out in Admiralty Court:

> No doubt that a large majority of shipowners of high reputation regard the provision of charts and their maintenance as matters which are quite properly left to the responsibility of the master. In the light of all the evidence, a prudent shipowner is entitled to regard the provision of charts as the responsibility of the master unless he has good reason to think that the master is not carrying out his responsibility. In that event, further action is required. It may even become necessary to relieve the master of his command.[35]

However, as Lord Brandon observed, the schedules instead were indicative of three main matters. The first matter indicated by them was that, while a substantial number of reputable shipowners did rely solely on their masters for obtaining and maintaining charts, without

29 *Scrutton on Charterparties and Bills of Lading*, 24th ed, pp. 7–028.
30 *Bills of Lading*, 3rd ed at para. 11.131.
31 *The Marion* [1984] 2 Lloyd's Rep.1 (H.L.).
32 Ibid, per Lord Brandon at p. 7.
33 Ibid, p. 8.
34 Ibid, p. 9.
35 *The Marion* [1982] 2 Lloyd's Rep.52, per Sheen J at p. 64.

exercising any supervision over them in this respect, a majority of such shipowners were not content with such a system or lack of system. That majority, while relying primarily on their masters for obtaining and maintaining charts, exercised a degree of supervision over them in order to satisfy themselves that they were carrying out properly their duties in that field. The forms of supervision used vary considerably, depending no doubt on the size of the companies concerned, the number and types of the ship which they operated, and the trades in which such ships were employed. The second main matter was that deliberate ignorance may well be attributable to the fear of the award of punitive damages by juries in the USA in the event of marine casualties caused by the use of obsolete or uncorrected charts, of which, if shipowners did exercise supervision, they might be found to have been actually or constructively aware. The third matter which the schedules indicate was that, during the last 20 years or so, an increasing number of shipowners had adopted a system involving at least some degree of supervision of their masters in relation to charts.[36]

7.5 Chart discrepancies and grounding

It is settled law that there must be a causal link between the order and the consequences relied upon. In short, there must be no break in the chain of causation between the order and the consequences.[37] This is clear from the *White Rose*,[38] where Donaldson J there accepted that it was necessary in every case to establish an unbroken chain of causation. That is the sense of Hobhouse of Woodborough's reference to the necessity for a direct causal link in the *Hill Harmony*.[39]

Similar to the nautical chart, the expired or un-updated chart and the accident must also be causally linked; if no such chain of causation, the shipowner need not bear the responsibility. In the *Torepo*,[40] the vessel grounded on 9 July 1997 on the coast of Wellington Island, which formed the western bank of the Paso del Indio. Salvors have subsequently engaged on LOF 95 terms, and the defendant owners declared general average. The claimants sought to recover the amount they were obliged to pay the salvors by way of salvage remuneration and the return of the general average security that they posted.

It is the claimants' case that the grounding and the consequences thereof were caused by actionable fault on the part of the defendants. The defendants contend that the grounding was caused by the negligence of the pilot in and about the navigation of the vessel for which they are not liable. In the alternative, the defendants contend that if, contrary to their primary case, there was causative unseaworthiness, they exercised due diligence to make the vessel seaworthy.

The issues for the decision were: (a) the sequence of events leading to the grounding; (b) the cause of the grounding, whether it was due to navigational error or whether it was due to (1) the unseaworthiness of the vessel, (2) the charts containing discrepancies, or (3) the pilot not being properly rested at the time when he boarded the vessel; (c) whether the

36 Ibid, per Lord Brandon in [1984] 2 Lloyd's Rep.1 (H.L.) at p. 6.
37 *The Polyglory* [1977] 2 Lloyd's Rep.353; *The Kos* [2012] 2 Lloyd's Rep.292 per Lord Clarke at p. 307.
38 *The White Rose* [1969] 2 Lloyd's Rep.52.
39 *The Hill Harmony* [2001] 1 Lloyd's Rep.147 (H.L.).
40 *The Torepo* [2002] 2 Lloyd's Rep.535.

defendants failed to exercise due diligence to make the vessel seaworthy; (d) whether the defendants could rely on article III, rule 2 to avoid liability if they were in breach of article III, rule 2; (e) the terms of the bill of lading; and (f) whether the defendants were in breach of a continuing obligation to exercise due diligence to maintain the vessel in a seaworthy condition arising from the incorporation of the terms of either the head charterparty or the sub-charterparty.[41]

David Steel J observed that there was, unsurprising, no issue as to the law. There was a helpful summary of the relevant principles, together with reference to many of the leading authorities, in the judgment of Cresswell J in the *Eurasian Dream*,[42] at paragraphs 120–136.

David Steel J viewed that the claimants had not established even a prima facie case of unseaworthiness in this respect. Mr Justice would add that also has considerable sympathy with the defendants' submission that a deficiency of the kind relied upon by the claimants was not likely to be identified whatever diligence was exercised by the owners.[43]

In David Steel J's view, passage planning was not a science, saying:[44]

> There was inevitably an element of judgment as to what annotations need to be added to the chart (or recorded elsewhere). I certainly accept that the passage plan would have been improved by the addition of the three matters referred to. But it must be remembered that the passage was not prepared by the master or officers of Torepo whose expertise in this field is criticized by the claimants. It was prepared by pilots who had regularly taken vessels through the Patagonian Channels with no recorded difficulty.

The last cause of the casualty relied upon by the claimants was the grid of discrepancy between chart 917 and chart 947. The short answer in David Steel J's judgment was that the vessel was not even arguably thereby rendered unseaworthy. It was not a material defect in the chart portfolio. Disparities in such matters as coordinates, contour lines, soundings, and so on are commonplace. In any event, the discrepancy was not causative.[45]

It was held by David Steel J that the discrepancy in the charts did not render the vessel unseaworthy; it was not a material defect in the chart portfolio and the disparity was not causative, and it was not arguable that there was any want of due diligence in furnishing the vessel with the only available large-scale charts.[46]

David Steel J observed that the discrepancy between the charts was not of itself the cause of the casualty; if the pilot's attention truly was deflected more than momentarily, it was, in any event, negligent navigation on his part, and a failure to arrange adequate rest periods between the pilots during the voyage itself constituted faulty navigation so that the defendants were not deprived of the protections of article IV, rule 1(2). Whatever charterparty was incorporated in the bill of lading, the effect was to create a continuing obligation of due diligence to render the vessel seaworthy.[47]

This case has raised some interesting questions in regard to passage planning in pilotage waters. In the event, David Steel J concluded for all these reasons that the claimants had failed to establish that the casualty was occasioned by causative unseaworthiness.

41 Ibid.
42 *The Eurasian Dream* [2002] 1 Lloyd's Rep.719.
43 *The Torepo*, per David Steel J at p. 548.
44 Ibid, p. 549.
45 Ibid, p. 551.
46 Ibid.
47 Ibid.

Their claim accordingly failed, and the defendants were entitled to judgment on their counterclaim.[48]

Therefore, not every discrepancy in the charts will render a vessel unseaworthy.

7.6 Out-of-date charts

In the *Isla Fernandina*,[49] the claimants alleged that the first defendant, Transnave, failed to exercise due diligence to make the vessel seaworthy at the commencement of the voyage or to properly man or equip the vessel or care for the cargo by reason of out-of-date charts and navigational equipment being on board, the conduct of the master, and the condition of its power and refrigeration plants. They also alleged breaches of the letter of instruction about care for the cargo. Transnave argued that the vessel was seaworthy and properly equipped, that the grounding was caused by negligence on the part of the master and/or the third officer and so excluded from their responsibility. The defects in the remaining cargo found at Genoa were caused by the natural ripening of the cargo consequent on the delay in the carriage, which itself resulted from the grounding and a latent defect in generator 3, and hence matters excluded from liability.[50]

While there are important issues on unseaworthiness and due diligence in relation to the grounding, the major battle has been fought on causation and, in particular, whether the absence of the light on the Salmedina Bank played any legally causative part in it. Langley J reached a clear conclusion that it did not.

In Langley J's view, it is not in doubt. Langley J took it from the speech of Lord Wright in the *Lilburn*.[51] It sufficed if unseaworthiness "is a cause, or if it is preferred, a real or effective or actual cause" and that "the question is . . . would the disaster not have happened if the ship had fulfilled the obligation of seaworthiness." Langley J pointed out that the obligation in this case, if such it was, was not to provide a light on the Salmedina Bank but to provide the information that there was no light on it. That, on Langley J's findings, would have made no difference. The "disaster" would still have happened. The issue was much more one of fact than a matter of expert opinion. In Langley J's view, the third officer should have been using visual bearings but was not. He should not have been fixing his position by single radar distance and bearings at all, let alone exclusively. The navigation was negligent and was the only effective cause of the grounding.[52]

Langley J discussed unseaworthiness and properly manning, on the evidence that the master's failings on this occasion were unpredictable and unprecedented. They might have been contributed to by the trauma of the bosun's death, his own illness, and the need to prepare for entering port at Cartagena, but whether that be so or not, they were not due to a failure by Transnave to exercise due diligence either to make the ship seaworthy or to properly man it.[53]

Langley J continued to say that the grounding was caused by a belief derived from the out-of-date chart that there was a light on the Salmedina Bank. Mr Kverndal nonetheless

48 Ibid, p. 552.

49 *The Isla Fernandina* [2000] 2 Lloyd's Rep.15.

50 Ibid.

51 *The Lilburn* [1940] 67 Ll.L. Rep.253 (H.L.).

52 *The Isla Fernandina*, per Langley J at p. 33.

53 Ibid.

submits that it was not the result of a failure on Transnave's part to exercise due diligence to make the ship seaworthy or to properly equip her, that even if it was, the grounding was again not caused by such failure, and that Transnave is, in any event, exempted from liability by article IV, rule 4 of the Hague Rules, as the damage resulted from a "reasonable deviation."[54]

As to the article IV, rule 4 submission, Langley J observed that it was untenable. It was a good example of the same misuse of the principles of causation which underlies the causation issue in relation to the light on the Salmedina Bank. The fact of deviation was not causative of the grounding, save in the sense that it would not have occurred had the vessel not deviated to Cartagena. Competent navigation would, and should, have avoided the grounding. The want of competence was the effective cause, not the fact that the vessel happened to divert before it occurred.

Langley J ruled that there was incontestable evidence that the state of the charts and navigational aids on board the vessel was inadequate; such materials could be more dangerous than nothing, and Transnave should have appreciated and been aware of that; however, it was improbable that either the master or the third officer would have consulted any list of lights had it been available. The vessel was navigated solely by reference to the charts, and if the charts had been up to date, no one would have been any the wiser.[55]

As Langley J stated in this case, any failings with regard to navigational aids had no causal connection to the master's navigational or supervisory abilities; on the evidence, the master's failings on this occasion were unpredictable and unprecedented, but they were not due to a failure by Transnave to exercise due diligence either to make the ship seaworthy or properly to man it.[56]

In this case, the cargo owners fell between two stools in their attempt to show loss by unseaworthiness, in that although the vessel was, it appears, unseaworthy due to a lack of up-to-date charts, this was not causative of any loss, as the judge held that the crew would have made no reference to relevant parts of the charts in navigating the vessel. However, the shortcomings of the master and crew did not themselves amount to unseaworthiness.[57]

7.7 Passage plan

The Guidelines for Voyage Planning adopted by IMO on 25 November 1999 state that passage planning is "of essential importance for the safety of life at sea, safety and efficiency of navigation and protection of the marine environment." It identifies four stages, namely, (1) appraisal (i.e. gathering all relevant information), (2) detailed planning of the whole voyage from berth to berth, (3) execution of the plan, and (4) monitoring of progress in the implementation of the plan. Strictly speaking, only the first two of these constitute passage planning, as the remaining two consist of executing (and modifying as necessary) the plan, which has been made before the voyage began. The guidelines require that, as part of the appraisal stage, account should be taken of "appropriate scale, accurate and up-to-date charts to be used for the intended voyage or passage, as well as any relevant permanent or

54 Ibid.
55 Ibid.
56 Ibid.
57 *Bills of Lading*, 3rd ed at para. 11.131, note 249.

temporary notices to mariners and existing radio navigational warnings." The passage plan should then be prepared "on the basis of the fullest possible appraisal," the intended route should be plotted on "appropriate scale charts" with an indication of "all areas of danger," and the plan should be "approved by the ship's master prior to the commencement of the voyage or passage."[58]

And the detailed voyage or passage plan should include the following factors:

1. The plotting of the intended route or track of the voyage or passage on appropriate scale charts: the true direction of the planned route or track should be indicated, as well as all areas of danger, existing ships' routeing and reporting systems, vessel traffic services, and any areas where marine environmental protection considerations apply.
2. The main elements to ensure the safety of life at sea, safety and efficiency of navigation, and protection of the marine environment during the intended voyage or passage.

The details of the voyage or passage plan should be clearly marked and recorded, as appropriate, on charts and in a voyage plan notebook or computer disk. Each voyage or passage plan, as well as the details of the plan, should be approved by the ship's master prior to the commencement of the voyage or passage.

Also, as per SOLAS,[59] for safe navigation and avoidance of dangerous situations:

1. Prior to proceeding to sea, the master shall ensure that the intended voyage has been planned using the appropriate nautical charts and nautical publications for the area concerned, taking into account the guidelines and recommendations developed by the organization.
2. The voyage plan shall identify a route which:
    1. takes into account any relevant ships' routeing systems;
    2. ensures sufficient sea room for the safe passage of the ship throughout the voyage;
    3. anticipates all known navigational hazards and adverse weather conditions; and
    4. takes into account the marine environmental protection measures that apply.
3. The owner, the charterer, or the company, as defined in Regulation IX/1, operating the ship or any other person, shall not prevent or restrict the master of the ship from taking or executing any decision which, in the master's professional judgement, is necessary for safe navigation and protection of the marine environment.

Refer to the Guidelines for Voyage Planning, adopted by the organization by Resolution A.893(21).

The Supreme Court handed down judgment on 10 November 2021 in the *CMA CGM Libra*,[60] its long-awaited analysis of seaworthiness and the due diligence obligation under the Hague and Hague–Visby Rules.

58 IMO Res. A.893(21). See also *Males LJ* [2020] EWCA Civ 293 at p. 86.

59 *Solas*, Chapter V, Regulation 34. Avoid as far as possible actions and activities which could cause damage to the environment.

60 *The CMA CGM Libra* [2021] UKSC 51.

The vessel is a large container ship, at the time of the grounding, which occurred as the vessel was leaving the port of Xiamen, where she had loaded cargo. The passage plan prepared for the voyage from Xiamen to the next port of Hong Kong was prepared by the second officer. The working chart contained a course line marked in blue on the chart to buoy 19, the pilot station, then from there to buoy 15, passing that buoy on the starboard-side edge of the fairway with a danger area marked on the chart passed to port. However, there were no "no go" areas, marked with hatched lines on the chart, on either side of the fairway.

In the Admiralty Court, Teare J made important findings:[61]

> Nevertheless prudent passage planning required the danger created by the presence of numerous depths less than those charted outside the fairway to be noted on the chart. Such a note, in the terms suggested by Captain Hart, would immediately remind the officer navigating the vessel that it was unsafe to navigate outside the fairway. Such a note would do that which the IMO guidance on passage planning requires, namely, it would give a clear indication of the danger in navigating outside the fairway. . . . My conclusion, having considered the expert and other evidence, is that whilst it would of course be prudent to note the warning in the passage plan it would also be necessary (and prudent) to mark the warning on the chart since that is the primary document to which the officer navigating the vessel would refer when making navigational decisions in the course of the outward passage.

Teare J discussed the test of unseaworthiness:[62]

> The usual test of unseaworthiness is whether a prudent owner would have required the relevant defect, had he known of it, to be made good before sending his ship to sea; see *The Cape Bonny* [2018] 1 Lloyd's Reports 356 at paragraph 118 and *Scrutton on Charterparties and Bills of Lading* 23rd.ed. at paragraph 7–025. The submission made on behalf of the Cargo Interests was that a prudent owner would have required defects in the vessel's passage plan to be corrected before the vessel set out to sea.

Teare J observed that the usual or conventional test on unseaworthiness was set out in *McFadden v Blue Star Line* [1905] 1 KB 697 at p. 706. The conventional test was taken by Channel J from *Carver on Carriage by Sea*, so it is not only a long-established but also an authoritative test. Teare J stated:[63]

> It is right to say, as counsel submitted, that passage planning is "the preparation" for safe navigation. However, it does not follow that "passage planning itself is not an aspect of seaworthiness." Seaworthiness extends to having on board the appropriate documentation, including the appropriate chart; see *Scrutton on Charterparties and Bills of Lading* 23rd.ed. at paragraph 7–028 and *Bills of Lading* by Aikens and others 2nd.ed. at paragraph 10.127. The presence on board a vessel of the appropriate chart is another aspect of the "preparation" for safe navigation. But the presence on board of the appropriate chart is also an aspect of seaworthiness. Further, where the Admiralty gives notice of a correction to the appropriate chart a vessel will not be seaworthy unless the chart has been corrected. If the vessel's navigating officer fails, before the commencement of the voyage, to correct the chart the vessel is thereby rendered unseaworthy. The correction of the chart is part of the "preparation" for safe navigation. A corrected chart does not cease to be an aspect of seaworthiness merely because its purpose is to assist in ensuring safe navigation. This can be illustrated by the facts of the present case. If the second officer had failed to correct the chart by noting the new soundings of

61 Ibid, per Teare J [2019] EWHC 481 (Admlty) at p. 70.

62 Ibid, p. 75.

63 Ibid, p. 79.

4.8 metres and 1.2 metres on the chart before the beginning of the voyage (as required by the April 2011 notice to mariners) such failure could have rendered the vessel unseaworthy at the beginning of the voyage.

Turning to causation, Teare J concluded that the master's decision to leave the buoyed fairway and navigate to the west of buoy 14–1 was negligent. Whether the defective passage plan was causative of that negligence depends upon whether or not the master was, in fact, cognisant of the notice and of its contents. If he was, then the material defect in the passage plan may not have been causative.[64]

As due diligence under Hague Rules article III, rule 1, Teare J found that the master and second officer failed to prepare an appropriate passage plan. Teare J pointed out:[65]

> An owner cannot expect to secure a finding that due diligence has been exercised if its SMS is inadequate. Indeed, as stated in *Maritime Law* 4th.ed. by Baatz at p. 352, "a well-documented Safety Management System would be of considerable help in establishing the exercise of due diligence and, as such, should be considered an important tool for defending claims based on unseaworthiness" . . . that in order to comply with Article III r.1 it is not sufficient that the owner has itself exercised due diligence to make the ship seaworthy. It must be shown that those servants or agents relied upon by the owner to make the ship seaworthy before and at the beginning of the voyage have exercised due diligence. That is because the duty is non-delegable.

Having dealt with various other authorities relied upon by the owners, Teare J concluded:[66]

> For these reasons the Owners' claim must fail. The Cargo Interests have established causative unseaworthiness and the Owners have failed to establish the exercise of due diligence to make the vessel seaworthy. That is the consequence of applying to the facts of this case established propositions of law, namely, the traditional test of seaworthiness, the principle that documentation is an aspect of seaworthiness and the non-delegable nature of the duty to exercise due diligence.

In conclusion, Teare J ruled that the vessel was unseaworthy before and at the beginning of the voyage from Xiamen because it carried a defective passage plan. That defective passage plan was causative of the grounding of the vessel. Due diligence to make the vessel seaworthy was not exercised by the owners because the master and second officer failed to exercise reasonable skill and care when preparing the passage plan. It follows that the grounding of the vessel was caused by the actionable fault of the owners, and so the cargo interests are not liable to contribute in a general average.[67]

The decision was upheld by the Court of Appeal.[68] The leading judgment in the Court of Appeal was given by Flaux LJ, with whom Males and Haddon-Cave LJ agreed. Males LJ gave a judgment with which Haddon-Cave LJ agreed.

In the Supreme Court,[69] Lord Hamblen, delivering the judgment, said:

> The seaworthiness obligation was fundamental to all contracts of carriage of goods by sea. At common law, the carrier was under an absolute obligation to provide a seaworthy vessel. Today the seaworthiness obligation was invariably governed by the terms of the parties' contract or by statute, such as the UK Carriage of Goods by Sea Act 1971.

64 Ibid, p. 89.
65 Ibid, p. 113.
66 Ibid, p. 114.
67 Ibid, p. 129.
68 Ibid, [2020] EWCA Civ 293.
69 Ibid, [2021] UKSC 51.

In the approach to the interpretation of the Hague Rules, Lord Hamblen observed that the start point was the ordinary meaning of the wording of the relevant rules in the context of the Hague Rules as a whole. The scheme of the relevant rules was clear. As foreshadowed by article II, article III sets out the responsibilities and liabilities of the carrier, and article IV sets out the rights and immunities of the carrier. The carrier's primary responsibilities under article III are (i) before and at the beginning of the voyage to exercise due diligence to make the vessel seaworthy, as provided in article III, rule 1(a)(b)(c), and (ii) to properly and carefully care for the goods, as provided in article III, rule 2. In relation to the obligation of seaworthiness, the relevant right and immunity of the carrier are set out in article IV, rule 1, which defines the circumstances in which the carrier shall not be liable "for loss or damage arising or resulting from unseaworthiness." This is limited to cases in which the carrier discharges the burden of proving that he has exercised due diligence.[70]

Turning to the prudent owner test, Lord Hamblen stated:[71]

> The origin of the prudent owner test is a passage in Carver, A Treatise on the Law relating to the Carriage of Goods by Sea in which it was stated that:
>
> > "... the duty to supply a seaworthy ship is not equivalent to a duty to provide one that is perfect, and such as cannot break down except under extraordinary peril. What is meant is that she must have that degree of fitness which an ordinary careful and prudent owner would require his vessel to have at the commencement of her voyage, having regard to all the probable circumstances of it. To that extent the shipowner, as we have seen, undertakes absolutely that she is fit; and ignorance is no excuse. If the defect existed, the question to be put is, Would a prudent shipowner have required that it should be made good before sending his ship to sea had he known of it? If he would, the ship was not seaworthy within the meaning of the undertaking."

The Supreme Court concluded that the carrier's obligation under the Hague Rules was not subject to a category-based distinction between a vessel's quality of seaworthiness or navigability and the crew's act of navigating. The crew's failure to navigate the ship safely was capable of constituting a lack of due diligence by the carrier. It makes no difference that the delegated task of making the vessel seaworthy involves navigation.[72] In particular:

(i) On the proper interpretation of the Hague Rules, the article IV, rule 2 exception of act, neglect, or default in the navigation or management of the vessel cannot be relied upon in relation to a causative breach of the carrier's obligation to exercise due diligence to make the vessel seaworthy.[73]

(ii) If the vessel is unseaworthy, it makes no difference whether negligent navigation or management is the cause of the unseaworthiness or is itself the unseaworthiness.[74]

(iii) The concept of unseaworthiness is not subject to an attribute threshold requiring there to be an attribute of the vessel which threatens the safety of the vessel or her cargo.[75]

70 Ibid, per Lord Hamblen at pp. 60–63.
71 Ibid, p. 98.
72 Ibid, p. 145.
73 Ibid, pp. 70–76, 83–84, 119.
74 Ibid, pp. 85, 121.
75 Ibid, pp. 86–96, 122.

(iv) Save for exceptional cases at the boundaries of seaworthiness, the well-established prudent owner test, namely, whether a prudent owner would have required the relevant defect to be made good before sending the vessel to sea had he known of it, is an appropriate test of seaworthiness, well suited to adapt to differing and changing standards.[76]

(v) The fact that a defect is remediable may mean that a vessel is not unseaworthy. This is likely to depend on whether it would reasonably be expected to be put right before any danger to the vessel or cargo arose.[77]

(vi) Given the "essential importance" of passage planning for the "safety . . . of navigation," applying the prudent owner test, a vessel is likely to be unseaworthy if she begins her voyage without a passage plan or if she does so with a defective passage plan which endangers the safety of the vessel.[78]

(vii) The fact that the defective passage plan involves neglect or default in "the navigation of the ship" within the article IV, rule 2(a) exception is no defence to a claim for loss or damage caused by unseaworthiness.[79]

(viii) The obligation of the carrier to exercise due diligence to make the vessel seaworthy requires that due diligence be exercised in the work of making the vessel seaworthy, regardless of who is engaged to carry out that task.[80]

(ix) The carrier may not be liable for lack of due diligence which occurs before he has responsibility for the vessel or for lack of due diligence which occurs before he has responsibility for the cargo. The carrier may nevertheless be liable if the defect or danger would be reasonably discoverable by the exercise of due diligence once the vessel or cargo has come within his control.[81]

(x) The carrier is liable for a failure to exercise due diligence by the master and deck officers of his vessel in the preparation of a passage plan for the vessel's voyage. The fact that navigation is the responsibility of the master and involves the exercise by the master and deck officers of their specialist skill and judgment makes no difference.[82]

(xi) The carrier's seaworthiness obligation in relation to passage planning is not limited to providing a proper system for such planning.[83]

The Supreme Court's decision confirms owners' overriding duty to exercise due diligence to make a vessel seaworthy under article III, rule 1 of the Hague Rules, resolving a number of long-standing controversies in this area of law. This landmark is notable and highlights the importance of an accurate passage plan. The decision increases the due diligence burden on ship owners, such as crew training, and the vessel's system.

Furthermore, as per the law established in *The Maurienne*,[84] where loss or damage was caused by a breach of the carrier's obligation to exercise due diligence to make the vessel

76 Ibid, pp. 97–101.
77 Ibid, pp. 102–103.
78 Ibid, pp. 124–128.
79 Ibid, pp. 118–119.
80 Ibid, pp. 133–134.
81 Ibid, pp. 135–136.
82 Ibid, pp. 137–139.
83 Ibid, pp. 141–143.
84 *The Maurienne* [1959] 2 Lloyd's Rep.105 (P.C.).

seaworthy under article III, rule 1, the article IV, rule 2 exceptions cannot be relied upon, including where the excepted matter is the cause of the unseaworthiness. If the carrier wishes to benefit from the immunities from liability in article IV, he must show that due diligence was in fact exercised.

7.8 Deratisation certificate

The Ship Sanitation Control Exemption Certificate/Ship Sanitation Control Certificate (SSCEC/SSCC) is regulated in articles 20 and 39, and annex 3, of the International Health Regulations (IHR) (2005). These certificates are valid for a maximum period of six months. This period may be extended by one month if the inspection or control measures required cannot be accomplished at the port.[85]

If a valid SSCEC/SSCC is not produced or evidence of public health risk is found on board a ship, the state party may proceed as provided in paragraph 1 of article 27. If clinical signs or symptoms and information based on fact or evidence of a public health risk, including sources of infection and contamination, are found on board a conveyance, the competent authority shall consider the conveyance as affected and may:

(a) Disinfect, decontaminate, disinsect, or derat the conveyance, as appropriate, or cause these measures to be carried out under its supervision.
(b) Decide in each case the technique employed to secure an adequate level of control of the public health risk as provided in these regulations. Where there are methods or materials advised by WHO for these procedures, these should be employed unless the competent authority determines that other methods are as safe and reliable.

The competent authority may implement additional health measures, including isolation of the conveyances, as necessary, to prevent the spread of disease. Such additional measures should be reported to the National IHR Focal Point.[86]

As advised previously, there are various governing laws in the shipping industry; these laws demand the vessel must carry some certain certificates before she can enter or leave ports. Without these certificates, the vessel will be not permitted to berth or sail, the result of which failure will make the ship unseaworthy.

In the *Madeleine*,[87] on 6 May 1957, the vessel's deratisation exemption certificate expired. On 9 May, the vessel completed the discharge of cargo at Calcutta, and the owners advised the charterers that the vessel would be delivered on the morning of 10 May. On 9 May, the vessel was inspected by port health inspecting officer, and a new deratting exemption certificate was refused and fumigation ordered. Fumigation could not be completed before midnight of 10/11 May. However, the charterers refused to accept delivery and cancelled the charter. The question of law for the court to be decided was whether, on the facts found and upon a true construction of the charterparty so varied, it was wrongfully repudiated by the charterers.

85 www.who.int/ihr/ship_sanitation_certificate/zh/.
86 *International Health Regulation 2005*, 3rd ed, Article 27, 39.
87 *The Madeleine* [1967] 2 Lloyd's Rep.224.

The charterers contended (1) that in the absence of deratting certificate, the vessel could not be effectively delivered. Owners contended (1) that they were entitled to deliver the vessel to charterers irrespective of her then physical condition, whether in relation to deratisation certificate or otherwise, and (2) that the words "in every way fitted for ordinary cargo service" in clause 1 referred only to the possession of adequate equipment by the vessel for the carriage of such cargo as charterers required her to carry.

Roskill J (as he then was) observed that must be a question of the true construction of the clause. He said:[88]

> It is well established that clauses in charter-parties cannot be construed in isolation from each other. A charter-party like any other contract must be construed sensibly and in its entirety. Where one has a series of clauses in a standard form which has been in use for a great many years, and which has been interpreted many times by the Courts and by arbitrators, the Court must look at the provisions as a whole.

Roskill J viewed that an owner delivered a ship to a time charterer under this form of charterparty by placing her at the charterers' disposal and by placing the services of her master, officers, and crew at the charterers' disposal, so that the charterers may thenceforth give orders (within the terms of the charterparty) as to the employment of the vessel to the master, officers, and crew, which orders the owners contract that their servants shall obey.[89]

Roskill J referred to the *Hong Kong Fir*,[90] in which case Diplock LJ (as he then was) said:[91]

> As my brethren have already pointed out, the shipowners' undertaking to tender a seaworthy ship has, as a result of numerous decisions as to what can amount to "unseaworthiness," become one of the most complex of contractual undertakings. It embraces obligations with respect to every part of the hull and machinery, stores and equipment and the crew itself. It can be broken by the presence of trivial defects easily and rapidly remediable as well as by defects which must inevitably result in a total loss of the vessel.

Roskill J pointed out that the point at issue in the *Hong Kong Fir* was the nature of the owners' seaworthiness obligation. The court was not there concerned with whether those obligations were express or implied, though the court clearly thought they were express obligations. Roskill J observed that it was clear that the same result would be reached whether those obligations arose from express words or by necessary implication. But the point in Roskill J's view was that the learned trial judge and all the learned lords justices clearly regarded the words in the Baltime 1939 charterparty, there as here, "in every way fitted for ordinary cargo service," as the equivalent of an express warranty of seaworthiness.[92]

Owners argued that the owners' obligations regarding the provision of the necessary documentation in the shape of the deratisation certificate were not part of their express obligations under clause 1. Therefore, whatever be imported from clause 1 into clause 22, there was no express right given by clause 22 to cancel merely because of the absence of

88 Ibid, per Roskill J at p. 238.
89 Ibid.
90 *The Hong Kong Fir* [1961] 2 Lloyd's Rep.478 (C.A.).
91 Ibid, per Diplock LJ at p. 494.
92 *The Madeleine*, sup. at p. 240.

the necessary documentation because the vessel was in the condition called for by clause 1, notwithstanding the absence of that documentation.

Roskill J ruled that clause 22 cannot be divorced from clause 1. Clause 1 required the owners to deliver in a condition in which the vessel was in every way fitted for ordinary cargo service. Clause 22 provided for the right of cancellation if she was not so timeously delivered.[93]

The umpire has found in clause 10 (d) that: "The vessel was in every way fitted for cargo service and seaworthy notwithstanding the absence of the necessary Certificate which resulted in a restriction of her movements for a period of 34 hours."

Roskill J was satisfied that it was agreed to be a conclusion of law and not a finding of fact. In Roskill J's judgment, the umpire, with all respect to him, has erred in reaching that conclusion. There was here an express warranty of seaworthiness, and unless the ship was timeously delivered in a seaworthy condition, including the necessary certificate from the port health authority, the charterers had the right to cancel.[94]

It was held by Roskill J in this case that a charterparty should be construed in its entirety and read as a whole. The obligation in clause 22 postulated that owners would not perform as their obligation under clause 1, that the phrase "in every way fitted for ordinary cargo service" was an express undertaking of seaworthiness and that seaworthiness required that the ship possess the documents necessary to enable it to sail.

7.9 RightShip approval

RightShip was formed in Melbourne in 2001, with BHP Freight and Rio Tinto committing to deliver an industry standard that all maritime workers could commit to. The program was rolled out across all BHP Billiton and Rio Tinto assets globally, at which point it was essential to open a US-based office. In 2006, Cargill joined as an equal-partner shareholder, and by 2007, the UK and European offices had been established. As RightShip has evolved, it has added a key sustainability focus.[95]

RightShip vetting has been a core component of RightShip's due diligence offering since its inception, and its criteria have been refreshed consistently over the years in line with global safety, sustainability, and human rights expectations. Initially, it was developed for charterers moving cargo, but today it is also utilised by ports and terminals as well as financiers and shipowners looking to review vessels before chartering in additional tonnage. The vetting criteria represents the RightShip minimum acceptable standard for them to recommend a vessel as a commercial partner. It has been designed in response to existing risks and challenges that occur in the daily practice of operating a vessel. This means that the criteria need to be updated as risks change over time, standards improve, and customers innovate new best practices in running and operating supply chains.

In January 2021, RightShip announced several updates to their vetting criteria. A priority during the expansion of the standard was responding to existing challenges that customers faced. Primarily, this involved providing clear insights into what delivers an acceptable outcome versus the reasons in which the outcome may be unacceptable. To improve that

93 Ibid, p. 241.
94 Ibid.
95 www.rightship.com/.

transparency, we made binary failings clearer in the new standard to remove confusion and ensure the path to an acceptable recommendation is easily understood.

RightShip's vetting standards are at the heart of RightShip's ecosystem. The vetting standard was the inspiration for the Safety Score rules, bringing these two products together as many of the rules which govern a Safety Score of 1 and Safety Score of 2 originate from the new vetting criteria. Improved social responsibility measures were also essential. For example, RightShip has included the following binary criterion: "Any vessel Flagged with a country that has not adopted and ratified the 2006 Maritime Labour Convention and without an equivalent level of compliance (for example a valid ITF Agreement)."[96]

In the *Silver Constellation*,[97] the vessel was chartered on the NYPE form. Disputes arose between the parties relating to the RightShip approval system. The system had been set up in 2001 with the aim of identifying vessels that were suitable and safe for the carriage of iron ore or coal cargoes.

The disputes under the charter and the sub-charter were referred to as back-to-back arbitrations. In each case, the tribunal was asked to determine (1) whether, pursuant to line 38 and/or clause 31 of the charters, the owners were obliged to provide a vessel with RightShip approval and to maintain such approval for the currency of the charters and/or (2) whether the owners were obliged to permit a RightShip inspection of the vessel and other vetting procedures as and when required by the charterers.

In respect of seaworthiness, Seagate contended that line 38 was only concerned with questions of seaworthiness and with official certificates such as arise from classification or flag state requirements in that respect. Glencore and Swissmarine contended that line 38 encompasses the current requirements of all ports regardless of whether they are concerned with such matters as class, seaworthiness, and flag state requirements or not: in any event, RightShip certification does relate to seaworthiness.

Seagate went on to submit that "fitness" in this respect was closely analogous to the requirement in line 22 that the vessel be "in every way fitted for service." It followed so the argument ran that, in the light of the decision in the *Derby*,[98] there was no obligation to comply with the requirements of "a self appointed and extra-legal organization." Read as a whole, it was contended that line 38 and clause 31 focus on certification and documentation, which in turn establish fitness and eligibility. Yet the RightShip scheme did not give rise to the provision of any documentary form of certification.

David Steel J observed that the passage from Kerr LJ in the *Derby* was of some assistance to the charterers since RightShip approval was, at least in part, concerned with the physical condition of the ship for the purpose of undertaking coal or iron ore cargoes. As the tribunal has found, the factors on which the assessment is made include such matters as conditions of class, terminal inspections, and so on, all with a view to assessing whether the relevant vessel is in a suitable condition to complete the voyage safely. Thus, the approval, as the tribunal put it, would confirm what a conscientious owner would seek to achieve "by way of maintenance of the vessel."[99]

96 *Shipowners Guide to Rightship's Vetting Criteria*, May 2021.
97 *The Silver Constellation* [2008] Lloyd's Rep.440.
98 *The Derby* [1985] 2 Lloyd's Rep.325 (C.A.).
99 *The Silver Constellation*, sup., per David Steel J at p. 449.

However, David Steel J pointed out that the focus was upon requirements legally imposed either by the law of the flag, the law of the country to which the vessel has been ordered, or the laws of the port of call. This was further emphasised by the heading to clause 31, "Certificates, Laws and Regulations." It was not suggested, however, that RightShip approval was "lawfully" required by the ports at which coal or iron ore may be loaded (albeit there may be some unidentified exceptions). It was simply a commercial requirement which had become progressively more widespread since 2001.[100]

David Steel J viewed this feature as a further reflection of the extra-legal and private nature of the system. Even accepting for present purposes the tribunal's finding that the system was not operated in an arbitrary fashion, the fact remains that the basis of any approval remains obscure. Whilst it was said that the requirements were no more than those which a conscientious owner would wish to achieve, it was clear that matters extend well beyond the physical state of the vessel (in respect of which there was already an obligation as regards the maintenance of seaworthiness).

There was also of considerable note that specific provision was made in the charterparty for a whole range of certificates. David Steel J agreed with Seagate that this gave rise to a strong inference that, given the absence of RightShip approval (something the tribunal would expect to be included), no such approval was required under the charterparty. This was all the more so where the charterparty focused almost exclusively on iron ore and coal cargoes and thus involved trading to the "hotbeds" of the RightShip system, such as Australia.[101]

David Steel J stated that on the true construction of the charter, the owners were not required to obtain and retain RightShip approval and the owners had complied with their obligation to maintain seaworthiness of the vessel.[102]

It noting in this case, the charterers' entitlement to direct the ship's employment may entitle them to have the ship inspected by third parties, where that was a commercial requirement of the charterers' ordered employment, and not only where it is a requirement imposed by local law. Thus, as David Steel J held that although the charter, which was on the NYPE form, did not oblige the owners to obtain or maintain a RightShip approval rating for the ship, clause 8 did oblige them to obey the charterers' orders to submit the ship to a RightShip inspection and vetting procedure. Similarly, an order to allow shore inspectors on board to inspect the cleanliness of holds prior to loading would be an order as regards employment under clause 8.[103]

7.10 ITF

The International Transport Workers' Federation (ITF) is a truly global organisation. It is a federation of around 700 unions from some 150 countries, representing over 4.5 million transport workers. The ITF was founded in 1896 in London by European seafarers' and dockers' union leaders who realized the need to organise internationally against strike-breakers. Today the ITF organises workers in ships, ports, railways, road freight and passenger transport, inland waterways, fisheries, tourism, and civil aviation.

100 Ibid.
101 Ibid, p. 450.
102 Ibid.
103 *Time Charters*, 7th ed at para. 19.31.

The ITF represents transport workers at the world level and promotes their interests through global campaigning and solidarity. It is dedicated to the advancement of independent and democratic trade unionism and to the defence of fundamental human and trade union rights. It is opposed to any form of totalitarianism, aggression, and discrimination. The ITF is one of several Global Federation Unions allied with the International Trade Union Confederation (ITUC).

The aims of the ITF are set out in its constitution (see the following). They are:

i. To promote respect for trade unions and human rights worldwide.
ii. To work for peace based on social justice and economic progress.
iii. To help its affiliated unions defend the interests of their members.
iv. To provide research and information services to its affiliates.
v. To provide general assistance to transport workers in difficulty.[104]

In the *Derby*,[105] the vessel was time-chartered for a period of 11 to 13 months. The charter was in the NYPE form, and line 22 provided *inter alia*:

> Vessel on her delivery to be ready to receive cargo . . . and in every way fitted for the service . . . (and with a full complement of officers, seamen . . .).

On 12 May 1981, the vessel arrived at Leixões in Portugal to discharge a cargo of logs from West Africa. She moved into a berth on 23 May. Discharge proceeded normally, albeit slowly, until 28 May. On 27 May, an ITF representative inquired if the vessel possessed an ITF blue card and found that it did not. At 1500 hours on 28 May, discharging operations ceased and the ITF demanded that either the blue card be produced or that the vessel be signed up on an ITF special agreement regarding manning.

The dispute was referred to arbitration, and the arbitrator held that the owners were in breach of their obligation under the charterparty in that the vessel was not in any way fitted for service since she had a Filipino crew employed on terms which did not meet with the approval of the ITF. The arbitrator further held that the charterers were entitled to any profits they would have earned on the cancelled sub-charter but refused to award them also the losses incurred on the Ghent sub-charter. The owners and the charterers appealed against that award.[106]

Hobhouse J, in the first instance, observed:

> In my judgment the correct construction of line 22 of the NYPE form was that in its context it related only to matters of seaworthiness. Seaworthiness included the legality of the vessel and her documentation and, in conjunction with the whole of lines 21–24, the adequacy and competence of her crew. It relate to matters which do not affect the seaworthiness of the ship or the ability of the owners to comply with orders given to them by the charterers. In the present case it thus does not, on any view, extend to characteristics of the crew which do not affect the crew's ability to preserve the safety of the vessel and her cargo and to fulfil owners' obligations under the charter-party nor does it extend to the provision of a blue certificate or any similar document demanded by some extralegal grouping.[107]

104 www.itfglobal.org/en/about-us/who-we-are.
105 *The Derby* [1984] 1 Lloyd's Rep.635; [1985] 2 Lloyd's Rep.325 (C.A.).
106 Ibid, p. 635.
107 Ibid, per Hobhouse J at p. 642.

Hobhouse J ruled that the arbitrator was not entitled to infer from lines 32 and 33 any warranty by owners that a visit to Portugal or Italy would not give rise to any ITF action; such an obligation was to be found, if at all, in line 22, and line 22 did not impose any such obligation.

In the Court of Appeal, Kerr LJ observed:[108]

> The context in which the words "in every way fitted for the service" occur shows that these words relate primarily to the physical state of the vessel. However, the authorities also show that their scope is wider, in at least two respects. First, in *Hongkong Fir Shipping Co. Ltd. v. Kawasaki Kisen Kaisha Ltd.*, [1961] 2 Lloyd's Rep.478; the words "she being in every way fitted for ordinary cargo service" in the Baltime form of time charter were treated as forming part of an express warranty that the vessel was seaworthy, and it was held that this warranty required the provision of a sufficient and competent crew to operate the vessel for the purposes of the charter service. I accept that precisely the same reasoning applies to the words "in every way fitted for the service" in the present case. To that extent, therefore, these words go beyond the purely physical state of the vessel as such. However, I cannot see any basis for any further enlargement of the scope of these words by extracting from them a warranty that the rates of pay and conditions of employment of the crew, with which they expressly declared themselves to be satisfied, must also comply with the requirements, not of any law which is relevant to the vessel, her crew or the vessel's operation under the charter, but also of a self-appointed and extra-legal organization such as the I.T.F. In my view this is not a meaning which these words can properly bear, let alone in the context in which they appear in the charter.

Kerr LJ continued to point out that the second respect in which the scope of these words in line 22 had been held to go beyond the physical state of the vessel was that they had been held to cover the requirement that the vessel must carry certain kinds of documents which bore upon her seaworthiness or fitness to perform the service for which the charter provides. Navigational charts which were necessary for the voyages upon which the vessel may be ordered from time to time were an obvious illustration.[109]

Kerr LJ viewed that the nature of such certificates may vary according to the requirements of the law of the vessel's flag or the laws or regulations in force in the countries to which the vessel may be ordered, or which may lawfully be required by the authorities exercising administrative or other functions in the vessel's ports of call pursuant to the laws there in force. Documents falling within this category, which had been considered by the authorities, were certificates concerning the satisfactory state of the vessel, which was, in some respect, related to her physical condition, and accordingly to her seaworthiness.[110]

Kerr LJ went on to state:[111]

> Their purpose is to provide documentary evidence for the authorities at the vessel's ports of call on matters which would otherwise require some physical inspection of the vessel, and possibly remedial measures – such as fumigation – before the vessel will be accepted as seaworthy in the relevant respect. The nature of description of such certificates, which may accordingly be required to be carried on board to render the vessel seaworthy, must depend on the circumstances and would no doubt raise issues of fact in individual cases. But I do not see any basis for holding that such certificates can properly be held to include documents other than those which may be required by the law of the vessel's flag or by the laws, regulations or lawful administrative practices of governmental or local authorities at the vessel's ports of call. An

108 Ibid, per Kerr LJ [1985] 2 Lloyd's Rep.325 (C.A.) at p. 331.
109 Ibid, p. 331.
110 Ibid.
111 Ibid.

> I.T.F. blue card does not fall within this category, and I can therefore see no reason for including it within the scope of the words in line 22, even in their extended sense as indicated above.

Sir Denys Buckley added that to discharge their obligations under this charterparty, the owners were bound to provide a vessel which was physically fit to encounter all such perils as would be reasonably foreseeable on any voyage the charterers could legitimately require the ship to make and to carry safely to its destination any cargo which the charterers could properly specify; they had to man the ship with a master and crew competent and sufficient for the purposes of any such voyages.[112]

In this case, issues as to a vessel's seaworthiness might involve questions of fact and the degree to which the decisions of arbitrators could not properly be regarded as open to review; the same might well apply to certificates or similar documents, depending upon the reasonable foreseeability that they would be needed for the purpose of performing the charter service in the circumstances of any particular case. The Court of Appeal dismissed the charterers' appeal.

As discussed previously, the courts have long recognised that a ship may need certain certificates or documents in order to be able to perform the charter service. The requirement that the ship is fit for the charter service imposes on the owners an obligation to ensure that the ship is seaworthy on delivery. However, as in this case, the owners do not undertake that the rates of pay and conditions of employment of the crew will comply with the requirements of ITF.

7.11 Documents

For a vessel to be ready, all necessary papers have to be in order; exceptions are made only when legal formalities are required. In other words, if the obtaining of an official document or permit is only a formality and the absence of such document or permit does not interfere with the ship's ability to perform the charter service, the lack of such documents will not prevent the ship being "ready" under a voyage charter and being "in every way fitted for the service" under a time charter.[113]

The vessel may be detained by PSCO if she is without maintenance record or documents on board. A detention or improvement order could be evidence of an unseaworthy ship. In general, the seaworthiness of a vessel is a matter of fact, and the presence of a certificate or otherwise is only evidential, not conclusive. However, article 2(9) of the European Council Directive on Port State Control states that a ship under detention is to be construed as "unseaworthy." It is also possible that the underlying defects leading to the detention of the vessel may be used as evidence of an unseaworthy vessel.[114]

In the *Devon*,[115] the cause of the engine breakdown is disputed and, in particular, whether it is attributable to unseaworthiness at the commencement of the voyage and whether the owners exercised due diligence within the meaning of the Hague Rules. CHS also alleged a failure to proceed on the voyage with all convenient speed as required by the contract of carriage.

112 Ibid, per Sir Denys Buckley at p. 333.
113 *Port State Control*, 2nd ed at para. 13.37.
114 Ibid, para. 13.41.
115 *The Devon* [2012] EWHC 3747 (Comm).

CHS alleged that the vessel was unseaworthy in the following respects:

> [T]he Claimants' case is that the Vessel was unseaworthy before and at the beginning of the voyage by reason of:
> 1. the poor condition of the Vessel's engine lubrication and lubrication cooling systems; and
> 2. the lack of adequate systems on board the Vessel to ensure that:
>   i) the temperature of the engine lube oil was properly regulated;
>   ii) the cooling system did not become blocked; and
>   iii) the engine was adequately lubricated.

The Honourable Cooke J observed:[116]

> In my judgment, there are only two possible explanations for this absence of disclosed documents discussing the cause of the damage, both of which bear unfavourably upon Owners. The most obvious explanation, and to my mind the most realistic, is that such documents did exist but have not been disclosed. . . . There can only be one reason for either course of action, which is that the cause or possible causes discussed were causes which the Owners wished to hide because it or they were causes which would not have assisted them in their dispute with CHS. It or they must have involved some unseaworthiness of the vessel at the commencement of the voyage from Varna.

Cooke J considered the possibility that neither expert has found the root cause of the problem. In such circumstances, Cooke J found that the cause of the lube oil problem was, on the material available, incapable of satisfactory explanation, with the potential result that CHS would fail to prove its case on unseaworthiness, unless such strong inferences could be drawn that he was persuaded of unseaworthiness without proof of the cause. The position was, however, that the parties have produced expert evidence on the issue, and the explanations they had proposed are the only ones which were put before the court, with all others discounted.[117]

Cooke J found that:[118]

> In consequence, I find that the vessel was unseaworthy at the commencement of the voyage by reason of the condition of the SW cooling system and its dirty and partially blocked state, which led to a failure in the LT FW cooling system which manifested itself within 3 hours of sailing from Varna in the form of high temperatures in the luboil for the main engine.

Cooke J continued to hold:[119]

> The Owners had no system in place for the proper monitoring of temperatures in the engine luboil or pressures in the SW system. Inspection in the 3 hours preceding the incident should have revealed the developing problem which manifested itself on the sounding of the luboil alarm. The vessel was unseaworthy by virtue of that lack of system also, which meant that the cooling system was prone to fail and the luboil to heat.

Cooke J ruled that CHS allegations as to the poor condition of the vessel's engine lubrication and lubrication cooling systems and the lack of adequate systems on board the vessel to ensure that the temperature of the engine lube oil was properly regulated, that the

116 Ibid, per Cooke J at p. 20.
117 Ibid, p. 40.
118 Ibid, p. 43.
119 Ibid, p. 44.

cooling system did not become blocked, and that the engine was adequately lubricated are made good.[120]

Turning to the question of whether due diligence was practiced on the part of the owners to make the vessel seaworthy, Cooke J viewed that there was no need to decide whether it was a failure in due diligence to adopt a system of recording information in the engine room logs only once a day in an automated engine room. The evidence before the court was that this was acceptable to class and to the flag authorities, although Mr Rossiter said it was inadequate. Mr Justice heard no evidence of any system for inspection of temperature and pressure gauges, however, or monitoring of them in watchkeeping duties, regardless of keeping records (of which there were, of course, none in the previous 5–6 days and only daily records prior to that). Had there been any monitoring of the pressure gauge at the SW pump or monitoring of the efficacy of the ballast pump, it would have revealed a change in pressure for the reasons given by the experts, if there was a blockage in the SW line.[121]

Cooke J pointed out that monitoring of the lube oil temperature would have revealed its increase before the alarm sounded also, with the possibility of remedial action. Cooke J found that there was a failure to institute a system to monitor such matters, which contributed to the casualty. The same feature that constitutes unseaworthiness also constitutes a lack of due diligence in this respect.[122]

Cooke J stated:[123]

> In these circumstances no defence is available to the Owners based on Art IV.1. As I have found unseaworthiness at the commencement of the voyage, neither Art IV.2 (p) (latent defect not discoverable by due diligence) or (q) any other cause arising without the actual fault or privity of the carrier, or without the fault or neglect of the agents or servants of the carrier, can assist the Owners either.

Another issue was, CHS alleged that the owners had, in breach of the obligation contained in the bill of lading, failed to proceed with all convenient speed to the nominated port. Cooke J observed that there was no need to decide whether there was such a breach or not, because of his findings of breach of the Hague Rules. Cooke J found that the repairs which were undertaken were necessary for the prosecution of the voyage and that there was no unreasonable delay in effecting them. The cause of the delayed voyage was the breakdown of the vessel, which resulted from her unseaworthiness. That was the operative causative breach which led to delay in the voyage and cargo damage.[124]

In this case, there were no internal documents disclosed by owners at all which showed any discussion of the cause, whether by reference to the crew's version of events or to the damage found. There were no photographs of the damage. There were no contemporary notes of any interviews or discussions with the chief engineer or the engine room personnel. No bearings or other parts were apparently sent for analysis, save that crankshaft hardness and crack tests were conducted by Goltens. The owners' expert said he would have liked to see the bearings, but they were not available to him. Those

120 Ibid, p. 45.
121 Ibid, p. 52.
122 Ibid.
123 Ibid, p. 54.
124 Ibid, p. 55.

who were present on board the vessel at Varna did see the engine damage and were in the best position to ascertain the cause, but nowhere do the disclosed documents show their conclusions on the subject.

Cooke J was not satisfied that the owners had disclosed all documents in their control in relation to the cause of the damage. In Cooke J's view, documents must have been engendered by the owners themselves regardless of documents emanating from the hull insurer's surveyors. This is only a specific application of the fundamental legal and moral rule that a man should not be allowed to take advantage of his own wrong. In the circumstances, CHS's claim for damages succeeds.

As discussed previously, in a nutshell, at common law, a shipowner, by contracting to carry goods on a voyage in a ship, in the absence of express stipulation, impliedly undertakes that his ship is seaworthy. Such seaworthiness includes all respects, especially the physical fitness of the vessel, cargoworthiness, human seaworthiness, and documentary element of seaworthiness. The seaworthiness required is relative to the nature of the ship, the particular voyage contracted for, and the particular stages of that voyage. The undertaking of seaworthiness requires not merely that the shipowners will do and have done their best to make the ship fit, but that the ship really is fit in all respects to carry her cargo safely to its destination, having regard to the ordinary perils to which such cargo would be exposed on such a voyage.[125]

The classic definition of seaworthiness, as set out by Thomas Carver himself in their edition of his treatise, states that:

> [T]he duty to supply a seaworthy ship is not equivalent to a duty to provide one that is perfect, and such as cannot break down except under extraordinary peril. What is meant is that she must have that degree of fitness which an ordinary careful and prudent owner would require his vessel to have at the commencement of her voyage, having regard to all the probable circumstances of it. To that extent the shipowner, as we have seen, undertakes absolutely that she is fit; and ignorance is no excuse. If the defect existed, the question to be put is, Would a prudent shipowner have required that it should be made good before sending his ship to sea had he known of it? If he would, the ship was not seaworthy within the meaning of the undertaking.

Put simply, the test of seaworthiness is: Would a prudent owner have required that the defect should be made good before sending his ship to sea, had he known of it? If he would, the ship was not seaworthy. This statement of the law was approved and applied by Channell J in *McFadden v Blue Star Line*[126] and by Scrutton LJ in *F C Bradley & Sons Ltd v Federal Steam Navigation Co Ltd.*[127] Since then, it has been applied in many cases, as discussed previously.

It has been said that, as a matter of construction, unless the contract clearly provides to the contrary, it will be presumed that it was not the intention of the parties that either should be entitled to rely on his own breach of duty to avoid the contract or bring it to an end or to obtain a benefit under it. The well-known principle is that, unless the contract clearly provides the contrary, a party is not entitled to rely upon his own breach of contract to excuse himself from the requirement of further performance. So if the owners breach their obligation of seaworthiness, the owners will be liable for damages. The general

125 *Scrutton on Charterparties and Bills of Lading*, 24th ed at para. 7-019–7-024.
126 *McFadden v Blue Star Line* [1905] 1 KB 697.
127 *F C Bradley & Sons Ltd v Federal Steam Navigation Co Ltd.* [1926] 24 Ll.L. Rep.446.

principle for the assessment of damages is compensatory, that is, that the innocent party is to be placed, so far as money can do so, in the same position as if the contract had been performed.

The fundamental principle governing the quantum of damages for breach of contract is long-established and not in dispute. The damages should compensate the victim of the breach for the loss of his contractual bargain. The principle was succinctly stated by Parke B in *Robinson v Harman*,[128], and remains as valid now as it was then.

> The rule of the common law is, that where a party sustains a loss by reason of a breach of contract, he is, so far as money can do it, to be placed in the same situation, with respect to damages, as if the contract had been performed.

128 *Robinson v Harman* 1 Ex 850.

INDEX